POCKET BEER GUIDE 2015

A FIREFLY BOOK

Published by Firefly Books Ltd. 2014

First printing

Publisher Cataloging-in-Publication Data (U.S.)

A CIP record for this title is available from the Library of Congress

Library and Archives Canada Cataloguing in Publication

Beaumont, Stephen, 1964–, author
    Pocket beer guide 2015 : the world's best craft and traditional beers / Stephen Beaumont and Tim Webb.
Includes index.
ISBN 978-1-77085-486-4 (flexibound)
    1. Beer. 2. Beer—Guidebooks. I. Webb, Tim, 1955–, author II. Title.
TP570.B42 2014   641.2'3   C2014-902506-8

Published in the United States by Firefly Books (U.S.) Inc.
P.O. Box 1338, Ellicott Station
Buffalo, New York 14205

Published in Canada by
Firefly Books Ltd.
50 Staples Avenue, Unit 1
Richmond Hill, Ontario L4B 0A7

Cover Design: Erin R. Holmes

Printed and bound in China

DEDICATION

I dedicate this edition to my mother, Jean Beaumont, who died during its final days of production. Although she seldom drank beer, she taught me to treasure and relish our time on earth, indirectly reinforcing the truth behind the maxim that life is indeed too short to drink boring beer.

— Stephen Beaumont

The publishers will be grateful for any information that will assist them in keeping future editions up to date. Although all reasonable care has been taken in the preparation of this book, neither the publishers nor the authors can accept any liability for any consequence arising from the use thereof, or the information contained therein.

First published in Great Britain in 2014 by Mitchell Beazley, an imprint of Octopus Publishing Group Limited, Endeavour House, 189 Shaftesbury Avenue, London WC2H 8JY

Head of Editorial Tracey Smith; **Senior Editor** Leanne Bryan; **General Editor** Jo Copestick; **Copy Editor** Jo Murray; **Art Director** Jonathan Christie; **Executive Art Editor** Juliette Norsworthy; **Designer** Jeremy Tilston; **Database Manager** Bill Hemsley; **Picture Researcher** Jen Veall; **Senior Production Manager** Katherine Hockley; **Cartography Digital mapping** Encompass Graphics Ltd, Hove, UK, www.encompass-graphics.co.uk

POCKET
BEER
GUIDE
2015

The World's Best Craft and Traditional Beers

**STEPHEN BEAUMONT
& TIM WEBB**

COVERS
3,500
BEERS

FIREFLY BOOKS

HOW TO USE THIS BOOK 6

INTRODUCTION 8

WHAT IS CRAFT BEER? 11

BEER STYLES 13

BEER AT THE TABLE 21

EUROPE 28

Belgium 28
Flanders 29
Brussels & Wallonia 38
The Lambic Makers of Brussels
   & Payottenland 43

Germany 46
Bavaria 48
Munich & Upper Bavaria 49
Bamberg & Upper Franconia 53
Rest of Bavaria 62
Baden-Württemberg 70
Cologne, Düsseldorf & North
   Rhine-Westphalia 73
Rest of Germany 77

Austria 83

United Kingdom 89
England 90
Scotland 108
Wales 111
Northern Ireland 113

Republic of Ireland 114

France 117

Netherlands 126

Scandinavia 134
Denmark 134
Norway 140
Sweden 143
Finland 146
Iceland 149

Iberia 150
Spain 150
Portugal 152

The Baltic States 153
Estonia 153
Latvia 154
Lithuania 155

Italy 159

Luxembourg 170

Switzerland 171

Eastern Europe & the Balkans 174
Czech Republic 174
Slovak Republic 182
Poland 183
Slovenia 186
Hungary 187
Ukraine 189
Greece 189

Russian Federation 191

NORTH AMERICA & THE CARIBBEAN 193

United States 193
California 194
Pacific Northwest 201
Rocky Mountains & the Midwest 208
East Coast 221
South 228

Canada 234
Western Canada 234
Eastern Canada 238

The Caribbean 246

LATIN AMERICA 248

Mexico 248

Brazil 251

Argentina 256

Chile 259

Rest of Latin America 261

ASIA & THE MIDDLE EAST 264

Japan 264

China 271

Southeast Asia 275
South Korea 275

Taiwan, China 276
Vietnam 277
Singapore 278
Rest of Southeast Asia 279

India 281

The Middle East 282
Turkey 282
Israel 283

Rest of the Middle East 284

AUSTRALASIA 285

Australia 285

New Zealand 292

The Western Pacific 298

AFRICA 299

South Africa 299

Namibia 302

Rest of Africa 302

Index of Beers 303
Acknowledgements 320

HOW TO USE THIS BOOK

Sample entry:

❶ **RODENBACH (PALM)**
Roeselare, West Flanders ——— **❷**

❸ Unique 1899 brewery full of huge oak
tuns, mostly ripening a single brown ale
for up to two years. Blended into fresh
beer this makes sour-edged, pleasant-
enough **Rodenbach ★★** but in its raw
form, filtered and slightly sweetened
it becomes **Grand Cru ★★★☆**, an ——— **❹**
ultra-tangy, red-brown ale of fine oaked-
aged character, often appealing to wine
drinkers. Selected runs in larger bottles
become **Vintage ★★★★**. **Vin de
Céréale ★★★★** is an occasional
and experimental single tun bottling
of a higher strength brew.

❶ Name: Breweries are identified by their most common name, with
either their parent company or, in some cases, operating business name
following in brackets. In languages where the local word for "Brewery" or
"Brewing Company" ordinarily precedes the brewery name, that word has
been deleted. However, where it usually follows, words such as "Brewing",
"Brewery" or their linguistic equivalent have been retained in the title.
So "Rodenbach" rather than "Brouwerij Rodenbach" and "Anchor Brewing"
rather than "Anchor Brewing Company".

❷ Location: This gives the village/town/city and the province/state.

❸ **Descriptions:** Efforts have been made to summarize the brewery's personality and efforts in as concise a fashion as possible. Descriptive reviews and ratings are then provided for a maximum of five brands for each brewery.

❹ **Ratings:** Each beer has been rated on a scale of one to four stars, with most qualifying for this book with a minimum of two. An outlined star (☆) indicates a half.

★ Dependable quality but unexciting
★★ Above average character
★★★ Highly impressive, worth seeking out
★★★★ One of the world's great beers, a champion

Where a beer has year-to-year, format-to-format or batch-to-batch variation, an arrow (→) has been employed to denote the range of quality. So for example, bottles of Rodenbach's Vin de Céréale tasted thus far have varied between one to three stars in terms of quality and character.

Value: Although beer prices have been on the rise of late, we believe that, with but a small handful of special release exceptions, the overwhelming majority of ales and lagers produced today remain modestly priced. Thus, no consideration has been given to ratings in terms of value for the money, although we acknowledge that there may arise a need to introduce this in the future.

Cross references to other entries have been made where applicable and are marked in small capital letters.

Destinations: Throughout the book are listed specific Beer Destinations. In some instances, these are individual bars, restaurants or shops, while in others they suggest a specific city. In all cases, they represent what we view as the "best of the best" for local or regional beer enjoyment.

> **DESTINATION OOSTAKKER**
>
> **Geerts Drankenhandel**
> (7 Ledergemstraat) is the finest beer supermarket in Belgium, just off the Ghent ring road, well-stocked, simply presented, full of rare Belgian and better imported beers. Good parking.

INTRODUCTION

The world today has more beers in a greater variety of styles, colours and flavours than has ever been the case before.

This assertion is, of course, pure conjecture. Yet at a time when brewers of interesting and engaging beers have not only achieved blanket coverage of all the archetypal brewing nations, but also made significant inroads in countries like Brazil, Italy, Japan and now India, we consider it a fairly safe bet.

This renaissance in hands-on brewing has been gradually sweeping the globe since its emergence in the 1970s. Following decades during which breweries grew larger and more impersonal, and beers became uniform and dull, those drinkers who did not react simply by migrating to wine or spirits were ready for beers with a sense of place and community, and most of all character and flavour. It was a movement that buoyed not only a new global breed of craft brewer, but also long-suffering brewers of traditional beer styles.

As real ales, *bières artisanales*, microbrews, *streekbieren* and *landbier* enter their fifth decade of revival, however, what we see globally is that such "craft brewing" is no longer a quaint cottage industry, but has become a juggernaut that can and is changing the world of brewing, even as the dominant and ever more massive multinational corporations struggle to maintain their hold on their trade.

We see also an industry enduring its own growing pains.

In the UK, for example, craft brewers face off not against the dominant major breweries, but increasingly the pioneering consumer champions of cask-conditioned ale. In North America, former "microbreweries" that have grown national in scope are sometimes looked upon with distrust, or as interlopers when entering new regions well equipped with established craft breweries of their own.

Concurrently, we have witnessed the emergence of superstar brewers and owners, so renowned and respected that they are sought-after speakers and advisers on national and international stages, even as other brewers have developed cult status for their breweries, producing small amounts of some of the most highly prized ales and lagers in the world.

We have also watched breweries multiply almost exponentially, marvelling at the latest remarkable small brewery count – over 50 in London alone! More than 2,500 in the United States! And almost 600 in Italy and in France – each quickly and now predictably eclipsed by another, notably higher number.

Taken together, these developments, and numerous others besides, point to a global industry that has reached an impressive level of scale, maturity and sophistication. No longer may it be said that craft brewing is but a passing fad, any more than one might claim that fine wine or high-end cuisine is a temporary trend of which society will eventually tire. The multinationals will likely continue to own the bulk of the global market for some time to come, just as fast food chains outsell Michelin-starred restaurants, yet almost regardless of where you look today, the appreciation of artfully brewed beer has an established and most likely growing following.

Given such an abundance of breweries and beers worldwide, it would be folly to suggest we could attempt complete coverage or even a comprehensive overview in a single volume, much less one that is sized for the pocket. We make neither of these claims.

Instead, what we have done is comb the globe for the foremost local beer authorities in a multitude of countries and regions, some of whom we have known personally for decades and others we met while researching Mitchell Beazley's *The World Atlas of Beer* in 2012. The challenge we lay down to each is to deliver a compilation of the best of the old school, the most promising of the multitude of new arrivals, and the most creative and exciting breweries in either camp, highlighting what are simply the finest beers in each brewery's portfolio, be they cutting-edge innovations in flavour and ingredients or textbook-perfect takes on traditional styles. We have assumed these same responsibilities for many areas ourselves.

We know we have assembled an exceptional team. In a majority of cases one or the other of us has enjoyed the opportunity of tasting alongside our experts, and in others we have sampled their recommended beers separately. This has allowed us to guide the tone and content of the reviews, and ensure that each beer is judged strictly on its individual merits, not relative to the maturity of its market or in consideration of how "out there" it might be, but assessed against the very best beers worldwide – although measuring the excellence of a brilliantly simple *kölsch*, say, against the full firepower of an Imperial stout will always be a challenge.

In this fashion, what we have crafted is not a guide to all the beers of the world, or even every single good beer, but rather an expertly curated selection of the best in brewing the planet has to offer – this year. We doubt you will agree with every rating that follows, and you will perhaps have personal favourite finds – beers or breweries – you feel should be included but are not, but what we have endeavoured to provide are new and exciting beer discoveries on almost every page.

Which is not to suggest that finding them will be always easy. Indeed, in many cases, a desire to sample the best will leave you no alternative but to visit their country or perhaps front door of origin. We make no apologies for this; excellence is like that sometimes.

Stephen Beaumont & Tim Webb

WHAT IS CRAFT BEER?

Although believed in some quarters to be a product of American small brewery marketers, the phrase "craft brewing" and its corollaries "craft brewed beer" and "craft beer" in fact date to at least the mid-1970s, during which time they were used to refer to small, artisanal and usually family-owned European breweries and their brands. Or more simply, whatever was not a large and usually multinational brewery or beer.

Today, the question of what makes a beer "craft" is a little thornier, but the answer remains in part the same. Brewing corporations that operate on a massive scale are, for the most part, devoted to the image of their beer rather than the flavour – although exceptions certainly do exist and, where appropriate, have been noted within these pages. Craft breweries are smaller by degrees – although with care it is possible to create assertively flavourful beers in massive single brew runs, this is only provided that no corners are cut in recipe or method, which omits most of the options for cost-cutting.

It is the flavour part of the equation that we consider most significant, and to that end there exist techniques generally used in convenience brewing that are normally shunned in the craft sector, beginning with high-gravity brewing.

Widely practised by multinational breweries, high-gravity brewing is the fermentation of beer to an alcohol content of 150% or higher than the intended packaging strength and the subsequent dilution of the beer at bottling, canning or kegging to that final potency. So, for example, a beer meant to appear in the bottle at 5% alcohol by volume might be fermented to 7.5% and watered back to 5% just prior to packaging, so rewarding a brewery with, say, 150,000 litres of bottled beer from a tank with a holding capacity of just 100,000 litres.

The use of brewing adjuncts is another area of differentiation between craft and convenience breweries. Where the latter often employ alternative sources of fermentable sugars, such as corn, rice or liquid sugar, to thin out and lighten the body of their already rather benign beers, craft breweries will tend to use smaller quantities of the same substances to achieve favourable flavour or balance, or both, moderating the weight of a strong ale, for example, or adding a grainy or caramelly accent to the taste of a weaker beer.

One rather romantic and superficially attractive definition of craft beer argues that it has "the brewer's thumbprint" on it, suggesting an ale or lager created by personality as well as technology and science. While we admire this notion, we would suggest that perhaps a less esoteric way to express it might be through a brewery's willingness to experiment, innovate and take risks.

Starting a business is always a risky undertaking, even more so when it must compete against established giants that not only dominate the market to near-exclusivity, but in many cases also control the means of distribution. Add in a determination to expand the market from the ubiquitous light lager to the rich tapestry of ales and lagers we enjoy today and it's clear that risk-taking and innovation are among the hallmarks of craft brewing.

On a related note, in a true craft brewing company, the ideas flow from the brewers to the marketing division, while in large-scale convenience brewing operations, the reverse is true. Looking at some of the delightfully illogical beers that craft breweries have created and made successful and comparing them with such big beer "innovations" as a can that changes colour when cold or a pink brew directed at the female market, it is an easy conclusion to draw.

Beyond size and risk and personality and intent, perhaps the single characteristic that most marks a craft brewery is a willingness and intent to lead. For all the most important steps forward the global brewing industry has taken over the last three or four decades have come as a result of craft beer instigation, marking the craft brewer as someone intent on changing the status quo, rather than being content to follow the herd.

BEER STYLES

The idea that a beer should be considered of a particular style was anathema to the 20th century industrialists who forged the notion of the universal beer. For them, the ideal was light gold, grainy sweet, almost bereft of bitterness and served as cold as possible, and the key was marketing.

The rise of modern craft breweries, on the other hand, has provoked a need for reliably recognizable terms to describe, distinguish and explain the myriad types of beer, old and new, that now adorn the shelves of bars, stores and home refrigerators around the world. The questions that remain are which terms to use and how to apply them?

We believe it was Michael Jackson, in his 1977 book, *The World Guide to Beer*, who first attempted to catalogue global beer styles, introducing readers to such beer types as "*münchener*," "Trappiste" and "(Burton) Pale Ale". His goal then was to provide readers with a context through which to discover – or rediscover – these beers. Our challenge, although addressed to a more beer-aware public, remains in essence the same.

While we would love to report that we have solved all the issues surrounding the current confusion and can provide readers with a simple map of the major beer styles of the world, this is not currently possible and, we admit, may never be. What we offer instead is a rough guide on how to pick your way through a linguistic and conceptual minefield in a fashion that adds to rather than detracts from understanding.

START WITH TRADITION

We believe the most reliable stylistic imperatives to be those based in centuries of brewing tradition and that most modern derivations are merely modifications of existing beer styles, however inventive or ingenious. Hence our first separation is according to method of fermentation.

Historically, the term **ale** has referred to a beer fermented at room temperature or higher, causing its yeast to rise to the top of the wort, or unfermented beer, hence references to top-fermentation or, sometimes, warm-fermentation. In contrast, a **lager** was fermented at a cooler temperature causing its yeast to sink, thus known as bottom-fermentation or, sometimes, cool-fermentation.

These main beer classes, comparable to red and white wine, still serve to define the overwhelming majority of beers, despite the temperature and yeast manipulation possible in a modern brewhouse. As a general rule, a beer fermented at warmer temperatures with a yeast of the family

Saccharomyces cerevisiae and conditioned, or lagered, at relatively warm temperatures for short periods – an ale – should tend toward a fruitier character. Those fermented at cooler temperatures with a yeast of the family *S. pastorianus* and lagered for longer periods of time at cool temperatures – lagers – should not. Combine ale yeast with a lager-style conditioning and you have the hybrid styles of **kölsch** and **altbier**, respectively native to Cologne and Düsseldorf in Germany, as well as the American **cream ale**. Flip it to lager yeast and ale-type conditioning and you have **steam beer**, also known as **California common beer**.

Beers that have no yeast added to them, most famously the lambic beers of Belgium, are said to undergo spontaneous fermentation, effected by a combination of airborne and barrel-resident microflora, including *Brettanomyces* and *Pediococcus*, which yield complex flavours from mildly lemony to assertively tart. Those fermented with the same types of microbes introduced deliberately are becoming known as **wild beers** or **sour beers**.

ADD COLOUR AND STRENGTH

Colour is a powerful force in beer and often used to define beer by style, with some references to hue reserved exclusively for certain types of beer, such as "white" (*blanche*, *wit*, *weisse*) for **wheat beers**, even when such beers are relatively dark in colour. "Pale" or "light" (in colour, not alcohol or calories) are also popular adjectives, yielding the now-international **pale ale** and **India pale ale**, or **IPA**, the German **helles** and the Czech **světlý**.

"Amber" in North America was and to some extent remains synonymous with ordinary ales or lagers with a blush of colour, while "red" has varying degrees of Irish and Flemish (northern Belgian) authenticity, but is just as often used to describe a beer of uncertain style. "Dark" is also used in fairly random fashion in the English-speaking world, but retains validity in Bavaria where its translation, **dunkel**, should indicate a brownish lager of a style once strongly associated with Munich, and in the Czech Republic, where the term is **tmavý**.

"Brown" implies the use of more roasted malts and, while historically associated with a class of fairly winey **brown ales** from England or a tart, fruity **oud bruin** style native to northern Belgium (related to the Flemish red, above), may now apply to a wide variety of flavours, from sickly sweet to forcefully bitter, mild to alcoholic. "Black" is usually reserved for **porters** and **stouts**, although bottom-fermented German **schwarzbier** also deserves inclusion.

As for alcoholic strength, although commonly used around the world, few words are less useful to a beer description than "strong". The difficulty is in terms of context, since in parts of Scandinavia, strong beer (**starkøl**) is defined as being above 4.7% ABV, not far from where the British would place the definition, while most Belgians, North Americans and Italians would be hard-pressed to consider anything below 6% or 7% to be "strong".

The terms *dubbel*/double and *tripel*/triple are monastic in origin and have proved both durable and international. Historically used to indicate a beer fermented from a mash with greater malt sugar content – often the "first runnings" of grain then reused to make a second beer – the modern context of *dubbel*/double generally indicates a beer of 6–8%. Most commonly, it appears in reference to the malty and sweet Belgian abbey-style **dubbel**, the German **doppelbock** and related Italian **doppio malto** – although use of the latter term appears to be waning – and the modern American **double IPA**, usually an ale of significant strength and aggressive bitterness.

Tripel/triple likewise owes its origins to monastery breweries, although its advent is more recent, having been first employed in the 20th century. It usually describes a very specific type of blond, sweet-starting but usually dry-finishing strong ale, although is today sometimes used with IPA to suggest an even stronger and hoppier brew. *Quadrupel*/quadruple/quad, on the other hand, is a modern affectation, the first variant originally used by the Dutch Trappist brewery, La Trappe, to designate its new high-strength ale in 1998, hence the Dutch spelling – to imply heritage.

Historically, the term barley wine was used to indicate a beer of wine strength, though the modern interpretation sometimes brings it closer to old ale in its British guise, that is, a beer requiring some period of bottle-ageing, or high hoppiness in its American interpretation, and sometimes both.

Imperial has experienced a recent transformation from its original **Imperial Russian stout** designation, meaning a strong, intense, sometimes oily stout, to the suggestion that any style may be "Imperialized", which is to say made stronger and more intense. **Imperial pale ale** as a synonym for double IPA is the most common of these, although Imperial pilsner, Imperial *saison* and even the hopefully tongue-in-cheek Imperial mild have been sighted.

Brewers have for centuries used subtle nudge and wink systems to highlight alcohol content. The best-known remnant of this practice is the Scottish "shilling" system, whereby ales are measured from **60 shilling**, or **60/-**, for the lightest ale, to **90/-** for the strongest, the last sometimes also called "**wee heavy**". In the Czech Republic, the old Balling system of measuring wort gravity defines beers by degrees, from **8°** for the lightest to **12°** for a beer of premium strength and on up into fermented porridge territory.

FACTOR IN THE GRAINS

Besides the basic four ingredients of beer – water, barley malt, hops and yeast – numerous other grains are used with varying degrees of regularity, in all but a handful of specialized cases in combination with barley malt.

Wheat is the most common of these, creating whole categories of beer such as the German-style wheat beers variously known as **weizen**, **weisse**, **hefeweizen** or **hefeweissbier**, all normally indicating a beer with added yeast in the bottle, unless specified **kristall**, meaning clear. Also included in this family are the derivatives **dunkelweisse** and **weizenbock**, respectively meaning dark and strong wheat beers. Quite different is the more obscure **Berliner weisse**, kept light (usually +/-3.5%) and made tart through the use of lactic acid during fermentation.

Spontaneously fermented Belgian **lambic** is by law a wheat beer, though more common in Belgium and elsewhere is **witbier (white beer, bière blanche)**, brewed with unmalted rather than malted wheat and spiced with orange peel and coriander, sometimes in conjunction with other spices.

Once ubiquitous but now more seldom seen are simple **wheat ales**, blond beers that have simply been made lighter of body through the use of malted wheat. Some craft brewers in the US and elsewhere have started to make strong wheat beers called **wheat wines**, referencing barley wine.

Other grains in general usage include oats, which brings sweetness and a silky mouthfeel to **oatmeal stouts** and other, more unconventional beers such as **oatmeal brown ales**; rye, which bestows a spiciness upon **rye pale ales** and **rye IPAs**, as well as the odd lager-fermented **roggenbier**, of German origin; buckwheat, blackened and used in the Brittany beer style, **bière de blé noir**; and an assortment of non-glutinous grains employed to create the growing class of **gluten-free beers**.

Malt and grain substitutes are mostly there for fermentable sugar to increase alcoholic strength, with or, more commonly, without adding flavour characteristics. The likes of maize (corn), rice, starches, syrups and candy sugar may bring balance to heavy beer by ensuring that it is suitably strong in alcohol, but are not seen as creating styles in their own right – though Japanese rice beers and a handful of related beers in the United States are having a go. The exception to this rule is where unfermentable sugars are added with the intention of adding sometimes considerable sweetness without alcoholic strength, fructose creating sweet stout and lactose contributing to milk or cream stout.

HOPS AND OTHER

Hops have been the primary flavouring agent in beer since the Middle Ages, but only in the last century or two have beer styles begun to be defined by the variety of hop used.

Perhaps most famously, what the world knows as the **Czech-style pilsner** is seasoned with a single variety of hop, the floral Saaz, grown near where the style was invented. Equally, the typical hops used in a **British best bitter** have always been Fuggle and Golding, not necessarily because it was planned that way, but because they are what Kentish hop farms were and are still growing. (A wider variety are typically employed in the stronger, maltier **Extra Special Bitter**, or **ESB**, but Fuggle and/or Golding are often still used.)

When what we now recognize as the **American pale ale** was established in the 1970s, the hop used to give the beer its trademark citrus bite was Cascade, although now a variety of other so-called "C-hops" are considered acceptable, including Centennial and Chinook. By extension, these hops have also grown to be emblematic of the **US-style IPA** and its recently developed sibling, the **black IPA**, which might equally be described as a hoppy porter.

More recent hop-defined beer styles include two from New Zealand, the **New Zealand-style pilsner** and the **New Zealand-style pale ale**, both flavoured with grapey, tropical-fruity Kiwi hops, notably Nelson Sauvin and Motueka. As hop cultivation becomes increasingly scientific and more hybridized varieties are created, we may and most likely will see more beer styles identified by the variety of hops used.

While hops can be considered a core ingredient of any beer, other flavourings are distinctly optional, including herbs and spices. While we still see the odd beer identified as **gruut** (sometimes grut or gruit), which is to say seasoned with a selection of dried herbs and flavourings, but no hops, certainly the most famously spiced beer is the **Belgian-style wheat beer**.

Although all manner of herbs and spices were used prior to the widespread use of hops in brewing, before Pierre Celis pitched coriander, cumin and dried Curaçao orange peel into the **witbier** he revived in the Belgian town of Hoegaarden in 1966, the extent to which brewers, Belgian or otherwise, spiced beers is questionable. Today, however, beers can and frequently are flavoured with all manner of ingredients, to the extent that lumping them all into a single **spiced beer** category seems to us rather random. Unfortunately, failing the creation of all manner of sub-categories – black pepper beers, white pepper and allspice beers, grains of paradise beers, and so on – it remains the best available option.

We can blame popular modern Belgian brewers for the arrival of fruit syrups in beer. While cherries and raspberries have for centuries been steeped whole in Belgian **lambic** beers to create respectively **kriek** and

framboise, the rash of beers made by adding juice, syrup, cordials or essence to ordinary lagers and ales is mostly a post-1980 phenomenon. While collectively known as **fruit beers**, this is often a misnomer as the additives are often a considerable distance from their time on the tree.

Stout in particular, but also **porter** and other types of **brown ale**, are increasingly having vanilla, cocoa and coffee added to them in formats that range from whole pods or beans to syrups and essences, with varying degrees of success.

One of the most curious additives is salt, once commonly and still variously used in **dry Irish-style stout** to fill out the palate, achieved with greatest aplomb in the 19th century by filtering the wort through a bed of shucked **oyster shells**, hence oyster stout. East German **gose** is essentially a salted wheat beer.

Italian brewers have sought to make a style out of adding chestnuts to their beer, whether in whole, crushed, honey or jam form. Whether it or any of the multitude of other additives and seasonings currently in use – from root vegetables to nuts to flowers and even tobacco leaf – stand the test of time once the initial excitement wears off, remains to be seen.

NATIONAL ADJECTIVES

Various nationalities and regionalities have grown in recent years into beer style descriptors. While some rankle – the term "Belgian" for a beer quite clearly brewed elsewhere than Belgium, for example – they do in most cases provide useful information.

Because some Belgian ales taste spicy, whether by dint of the yeast used or spices added, yeast propagation companies have developed yeast strains meant to mimic this effect, hence **Belgian-style** has come to mean a spicy or sometimes somewhat funky take on an understood beer style – i.e. Belgian pale ale, Belgian IPA, and so on.

Hop-related styles already discussed include US-style for pale ales and IPAs seasoned with Cascade and other such hops, and **New Zealand-style (Aotearoa-style)** pilsner and pale ale. **British-style**, usually used in conjunction with pale ale, IPA or barley wine, generally indicates not only the less aggressive hop character of a Golding, Fuggle or Northern Brewer hopping, but also a pronounced maltiness.

Scotch ale or **Scottish-style ale** suggests a beer of quite significant maltiness, with strength of up to 8% indicated by the former. Long-standing confusion about Scottish brewing methods means that beers so described sometimes also feature a potion of peated malt.

Other geographical qualifiers are more restricted. **Baltic porter** defines a beer that is not a porter at all, but rather a strong, dark and usually sweet bottom-fermented ale; **Irish red ale** is a popular descriptor of questionable authenticity; **Irish stout** has both legitimacy and utility in describing a low-strength, dry, roasty form of stout; **Bohemian-** or **Czech-style** generally modifies pilsner and suggests one more golden than blond, softly malty and floral; and Bavarian or German implies crisper, leaner and blonder when referencing pilsner, clovey and/or banana-ish when applied to a wheat beer.

AND THE REST
Several other old and new styles and derivatives also deserve mention here.

The need for beer during the non-brewing months of summer has historically led to the creation of several somewhat related styles, including *märzen* in Germany, *bière de garde* in France and *saison* in southern Belgium. Each is distinguished by a slightly elevated alcohol content and normally increased hopping rate, both employed for preservative effect.

Come harvest, German, Austrian, Dutch and Norwegian brewers would clear the stocks of malt from the previous year's barley by brewing a dark *bok* or *bock*, a custom mirrored in the spring in all but Norway with a pale **maibock** or **lentebok**. The latter fell in line with a tradition across much of northern Europe to produce stronger beers around the Lenten period.

The Germans also claim a host of local variants on usually blond lagers that are only partially filtered, sometimes known collectively as *landbier* and including various types that are simply cloudy (**zwickelbier**), some which continue some fermentation during storage in the pub cellar (**kellerbier**) and a few in which carbon dioxide is allowed to be released during the lagering process (**ungespundetes**).

Franconian brewers claim a slice of history by perpetuating the use of wood-smoked malt in their **rauchbiers** – at the same time inspiring a host of New World smoked beers – while Finnish and Estonian brewers do the same with their **sahti**, a beer filtered through juniper boughs and fermented with bread yeast, served by necessity very young and fresh.

Finally, the craft brewing renaissance has witnessed the emergence of a cacophony of new styles, both real and imagined, classifiable and almost ethereal. In the last group we place **barrel-aged** and **barrel-conditioned beers**, which begin in a multitude of styles and spend time in a variety of different sorts of barrels, from those which previously held wine, to bourbon barrels, to, in at least one extraordinary case, a barrel previously used to age maple syrup. Of particular interest in this area, we find, is what Brazilian brewers are currently doing with the exotic woods of the Amazon.

In a similar vein, fresh or unkilned hops are used in a new class of **wet hop beers**, mostly ales and primarily in the United States but otherwise of almost any hop-driven style the brewer wishes to brew. And beers named for occasions or seasons, including **Christmas** and **winter ales**, **summer beers** and **harvest ales**, suggest general character traits – heavier in winter, lighter for summer – but little else.

BEER AT THE TABLE

by Stephen Beaumont

Although through the millennia beer has been enjoyed in all manner of ways, from workplace restorative to meal accompaniment and evening refresher, over the past two centuries or so it has been largely confined to the role of social elixir, what you go out for "a couple of" with colleagues after work or enjoy with friends on a Friday or Saturday night.

With the emergence of craft breweries and their vast array of beer styles, however, beer has rediscovered its place at the table. And with the remarkable diversity of aromas and flavours currently being brewed all over the world, it's no wonder. Indeed, with its multiple ingredients and diverse fermentation possibilities, it can be argued that beer has even greater versatility in food pairing than does wine.

Included in that versatility are the myriad of flavourings that may be used, from coffee and chocolate to a host of herbs, spices, fruits and so on. We have, for the most part, excluded these beers from our pairings – except for dessert – but they should be considered whenever the beer's flavouring is harmonious with the food's.

The following is my attempt to demystify the process of partnering food with beer, although I caution that while a well-orchestrated match can be a most delicious and enjoyable experience, the best pairing is always the beer you want with the food you desire.

BREAKFAST

Waiting "until the sun is over the yard-arm" before having a drink is a popular aphorism in parts of the world, but hardly a universal truth. Although it is becoming less common to find beer consumed early in the day, the practice is far from extinct and does come with certain gastronomic benefits.

Bagel and cream cheese: A not-too-hoppy pale ale.

Churros: A chocolaty stout or porter or, if you're feeling adventurous, a malty and not-too-strong barley wine.

Croissant: You'll likely be having this with an espresso or café au lait, but try a chocolaty porter for something different.

Eggs Benedict: Cut the richness of the hollandaise with a crisp *helles* lager.

French toast with fruit: Here a sweeter *kriek* or *framboise* is a good choice.

Fresh fruit with yogurt: A dryish fruit lambic or a *Berliner weisse* with or without syrup.

Full English breakfast: With so much on the plate, best keep the beer light. A golden bitter will do the trick.

Granola: If with milk, a nutty brown ale. With yogurt, a Flemish brown or red ale.

Oatmeal: Oatmeal stout, of course.

Pancakes with maple syrup: Oatmeal stout, preferably a sweeter and not so roasty example.

Raw or cured ham: A crisp pilsner, especially if mild cheese is also served.

Scrambled eggs: A Belgian-style wheat beer is a natural.

Smoked salmon: Dry stout or a softly smoky *rauchbier* or smoked porter.

Weisswurst: *Weissbier* is the traditional accompaniment, and for good reason.

LUNCH

While almost anything may be eaten for lunch, the key to pairing beer with the midday meal is to keep the alcohol content low and the refreshment element high, so the effect is restorative and invigorating rather than filling and dulling.

Chicken, fried: Anything light and hoppy, from US-style pale ale to pilsner or *kölsch*.

Chicken wings, spicy: For medium heat, pilsner; for hot, US-style pale ale or IPA.

Chicken sandwich with mayonnaise: *Bière de garde* or *märzen*.

Clam chowder: (New England-style) A hoppy blond ale or golden bitter; (Manhattan-style) Vienna lager or *altbier*.

Crab cakes: Dry porter or a *schwarzbier*.

Croque monsieur: A spicy, Belgian-inspired blond ale.

Hamburger: Dry, hoppy and aromatic US-style pale ale, or crisp pilsner.

Nachos: Spicy, cheesy and sloppy, this dish needs a beer to clean it all up: a crisp pilsner or restrained UK- or US-style IPA.

Oysters, raw or cooked: Dry stout, or *gueuze* lambic for a tasty variation.

Pizza: (Tomato) Vienna lager or *bock*; (White) *Weissbier* or, if cheesy, *weizenbock*; (With the works) A big US-style IPA.

Ploughman's lunch: Best bitter or UK-style pale ale.

Pulled pork: *Märzen* or *bock*.

Quiche Lorraine: *Altbier* or dark mild ale.

Salad, cobb: Pale ale or *saison*.

Salad, green with vinaigrette: *Helles* for a conventional approach; *gueuze* lambic for a refreshing alternative.

Salad, tuna: Brown ale if served without pickles; porter or light stout if served with.

Soup, cream: Pilsner.

Soup, French onion: Pale ale or best bitter, or one of the hoppier and darker examples of *bière de garde*.

Veal schnitzel: Pilsner if greasy; *märzen* if not.

DINNER

FISH

The key to pairing beer with fish is to start light and increase the weight of the beer according to the oiliness of the fish, the richness of the sauce, and so on. Also, fish generally don't take terribly well to hoppiness, often producing a metallic or minerally flavour in response, so well-hopped pilsners, pale ales, IPAs and the like should be employed judiciously.

Brandade: A simple, fruity blond ale.

Ceviche: The citrus makes this a fairly acidic dish, so match with the acidity of a fruit lambic or a tamer coriander-forward Belgian-style wheat beer or a *kölsch*.

Cioppino: This fennel and seafood stew from San Francisco pairs wonderfully with that city's beer claim to fame, steam beer, also known as California common beer.

Crab: Almost any way it's prepared, a sweetish porter will be crab's best friend. Make it hoppier if the crab is softshell and fried or heavily spiced.

Fish and chips: Best bitter or British-style pale ale, please.

Fish baked in a salt crust: This technique yields profoundly moist and flavourful flesh, suitable for pairing with a *märzen* or *schwarzbier*.

Haddock, halibut, cod and other firm and meaty fish, poached, sautéed or roasted: Meaty but light in flavour, these fish will accept almost any sort of non-hoppy ale or lager, from *bière de garde* to *bock* to light porters and dry stouts.

Lobster, steamed with butter: A nutty and sweetish brown ale will accentuate the flavours of the lobster.

Lobster, cold with mayonnaise: *Bock* or malty *dubbel*.

Mackerel, sardines, herring or other dark and oily fish, grilled: The fattiness of these fish beg for some hops to cut through the oil, so try a balanced, citrusy pale ale.

Monkfish, roasted: Oatmeal stout or Baltic porter.

Mussels: It's a myth that mussels should be enjoyed with the beer used to steam them, since a few cloves of garlic or a bunch of herbs can change the flavour playing field completely. Start with a Belgian-style wheat for lighter preparations such as lemon and parsley and increase the beer's weight as the flavours grow bolder. Avoid high bitterness in all cases, though.

Pad Thai: This dish mixes salty, sweet and sour, usually with a decent amount of spice, so reach for the workhorse of beer and food pairing, pale ale.

Paella: Garlic and a multitude of different flavours suits this to a Czech-style pilsner or British-style pale ale. Or if it's a very rich version, try one of the lighter Trappist ales.

Prawns (shrimp), barbecued New Orleans-style: This dish begs an IPA or double IPA. Alternatively, go for a severe, refreshing contrast with a crisp pilsner.

Prawns (shrimp), garlic: German- or Czech-style pilsner, light pale ales.

Red snapper, sea bass and other light and lean fish, poached, sautéed or roasted: Keep the beer light and fresh. Almost any wheat beer will work, or a *helles* if a little garlic or spice is involved.

Sablefish, black cod, sturgeon and other firm, oily whitefish, poached, sautéed or roasted: Although delicate of taste, the oils in these fish allow for a little hoppiness and their firm flesh invites a bit of weight. *Märzen*, or a not overly hoppy *altbier* or UK-style pale ale.

Salade Niçoise: Dressed with vinaigrette and prepared with the traditional canned tuna, this *salade composée* suits a *saison*.

Salmon, seared or grilled: Dry stout.

Scallops: On their own, sautéed or baked, their sweet and delicate taste begs for *kölsch* or Belgian-style wheat beer.

Seafood curry: Break out the pilsner and make it hoppier as the curry gets hotter. For a rich coconut milk curry, try an abbey-style *tripel*.

Sushi or sashimi: Varies according to the fish and other ingredients included, but if disinclined to drink sake, a *kölsch*, *altbier* or *schwarzbier* can be quite nice.

Trout, grilled or fried: New Zealand-style pilsner, if you can find it, or a light and fruity blond ale if you cannot.

Tuna, grilled or seared: Properly served raw in the middle, so any suggestion of hoppiness will bring out metallic tastes in the fish: stick to a *dubbel*, sweet *bock* or other medium weight and malty ale or lager.

MEAT

Red meat allows you to bring out the big guns of beer – abbey-style ales, double IPAs, barley wines and such. Poultry, on the other hand, allows for great leeway from lagers and lambics all the way to brown ales and porters. And everything German is good with pork.

Beef cheeks, braised: Imperial stout or strong abbey-style ale.

Beef, roast, medium to well done: The browner the meat, the browner the ale. Try a nutty brown ale for medium and head towards a porter for more well-done beef.

Beef, roast, rare: Rich, meaty sweetness is best balanced by pale ale or best bitter.

Beef stew with potatoes, carrots, etc: Brown ale or porter.

Beef Stroganoff: Something big and beefy, like a malt-driven barley wine, strong abbey-style ale or even a whisky-barrel-aged stout.

Carbonade de boeuf: The Belgian equivalent to boeuf bourguignon, cooked with beer. A tart Flemish red or brown ale, or a moderately strong wild ale, is wonderful if the stew is finished with a little acidity, or a malty Trappist or abbey-style brown ale if not.

Cassoulet: Deliciously rich, this dish calls for hoppiness without excess weight, meaning a *tripel* or traditional *saison*.

Chicken or turkey, roast: Traditional (*oude*) *gueuze* is a superlative match.

Chicken or prawn vindaloo: The ultimate accompaniment to spicy curries is, coincidentally, India pale ale.

Chilli con carne: A dish with many guises — meaty, bean-forward, spicy, turkey — calls for a beer with great flexibility of flavour, pale ale or, if very spicy, IPA.

Coq au vin: Properly deserving of red wine, but a brown ale can do at a pinch. (Or try *coq à la bière*.)

Duck or goose, roast: An ideal occasion for a proper *tripel* or a New World wine-barrel-aged strong golden ale.

Duck two ways (roast breast and confit leg): Hoppy *bocks* love this dish, or a new style "*hopfen*" *weissbier* otherwise.

Goulash: Balance refreshment with fat-cutting hoppiness and serve a restrained American pale ale.

Haggis: Whisky-barrel-finished porter or stout, peated malt ale or a single malt.

Ham, cooked: You can't go wrong with German beers whenever pig is on the menu. *Märzen*, *bock*, *rauchbier* and *weizenbock* can all be marvellous here.

Jambalaya: The hotter, the hoppier; start with a pale ale to partner with a mild spiciness and move to IPA when the hot sauce takes over.

Lamb, roast: Rare to medium-rare lamb is wonderful with a rich, malty and — dare we say it? — winey brew. Try an old ale, British-style barley wine or strong porter or brown ale. Medium-strength Trappist or abbey-style ales work, too.

Lamb rogan josh: A wonderful dish with lots of grease, calling for a malty double IPA or strong British-style IPA.

Pork, roast: An earthy *dunkel* or *bock*.

Rabbit: Full-bodied *dunkel*, sweetish brown ale or light porter.

Sausages: Best bitter for beef; *helles* or *bock* for pork; *weissbier* for veal. Choose hoppier styles like pilsner, pale ale and IPA for spicier sausages such as Italian, chorizo and merguez.

Shepherd's pie: Best bitter or brown ale; sweet porter if properly (but now rarely) made with lamb.

Spaghetti and meatballs in tomato sauce: *Bock* or *doppio malto*.

Steak and kidney pie or Steak in stout pie: Brown ale, porter or stout as a catch-all; Flemish brown ale for the kidneys and Imperial stout for the steak-in-stout as perfection.

Steak frîtes: Flavours that will crush any lager; choose instead an ESB or British-style pale ale.

Steak tartare: A spiced or spicy strong abbey-style ale is a great match, or a malty pale ale if potency is a consideration.

Sweetbreads: The most elegant and balanced strong golden ale you can find, with extra points for a lean and spicy body.

Veal, roast: Brighten its character with a *bock*, or if served with gravy, a spicy *dubbel*. Berry-based and not overly sweet fruit beers are also an option.

Venison: Either a traditional (*oude*) fruit lambic with lots of fruitiness or a wild ale fermented with berry fruit.

Wild boar: Not to be treated as pork, boar deserves a strong *bock* or strong, rich, barrel-aged wild ale.

VEGETARIAN DISHES

Vegetarian food arrives in such a vast variety of flavours that it's difficult to make pairing generalizations. Below is a small sample offered for guidance.

Baked pasta dishes: Best is often a dark lager with a degree of hoppiness, an earthy *dunkel* or an *altbier*.

Cheese soufflé: A hoppy *kölsch* or wheat beer would work best.

Couscous with vegetables: Mild and light, a Vienna lager suits this to a T.

Grilled vegetables: With olive oil and herbs, a hoppy *helles* is a delight.

Lentils: *Altbier* is a great match for their earthy flavour, but a dry brown ale will do if none are available.

Macaroni cheese: Pair to the cheese, so a *bock* or brown ale if mild and best bitter or UK-style pale ale if sharper.

Mushrooms: Pair wonderfully with any beer that emphasizes dark, earthy malts, from *altbier* to stout.

Ratatouille: Richness plus garlic calls for a hoppy brown ale, equally hoppy *bock*, or perhaps a rye pale ale.

Spicy vegetarian dishes: Lager or ale suit, with pale ales/IPAs serving as well as hoppy *bocks* or 12°-or-stronger Czech or Czech-style lagers or Imperial pilsners.

Stuffed peppers: Green peppers call for a contrasting, cleansing flavour to balance, like a pilsner or *helles*. Switch to British-style pale ale if the peppers are sweet, and US-style IPA if the stuffing is spicy.

DESSERTS

Beer shines when it comes to dessert, especially when chocolate is involved. It is wise, in most cases, to choose a beer that is at least as sweet as the dish, if not sweeter, in order to avoid the beer's flavour being trampled by the dessert's sugar.

Apple pie, strudel: An apple-flavoured, allspice- or cinnamon-spiced strong ale.

Cakes and cupcakes; sponge cake with icing: Pale, sweet *bock* or a sweet Belgian or Belgian-inspired golden ale.

Cheesecake: For a fruit-topped cake, pick a beer flavoured with the same or a complementary fruit. For liqueur-flavoured or caramel cheesecake, opt for a malty barley wine or more youthful old ale.

Chocolate: Pair flourless chocolate cake with Imperial stout; chocolate pudding with *doppelbock*; nutty chocolate truffle with brown ale; milk chocolate with sweet porter; chocolate cheesecake with milk stout.

Christmas pudding, mince pies: Barley wine or spiced winter ale.

Coffee desserts: Coffee-flavoured stout; regular stout and porter; or Imperial stout or Trappist ale for strongly flavoured dishes.

Crème brûlée: Strong and sweet blond ale, fruity or spicy or spiced.

Fruit: For a fruit salad, *hefeweizen*; for berries in cream, milk stout, Flemish red ale or chocolaty brown ale; for fruit tarts, match the custard with a sweet, fruity blond ale.

Lemon flavours: Wheat beers of varying types, selected according to intensity of the dish, or sometimes pilsners.

Nuts: Brown ale, some *bocks*, old ale.

Pecan pie: A bourbon barrel-conditioned stout or barley wine is a beautiful match.

Sticky toffee pudding: Sweet Scotch ale.

Tiramisú: Highlight the coffee with a sweet stout, or emphasize the creaminess with an abbey-style *dubbel* or stronger ale.

Trifle: Scotch ale.

CHEESE

Wine and cheese may get all the press, but beer and cheese is a more natural and harmonious pairing, as even many sommeliers now admit. The suggestions below are a mere starting point for a long and delicious journey.

Bloomy rind cheeses (Brie de Meaux or Camembert): Porter or oatmeal stout.

Firm, sharp and fruity-nutty cheeses (aged Cheddar, Gruyère, Manchego): Best bitter or UK-style pale ale (much the same thing) or dry porter or stout.

Goats' cheese, semi-soft and dry: Some hoppier versions of *kölsch*, *bière de garde* or *saison* fare well, but best is a traditional *oude* (old) *gueuze* lambic.

Goats' cheese, soft and moist: Belgian- or German-style wheat beer or *helles*.

Hard, grainy, crumbly and sharp cheese (Parmigiano Reggiano, aged Gouda): Nutty brown ale, malty porter or *rauchbier* is nice, but a bourbon-barrel-aged porter or strong brown ale is bliss.

Mild to moderately sharp and creamy blue cheeses (Cambozola, Cashel Blue, Stilton): Sweet stouts, strong, malty abbey-style *dubbels* and *doppelbocks* fare well with milder versions; for Stilton break out a malty, UK-style barley wine.

Semi-soft, mild-mannered cheese (Edam, Havarti, Morbier): *Bock*; Irish ale; Scottish ale; some light and sweeter versions of abbey-style *dubbel*.

Sharp, aggressive and mouth-drying blue cheeses (Roquefort, Cabrales, Gorgonzola): Break out the big guns, such as double IPA, US-style barley wines or strong Trappist or abbey-style dark ale.

Washed rind, strong and pungent cheeses (Epoisses, Münster, Chimay à la Bière): Strong spiced or spicy Belgian or Belgium-inspired ales, the strongest of almost any Trappist brewery's portfolio.

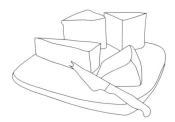

EUROPE

BELGIUM

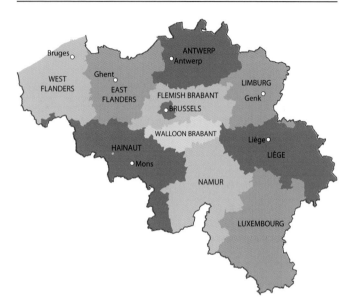

When the new appreciation of beer began, back in the 1970s, what Belgium brought to the table was its unique, almost limitless tradition of local beer styles, from the near impossibly delicate, to extremes of spicy sweetness, frank acidity or balanced power, appearing in all variety of colours, strengths and presentations.

Above all, Belgian brewing stood for an attitude that brewers need not be bound by officious rules dictating the appearance, production methods or ways to serve their beer. What matters in the end is the taste.

Nationally, influences include the traditions of monastic brewing kept alive by six brewing abbeys of the Trappist Order; the lambic brewers of Payottenland, whose lambic beers rely on wild fermentation and barrel-ageing; farmhouse traditions of seasonal brewing; and, since the country's last occupation ended in 1945, a plague of industrial lagers.

The breweries and beers we have selected demonstrate Belgian brewing's core strength of conditioning beers slowly to perfection at or near the brewery, omitting some older, safer breweries in favour of newer ones intent on maintaining their country's position at the top of global brewing.

FLANDERS

In the northern, Dutch-speaking part of Belgium the Flemish weakness for putting spice in beer may owe its origins to the *gruut* barons of ancient Bruges, or arguably the influence of well-intentioned British beer writers of the late 20th century. Eighty years earlier it was an expat British brewer who popularized sweet stout and lightweight pale ales called *speciaal*. By that time, firm brown ales, some aged to sourness, had been a renowned feature of better Flemish taverns for centuries. Oak-ageing of ales continues to this day in West Flanders.

ACHEL
Hamont-Achel, Limburg

Newest Belgian Trappist brewery, near Hamont-Achel since 1999. Delicate, hazy, hoppy, aromatic **5° Blond** ★★☆ appears only on draught and on-site; while the Trappist Achel bottle-conditioned beers are slightly spicy, straw-coloured lighter *tripel*, **Blond** ★★☆; more typically monastic, richer, fruitier *dubbel*, **Bruin** ★★★; and chestnut-coloured, sweetish, chocolaty barley wine, **Extra Bruin** ★★★☆.

ALVINNE
Moen, West Flanders

Restless craft brewery, now at Moen, south of Kortrijk. Mostly experimental, sometimes wildly. Chinook and Amarillo hops dominate Belgo-US-style pale ale **Alvinne Extra Restyled** ★★★; the **Freaky** brands ★★ pack significant flavour into lightweight beers; and variants of the Three Wise Men Christmas beers **Gaspar**, **Balthazar** and **Melchior** ★→★★★ repeat the same at the heavy end. Slowly getting there.

ANKER, HET
Mechelen, Antwerp

Ages-old brewery, expanded after 1945 and kicked into shape by the current team since 1998. Its Gouden Carolus beers include clear, heavily caramelized, dark brown **Classic ★★★**; US-influenced strong, pale, hoppy-faced but modestly bitter **Hopsinjoor ★★☆**; clean, precise, sweetish and light golden **Tripel ★★☆**; and premium-priced, annually recreated deep brown monster **Cuvée van de Keizer Blauw ★★★→★★★★**.

BOELENS
St Niklaas, East Flanders

Brewery founded 1993 at a drinks merchant near St Niklaas, west of Antwerp. Former honey beer specialist evolving into a star brewer. **Waase Wolf ★★☆** is a light copper-coloured, spiced ale best described as Flemish; brown **Dubbel Klok ★★★** is confident, caramel-laced, fruity and robust; blond **Tripel Klok ★★★☆** matches an intense herbal hop aroma to a substantial, mellow, grainy body; leaving only golden **Bieken ★★☆** flying the flag for honey beer.

BOSTEELS
Buggenhout, East Flanders

Family brewery northwest of Brussels, famed for glassware. Candied amber **Pauwel Kwak ★★** is served in a stand-mounted coachman's flask; spicy blond **Tripel Karmeliet ★★☆**, sweetened by wheat and oats, has a painted goblet; and **DeuS ★★☆** is presented in Champagne flutes; a production method like that of classic sparkling wine is used to create a highly carbonated, pungent and expensive pale blond sparkling barley wine.

BZART
Niel-bij-As, Limburg

Our riskiest Belgian entry by far not only is missing a brewery, but also has no intention of acquiring one. Instead, this small group of friends has invested in oak casks in which they referment existing beers using Champagne yeast, creating extraordinary results with beers based on and designated as **Blonde**, **Lambiek**, **Krieklambiek** and **Oude Geuze ★★★→★★★☆**.

CNUDDE
Eine, East Flanders

Not so much a brewery as a working antique, near Oudenaarde. This occasional brewhouse puts out one brown ale and ages it in metal tanks. **Cnudde Bruin ★★☆** is a dry, sourish, grainy brown ale with strong lactic presence, in which cherries are sometimes steeped to create rare, grab-it-if-you-see-it **Bizon Bier ★★☆**.

CONTRERAS
Gavere, East Flanders

Farm-based brewery south of Ghent. Gradual renovation of equipment and

VALEIR
D I V E R S

ARTISANAAL GEBROUWEN TRIPEL BIER VAN HOGE GISTING - HERGIST IN DE FLES
BIÈRE TRIPLE ARTISANALE DE HAUTE FERMENTATION - REFERMENTÉE EN BOUTEILLE
TRIPLE TOP FERMENTATION BEER - REFERMENTATION IN THE BOTTLE
BIRRA TRIPLE ARTIGIANALE AD ALTA FERMENTAZIONE - RIFERMENTATA NELLA BOTTIGLIA
CERVEZA TRIPLE ARTESANAL DE ALTA FERMENTACIÓN - REFERMENTADA EN BOTELLA

brands brought a reliable range of Valeir beers. Blond is better double-hopped as **Extra ★★**; **Donker ★★** is medium-brown and liquorice-laced; and **Divers ★★☆** is a soft light golden *tripel*. Light copper local pale ale **Tonneke ★★☆** baffles those drawn to big tastes and clear styles, as does its seasonal variant **Especial Mars ★★**.

DESTINATION
OOSTAKKER

Geerts Drankenhandel
(7 Ledergemstraat) is the finest beer supermarket in Belgium, just off the Ghent ring road, well-stocked, simply presented, full of rare Belgian and better imported beers. Good parking.

DE BRABANDERE
Bavikhove, West Flanders

Family-dominated brewery northeast of Kortrijk. Five low-alcohol *tafelbieren* ("table beers") like **Triple Bock ★★** are of historic interest; summer and winter versions of **Wittekerke** wheat beer **★→★★** are popular; acidic,

ultra-dry, oak-aged **Petrus Aged Pale ★★☆** is an acquired taste; while ruby-tinted **Petrus Dubbel Bruin ★★☆** coalesces polish with a nice malt mix and adequate hopping.

DE KONINCK (DUVEL MOORTGAT)
Antwerp

Brewed in Antwerp and part of the city's soul. Saved from closure by a takeover in 2010. Its main beer, an amber quaffer made with 100% malt and Saaz hops, is **De Koninck**, best unpasteurized on draught, OK in bottle, rough when in cask **★★☆→★☆**. All other brands seem to fail, though neat and polished *dubbel*, **Winter ★★**, and clean, finely balanced, light amber **Triple d'Anvers ★★** almost work.

DE RYCK
Herzele, East Flanders

Small century-old family brewery, between Ghent and Brussels. Pale ale **Special De Ryck ★★☆** is soft but rugged-edged; while the newish range of Arend beers includes the interesting, zesty and yeasty **Blond ★★**; a workmanlike, dryish, caramelled brown **Dubbel ★★**; and a nicely evolving orange-blond **Tripel ★★★** in which floral, citrus and sweet elements complement each other.

DILEWYNS
Dendermonde, East Flanders

This 2011 brewhouse is the Dilewyns family's first in decades, arriving as precisely designed as their Vicaris beers. The **Tripel ★★☆** is reliable, balanced, biscuity and full-flavoured; sometimes found blended with lambic as the clunky-sounding **Tripel-Gueuze 7%** ★★☆; while **Generaal** ★★★☆ is a star-quality, liquorice-laced, sumptuous brown ale, gifted by the brewer to her grandmother.

DOCHTER VAN DE KORENAAR, DE
Baarle-Hertog, Antwerp

Founded in 2007 at Baarle-Hertog, a Belgian enclave in the Netherlands, a small brewery with minimal production that will grow when it soon moves location. **Noblesse** ★★☆ is a spicy-ending quencher of a golden ale; strong, spicy, rye-seeded **Finesse** ★★☆ is changed but not improved when barrel-aged; beefy brown **Embrasse** ★★★ is a lovely, chocolaty, strong abbey-ish ale that marries well with Islay barrel-conditioning in special editions; and **L'Ensemble** ★★★☆ is a powerful, limited edition barley wine with berryish malt and outstanding complexity.

DESTINATION
ANTWERP

Kulminator (32 Vleminckveld) is a charming old drinks café just off the city centre, with perhaps the largest range of aged beers found anywhere, mostly Belgian but with some other extreme rarities.

DUVEL MOORTGAT
Breendonk, Antwerp

Belgium's most successful independent brewery, near Antwerp. Flagship strong golden ale **Duvel** ★★☆ has lost a step over the years, but is redeemed in its **Triple Hop** incarnation ★★★☆;

best light beer is **Bel Pils** ★★; while the declining Maredsous brands include **8 Bruin** *dubbel* ★★, which no longer cedes sweetness to complexity on ageing. Acquiring Liefmans of Oudenaarde led to an upgrade of its cherried ale to **Cuvée-Brut** ★★★.

EUTROPIUS
Heule, West Flanders

In the same premises, near Kortrijk, vacated by **ALVINNE** when it moved to Moen. Still finding its feet but unafraid to experiment with beers that sport prominent hoppy flavours, including its original US-hopped *tripel*, **First Angel** ★★★; honeyed, floral, bitter brown **Remembrance Beer '14-'18** ★★☆; and sweet, strong, amber-blond **Vinkenier** ★★☆.

GLAZEN TOREN
Erpe-Mere, East Flanders

Small brewery run by beer writer Jef Van Den Steen and friends at Erpe-Mere, near Aalst. Tries to use locally grown hops in sweetish beers like amber **Saison d'Erpe Mere** ★★☆ beyond any *saison* style we know; perfumed, citrus, murky oats and buckwheat "double *wit*" **Jan De Lichte** ★★☆; orange-blond and prominently hopped **Ondineke Oilsjtersen Tripel** ★★★; and the excellent dark, rich **Canaster Winterscotch** ★★★☆.

HALVE MAAN, DE
Bruges, West Flanders

The Vanneste family reacquired its brewery in 2007. The Brugse Zot beers tend to be safe, though the grassy, pale **Blond** ★★☆ makes an excellent fallback beer and equally reliable **Dubbel** ★★ is growing pleasant edges. Straffe Hendrik brands are bolder: **Tripel** ★★★ being a crisp, golden-amber strong ale; and **Quadrupel** barley wine ★★★☆ being deep brown, rich and fruity. Persistently improving.

DESTINATION BRUGES

't Brugs Beertje (5 Kemelstraat) is a simple, charming and welcoming backstreet café in old Bruges, where a quiet revolution in beer appreciation began in 1985, renewing its vows daily with a list of 300 beers.

HOFBROUWERIJKE, 'T
Beerzel, Antwerp

One-man hobby brewery east of Antwerp, with a prodigious output of beers, some regular and impressive. Top of the tree is lightish, roasty, dry Irish-style stout **Hofblues** ★★★; unmistakably Belgian pale ale **Hoftrol** ★★☆ is a reliable all-malt creation; and lighter, slightly tangy pale ale **Hofnar** ★★, with whisky malt, is worth sourcing.

KERKOM
Kerkom, Limburg

Brewing at the old farmstead in Kerkom, near Sint-Truiden, has ceased for now, forcing the hire of facilities elsewhere to produce classically light, aromatic, super-hoppy **Bink Blond** ★★★; assertive, fulsome, golden **Kerckomse Tripel** (US: Bink) ★★★☆; ruby-brown, bittersweet and spiced seasonal **Winterkoninkske** ★★; and its blockbuster namesake, the huge and complex barley wine **Grand Cru** ★★★☆.

LEROY
Boezinge, West Flanders

In Boezinge since 1720 but averse to limelight. Owned by the same family as VAN EECKE. **Leroy Stout** ★★ is a dark, sweet, ruddy-brown, low-alcohol milk stout; **Sas Pils** ★★ is precise with true pilsner character; **Yperman** ★★☆ is a ginger-coloured and caramelized Flemish pale ale; and **Christmas Leroy** ★★☆ is deeper and richer, usually achieved at medium gravity.

LOTERBOL
Diest, Flemish Brabant

A recovered brewery that restarted brewing in 1995 next to the wholesaler that handles the interests of Trappist brewers. Its light amber draught **6°** ★★☆ has banana edges; bottled, dry-hopped **Blond 8°** ★★★ and burnt, bittersweet **Bruin 8°** ★★☆ are steadily improving; while errant maniac **Tuverbol**, a blend of strong ale and 3 FONTEINEN lambic, needs five years' cellaring to reach its proper character ★★☆ → ★★★☆.

MALHEUR
Buggenhout, East Flanders

A 1997 brewery added to a drink merchant's business. Regular Malheur beers include golden-blond **6 ★★**, an English-style pale ale; and over-pepped blond *tripel* **10 ★★**. Like near neighbour **BOSTEELS** it dabbles in classic-sparkling-wine-style, high carbonation beers but without pungent spicing. Of these, straw-coloured **Bière Brut Reserve ★★★** is strong and appealing; while **Brut Noir ★★★** is an effervescent dark malt drink spewing coffee and chocolate in its after-burn.

NIEUWHUYS
Hoegaarden, Flemish Brabant

This tiny 2006 brewery expanded to small in 2013. Its soft but tangy Flemish pale ale **Rosdel ★★** is a rarity; as is the faintly floral, lightly coriandered *witbier* **Huardis ★★**; though the limelight beckons for its accomplished heavyweight brown *tripel* **Alpaïde ★★★**.

PALM
Steenhuffel, Flemish Brabant

The second largest independent ale brewer in Belgium, based northwest of Brussels. Owns **RODENBACH** and half of **BOON**. Surprisingly good pilsner **Estaminet ★★** is made with Saaz hops and tastes of a brewery; easy-drinking staple **Palm Speciale ★★** is well made and clean; amber-blond **Royale ★★** is smoother, sweeter and stronger; and **Steenbrugge Dubbel Bruin ★★** is a polished interpretation with added *gruut*.

PIRLOT
Zandhoven, Antwerp

Brewing for several years at **PROEF** before installing first-rate kit to make well-practised Kempisch Vuur beers such as fulsome, oat-filled **Haverstout ★★☆**; roasted, sharpish, red-brown **3-Dubbel ★★★**; and unusual stronger blond, rustic **Tripel ★★★**. **Kerstvuur** is a rarely dull but changeable Christmas brew **★★☆→★★★**.

PROEF
Lochristi, East Flanders

Top-rate modern brewery between Ghent and Antwerp, creating bespoke beers of high technical quality for hundreds of wannabe and established brewers. The in-house Reinaert range includes one of few examples of a 100% malt **Tripel ★★☆**; and heavy, chestnut-coloured barley wine, **Grand Cru ★★☆**. Its efforts for others too often go unacknowledged.

RODENBACH (PALM)
Roeselare, West Flanders

Unique 1899 brewery full of huge oak tuns, mostly ripening a single brown ale for up to two years. Blended into fresh beer this makes sour-edged, pleasant-

enough **Rodenbach** ★★, but in its raw form, filtered and slightly sweetened it becomes **Grand Cru** ★★★☆, an ultra-tangy, red-brown ale of fine oak-aged character, often appealing to wine drinkers. Selected runs in larger bottles become **Vintage** ★★★★. **Vin de Céréale** ★→★★★ is an occasional and experimental single tun bottling of a higher strength brew.

SLAGHMUYLDER
Ninove, East Flanders

Family-owned 1860 brewery, west of Brussels, becoming one of Belgium's first lager breweries in 1926. Its seasonal **Paas-** and **Kerstbier** ★★☆ are variations on its regular pilsner. Better known for its Witkap range, including slightly peppery pale ale **Special** ★★; fruity, aromatic, light blond **Stimulo** ★★☆; and unusual, yeast-spiced, straw-coloured **Tripel** ★★★.

SMISJE
Mater, East Flanders

The hamlet of Mater's smaller brewery. The **Smiske Nature-Ale** ★★ is an instantly likeable pale ale using Poperinge hops and 100% malted barley, appearing dry-hopped as **Extra** ★★☆. Newer are ruddy-brown work-in-progress **Bruin** ★★; and the annually revamped heavyweight spiced barley wine **Winter** ★★☆.

ST BERNARDUS
Watou, West Flanders

Opened in 1946 to brew commercial scale beers for **WESTVLETEREN**. Went on to develop its own range, including highly spiced **Wit** ★★☆, a wheat beer

of character; a blond, oddly bitter, lighter **Tripel** ★★★; dark, mellow, sweet, stronger *dubbel*, pear-dropped **Prior 8** ★★★☆; massive golden-brown, fruity, alcoholic barley wine **Abt 12** ★★★☆; and darker, spicy winter indulgence **Christmas Ale** ★★★.

DESTINATION KORTRIJK

Boulevard (15 Groeningelaan) is a beautiful, ancient, laid-back café bistro with a wide range of beers and simple delightful snacks to enjoy in Burgundian style inside or overflowing onto the grass.

STRUBBE
Ichtegem, West Flanders

Family brewery (1830) at Ichtegem. Well-hopped **Strubbe Pils** ★★☆ is perhaps Belgium's best; though easy-drinking, sour-edged brown ale **Ichtegems Oud Bruin** ★★ and the slightly sweetened form of its oak-aged parent beer, **Grand Cru (6.5%)** ★★★, are better known. Brews many other beers every year including **Vlaskop** ★★, a wheat beer made with unmalted barley.

DESTINATION OSTEND

To experience the whole of Belgian beer culture under one roof, stay at the family-run **Hotel Marion** (19 Louisastraat), drink in its **Botteltje** beer café and take in its Flemish restaurant, too. Over 300 beers and barely a lager in sight.

STRUISE BROUWERS
Woesten, West Flanders

Rock-star craft beer makers, less well recognized at home, brewing mostly at Deca in Woesten. First attracted attention with aged variations on dark barley wine **Pannepot** ★★★→★★★★; twisting and turning with fruit-steeped, equally strong winter equivalent **Tsjeeses** ★★★; and creating an absurdly strong, surprisingly approachable Imperial stout **Black Albert** ★★★☆. To prove it can brew normal beers, try the disarmingly simple unfiltered, slightly hopped-up **Koeke Blond** ★★☆. Experimental and collaboration beers abound.

TRIEST
Kapelle-op-den-Bos, Flemish Brabant

One to watch in 2015. After winning prizes in some prestigious contests, this respected hobby brewer from west of Mechelen is expanding the production of hoppy-for-Belgium **IPA** ★★☆; confused but effective light brown **Dubbel** ★★★; and cleverly spiced, ruby brown **X-mas** ★★★.

VAN DEN BOSSCHE
Sint-Lievens-Esse, East Flanders

Fourth-generation 1897 tower brewery in a large village south of Ghent. Reputable for middle-strength dark ales like dryish, caramelled **Buffalo 1907** ★★☆, which spawned stronger **Belgian Stout** ★★☆ for the US market. Pater Lieven brands include moderately sweet and toasty **Bruin** ★★☆; and variable big brown spice-bomb **Kerst Pater Special Christmas** ★★→★★★, always with a smack of chocolate.

VAN EECKE
Watou, West Flanders

Small 1862 brewery in the West Flanders hop belt. Its Kapittel range includes well-rounded, easy-drinking dry-hopped **Blond** ★★☆; and medium-dark *tripel* **Prior**, which becomes epic after a few years' cellaring ★★★→★★★★. Misty **Watou's Witbier** ★★☆ is light and lemony; while long-established, far-sighted, proto-IPA **Poperings Hommelbier** blossoms annually when brewed with new harvest hops ★★→★★★.

VAN STEENBERGE
Ertvelde, East Flanders

Started in 1768 and went commercial in the 1900s, at Ertvelde, north of Ghent. Once famed for sour brown ales, now concentrating on abbey beers and export. A once confused range has been trimmed to leave sweet and spicy legacy wheat beer **Celis White** ★★★; well-judged stronger **Augustijn Blond** ★★☆; and **Gulden Draak** ★★★, its opaque bottles obscuring a serious, intensely spicy barley wine finished with a vintner's yeast.

VANDER GHINSTE, OMER
Bellegem, West Flanders

The fifth Omer Vander Ghinste to head up his family's 1892 brewery south of Kortrijk is changing things. A new strong golden ale was also christened **Omer** ★★☆; the blended, faintly sour brown ale has relaunched as **VanderGhinste Oud Bruin** ★★; and the sour, 18-month-old lambic-like beer that adds its zing has been released to the US market as **Cuvée des Jacobins Rouge** ★★★.

VERHAEGHE
Vichte, West Flanders

Fourth-generation family brewery near Kortrijk, making regular beers for its drinks warehouse and blends of aged brown ales for the world. Those who like their oak-aged browns sharper, lighter and woodier should prefer **Vichtenaar** ★★★☆; while for darker, sweet-sharp and buttery, choose **Duchesse de Bourgogne** ★★★☆; **Echt Kriekenbier** ★★☆ has whole cherries steeped in it. Best of the rest is **Noël Christmas Weihnacht** ★★☆, a yellow-ochre, lightly spiced seasonal ale.

VIVEN
Sijsele, West Flanders

Beer commissioner and wholesaler helping create an excellent series of Viven beers with PROEF from simpler varieties like pale, hazy, rustic **Belgian Ale** ★★ and hazy golden, off-centre, spice-effect **Blond** ★★, to impressive US-influenced hoppy, roasty, aromatic **Porter** ★★★ and slightly over-hopped **Imperial IPA** ★★☆.

WESTMALLE
Westmalle, Antwerp

Largest of the Trappist brewers, northeast of Antwerp. Responsible for popularizing the dark-*dubbel*, blond-*tripel* divide of stronger ales in the 1950s. Ruddy-brown Trappist **Westmalle Dubbel** appears in large and small bottles and on draught, simplicity rising and chocolaty-fruity edginess falling accordingly ★★→★★★; while stronger pale orange-golden benchmark **Tripel** ★★★ gains colour, allure and a honeyed glow with cellar ageing. Delicate, light golden **Extra** ★★★ is brewed occasionally for the abbey community and some of its friends.

WESTVLETEREN
Westvleteren, West Flanders

Low-production Trappist brewery, afflicted by adulation, the scarcity of its beers being mistaken for magnificence. The only one that uses whole hops is the skilful, light, rustic **Blond** ★★★☆, with its intense floral aroma and just enough grain; **Extra 8°** ★★★ is a liquorice-edged, strong *dubbel* that improves grudgingly in the cellar; and **Abt 12°** ★★★☆ is a dark, intense barley wine that used to grow with keeping but less so now. Special releases for a supermarket chain and US importer were unlikely to have been brewed here exclusively.

BRUSSELS & WALLONIA

The beer of the south is *saison* and it probably does not exist – at least not as a single form. To one side, historically, is French *bière de garde*, ale stored in bottles and casks while its character matures like a fast-motion Alpine lager without the ice. To the other is agricultural practicality, farm brewing being easier in the winter for the availability of a workforce and the absence of insect life. In truth the Wallonian *saison* tradition is as authentically imprecise as that of German *landbier*.

3 FOURQUETS, LES
Bovigny, Luxembourg

Created in 2004 at Les 3 Fourquets restaurant deep in the Ardennes as a retirement hobby for a successful craft brewer. Now making Lupulus ales in 75cl bottles, beginning with spicily hopped **Blonde ★★★☆** and expanding to include dark, sweet citrus-peeled **Brune ★★★☆** and dark winter special **Hibernatus ★★★**.

ABBAYE DES ROCS
Montignies-sur-Roc, Hainaut

Second-generation family brewery, southwest of Mons. The original **Brune ★★★** is a huge, spiced, ruddy-brown ale; **La Montagnarde ★★☆** is a darkish amber *tripel* full of malt with spicy edges; while best of the lighter brews are **Blanche des Honnelles ★★**, a "double" wheat beer with malted oats and minimal spicing, and complex, unspiced blond ale **Altitude 6 ★★☆**.

BASTOGNE
Vaux-sur-Sûre, Luxembourg

Brewing began in 2007 at RULLES, then moved to its own brewery in 2009,

near Bouillon in the far southwest. Started safe but becoming more daring. The La Trouffette range includes grainy, herbal **Blonde ★★☆**; a fruity, tangy unspiced **Brune ★★☆**; playful, light, dry bitter **Belle d'Été ★★☆**; and light blond, hop-laced spelt beer **Bastogne Pale Ale ★★☆**.

BLAUGIES
Blaugies, Hainaut

Second-generation family brewery on the French border, southwest of Mons, since 1988. Dry amber-blond, hazy, grainy **Darbyste ★★** has a dab of fig juice and is best drunk fresh; **Saison de l'Epeautre ★★★★** has clumpy turbidity, the aroma of a hay barn and a hop-yeast-buckwheat combo that delivers a rural idyll to the glass; and **La Moneuse ★★★** is a punchy, stronger *saison* tasting like a huge best bitter made with its characteristic yeast-hop double act.

BRUNEHAUT
Rongy, Hainaut

Brewing since 1992, south of Tournai. Technical quality has always been high but a new owner-brewer has brought more interest. Organic **Bio Blanche** ★★☆ is the best of a range in which others are gluten-free, while the St Martin beers had peaked with fruity, liquorice **Brune** ★★ and floral, bready **Tripel** ★★ before the massive, cask-aged black barley wine **Cloak of St Martin** ★★★ arrived.

CARACOLE
Falmignoul, Namur

Well-respected 1994 brewery in an ancient brewhouse in the Meuse valley. **Troublette** ★★★ is an interesting, cloudy, lightly spiced wheat beer; flagship **Caracole** ★★★ is a strongish amber ale made with five malts and orange peel; **Saxo** ★★☆ is a strong golden-blond ale; and **Nostradamus** ★★★ is the rich, warming, spiced barley wine.

CAZEAU
Templeuve, Hainaut

Farm brewery west of Tournai, in its third incarnation; the original started in 1753, this one in 2004. Tournay beers include solid, dependable, crafty-edged **Blond** ★★★; **Noire** ★★★, a roasted strong porter of promise; and **Noël** ★★★, a large, sweetish brown ale reminiscent of old-style Gauloise. **Saison Cazeau** ★★★ is a wispy summer ale that mixes floral hops with elderflower.

CHIMAY
Chimay, Hainaut

Second largest Trappist brewer, at the Abbaye Notre-Dame de Scourmont in southern Hainaut. Began small scale in 1862, expanding in the 1920s. Brewed and fermented at the abbey, bottled and matured in Bailleux. Adopts different names for 75cl bottles. **Rouge (Première)** ★★ is a slim-bodied red-brown *dubbel* with light, crude bitterness; **Blanche (Cinq Cents)** ★★☆ is an improving, well-balanced *tripel* that appears part-filtered on draught; and **Bleue (Grande Réserve)** ★★★ is a giant barley wine that avoids cloying.

DUBUISSON
Pipaix, Hainaut

Family-run brewery east of Tournai, which began brewing a super-strong English-style beer in 1931, its sole product until 1991. The original sweet, heavy, 12% ABV Bush (US: Scaldis) barley wine is now **Ambrée** ★★☆, which also comes oak-aged as **Prestige** ★★★☆; and again aged rather variably in old barriques of Nuits-St-Georges, hence **Bush de Nuits** ★→★★★. Also makes lighter, hazy, spiced blond **Cuvée des Trolls** ★★.

DUPONT
Tourpes, Hainaut

Photogenic farm brewery with ultra-modern kit, east of Tournai. Its

thumbprint yeast mix screams farmhouse. Brewing since 1844, in the family since 1920. Faintly musty, hopyard, barn-in-autumn, style-defining **Saison Dupont ★★★★** even outshines its Wallonian *tripel*, **Moinette Blonde ★★★☆**. Other greats include curiously attractive, unfiltered **Rédor Pils ★★★**; and strong amber **Bière de Beloeil ★★★**. Makes many organic beers including florally hopped **Biolégère ★★★**, in an older, lighter *saison* style.

ELLEZELLOISE (LÉGENDES)
Ellezelles, Hainaut

This 1993 farmhouse brewery near Ellezelles in northern Hainaut, is the folksier half of Brasserie des Légendes (*see* GÉANTS), and uses flip-top bottles. **Blanche de Saisis ★★** is a tasty dark blond unspiced wheat beer; **Quintine Blonde ★★☆** is an unusually bitter, peel-edged stronger blond; but the pride of place goes to Imperial-strength **Hercule Stout ★★★☆**, whose chocolate and prune flavours are offset by something Irish.

GÉANTS (LÉGENDES)
Ath, Hainaut

Légendes' other half (*see also* ELLEZELLOISE) brews in a 21st-century brewery at a 12th-century castle on the outskirts of Ath, east of Tournai. Sweetish, light amber **Saison Voisin ★★** foils style junkies through low hopping but has genuine 1884 pedigree; **Gouyasse Triple ★★☆** has a fulsome, grainy character with aged edges; while the most impressive regular is quirky, red-brown, off-peaty, yeast-spiced **Urchon ★★★**.

JANDRAIN-JANDRENOUILLE
Jandrain-Jandrenouille, Walloon Brabant

This brewery, established in 2007 in a converted barn at a double-barrelled village south of Brussels, uses American kit and hops to make Belgian beers. Its **IV Saison ★★★** is in the modern floral bitter style that influenced early US craft brewers; the red-brown **V Cense ★★★** would be a black *saison* if such a thing existed; and **VI Wheat ★★☆** is a mid-Atlantic wheat beer that begins with Simcoe hops, ends with Belgian spicing and does fresh bread throughout.

MILLEVERTUS
Breuvanne, Luxembourg

This lovably adventurous 2004 Luxembourg brewery moved in 2011 to Breuvanne. An overly large portfolio of products includes the plum-tinged, aromatic wheat beer **Blanchette de Lorraine ★★**; a Belgian take on US-style IPA called **La Bella Mère ★★☆**; and **La Douce Vertus ★★**, a lush, sweetish, full and dark French-style *bière brune*.

ORVAL
Villers-devant-Orval, Luxembourg

When the Trappist abbey of Orval, near Florenville, was reconstructed in 1926 the Order added a brewery to assist with costs. **Orval ★★★☆** is a unique dry-hopped, bottled pale ale presented in a distinctive bottle, full of hops in the nose but not on the palate, flirting with genius by adding musty overtones to both by using brettanomyces in bottle-fermentation.

RANKE, DE
Dottignies, Hainaut

Small brewery north of Tournai, run by a great Flemish brewing team who led the return of hops to Belgian brewing and revived mixed fermentation beers. **Saison de Dottignies ★★★** is the cleanest of the hoppier *saisons*; **XX Bitter ★★★☆** is a pale golden ale of thirst-quenching bitterness; **Guldenberg ★★★☆** is what happens when herbal hops are loaded into a well-made *tripel*; and dark, strong **Noir de Dottignies ★★★** defies classification deliciously. **Cuvée de Ranke ★★☆** is a sparkling musty concoction made by mixing blond ale with young lambic.

ROCHEFORT
Rochefort, Namur

Small Trappist brewery near Rochefort, south of Namur, cursed by being considered among the best in the world. Trappistes Rochefort **6 ★★★** is a light ruddy brown, dryish *dubbel* that gained character in a recent revision; **8 ★★★☆** is the staple – an interesting,

CUVÉE DE RANKE

70% BELGIAN SOUR ALE WITH 30% LAMBIC ADDED

Unpasteurised - Unfiltered.

red-brown, often hazy ale with firm chocolate backtastes; while **10 ★★★★** is the supremely complex barley wine, best sipped or inhaled from a chalice, while seated in the glow of an open fire.

DESTINATION
LIÈGE

Bars with a huge range of beers are rare in Wallonia, but the chain that began with suburban **Vaudrée 1** (109 rue du Val Benoît, Angleur) and central **Vaudrée 2** (149 rue Saint-Gilles) has expanded to seven, each opening daily until the small hours, with 250–500 beers and a huge menu.

RULLES
Rulles, Luxembourg

Small 1998 brewery in the southernmost part of the Belgian Ardennes. From a strong range we recommend in particular punchy, hop-packed, light pale ale **Estivale ★★★**; original perfectly balanced, faintly spicy and characterful **Blonde ★★★**; workmanlike **Brune ★★☆** with its dried- and tropical-fruit edges; and superb **Triple ★★★☆**, a beer that manages distinctive character with meticulous delivery.

SENNE
Brussels

Fully formed new arrival, making beers that capture past and future equally well. Hoppy light ale **Taras Boulba ★★★** is best bottled or in Brussels; near-perfect prize-winning **Stouterik ★★★☆** is a lighter stout that defies subtyping; precisely hopped pale ale **Zinnebir ★★★** similarly avoids being American, British or a modern *saison*; while sweetish, yeast-spiced, orange-blond *tripel* **Jambe-de-Bois** ★★★☆ has snuck up to become one of Belgium's most enjoyable beers.

DESTINATION
BRUSSELS

Moeder Lambic Fontainas (8 place Fontainas) is a modern café next to Anneessens metro, with the best range of rare draught Belgian beers in the country, a few special foreign beers and top-quality finger food. In contrast, **Poechenellekelder** (5 rue du Chêne) is a delightfully eccentric drinks café opposite the Manneken Pis, with a superbly chosen beer list, puppetry and an atmosphere that is hard to beat.

ST FEUILLIEN
Le Roeulx, Hainaut

Handsome 1873 brewery between Charleroi and Mons. Recent years have seen some confident new beers such as **Saison** ★★★, which has grown steadily to be up with the best; the

house staple **Blonde** ★★☆ is well rounded and aromatic; newer **Grand Cru** ★★★ is restrained and delicate for a heavyweight pale golden *tripel*; and light-red-brown **Cuvée de Noël** ★★☆ is an indulgent soup of spices. Occasionally sold in massive bottles.

DESTINATION
MONS

A dozen bars around the Grand Place have good selections of Wallonian beers, including two, **Excelsior** (no 29) and **Cervoise** (no 25), where the exceptional choice includes many that are hard to source.

VAL-DIEU
Aubel, Liège

Brewing since 1997 in the impressive setting of a 13th-century abbey in rural northern Liège. High technical quality has not always been accompanied by full-on flavours but their firm, caramelled **Brune** ★★☆, fruity, alcoholic **Triple** ★★☆ and dark, warming and assertive **Grand Cru** ★★★ are all gradually maturing.

VAPEUR, À
Pipaix, Hainaut

Saved from extinction in 1984 by idealists and still steaming away three decades later. The Vapeur brands are **Légère** ★★, a light ale sprinkled with vanilla and cinnamon; microbiologically odd, spiced, strong amber-blond **En Folie** ★★; and herbal, amber heavyweight **Cochonne** ★★☆. Frankly acidic and highly spiced **Saison de Pipaix** ★★ is as per the original, allegedly.

THE LAMBIC MAKERS OF BRUSSELS & PAYOTTENLAND

The lambic beers of Brussels and the rural area to its west, Payottenland, are the ultimate examples of folk brewing. In a tradition of dry to sourish wheat beers that had been present in western and central European brewing for centuries, they take the idea of local variation to a new level by fermenting only with "wild" yeast, initially air-borne and found growing around the maker's storage areas or caves, and inside the oak casks in which lambics ferment. Few flavour characteristics are shared with ale or lager, most ending blended as *gueuze* or fruit-steeped as *kriek* or *framboise*.

3 FONTEINEN
Beersel, Flemish Brabant

Recently restyled 3F, a passionately committed lambic maker and now brewer, south of Brussels. Distinctive, dry and delicately bitter, pungent **Oude Gueuze** is also available as **Vintage ★★★→★★★★**; while its neatly balanced, big fruit and lambic **Oude Kriek** takes on historically traditional flavour as **Schaarbeekse ★★★→★★★★** when made with small, hard bitter Schaarbeek cherries. Ancient oddity **Doesjel ★★★** is a bottled lambic from a cask that fails to ferment properly. For a modern twist try near-black, mixed fermentation **Zwet.be ★★☆**, ale-fermented and *Brettanomyces*-conditioned, its taste heading off toward oak-aged brown ale.

BOON
Lembeek, Flemish Brabant

The southernmost lambic brewer, at Lembeek, south of Halle, and the most influential. Kept aloft by a commercial cherry beer but better represented spiritually by surprisingly approachable, grapefruit-tinted **Oude Gueuze ★★★** and

sharp, slightly sour but high-fruited **Oude Kriek ★★★☆**. **Oude Geuze Mariage Parfait ★★★☆** is delightfully dry but with a softness that comes from higher gravity. Also makes a lambic-free malt-driven dark brown ale with liquorice overlay called **Duivels Bier ★★☆**, for fun.

CAM, DE
Gooik, Flemish Brabant

Blender and steeper of other brewers' lambics. Most frequently encountered are the tart, lemon-grapefruit and horse-blanket mélange called **De Cam Oude Geuze ★★★☆**; and dark, vinous, sour-cherry, ultra-dry **Oude Kriek ★★★**; though the occasional, musty, lemony, late-bottled **Oude Lambiek ★★★** and sharp, spritzy, candy-coated, light amber bottled **Oude Faro ★★★** will amuse or amaze too.

CANTILLON
Brussels

Not far from Midi station near the centre of Brussels, part museum but mostly revered creator of astonishing drinks. 100% lambic and mostly organic ingredients. Half the output is accomplished, dry, slightly bitter, light citrus **Cantillon Gueuze 100% Lambic ★★★☆**. The rest is mostly fruit-steeped lambics such as the sharp, wild, lightly cherried regular **Kriek**, and its *grand cru* version **Lou Pepe ★★★→★★★★**; hybrid, black-graped **St Lamvinus ★★★☆**, aged in burgundy casks; and flowery, pink, extra dry and delicate framboise **Rosé de Gambrinus ★★★☆**. Darker, more assertive **Iris ★★★☆** cannot be a *gueuze* as it is all barley.

DE TROCH
Wambeek, Flemish Brabant

Oldest of the surviving lambic makers, probably at Wambeek since 1780. Troubled for decades, fruit syrups being added to lambics drifting toward eccentricity. New dynamics are now in play and the latest stock of **Chapeau Cuvée Oude Gueuze ★★☆** has raised heads. A dry and challenging **Oude Kriek ★★** appears occasionally too.

GIRARDIN
Sint-Ulriks-Kapelle, Flemish Brabant

Fourth-generation family brewers, on the farm at Sint-Ulriks-Kapelle since 1882. Most of the flat draught lambic found in Payottenland cafés will be its lightly carbonated, fungal, beery **Jonge ★★★**, or sharper, flat, musty, vinous **Oude Lambic ★★**. **1882 Gueuze** still appears in white- and black-labelled versions, respectively dominated by filtered young lambic or else masterfully blended with older casks **★★→★★★**. The **1882 Kriek** is filtered and sweetish in the bottle but drier and hazy on draught **★★→★★★**.

HANSSENS
Dworp, Flemish Brabant

Longest established of the lambic caves. Tart and slightly bitter **Hanssens Artisanaal Oude Gueuze ★★★** ages beautifully for five years and more to become slightly smoky; unusually, its well-cherried but sharp **Oude Kriek ★★★☆** also gains maturity for a couple of years; while unique, must-try traditionally made **Oudbeitje ★★★** gains little colour but much aroma from its strawberries. **Lambic Experimental** beers **★★★** in raspberry and blackcurrant are just that.

DESTINATION DWORP

On the main road east from the E19 junction 20, south of Brussels, are two contrasting bars, each with an exceptional selection of authentic lambics. For a stylish but cosy corner café visit **De Zwaan** (1 Gemeentehuisstraat); for reliable cooking in a barn of a place make it **Boelekwis** (856 Alsembergsesteenweg).

LINDEMANS
Vlezenbeek, Flemish Brabant

Seventh-generation lambic brewer. The single lambic is lighter in colour and strength than most and is put to best effect in the sharp, light, lemony and faintly hoppy **Cuvée René Grand Cru Oude Gueuze ★★★** and the steadily evolving **Kriek Cuvée René ★★★**. Among a clutch of sweeter beers, the semi-authentic darkish

Faro Lambic ★★ is most enticing when served iced on a hot day.

MORT SUBITE (HEINEKEN)
Kobbegem, Flemish Brabant

This is part of a global group that possesses a handful of massive century-old, oak tuns in which its better lambics are aged. Most of its production consists of commercial fruit beer but two of its products are made in the old-fashioned way. The rarely encountered, faintly acetic and not so agricultural **Oude Gueuze** ★★☆ is not as balanced as the sweeter-fruited, mouldy-in-a-good-way **Oude Kriek** ★★★.

OUD BEERSEL
Beersel, Flemish Brabant

Lambic cave in a preserved former brewery, brewing own-recipe lambics at BOON. These are blended to become an increasingly distinctive, bitter, citrus **Oude Geuze** ★★★☆ that has begun to win prizes, and steeped to produce a pretty confident, sharpish, bottled **Oude Kriek** ★★★. The base beer, draught, flat, youngish **Oude Lambiek** ★★★ can be found in a few dozen cafés locally and in Brussels.

TILQUIN
Bierghes, Walloon Brabant

The newest lambic cave or *gueuzerie*, just south of Payottenland, has settled swiftly into creating good things from the lambics it matures. The **Oude Gueuze Tilquin à l'Ancienne** ★★★☆ has grown impressively; its first whole-fruit lambic, uniquely steeped with plums, **Oude Quetsche** ★★★☆ turned heads; and you can even find a draught **Faro** ★★☆ occasionally. The draught **Gueuze** ★★☆, said by some to be typical of old Brussels, continues to be controversial.

TIMMERMANS
Itterbeek, Flemish Brabant

Brewery (1850) owned by a drinks and leisure group. Mostly commercial fruit beers but its **Oude Gueuze** ★★☆ is perhaps the driest and tartest of all; as is experimental **Oude Kriek** ★★☆. Among the rest are lambic-*witbier* hybrid **Lambicus Blanche** ★★; and dark, fruity **Bourgogne des Flandres Bruin** ★★, made by mixing lambic into brown ale to imitate ageing.

GERMANY

As recently as 1980 half the breweries in the world and 80% of those in the European Union were to be found in Germany. Since then the number of breweries in Germany has risen to nearly 1500 but the proportion of breweries in the world this represents has fallen to 12% and in Europe to 25%.

The type of German brewery has also changed. Brewpubs, or *hausbrauereien,* have increased in number enormously, particularly in the north, and more recently a typical new brewery has been a tiny operation, the size of a mechanized home-brew kit. Meanwhile, the typical, small, old family-owned and run village and town breweries have been on the wane.

The hallmarks of German beer are delicacy and purity. Classically, it is made with one or more of the four "noble" (*edel* in German) hops: Hallertau, Spalt, Tettnang and Saaz. It is designed to adhere to the now defunct *Reinheitsgebot* (*see* box, page 48). While most of it is bottom-fermented, even those that are top-fermented are lagered for several weeks at Alpine temperatures.

Given that the global picture for beer is that total volumes remain static, with significant growth in craft beers and gradual falls in basic ones, the German brewing industry's unique ability to make pure beers in massive volumes should put it in good stead to make inroads. Sadly, the larger brewery groups seem to be rising to the challenge by making economies of scale and starting to cut corners.

Most of the better-known beer brands in Germany are owned by the ever-conflating brewing groups that control much of the market. AB InBev owns Becks, Diebels, Löwenbräu and Franziskaner; Carlsberg owns Holsten; and Heineken controls Paulaner and many others. Thus far the Bitburger, Oettinger, Oetker and Krombacher groups remain in German hands.

While it is correct to see most German beer as orderly, it would be wrong to see it as either monochrome or monotonous. To consider

all German beer to be clear blond lager would be wrong. While a broad take on "pils" might encompass 70% of German beer – a figure lower than many nations – this will include many styles correctly divisible into *helles*, export, *märzen*, *spezial* and even the occasional longer-aged, darker-hued *lagerbier*.

More interesting are the types of beer that clearly owe their origins to particular regions, or those amorphously described as *landbier*, k*ellerbier* or z*wickelbier.* Our brewery choices feature heavily those breweries that represent older regional and local traditions, and those that are trying to revive German interest in the diversity of beer. Brewers of adequate, shiny froth-tops have fared badly.

BAVARIA

The Free State of Bavaria is home to 15% of the German population and over half its breweries. It only became part of Germany in 1919, though it had influenced brewing in the region for centuries. Of its seven districts, two in particular – Oberfranken (Upper Franconia) in the north around Bamberg and Bayreuth, and Oberbayern (Upper Bavaria) in the south around Munich – warrant the special attention of, and deserve a visit from, any serious beer lover for what they say about the nature of beer.

THE REINHEITSGEBOT

The German beer-purity order, or *Reinheitsgebot*, was seen in turns as the world's first and longest-lasting piece of consumer protection law; a lucrative patronage scam; and ultimately, by the EU, a restraint of trade.

In 1516 at Ingolstadt, after price wars developed between brewers and bakers over the purchase of wheat, and concerns grew that brewers were polluting local beers with anything from pulses and root vegetables to mushrooms and animal products, the rulers of Bavaria instigated the *Surrogatvebot*, an order banning brewers from making beer from anything other than barley, hops and water, yeast escaping mention for being undiscovered.

Wheat was soon excluded from the ban, though brewers who used it had to be licensed directly by the royal household.

As the German states came together slowly over the centuries, then precipitately under Bismarck, the regulation spread northward, becoming woven into a notion of German-ness. By 1906 it had become universal, Bavaria having made its adoption a precondition for becoming part of Germany, which it eventually did in 1919.

Critics of the *Reinheitsgebot* tend to decry the restraints it put on recipes and thereby the brewer's imagination, while its supporters cite exactly the same concerns, only from a different perspective.

MUNICH & UPPER BAVARIA

Munich's Oktoberfest may steal the publicity, but the city's famous beer halls are far more enjoyable and available all year round, while outside the great beer gardens of Oberbayern beckon visitors to sit under the linden trees from May to October, here to drink beer by the litre-sized *maß* in preference to the half-litre *seidla*.

ANDECHS, KLOSTERBRAUEREI
Andechs, Bavaria

Famous brewery below Andechs monastery, founded by Benedictine monks in 1455. Still owned by the order, but brewing is now carried out by secular staff. Andechser beers include **Export Dunkel ★★** with hints of bitter chocolate; the complex **Weissbier Dunkel ★★** with banana, chocolate and caramel flavours; clove- and banana-dominated **Weissbier Hell ★★**; and the frustrating **Doppelbock Dunkel ★★☆** with insufficient weight to be a classic.

AUGUSTINER-BRÄU
Munich, Bavaria

One of only two large Munich breweries not attached to global brewers – Hofbräu

is owned by the state of Bavaria – and so loved locally that it no longer needs to advertise. The name Augustiner-Bräu München is most associated with the sweet, pale **Edelstoff ★★★**; the bready **Lagerbier Hell ★★★☆** sets the standard for *helles* lagers; the **Dunkel ★★☆** does the same for darker beers; aromatic hop character abounds in the **Pils ★★**; while powerful **Maximator ★★★** is all about molasses and dark fruits.

DESTINATION **INTERNET: WWW.BIERKOMPASS.DE**

Germany's leading internet beer shop, importing a fabulous selection of craft beers old and new from around the world, and shipping across Germany and beyond.

AYINGER
Aying, Bavaria

Family-run brewery southeast of Munich named after its village. Ayinger beers enjoy widespread distribution in the US. Best known to enthusiasts for the rich and complex *doppelbock* **Celebrator ★★★**, of which there are echoes in the coffee- and caramel-accented **Altbairisch Dunkel ★★☆**. The stronger and more traditional of two citrus-spicy wheat beers is **Ur-Weisse** ★★; while the pick is **Weizen-Bock** ★★★, which shows up in time for Christmas.

BAUMBURG, KLOSTERBRAUEREI
Altenmarkt, Bavaria

Small brewery in a disused hilltop monastery outside Altenmarkt, brewing since 1612 and owned by the Dietl family since 1875. Ten solid enough beers are made, with lightly roasted, caramel-edged **Baumburger Dunkle Weiße** ★★ and creamy, citrus, seasonal **Weissbier Bock** ★★ hovering above the rest.

CAMBA BAVARIA
Truchtlaching, Bavaria

This 2008 pub brewery was opened to showcase the equipment of brewery manufacturer Braukon but quickly gained a following for its wide range of ales and lagers, many daringly experimental for Bavaria. The regular range of 20 or so Camba or Camba Bavaria beers includes the US-style citrus-hoppy **Pale Ale** ★★☆, and über-pepped **Eric's IPA** ★★☆, while the roasty **Eric's Porter** ★★☆ is head and shoulders above most other German examples. Best of the indigenous beers is the dark and fruity **Truchtl'inger Wilderer Weisse** ★★☆, though the whole shebang is worth a detour.

CREW ALEWERKSTATT
Munich, Bavaria

Cuckoo brewers Mario Hanel and Timm Schnigula use the kit at Schlossbrauerei Hohenthann to make the two ales that around Munich seem to define those bars serving them as interested in the future of beer. Each is a work in progress US-

style, the lighter **CREW Pale Ale** ★★ being hop-heavy, while *bock*-strength **CREW IPA** ★★ is rather subdued. They will get there.

ERDINGER WEISSBRÄU
Erding, Bavaria

The largest wheat beer producer in the world, still owned by the Brombacher family, at Erding just outside Munich. Erdinger beers enjoy global distribution and as often occurs with one so large, are predictably inoffensive. Its **Weißbier** ★☆ is for beginners, while **Urweisse** ★☆ manages to be thin and sweetish despite a claim to be brewed to an 1886 recipe. By far the best is the banana-spicy *weizenbock* **Pikantus** ★★.

ETTAL, KLOSTERBRAUEREI
Ettal, Bavaria

Another monastic brewery where secular staff produce the beer, in a high pass near Oberammergau. Of the Ettaler beers the best for regular drinking is the fruity-caramel **Kloster Dunkel** ★★☆; while the powerful and heavily roasted *doppelbock* **Curator** ★★★ should be approached with care.

FORSCHUNGSBRAUEREI
Munich-Perlach, Bavaria

Interesting small brewery in the Perlach district of greater Munich, founded in 1930, since when four generations of the Jakob family have made experimental beers, mainly for other brewers. Until recently, the only Forschungsbrauerei beers were the generously hopped yet malt-led **Pilsissimus** ★★★, described by the brewery as a *spezial* or export beer but by outsiders as a Bohemian-style pils; and **St Jakobus Blonder Bock** ★★★, which somehow starts out sweet but has a hoppy ending. Seasonal beers have started to appear.

DESTINATION
MUNICH

To understand the whole Bavarian beer thing, find your way around **Weisses Bräuhaus** (7 Tal) for mid-morning white sausage and wheat beer; the **Viktualienmarkt** beer garden for a pre-lunch one from the cask; the **Augustiner Bierhalle** (27 Neuhauser Straße) for pomp and lunch; the **Chinesischer Turm** (3 Englischer Garten) for an afternoon in the park; **Ayingers Speis & Trank** (1a Platzl) for proper food and drink; finishing with the **Hofbräuhaus** (9 Platzl) for oompah, kitsch and the shadow of history.

FREILASSING, WEISSBRÄU
Freilassing, Bavaria

As its name suggests, this tiny 1910 family brewery on the Austrian border near Salzburg makes only wheat beers. The two standard Weißbräu Freilassing beers are a pale, yeasty and citrus-tart **Hefe-Weizen** ★★☆ and equally impressive **Hefe-Weizen Dunkel** ★★. There are also two strong seasonal beers that we infer would reward finding.

GUTMANN
Titting, Bavaria

In the delightfully named Titting, close to the border with Franconia, this sizeable brewery makes mainly a full range of wheat beers, meaning pale, dark, strong, light and alcohol-free. The soft, banana-heavy, fruit-accented **Hefeweizen** ★★☆ is among the best in style; fruity-yeasty down-banana **Dunkles Hefeweizen** ★★ is not far behind; and the powerful yet quaffable pre-Christmas seasonal **Weizenbock** ★★★ also performs well.

HERRNGIERSDORF,
SCHLOSSBRAUEREI
Herrngiersdorf, Bavaria

Founded in 1131 by Benedictine monks, this small brewery south of Regensburg has a strong claim to be the oldest brewery in the world in private ownership. Its main beer is the herbal-hoppy **Schlossbräu Trausnitz Pils** ★★☆; though the equally interesting, aromatic, recent arrival **Hallertauer Hopfen-Cuvée** ★★☆ features Perle, Saphir and two types of Hallertau hops in its recipe.

KARG
Murnau, Bavaria

This wheat beer brewery makes some of the cloudiest beers known to man. Its Karg beers include chewy and yeasty **Helles Hefe-Weißbier** ★★☆; the often lump-infested but tasty **Dunkles Hefe-Weißbier** ★★; and star performer, the rich and fruity winter seasonal **Weizen-Bock** ★★★.

MAXLRAIN, SCHLOSSBRAUEREI
Maxlrain, Bavaria

Seventeenth-century castle brewery west of Rosenheim owned by the Princess von

Lobkowicz. Go for the Maxlrainer chocolaty and bitter **Aiblinger Schwarzbier** ★★; bready and bitter-sweet **Schloss Trunk** ★★; and the rich and fruity Lenten *doppelbock* **Jubilator** ★★☆.

PAULANER (HEINEKEN)
Munich, Bavaria

Part of a group in which Heineken has virtual control, with around 50 beers made in the Munich brewery. Under the Paulaner brand it makes the solid **Hefe-Weißbier Naturtrüb** ★☆ and the legendary if diminished *doppelbock* **Salvator** ★★. Under the Hacker-Pschorr brand it makes the popular seasonal **Oktoberfest Märzen** ★★ and the group's most impressive beer, the stronger, toffee-raisin *doppelbock* **Animator** ★★☆. It makes the Thurn & Taxis brands too.

REUTBERG, KLOSTERBRAUEREI
Sachsenkam, Bavaria

Small brewery founded near Sachsenkam in 1677 and working as a cooperative since 1924. Its best Reutberger performers are the soft and aromatic **Export Hell** ★★; the nutty and drier than average **Export Dunkel** ★★; and well-balanced, honey-tinged Lent seasonal **Josefi-Bock** ★★☆.

SCHÖNRAM, PRIVATE LANDBRAUEREI
Petting/Schönram, Bavaria

Eighteenth-century family-owned brewery near the Austrian border not far from Salzburg. One of the first traditional brewers to introduce a range of bottled beers in foreign styles, called Bavaria's

Best, at a price, among which the double IPA, **India Pale Ale** ★★☆, in particular hints at more to come. Among the Schönramer beers, the dry, crisp Pils is better when unfiltered and dry-hopped as **Grüner Pils** ★★; the dry **Altbayrisch Dunkel** ★★ is also nutty; and **Saphir Bock** ★★☆ is so sweet and fulsome it could be mistaken for a Belgian *tripel*.

STIERBERG
Stierberg, Bavaria

Small brewery in a village near Obertaufkirchen, from which few of owner-brewer Annemarie Kammhuber-Hartinger's four beers escape. If touring, try the aromatic and bittersweet **Stierberg Eispils Monte Torro** ★★ and copper-coloured, caramel-accented, fruity *Münchener* **Stierberg Hochzeitsbier** ★★☆ before the others.

UNERTL WEISSBIER
Haag, Bavaria

One of two similarly named wheat beer breweries in the region (*see* UNERTL, WEISSBRÄU), owned by cousins. This one is in Haag and owned by the fifth generation of first-born males in the family to take the name Alois. The standard Unertl offering is a fruity and slightly acidic **Weissbier** ★★☆; the darker and sourer *dunkelweisse* **Ursud** ★★ comes bottled only; and gently tart **Weissbier Bock** ★★☆ hints at chocolate and dark fruit.

UNERTL, WEISSBRÄU
Mühldorf am Inn, Bavaria

The second smallish brewery in the Unertl family (*see* UNERTL WEISSBIER) was founded at Mühldorf in 1929 and has been known to export its beers even to the UK. The best of these Unertl beers is the organic **Bio-Dinkel Weisse** ★★☆ made with spelt; the yeasty and citrus **Oberland Export Weissbier** ★★ is a new addition. The local **Steer Weiße** ★★ and seasonal **Steer Weißbierbock** ★★ are also currently made here by brewer Rudi Steer, whose own brewery is over capacity.

WEIHENSTEPHAN
Freising, Bavaria

Officially the world's oldest brewery, adjacent to a renowned brewing school of the same name. Owned by the state of Bavaria since the dissolution of the monasteries in 1803. Brewing began on this hill southwest of Freising in 1040 when Abbot Arnold obtained a licence from the town. The biggest-selling Weihenstephaner beer is the thinnish and banana-spicy **Hefeweissbier** ★★★; the **Hefeweissbier Dunkel** ★★ has chocolate and banana but is light; the best is the powerful, citrus *weizenbock* **Vitus** ★★☆; and the odd one out is malty-sweet *doppelbock* **Korbinian** ★★.

BAMBERG & UPPER FRANCONIA

Many Franconians will tell you, without rancour, that they do not wish to separate from Bavaria as they have never been a part of it. Those who live in Oberfranken (Upper Franconia) often harbour similar thoughts about its lower parts.

Historically, there are more breweries per head in this area than anywhere else in Europe, and possibly the world. Most have been established for several generations. Bamberg alone has 10, making it one of the great beer-exploring destinations.

As well as an abundance of local beers self-styled as *vollbier*, *landbier*, *zwickelbier*, *kellerbier* or *ungespundetes*, this is the spiritual home of *rauchbier*, a type of lager made with wood-smoked malted barley. The brewers we recommend will rarely send their products to you. Rather you will need to take yourself to them.

BINKERT BRAUHAUS
Breitengüßbach, Bavaria

Started as a sideline in 2012 by an employee of famous Bamberg brewing equipment manufacturer Kaspar Schulz. His Main Seidla beers have proved as impressive as the kit in which they are brewed. **Amber Spezial** ★★ is a crisp yet grainy stronger lager that hides its strength well; the **Weizen** ★★ is a highly enjoyable fruity and unusually aromatic wheat; but best is the citrus, bitter and highly aromatic **Kellerbier** ★★☆, sometimes sold as Kellerpils on draught.

DREI KRONEN (MEMMELSDORF)
Memmelsdorf, Bavaria

Fifteenth-century pub brewery a few doors up from **Höhn**. Three beers are available year-round alongside one for each of the four seasons and a few experimental brews. Drei Kronen regulars include **Stöffla** ★★☆, a lightly-smoked and sweeter than average *kellerbier*; and the draught-only, beautifully balanced, aromatic **Kellerpils** ★★.

DREI KRONEN (SCHESSLITZ)
Scheßlitz, Bavaria

A few kilometres up the road at Scheßlitz and unrelated to the Memmelsdorf **DREI KRONEN**. En route you will see the Drei Kronen at Straßgiech, a former brewery that is now the tap for **GÄNSTALLER-BRÄU**. The beers here are called Schäazer and

include an aromatic **Original Premium Pils** ★★☆ that finishes dry and bitter; and the maltier draught **Kronabier**, which loses something when bottled ★★☆→★★.

EICHHORN
Hallstadt-Dörfleins, Bavaria

Small brewery also known as Schwarzer Adler, north of Bamberg, unrelated to Eichhorn of Forchheim. Its five Eichhorn beers make it out of the village but not far. The crisp, well-rounded **Pils** ★★☆ is better as a session beer than the more generously hopped **Export** ★★; but pick of the bunch is the pale, perfectly balanced **Kellerbier** ★★★.

FÄSSLA
Bamberg, Bavaria

Ambitious brewery that has increased output tenfold in the past quarter century. All Fässla beers are well made. Nutty and bittersweet *dunkel* **Zwergla** ★★ belies its strength; **Gold-Pils** ★★ is stronger and maltier than most; the blond **Lagerbier** ★★ is malty and herbal; and the city's strongest beer is the *doppelbock* **Bambergator** ★★☆.

GÄNSTALLER-BRÄU
Schnaid, Bavaria

The former Friedel brewery in Schnaid, now used by Andy Gänstaller to brew "extreme interpretations" of classic

German styles. Beers are badged Drei Kronen when sold at the tap at Straßgiech but Gänstaller-Bräu elsewhere. The three regulars are the punchy, well-balanced **Kellerbier** ★★☆; the well-hopped **Zwickelpils** ★★☆; and stronger than typical **Zoigl** ★★★. Specials include the surprisingly subtle smoked *märzen* **FXA** ★★☆, and the astonishing smoked *doppelbock* **Affumicator** ★★★☆, brewed at the behest of Ma Che Siete Venuti a Fà in Rome but now sold elsewhere.

GOLDENEN ADLER
Rattelsdorf-Höfen, Bavaria

Diminutive 18th-century brewery in tiny Höfen, near Rattelsdorf, making a single amber, toffee-accented beer, **Goldenen Adler Ungespundetes Lager** ★★☆, brewed every couple of months and only available at the brewery.

GRASSER
Königsfeld-Huppendorf, Bavaria

Four regular Huppendorfer beers are made at this small brewery near Königsfeld, supplemented by a few seasonals. Optimistically described by the brewery as a *dunkel* is gently-bitter amber standard **Vollbier** ★★; the **Hefeweizen** ★★ has plenty of banana and clove; while in winter it offers herbal sweet and bitter **Heller Katherein-Bock** ★★☆.

GRIESS
Geisfeld, Bavaria

The village of Geisfeld, due east of Bamberg, manages to support two breweries (*see* KRUG). Output here

barely reaches 1000hl a year and Griess beers are rarely seen elsewhere. The bestseller is dry and hoppy **Kellerbier** ★★★, which appears in a concentrated form in winter as **Bock** ★★★. Less well hopped but still excellent is the **Pilsner** ★★☆.

HEBENDANZ
Forchheim, Bavaria

Founded in 1579, one of four breweries in Forchheim. The standard Hebendanz session beer is the aromatic and well-rounded **Export Hell** ★★; equally good is the herbal-spicy **Edel Pils** ★★; chewy **Erstes Forchheimer Export-Hefe-Weissbier** ★★ has banana in abundance; while its low-hopped, grassy, copper-coloured *märzen* **Jubiläums Festbier** ★★ appears under different names through the year.

HÖHN
Memmelsdorf, Bavaria

Heavily rebuilt, substantial pub brewery and hotel a few seconds' walk from DREI KRONEN, housing a wood-fired brewery that makes a single, unplaceable beer, a soft and herbal, unfiltered rustic pale lager called **Görchla** ★★.

HÖNIG
Tiefenellern, Bavaria

The Gasthof zur Post at Tiefenellern has brewed since 1478, the Hönig family taking over in 1812. Six Hönig beers are made, two of them seasonal. Best are the gently fruity and grassy **Lagerbier Ungespundet** ★★ and **Posthörnla** ★★☆, a subtle *rauchbier* light on both smoke and colour.

HUMMEL-BRÄU
Merkendorf, Bavaria

This, the smaller of Merkendorf's brewers (*see* **WAGNER**), dates from the 16th century but is nevertheless relatively adventurous, making more than a dozen Hummel-Bräu beers. The smoky but smooth **Räucherla** ★★★ is possibly the best regular *rauchbier* to be made outside Bamberg; its golden, toffee-tinged **Kellerbier** ★★★ has superb balance; the chewy Lent and Advent **Weizen-Bock** ★★☆ drips with banana; and in winter the powerful **Räucherator Doppelbock** ★★★☆ takes *rauchbier* brewing to a step beyond.

KEESMANN
Bamberg, Bavaria

This, the youngest of Bamberg's established brewers, is not yet 150 years old. The exceptionally pale but impressively grainy **Keesmann Bamberger Herren Pils** ★★☆ accounts for more than 90% of its production and is the most widely available beer in the city. The best try-also is the nutty-caramel **Sternla Lager** ★★.

KNOBLACH
Schammelsdorf, Bavaria

A small, late-19th-century, family-run brewery located to the east of Bamberg. The regular Schammelsdorfer beers are the fruity, dry and bitter **Ungspund's Lagerbier** ★★☆; the spicy-fruity **Knoblach Weißbier** ★★; and the **Räuschla** ★★, a malt-accented, dark, lightly smoked *märzen*.

KRAUS
Hirschaid, Bavaria

A family-run brewery and hotel in the centre of Hirschaid. Its nine Kraus beers have some local distribution. The best are the dryish and hoppy **Lager Hell** ★★☆; the lightly smoked **Hirschen-Trunk** ★★☆, an excellent *rauchbier* for the uninitiated; and the good all-rounder, winter-only **Bock** ★★☆.

KREUZBERG, BRAUHAUS AM
Hallerndorf, Bavaria

When the old Friedel Keller on much-visited Kreuzberg hill morphed into this bold brewpub in 2007 feathers were ruffled. It took a few years to settle down but its brewer now wins prizes for draught beers like bestselling, grainy, citrus **Zwickelbier** ★★☆, reworked from the old brewery's Kellerbier; dark, roasty *rauchbier* **Schlotfegerla** ★★; and a range designed to illustrate the diversity of traditional local beers, such as seven-grain session brew **Pilgertrunk** ★★☆, a collaboration brew with the monks of **KLOSTERBRAUEREI KREUZBERG**.

KRUG
Geisfeld, Bavaria

Geisfeld's other brewer (*see* **GRIESS**) makes a single regular beer, which is rarely seen outside its traditional taphouse and summer terrace. Usually served in ceramic mugs, **Krug Lagerbier** ★★★ is actually a hazy, golden-amber *kellerbier* that is predominantly fruity and devilishly easy to drink. Three seasonal beers are rumoured to appear.

KUNDMÜLLER
Viereth-Trunstadt, Bavaria

Family-owned brewery (since 1835) has expanded both its range and output in recent years. Among its Weiherer beers the bestseller is flowery, golden, modestly proportioned **Lager** ★★; hoppy new addition **Urstöffla** ★★☆ is billed as a *dunkel* but is more an amber *kellerbier*; hazy, herbal **Weiherer Keller-Pils** ★★☆ beats the ordinary one; and amber **Rauch** ★★☆ is a lightly smoked, pale *rauchbier*.

LINDENBRÄU
Gräfenberg, Bavaria

This small brewery and distillery is at the end of the rambling railway line from Nürnberg Nordost. Of six Lindenbräu beers, two are seasonal. The bread-and-butter brand is the bitter but malt-led *dunkel* **Vollbier** ★★; the pale, citrus **Weizen** ★★ goes down best on a summer's day; while ruddy-brown and toasty **Festbier** ★★☆ is the Vollbier enhanced.

LÖWENBRÄU BUTTENHEIM
Buttenheim, Bavaria

The smaller of Buttenheim's two breweries, though its beers are fairly common in the region. Its Löwenbräu Buttenheim beers have changed a bit, the draught *kellerbier* **Ungespundetes Lagerbier** ★★ lacking its former punch, while the recently added **Pilsner** ★★ has inherited some of its hops.

MAHR'S BRÄU
Bamberg, Bavaria

This family-owned Bamberg brewery, almost opposite KEESMANN, is well

established in the US market, with a couple of export-only products. The best known of the Mahr's Bräu beers is the unfiltered, light amber-coloured **Kellerbier Ungespundet** ★★★, which is best when served from the barrel; the **Festtags Weisse** ★★ combines citrus and banana; the pale winter seasonal **Bock Bier** ★★☆ has bread and spice notes; while the other winter brew **Der Weisse Bock** ★★☆ is punchier.

DESTINATION BAMBERG

Café Abseits (39 Pödeldorfer Straße), a couple of blocks out of town from the railway station, has accumulated a fine range of better Franconian beers and showcases some Weyermann experiments. Meanwhile, the world's best brewery crawl – 10 in all – must include **Fässla** and **Spezial** on Obere Königstraße, **Mahr's** and **Keesmann** on Wunderburg, **Greifenklau** on Laurenziplatz and the **Schlenkerla** tap on Dominikanerstraße.

MAISEL
Bayreuth, Bavaria

Bayreuth's last large brewery company no longer has a second site in Bamberg but is otherwise expanding its horizons. Best known for its Maisel's Weisse wheat beers, the citrus-spicy flagship *weizen* **Original** ★★ and caramel-fruity **Dunkel** ★☆; new ventures include a range of Maisel & Friends craft-style beers and experimental up-hopped, organic and spiced beers.

MEINEL-BRÄU
Hof, Bavaria

Gisela Meinel-Hansen's family has run this brewery for 12 generations. Its Meinel-Bräu beers are fairly easy to find in the area but are rarely seen elsewhere. The hugely aromatic **Classic Pils ★★☆** lives up to its name thanks to a generous dose of aromatic hops; while caramel features largest in the toasty **Märzen ★★**; and smooth, sweet, caramelized *doppelbock* **Absolvinator ★★☆** travels from sweet to bitterish via fruity.

MEISTER
Pretzfeld-Unterzaunsbach, Bavaria

Small family-run brewery at Unterzaunsbach, near Pretzfeld. Georg Meister makes his copper-coloured, toasty and slightly bitter *dunkel*-ish **Meister Vollbier ★★☆** year-round and sells it unfiltered in spring and summer as **Zwickelbier ★★☆**. An amber-coloured *märzen*-ish winter offering called **Festbier ★★☆** is stronger and a little sweeter.

MEUSEL-BRÄU
Dreuschendorf, Bavaria

Perhaps uniquely, three generations of the same family brew at their small brewhouse in Dreuschendorf. Of the regular Meusel-Bräu beers, **Kellertrunk ★★** is a little sweeter than most *kellerbiers*; while the deep red-brown **Bamberger Landrauchbier ★★☆** might be termed a middle-smoke; and vanilla and clove are to the fore in soft **Ottmar Weisse ★★**. It will be interesting to see how the youngest generation's impressive charge into ever-changing seasonal beers (30-plus to date) settles down.

MÜHLENBRÄU
Mühlendorf, Bavaria

Small family brewery, a bus ride southwest of Bamberg. Typical Franconian village set-up, its Mühlenbräu beers rarely being seen elsewhere. Its **Dunkles Lagerbier ★★☆** is full-flavoured with dabs of liquorice and caramel; while the **Pils ★★** is light, malt-led and herbal.

MÜLLER
Debring, Bavaria

Recently rebuilt but still tiny brewery between Bamberg and Würzburg. Another high-quality village brewery, making five Debringer beers, rarely seen beyond the parish. Go for the herbal, well-balanced **Pilsner ★★☆**, or **Micherla ★★☆**, its immediately likable unfiltered *kellerbier*.

OTT
Oberleinleiter, Bavaria

Seventeenth-century family-run brewery in a village in the Franconian Jura. Its six beers are not as rare as some but rarely stray more than 20km (12 miles) from home. Herbal hops lift **Ott Edel-Pils ★★** from its grainy base; and nutty malt is to the fore in the curiously named *dunkel*, **Ott Obaladara ★★**.

PENNING-ZEISSLER
Hetzelsdorf, Bavaria

Hillside brewery in tiny Hetzelsdorf, east of Forchheim. The eight Hetzelsdorfer beers are split equally between regular and seasonal and include the sweetish, malty **Pilsner** ★★ and bready, bitter, *dunkel*-ish Fränkisches Vollbier, also available unfiltered and slightly diminished as **Lagerbier** ★★.

RECKENDORF, SCHLOSSBRAUEREI
Reckendorf, Bavaria

Decent-sized brewery dating from 1597, when it opened to serve the now-demolished Reckendorf castle. Recently rebranded Recken, its beers are readily found within a 30km (19 mile) radius. Soft and aromatic **Edel-Pils** ★★ just passes muster; while the citrus-spicy **Weissbier** ★★ is perhaps its best everyday beer. A spicy, strong, seasonal **Weizenbock** ★★☆ was introduced in 2010.

REH
Lohndorf, Bavaria

Early-20th-century family-run brewery in the Eller valley. Its seven Reh-Bier brands do make it out of the valley and can be found up to 50km (31 miles) away. The local favourite is the fruity, hoppy **Pils** ★★; the **Zwick'l** ★★ is fruity but dry; while winter-warmer **Der Dunkle Reh Bock** ★★★ has sweet fruit initially, insinuates caramel and ends with a gentle bitter kiss.

RITTMAYER
Hallerndorf, Bavaria

Hallerndorf's larger brewery, Lieberth, has expanded its range of Rittmayer beers to more than 15 and also bottles in flip-tops for other brewers. One to watch for new directions, but for now head for the light brown, slightly sour *zoigl*-ish **Hausbrauerbier** ★★, a *kellerbier*

created in remembrance of the citizen's right to brew; or the winter-only, banana-packed, slightly spicy, bit-too-sweet **Weizenbock** ★★☆.

ROPPELT
Stiebarlimbach, Bavaria

At the foot of the Kreuzberg, Franz Roppelt's tiny village brewery is considerably more traditional than near neighbour BINKERT. His beers are best on draught at their wonderful tap, where the appropriately designated fruity-hoppy **Kellerbier** ★★☆ shines and the soft **Weizenbier** ★★ packs more banana than we thought possible.

ROTHENBACH
Aufseß, Bavaria

The largest of four small breweries in the municipality of Aufseß, a collection of 10 communities with a combined population of barely 1300. It's located in Aufseß village itself, hence Aufsesser beer. Its star performer is the dry and chocolaty **Dunkel** ★★★; with the herbal-hoppy **Pils** ★★☆ and equally well-hopped winter **Bockbier** ★★☆ not far behind.

SCHEUBEL
Schlüsselfeld, Bavaria

This small brewery with modern kit, originally established in 1828, is run by the Scheubel family at Schlüsselfeld, where it makes two beers called Stern-Bräu for general consumption. The **Vollbier** ★★ is a well-hopped *helles*, while the superb **Festbier** ★★★ is a lightly smoked, fairly dry *rauchbier* that is among the best.

SCHLENKERLA (HELLER)
Bamberg, Bavaria

Legendary 16th-century Bamberg brewery better recognized by the name of its beers and brewery tap, Aecht Schlenkerla. Its most often encountered beer is the extraordinary and unrelentingly smoky **Rauchbier Märzen** ★★★☆; more subtle is the unsmoked wheat and smoked barley combination in **Rauchweizen** ★★☆; best is chewy autumn treat **Aecht Schlenkerla Rauchbier Urbock** ★★★★; the powerful winter special **Eiche** ★★★★ is sweeter and less assertively smoked; and **Fastenbier** ★★★☆ appears for Lent at the brewery tap only.

SCHROLL
Nankendorf, Bavaria

Mid-19th-century brewery out in the sticks between Bamberg and Bayreuth. The two regular Nankendorfer beers and one seasonal are seen occasionally elsewhere. Caramel and bitter hops are evident in the chewy **Landbier** ★★☆; while the toasty **Bockbier** ★★☆ starts sweet before aiming toward a stronger hop finish.

SCHWANENBRÄU BURGEBRACH
Burgebrach, Bavaria

Tiny brewery that seems to have expanded from its pub brewery base. Its Schwanenbräu Burgebrach brands include a spicy, bittersweet, unfiltered amber *münchener* called **Lagerbier** ★★☆; a stronger, grassier, golden **Kellerbier** ★★; and the elusive, powerful, slightly tart but interesting seasonal **Der Weisse Bock** ★★☆, which deserves wider attention.

SESSLACH, KOMMUNBRAUHAUS
Seßlach, Bavaria

Community brewery built into the town wall of picturesque Seßlach. The only regular Seßlacher beer is nutty, bittersweet **Hausbräu** ★★, joined occasionally by similar but slightly stronger and hoppier **Festbier** ★★☆. Two pubs on the nearby square are supplied with wort that they lager themselves to make *zoigl* beers.

SPEZIAL
Bamberg, Bavaria

Smallish family-run Bamberg brewery, located directly opposite FÄSSLA. Owner-brewer Christian Merz smokes his own barley malt as they do at fellow *rauchbier* specialists Heller (*see* SCHLENKERLA (HELLER)), only on a much smaller scale. The "ordinary" Spezial beer is the near-perfectly balanced, understated **Rauchbier Lager** ★★★★; more robustly smoked **Rauchbier Märzen** ★★★ is often preferred by those seeking a Schlenkerla; *kellerbier* **Ungespundet** ★★★ is well hopped but completely unsmoked; and **Rauchbier Bock** ★★★☆ again involves subtle end smoking, this time applied to quite a delicate but interesting *bock*. Its Weissbier is made by Schneider at Essing.

ST GEORGEN BRÄU
Buttenheim, Bavaria

This is one of rural Franconia's larger brewers, located next door to **LÖWENBRÄU BUTTENHEIM**. The best known of the St Georgen Bräu range is the hoppy and darker-than-average **Keller Bier ★★★**; the **Landbier Dunkel ★★☆** has caramel-chocolaty notes and is almost as good; the crisp, hoppy **Pilsener ★★★** is tastily balanced; while the **Doppelbock Dunkel ★★☆** is more like the Landbier Dunkel on steroids.

STAFFELBERG-BRÄU
Bad Staffelstein-Loffeld, Bavaria

The largest of five breweries along the valley southeast from Bad Staffelstein, named after the peak that looms above its home town, Loffeld. The best of the Staffelberg-Bräu range is the **Hopfen-Gold Pils ★★☆**, which manages to balance bitter hops with quite intense malt; roasted malt and caramel are to the fore in **Loffelder Dunkel ★★**; while spicy banana marks out the **Hefe Weißbier ★★**.

TRUNK
Lichtenfels, Bavaria

Brewery located near Lichtenfels, just behind the baroque basilica at Vierzehnheiligen. This small family-run brewery, founded in 1803, names its beers Vierzehnheiligener Nothelfer, after the 14 holy helpers who are said to have appeared on the site in 1446. **Trunk ★★☆** is a nutty-caramel, dryish *dunkel*, and **Bio-Weisse ★★** is a banana-fruity organic wheat.

VASOLD & SCHMITT
Neunkirchen am Brand, Bavaria

Once much larger than it is now, this late-19th-century brewer, typical of its breed, makes beers that can prove hard to find but reward the effort to do so. Well-hopped and nutty, **Benedikt Dunkel ★★** is drier than most, a theme continued in the grassy, hoppy **Vasold Lager Hell ★★**.

WAGNER
Merkendorf, Bavaria

Merkendorf's other brewery (*see* **HUMMEL**) has an output of 17,000hl a year and its Wagner beers are a relatively common sight to the east of Bamberg. Its main product, a golden, moderately hopped, grassy *kellerbier* called **Ungespundetes Lagerbier**, sings on draught but mumbles in the bottle **★★→★★★**; **Märzen ★★☆** is full-flavoured, biscuity and hoppy; fruity-hoppy **Festbier ★★** appears so often it barely remains seasonal; and bittersweet **Bock Hell ★★☆** heralds Christmas.

WAGNER BRÄU
Kemmern, Bavaria

This small family-run brewery at Kemmern near Bamberg is unconnected to **WAGNER** or to a similarly named producer in nearby Oberhaid. The best of its 10 Wagner-Bräu Kemmern beers are the grassy and bitter **Ungespundetes Lagerbier ★★☆**; and dry, hoppy **Pils ★★☆**.

WEISSENOHE, KLOSTERBRAUEREI
Weißenohe, Bavaria

They first brewed at this former monastery near Gräfenberg around

1050. Urban Winkler's family took over in 1827 and they now brew around 20,000hl each year. The signature Weißenoher Klosterbrauerei beer is the nutty, copper-amber, unclassifiable **Altfränkisch Klosterbier ★★**; bread and caramel come through in the **Eucharius Märzen ★★**; and chocolate-raisin-caramel can be tasted in the Lent seasonal **Bonator Doppelbock ★★☆**.

ZEHENDNER
Mönchsambach, Bavaria

Late-19th-century brewery in a hamlet to the west of Burgebrach. Its five Mönchsambacher beers include well-rounded bestselling **Lagerbier ★★☆**; chewy banana milkshake **Hefeweizen ★★☆**; and fruity-alcoholic Christmas golden treat **Weihnachts-Bock ★★★**.

REST OF BAVARIA

The remainder of Bavaria consists of Lower and Middle Franconia, Schwaben (Swabia), Oberpfalz and Lower Bavaria. While there are fewer established brewers here the figure is relative – the town of Amberg alone has six. There are also remnants of the *zoigl* tradition (*see* box, page 68). In the north one goes to the *bierkeller,* in the south to the *biergarten* – though they amount to the same thing. The western side is particularly associated with the production of heavily clouded, spicy *hefeweizen* and numerous other variants of wheat beer. Lower Franconia is considered more of a wine region.

ADLER BRÄU
Stettfeld, Bavaria

Recently rebuilt and relocated, this smallish brewery bottles for a number of even smaller ones. Best of the Adler Bräu beers are light amber, toasty-caramel *kellerbier* **Alt Fränkisches Lagerbier ★★**; aromatic and hoppy pilsener **Stöpfelder Classic ★★☆**; herbal-hoppy **Stettfelder Pils ★★**; and biscuity, beautifully hopped **Stettfelder Heller Bock ★★★**.

ALTSTADTHOF
Nuremberg, Bavaria

This Nuremberg pub brewery kick-started the German *hausbrauerei* renaissance in 1984. Better known for its smooth, roasted **Altstadthof Schwarzbier ★★**, it is its fruit-accented **Altstadthof Maibock ★★☆** that has the edge for being dangerously sophisticated yet approachable.

DESTINATION
NUREMBERG

Few local places seem to stock a wide range of Franconian beers but **Landbierparadies** (60 Galgenhofstraße and other locations) is an exception, selling over 100 brands by the bottle and the case.

ANDORFER, WEISSBRÄU
Passau-Ries, Bavaria

Tiny brewery on a hill above Passau, by the Austrian border, making only wheat beers. The Andorfer house staple is the grainy, rustic **Weizen ★★☆**; while orange and clove stand out in the slightly sour **Weizen-Bock ★★☆**.

AUTENRIED, SCHLOSSBRAUEREI
Autenried, Bavaria

Mid-17th-century brewery near Ichenhausen that grows and malts most of the grain it uses. Around 60,000hl of beer passes out of its gates annually, most of it toward northwestern Schwaben. Autenrieder brands include **Urtyp Hell ★★**, with a good presence of noble hops; **Weizen ★★** with clove and fruits to the fore; **Weizen-Bock ★★☆**, with so much spicy fruit presence you may want to chew before swallowing; and the understated, caramel-laced **Leonhardi Bock ★★☆**, which hides its strength well.

BAYER
Theinheim, Bavaria

This small family-run brewery is fast approaching its 300th anniversary. Its only regular beer is the excellent unfiltered, gravity-drawn **Bayer Theinheim Ungespundetes Landbier ★★☆**, a pale and grassy *kellerbier*. A pale *bock* appears for Lent.

BRUCKMÜLLER
Amberg, Bavaria

Sedate Amberg, on the river Vils, boasts six breweries, the largest of which began life in a Franciscan monastery in 1490. In 1803, following dissolution, the Bruckmüller family bought all bar the church. Still produces some beers under the Weizen Falk ("White Falcon") brand, leading to Germany's most confusing beer name, **Weizen Falk Dunkles Falk ★★**, for a nuts-and-toffee, bottom-fermented, bottle-conditioned brown beer without wheat. Of the Bruckmüller brands, the fruity-hoppy, golden-orange **Kellerbier ★★** and lightish coloured, sweet-fruity-bitter *doppelbock* **Superator ★★☆** are the best.

DORN-BRÄU
Bruckberg, Bavaria

Recently modernized family brewery near Ansbach making five beers rarely seen beyond the town. Caramel-tinged **Bruckberger Dunkel ★★** has clearly been designed with the session drinker in mind; while yeasty **Gambrinus Weisse ★★** displays a malt character normally absent from most wheat beers.

EICHHOFEN, SCHLOSSBRAUEREI
Eichhofen, Bavaria

Late-17th-century village brewery near Regensburg. Six beers include the powerful treacle-toffee seasonal **Eichator Doppelbock ★★☆**; and the unfiltered, strongly chocolaty **Eichhofener Spezial Dunkel ★★**, sold as Premium Dunkel when bottled.

FALTER
Regen, Bavaria

The largest brewery in the Bavarian Forest was founded in 1649 and acquired for J B Falter and his descendants in

1928. Best of the Falter wheat beers is the soft and spicy **Weissbier Premium Gold** ★★, with typical banana and clove flavours; while best of the rest is **Regenator** ★★☆, an unusually dry, liquorice-fruity *doppelbock* for the carnival season.

FAUST
Miltenberg am Main, Bavaria

Miltenberg's only remaining brewery is the last left in what is principally a wine-producing area. The Faust beers from this small-to-medium-sized firm are widely available in the area and include the new heavily hopped US-style pale ale **Auswandererbier 1849** ★★☆; more traditional dry and yeasty **Kräusen** ★★☆; and an alcohol-infused **Doppelbock Dunkel** ★★☆ draped in molasses.

FISCHER
Höchstadt-Greuth, Bavaria

Norbert Fischer's family has been brewing at Greuth, near Höchstadt, since 1702. The pick of the three regular Fischer beers is the delicately smoked, none-too-assertive **Rauchbier** ★★☆, which makes a good starter for newcomers to the style; staple **Lagerbier** ★★ is bready; while the dark **Bockbier** ★★ is a sweet and malty winter warmer.

FRIEDEL
Zentbechhofen, Bavaria

Two kilometres from the previous entry, the village of Zentbechhofen is home to this 15th-century brewery, slightly larger than its near neighbour but every bit as local. Favourites of the Friedel range are the grassy **Vollbier** ★★; and darker, stronger and sweeter **Lagerbier** ★★.

FUCHSBECK
Sulzbach-Rosenberg, Bavaria

Small brewery immediately below the castle at Sulzbach-Rosenberg. Nine Fuchsbeck beers are made but they rarely travel further than Amberg. The bittersweet **Hell** ★★ makes an excellent session beer, as does the stronger, more fragrant and sweet-bitter **Export** ★★; while **Primus** ★★ is a spring *weizenbock* that has been pleasantly toned down to make it more approachable.

FUCHSBERG, SCHLOSSBRAUEREI
Fuchsberg, Bavaria

A schlossbrauerei actually based in a castle rather than simply named after one. Its five Fuchsberger beers rarely get more than 30km (19 miles) from Fuchsberg, though **Urhell** ★★ is a remarkably easy-drinking, mild and grassy *helles*; and **Pilsener Premium** ★★ has great balance before a bittersweet finish.

GÖLLER
Zeil am Main, Bavaria

Dating from 1514 and in the Göller family for barely a century, this busy brewery, between Bamberg and Schweinfurt, is in a wine town. It still brews on the original site but tanks beer to a newer bottling plant on the outskirts, which also bottles beers for other smaller breweries, some of which, particularly wheat beers, are made at Göller. The **Göller Rauchbier** ★★

is lighter than some; and its seasonal **Weizenbock ★★** has a hint of tartness among the clove and banana.

GRAF ARCO
Adldorf, Bavaria

Sizeable brewery at Adldorf not to be confused with the south German giant Arcobräu of Moos. It makes 10 or so acceptable year-round Graf Arco beers but it is the seasonal brews that impress here. Autumn sees dependable golden **Grafentrunk Festbier ★★**, which starts sweet and finishes dry; while Lent sees the arrival of the raisin-scented, burnt-grain, darker *bock* **Arcolator ★★☆**.

HEMBACHER
Igelsdorf, Bavaria

One-man band set up in 2008 on an industrial estate near Rednitzhembach. Experienced brewer Jürgen Müller makes four regular beers, best of which is the superbly aromatic and bitter **Zwickel-Pils ★★☆**; while **Goldweisse ★★** is a pale, citrusy wheat beer with a gently tart finish; and amber *landbier* **Stöffla ★★☆** is rural Franconian brewing in a glass.

HIRSCH
Dirlewang, Bavaria

Owned by Hans Lederle's family since opening in 1806, this small brewery in Dirlewang supplies few other places. Two Dirlewanger beers are made all year, the grainy and hoppy **Vollbier Hell ★★☆**; and softer, sweeter blond **Export ★★**; joined during winter by the fruity *märzen* **Festbier ★★**.

HÖSL
Mitterteich, Bavaria

This medium-sized, independent, family-dominated brewer makes around a dozen regular beers under its own name and numerous own-brand labels commissioned by others. They peak with **Hösl Whiskey-Weisse ★★☆**, an unusual, slightly smoky wheat beer that is brewed with Scottish whisky malt to celebrate 20 years of town twinning, now hopefully to remain.

HÜTTEN
Hütten, Bavaria

Long-established but small family-run brewery east of Bayreuth in the Fichtelgebirge mountains, making nine beers that include an unusually highly hopped grassy and dry **Hell ★★☆**; and a spicy amber **Helle Fränkische Hefe Weisse ★★☆** that ploughs its own furrow.

IRSEER KLOSTERBRÄU
Irsee, Bavaria

The owners of this former monastic brewery have ducked the opportunity to claim that brewing started here in this spot in the 12th century – which it more than likely did – for an official founding date of 1803, the year in which Bavarian monasteries were secularized. Of the Irseer beers, the unfiltered **Kloster-Urtrunk ★★** is an unusual, malty-herbal, hazy, slightly musty golden beer, similar in ways to its darker, hazy sister **Kloster-Urdunkel ★★**, which is full of caramel and laced with chocolate.

JACOB
Bodenwöhr, Bavaria

Lakeside brewery at Bodenwöhr, a small town in the Upper Bavarian Forest nature park. Better known for its wheat beers, some brewed for other companies, the Jacob range of bottom-fermented beers includes an aromatic, bitter and oddly Bohemian **Edel Pils** ★★☆. The pale **Weissbier** ★★☆ is assertively doused in banana and clove; the spicier **Dunkles Weissbier** ★★ could be drier; but the dark **Weizen-Bock** ★★★ manages a delicate balancing act best.

KNEITINGER
Regensburg, Bavaria

Brewery in the centre of Regensburg, dating from 1530 and used to producing two regular Kneitinger beers plus a winter *bock*. The **Edel-Pils** ★★ has good herbal bitterness; nutty caramel and chocolate flavours are evident in **Dunkel** ★★☆; while the dark winter **Bock** ★★★ is sweeter and stronger.

KREUZBERG, KLOSTERBRAUEREI
Bischofsheim an der Rhön, Bavaria

This small brewery is at a remote Franciscan monastery in the picturesque Rhön region. Although there are still monks here, they have no direct involvement in day-to-day brewing operations. Unusually for a brewery with 8500hl a year production, none of the beer is bottled. All four beers are unfiltered, among them the almost famous **Kreuzberger Klosterbier Dunkel** ★★★, a copper-coloured, bittersweet form of "liquid bread".

KUCHLBAUER
Abensberg, Bavaria

This substantial brewery at Abensberg claims it was founded in 1300. Best known for wheat beers, though there are also a couple of Kuchlbauer lagers. **Turmweisse** ★★☆ is citrus and almost *bock*-strength; while well-intentioned **Aloysius** ★★, its dark and fruity *weizenbock*, has room for improvement.

MÄRKL
Freudenberg, Bavaria

A small family-run brewery dating from 1466, near Amberg. Its Freudenberger beers are delightfully straightforward, the **Pils** ★★☆ being recognizably of the crisp, herbal Oberpfalz sub-style; while the **Dunkel** ★★☆ has clear caramel and roasted malt flavours and the powerful, no-nonsense *doppelbock* **Märkator** ★★☆ is packed with molasses and dark fruit. Its wheat beer is brewed elsewhere.

NAABECK, SCHLOSSBRAUEREI
Naabeck, Bavaria

One of the larger breweries in Oberpfalz, close to Schwandorf. Brews about a dozen Naabecker beers for itself and a similar number under contract to other companies. Its golden **Edel-Märzen** ★★ combines toasted malt and floral hops; while dark fruits dominate the slightly sweet **Bock Dunkel** ★★.

PYRASER
Thalmässing, Bavaria

This sizeable rural brewery south of Nuremberg has an extensive range of good-enough regular Pyraser beers such as the pale, sweet-and-sour **Angerwirts Weizen ★★**, but a smattering of better seasonal varieties such as unfiltered, hugely refreshing **Hopfenpflücker** ("Hop pickers") **Pils ★★★**; and the deceptively powerful, caramel-laden **Ultra ★★☆**. Its new Herzblut brand beers play with heavier international craft styles.

REINDLER
Jochsberg, Bavaria

Now in the eighth generation of ownership by the Reindler family, this small brewery, west of Ansbach, makes seven beers, among them the fruity and relatively high-hopped **Hefe Weizen ★★☆**; dark toffee, roasted and dry **Dunkel ★★**; and a winter *doppelbock*, the sweetish, spicy-peach **Seckenator ★★**.

RHANERBRÄU
Schönthal-Rhan, Bavaria

Village brewery near Schönthal that claims to have originated in 1283. Its 14 Rhaner beers are fairly easily found in the region. The slight sweetness in the **Pils ★★☆** fails to spoil great hopping; the **Panduren Weisse ★★** has plenty of spice and clove; while **Lilly Bock ★★☆** is a sweet, sour and spicy take on *weizenbock*.

RIEGELE
Augsburg, Bavaria

Sizeable brewery close to Augsburg's main railway station with a prodigious output of different beers for its own brands and numerous other companies. **Augsburger Herren Pils ★★** is reliably crisp and bitter, aromatic and light; while at the other end of the spectrum

its thick and malty *doppelbock* **Riegele Speziator ★★☆** is full of toffee and caramel with burnt notes. Its alcohol-free wheat beers are remarkably tasty and it has even started to play with some craft-style ales.

RITTER ST GEORGEN
Nennslingen, Bavaria

Knight-themed brewery at Nennslingen. Makes the best of packaging, with some distinctive labels and a couple of beers available in flip-top jeroboams. Hoppier-than-average **Ritter 1645 Ur-Märzen ★★** celebrates the founding year of the brewery; while its winter offering is a spicy *weizenbock* called **Starker Ritter ★★**.

ROPPELT
Trossenfurt, Bavaria

Attractive little brewery at Trossenfurt. The two Roppelt-Bräu beers are the **Lagerbier ★★**, a golden *kellerbier* with a grainy start and dry finish; and toasty, nutty, caramel-graced **Dunkel ★★**. We suspect its Steigerwald Gold Pils is brewed elsewhere.

SCHNEIDER
Kelheim, Bavaria

World-renowned Kelheim wheat beer producer originally from Munich, credited with the reinvention of high-quality wheat beers in Germany. Recent years have seen both extensive experimentation and rebranding of all beers as Schneider Weisse. The **Tap 7 Unser Original ★★★★** is the rebadged spicy *weisse* against which all others are judged; while the remarkable **Tap 6 Unser Aventinus ★★★☆** sets the same standard for *weizenbock*. Up-hopped **Tap 4 Mein Grünes ★★★** is a better balanced, weaker version of **Tap 5 Meine Hopfenweisse ★★☆**, initially a collaboration with New York's Brooklyn Brewery. However, **Aventinus Weizen-Eisbock ★★★★**, a spit for Tap 6 with less water, is an intense, berry-loaded, Sauternes of the grains, best poured to release its CO_2 and become silky-smooth.

THE ZOIGL BEER TRADITION

In Bavaria and Bohemia, the tradition of communal brewing goes back centuries, with town breweries gradually supplanting home-brewing from the 11th century onward. In Oberpfalz five "*Echter Zoigl*" brewhouses remain, brewing wort that can be bought and taken away by customers to finish preparing on their own premises.

Though identical on leaving the brewhouse, the subtle effects of different ambient microflora in each of the *zoigl* houses, typically pubs, where this happens means that every version tastes different. At the last count there were about 25 such beers coming from brewhouses in Eslarn, Falkenberg, Mitterteich, Neuhaus and Windischeschenbach. Exploration may be assisted by *www.zoigl.de.*

SEINSHEIMER KELLERBRÄU
Seinsheim, Bavaria

Seinsheim is a tiny town near Marktbreit with a suitably tiny brewery. Opened in 2002 by Frank Engelhardt and Winfried Zippel, next to the church, it opens for

sales each Friday (brewing day). Its regular offering is the superbly balanced, ruddy-brown, bitter **Seinsheimer Kellerbier ★★★**.

SIMON
Lauf an der Pegnitz, Bavaria

One of two small breweries in Lauf and that rarest of beasts, a Franconian wheat beer specialist. There is one bottom-fermented Simon beer but its best works are the chewy, spicy **Weißbier ★★**; and the sweeter, darker **Schwarze Kuni ★★☆**, a seasonal *weizenbock*.

SPALT, STADTBRAUEREI
Spalt, Bavaria

Having given its name to one of the four noble hops, it is appropriate that the 19th-century brewery better known as Spalter Bier is actually owned by its town. Among the 15 or so brands made here the obvious standout is crisp and bitter **Premium Pils No.1 ★★☆**, a showcase for the local hops; though spicy, peppery **Weißbier ★★**, surprisingly delicate **Bockl Hell ★★**, a *bock* light enough to convert

those scared of stronger beers, and the unusually dry and hoppy **Edel-Export Hell** ★★ are also worth a dip.

SPERBER BRÄU
Sulzbach-Rosenburg, Bavaria

Sulzbach-Rosenberg's other brewery (see **FUCHSBECK**) is another that keeps its ambitions local. Unusually it makes a couple of beers that mimic the *zoigl* style of brewing, the more authentic being the generously hopped, citrus **Sperber Bräu Zoiglbier** ★★☆; while the refreshing and more mainstream **Rosenburg Pils** ★★ is similarly well endowed.

WELTENBURGER
Weltenburg, Bavaria

Dating from 1050 and perhaps the most attractively situated brewery in all Germany. The Danube turns through 180° as it passes Weltenburg Abbey and on occasion has been known to pass through it. Most Weltenburger Kloster beers are brewed by Bischofshof in Regensburg but these are made on site. **Anno 1050** ★★ is a malt-driven amber lager; **Winter-Traum** ★★ is a pale and seasonal *märzen*; **Barock-Dunkel** ★★☆ is complex, bittersweet and dark, and appears super-charged as *doppelbock* **Asam-Bock** ★★★.

WIESEN, BÜRGERLICHES BRAUHAUS
Wiesen, Bavaria

A stone's throw from the border with Hesse, this small family-run brewery is at the northern end of the Spessart hills. It makes nine Wiesener beers of solid quality, among them the green-grassy **Pils** ★★; a

copper-brown and hoppy **Keller Bier** ★★ that has echoes of the ST GEORGEN version; and **Räuber Weisse Dunkel** ★★, a spicy, characterful dark wheat.

WINKLER
Amberg, Bavaria

Seventeenth-century brewery tucked inside Amberg's city wall. Its annual output of 25,000hl includes beers brewed under contract to a couple of other brewery companies. The pick of its own Winkler range are the dry and grassy-hoppy **Amberger Pils** ★★☆; and sweet and nutty winter **Alt-Amberger Doppelbock** ★★☆.

WINKLER BRÄU
Lengenfeld, Bavaria

Winkler is a popular brewery name in this part of Germany. The beers from this 1628 brewery-hotel and bottler, between Regensburg and Nuremberg, are distinguished as Winkler Bräu Lengenfeld on its labels. The spicy and aromatic **Hefe-Pils** ★★★ remains bitter to the bottom of the glass; while a fruity lacing of dark caramel comes through the *dunkel*, **Kupfer Spezial** ★★☆.

WOLF
Rüdenhausen, Bavaria

One-man brewery at Rüdenhausen, founded in 1746. Output is around 500hl a year and the beers do not get far. We include it as typical of a dying breed of small brewhouse making worthy beers that deserve a wider audience, in this case dry and nutty **Wolf Urtyp Dunkel** ★★☆ and the **Wolf Pils** ★★, which tastes of the country.

BADEN-WÜRTTEMBERG

The least well known of the German brewing regions sits at the country's southwestern corner, with the Rhine to its west, Switzerland to the south and Bavaria eastward. In contrast to the cystal-clear image of frothy-topped pils, here the beers are hazy. As well as sharing the wheat beer culture of western Bavaria, Baden-Württemberg is the home of *kellerpils* and *zwickelbier*, unfiltered draught lagers that are found increasingly in the bottle, spreading their fame.

ADLERBRÄU
Dellmensingen, Baden-Württemberg

There are six unrelated Adler ("Eagle") breweries in Baden-Württemberg. This one is at Dellmensingen, southwest of Ulm. Founded in 1349, its seven beers are rarely available elsewhere. Pick of the beers are **Haferbier ★★☆**, an unfiltered, top-fermented beer made with oats; and the aromatic, bittersweet **Keller Pils ★★**.

ANDREASBRÄU
Eggenstein-Leopoldshafen, Baden-Württemberg

One of many newish pub breweries around Karlsruhe, this above-average example being at Eggenstein-Leopoldshafen. Its only regular beer is the herbal, hoppy **Andreasbräu Pils ★★☆**, though there are also several worthy seasonal beers through the year.

BAISINGER BIERMANUFAKTUR
Rottenburg-Baisingen, Baden-Württemberg

Formerly badged Löwenbräu, this recently renamed family brewery near Rottenburg am Neckar has been owned by the Teufels ("Devils"!) for nine generations. The full Baisinger range is typical of the region and features the citrus, grassy, unfiltered **Keller-Teufel ★★**; and peak performer, the yeasty **Teufels Weisse Helles Hefe ★★**.

BAUHÖFER
Renchen-Ulm, Baden-Württemberg

Mid-19th-century, family-owned brewery at Ulm village, near Renchen. Its Ulmer beers include the grassy **Keller No. 5 ★★**, which is a little sweeter than might be expected; the slightly tart, fruity **Hefeweizen Dunkel ★★**; and a uniquely year-round, relatively dry and high-hopped **Maibock ★★**.

BRÄUNLINGER LÖWENBRÄU
Bräunlingen, Baden-Württemberg

Small family business in Bräunlingen, at the southern end of the Black Forest. Its four regular beers are all worthy of attention but the soft, spicy wheat beer **Bräunlinger Löwenbräu Weisser Leo ★★** and the hazy, hoppy **Keller-Pils ★★☆** stand out.

GOLDOCHSENBRAUEREI
Spielbach, Baden-Württemberg

A much-loved farm brewery, located just a few kilometres from historic Rothenburg-ob-der-Tauber. Unchanged for many decades, its sole regular beer rarely travels beyond Rothenburg. **Spielbacher Spezial Hell ★★☆** is a soft, grassy, golden *helles* that is made with love.

HÄFFNER BRÄU
Bad Rappenau, Baden-Württemberg

Nineteenth-century brewery that has recently developed two distinct faces. The Häffner Bräu range of traditional beers includes the biscuity, unfiltered blond **Raban ★★** and the spicy banana **Kurstadt Weizen ★★**. More edgy is the Hopfenstopfer range, among the first German beers to ape modern America. These include the grapefruity US-style pale ale **Citra Ale ★★**; and the double IPA **Citra Strong Ale ★★☆**, a 10% ABV beer that suggests that the brewery intends to become bolder.

HERBSTHÄUSER
Bad Mergentheim, Baden-Württemberg

Rural producer of over a dozen beers near Bad Mergentheim, in a part of the state that still sees itself as Franconian. The best Herbsthäuser beers tend to be the dry, herbal **Edel-Pils ★★**; fruity **Hefe-Weizen Hell ★★** with its slightly sour edge; equally fruity and moreish *dunkelweisse* **Alt-Fränkisch ★★**; and **1581 ★★☆**, the new yeasty *kellerbier* that recalls the year the brewery was founded.

HIRSCHEN-BRÄU
Waldkirch, Baden-Württemberg

Attractive, well-grounded, 19th-century regional brewery at Waldkirch, the home of German organ production. Its six-beer Hirschen-Bräu range is best represented by grassy, slightly spicy blond **Export ★★**; and banana-spice-laden **Hefe-Weizen ★★**, which is as pale as they come.

LAUPHEIM, KRONENBRAUEREI
Laupheim, Baden-Württemberg

Laupheim's last remaining brewery dates from 1753, supplying a handful of local pubs with beer made from their own barley malt. The staple Laupheimer beer, the biscuity **Kronen-Spezial ★★**, is slightly herbal, a characteristic it shares with the **Kronen-Pils ★★☆**. The recently arrived **Weisse ★☆**, the malted wheat for which is bought in, shows promise.

MÜLHAUPT
Lörrach- Brombach, Baden-Württemberg

This tiny brewery occupies the front room of Andreas Mülhaupt's home in Lörrach. Despite its size he produces 350hl of beer a year, mostly for bottling. Each of his regular Hausbräu Mülhaupt beers is surprisingly good. The dry **Helles Lagerbier ★★☆** hints at raspberries, and equally fruity, copper-coloured **Dunkles Exportbier ★★☆** finishes bitter.

PFLUGBRAUEREI
Hörvelsingen, Baden-Württemberg

Another of the small breweries around Ulm that still harvests ice to keep its lagering cellars cool through the warmer months. This one produces four year-round Pflug beers that include the soft, herbal **Pils ★★**; and pale, citrus **Hefe-Weizen ★★**, which finishes drier than most.

ROTHAUS
Rothaus, Baden-Württemberg

Germany's highest brewery (959m/3145ft above sea level), in a hamlet of the same name, is owned by the state of Baden-Württemberg. It has been expanding rapidly in recent years, its three beers now being found far and wide. Assertively hoppy **Rothaus Pils ★★** is the flagship; banana and citrus are to the fore in **Rothaus Hefeweizen ★★☆**; with the stronger **Rothaus Märzen Export ★★** less impressive. In 33cl bottles, they are known respectively as Tannenzäpfle, Hefeweizen Zäpfle and Eis Zäpfle.

RUSS, KRONENBRAUEREI
Ulm, Baden-Württemberg

This is another "Crown" brewery, unrelated to the Krone at TETTNANGER (KRONE). It is located at Söflingena, a suburb of Ulm, where its Söflinger beers are mostly found. It is one of the few remaining breweries (see PFLUGBRAUEREI) to harvest ice for lagering. Its **Kronen Bier Keller Pils ★★** is sweeter than most. Bittersweet and aromatic **Kronen Bier Spezial Hell ★★** is the standard light session beer, contrasting with the year-round, spicy and warming **Kronen Bier Natureis-Bock Hell ★★☆**.

SCHÖRE
Dietmannsweiler, Baden-Württemberg

Traditionally presented but modern-kitted pub brewery, distillery and farm, located deep in the Tettnang hop region at tiny Dietmannsweiler. It grows and uses its own hops in dry, bitter **Schörepils ★★☆**; the more subtly constructed, unfiltered **Schörebräu Hell ★★☆**; and the superb full-bodied, fruity **Schöre Weisse ★★★**.

SONNE
Herrenzimmern, Baden-Württemberg

Brewing again for barely a decade, this revived pub brewery sits at the centre of Herrenzimmern, a village high above the Neckar north of Rottweil. There are two regular beers, the toasty and bittersweet **Sonne Spezial ★★**; and **Sonne Weizen ★★**, dominated by banana but with a spicy side; **Sonne Keller-Pils ★★** is the easy-drinking summer special.

TETTNANGER (KRONE)
Tettnang, Baden-Württemberg

As you might expect from a brewery in Tettnang, hops are generously used by this small family business in the town centre. The Tettnanger range includes three pilsners of which the organic **Keller-Pils ★★☆** is the hoppiest and best; while **Kronen-Bier ★★** is a bittersweet, herbal *helles*; and sweet, fruity **Coronator Dunkel ★★☆** is one of two winter *doppelbocks*.

VOGELBRÄU
Karlsruhe, Baden-Württemberg

Representative of a new trend in German brewing, Rudi Vogel opened his first pub brewery at Karlsruhe in 1985 and has added two others at nearby Durlach and Ettlingen. These make and serve a regular range of 22 seasonal brews covering most of the compass of German brewing, plus one year-round regular, the unfiltered and lavishly hopped **Vogelbräu Pils** ★★☆.

WALDHAUS
Waldhaus, Baden-Württemberg

This smallish but not insignificant brewery dominates its hamlet. The wide range of Waldhaus beers is headed up by the beautifully balanced, generously hopped **Diplom Pils** ★★★; a second, unfiltered, extra-hoppy pilsner, **Ohne Filter Extra Herb** ★★☆, deliberately contains hops from all round the country; the low-alcohol **Classic 2.9** ★★ has far more character than most light beers; while the **Schwarzwald Weisse** ★★☆ demonstrates how to up-hop a wheat beer.

COLOGNE, DÜSSELDORF & NORTH RHINE-WESTPHALIA

The most interesting area of northern Germany for beer is also its most populous state, home to two famously regional styles of session beer and one foreign misunderstanding.

Düsseldorfer *alt*bier, or *alt* for short, is a darkish pale ale, while *kölsch*, from just up the Rhine at arch-rival Cologne is light blond. Each is fermented as an ale before being lagered for about six weeks. Sharing some qualities with other northern European specialities such as British bitter, Belgian *speciaal* and lighter forms of French *bière de garde*, they are unquestionably at their best served direct from an uncarbonated upturned cask lodged on top of the bar.

In contrast the Dortmunder "style" of stronger blond lager does not exist in Germany, where such beers are termed export or *märzen*, implying a blond lager that is bolder and slightly sweeter. Düsseldorf and Cologne deserve a visit for their beers and taphouses alone, Dortmund only for its zoo and rosarium.

BOSCH
Bad Laasphe, North Rhine-Westphalia

A world away from the industrial Ruhr, in genteel Bad Laasphe, two distinct brands of beers are made. Of the eponymous and largely traditional Bosch beers, bready, caramel-accented **Braunbier** ★★★ is perhaps the finest example of its plain-ish style. The altogether more unusual-for-Germany, American-influenced Propeller brand features entertaining enough **Aufwind** ★★, which lacks the hoppy punch of a regular double IPA; and roasty, bittersweet **Nachtflug** ★★, billed as an Imperial stout but lacking the expected body and complexity.

BRAUSTELLE
Cologne, North Rhine-Westphalia

Street-corner pub brewery in the Ehrenfeld suburb of Cologne that was for a time single-handedly changing the face of German beer. Around 100 different beers have been made here to date including several dozen for beer commissioners Freigeist Bierkultur in Stolberg and Fritzale of Bonn. With the range ever-changing, our best advice is to try any of the beers that bear one of these two brands, or a Braustelle. The most reliably encountered tend to be the bestseller, **Braustelle Helios ★★**, a hoppy, unfiltered *kölsch*; **Freigeist AbraxXxas ★★☆**, a stronger modern interpretation of a traditional and defunct style of salty, smoked and sour wheat beer called a *Lichtenhainer*; and any of the various incarnations of **Fritzale India Pale Ale ★★→★★★**, which go as hoppy as any German beer gets.

FRÜH
Cologne, North Rhine-Westphalia

Probably the best known of the *kölsch* producers for its export presence and its legendary tap near Cologne's towering Gothic cathedral. The brewery is now in an industrial area outside the city and makes just the one alcoholic product, the soft, light and predictably understated **Früh Kölsch ★★** that like all of its ilk is far superior when served fresh from the upturned, uncarbonated barrel.

FÜCHSCHEN
Düsseldorf, North Rhine-Westphalia

The Little Fox, one of the four remaining established *altbier* producers in Düsseldorf's old town. Three Füchschen beers are made, the soft and dry hoppy classic **Alt ★★★**; yeasty-citrus *weizen* **Silber Füchschen ★★**; and a slightly stronger and hoppier version of the ordinary *alt* called **Weihnachtsbier ★★★**, available bottled for six weeks before Christmas and sold on draught at the tap only on Christmas Eve.

GAFFEL
Cologne, North Rhine-Westphalia

Brewery operated by the Becker family for over a century, with a flagship pub near the famous cathedral. **Gaffel Kölsch ★★☆** is oft-derided as too commercial a brand, with production of over 400,000hl in bottles, cans and kegs, but its hop-forward, aromatic and only marginally fruity character makes it worth a visit.

DESTINATION
COLOGNE

The city centre's two genuine taphouses are **Päffgen** (64 Friesenstraße) and the beautiful **Malzmühle** (6 Heumarkt), though renegade **Pfaffen** (62 Heumarkt) and big boy **Früh** (12–18 Am Hof) have a presence too.

GEMÜNDER
Gemünd, North Rhine-Westphalia

Smallish village brewery in the northern Eifel. It produces more than a dozen beers under various names including the unfiltered, herbal-hoppy blond **Eifeler-Landbier ★★**; and the nutty, fruity, deep ruby-brown winter-only *bock*, **Eifeler-Böckchen ★★☆**.

GLEUMES
Krefeld, North Rhine-Westphalia

A handsome traditional pub brewery that dates from 1807 and is the last of its kind in the city. Three Gleumes beers are made there. The slightly roasty, bitter, light amber **Lager** ★★☆ is an *altbier* in disguise, the banana-yeasty **Weizen** ★★ is an incomer; and the newish, unexceptional but well-constructed **Pils** ★★ has been introduced to replace a perfectly respectable *helles*.

HÜCHELNER URSTOFF
Hücheln, North Rhine-Westphalia

This small brewery, located just west of Cologne, is named after its principal product. Four beers are made here, all of them top-fermented and then lagered. The best are **Bartmann's Kölsch** ★★, which is typically soft, light, fruity and bittersweet; and fruity-yeasty and refreshing **Hüchelner Urstoff** ★★, another rare example of the type of unfiltered *kölsch* traditionally called *weisse*.

IM DOM
Neuss, North Rhine-Westphalia

A revived *hausbrauerei* in the old town at Neuss. It was brewing here from 1601 until 1971 and again between 2008 and 2010. The new owner has thus far made mainly the dark, unfiltered, fruity and toasty-bitter **Dom's Alt** ★★, with a darker, stronger *altbier* that appears only occasionally.

KÜRZER
Düsseldorf, North Rhine-Westphalia

Started in 2010 in the city's Altstadt, producing a fairly full-bodied and sweetish **Altbier** ★★ with some dried-fruit notes and a comparatively ale-like character, attributable no doubt to its two-week brew and fermentation cycle. Worth a visit if only to see the unique "glass cask" used for dispensing.

MALZMÜHLE
Cologne, North Rhine-Westphalia

Small brewery at the southern end of Cologne's old town. Until recently it produced just one beer, the classically made, light but somehow grainier than average **Mühlen Kölsch** ★★★★. However, since 2012 a series of experimental beers in other styles have flowed, none yet sticking.

PÄFFGEN
Cologne, North Rhine-Westphalia

The most traditional of the Cologne breweries, Päffgen makes a single *kölsch* that is available only from the (usually wooden) barrel. The perfectly

balanced, hoppy **Päffgen Kölsch**
★★★☆ is available only in four pubs, all in the city. The only nod to the modern world is that the beer can now be bought in siphons, filled to order, to take away.

PFAFFEN
Lohmar, North Rhine-Westphalia

Following a difference of opinion with brother Rudolf, owner of the aforementioned family brewery, Max Päffgen founded his own small brewery on a farm near Lohmar. As his Pfaffen (roughly "faffing about") beers are brewed outside the area of metropolitan Cologne that has been designated for the production of official *kölsch* beers, it is better to term his pale blond, light-bodied, fruity, malt-driven, top-fermented and lagered **Original** ★★☆ of indefinable style. A second beer, the bready and sweet-bitter pale **Bock** ★★☆, appears in the spring and at Christmas. Both are sold mostly at the tap, Zum Pfaffen, in Cologne.

PINKUS MÜLLER
Münster, North Rhine-Westphalia

Pinkus Müller, a true Münster institution, boasts one of the most traditional taprooms of any north German brewery and was the first brewer anywhere to be certified organic. The beer range is gradually increasing to include the unfiltered, yellow-golden, dry and grassy **Müller's Lagerbier** ★★; the deep golden, crisp and malty **Original Pinkus Obergärig** ★★☆ (US: Münster Alt), available with fresh fruit syrup at the tap, sadly; and the dark, fruity, well-malted *dunkel* **Pinkus Jubilate** ★★.

RATINGER BRAUHAUS
Ratingen, North Rhine-Westphalia

A pub brewery since 2005 between Düsseldorf and Essen, making only **Ratinger Alt** ★★☆, a fine, traditionally designed, produced and tasting *altbier* that comes close to the classics, an impression boosted by the fact that as in Düsseldorf, it is served by *kobes*, the essential wise-cracking and blue-aproned waiters.

SCHLÜSSEL
Düsseldorf, North Rhine-Westphalia

Brewery in the heart of Altstadt that makes the lightest of the classic *alts*. Deep amber in colour, with dabs of fruit and nut, **Schlüssel Alt** ★★☆ has a lasting bitterness. A stronger alt called **Schlüssel Stike** ★★★ is available on two days each year, in March and October.

DESTINATION DÜSSELDORF

The city's Altstadt area hosts four taphouses – **Füchschen** (28 Ratinger Straße), **Schlüssel** (41 Bolkerstraße), **Kürzer** (18 Kurze Straße) and must-see **Uerige** (1 Berger Straße), all serving *alt* from the cask. A fifth, **Schumacher** (123 Oststraße), sits halfway between the old city and the railway station.

SCHMITZ MÖNK
Anrath, North Rhine-Westphalia

Pub brewery north of Mönchengladbach, that was founded around the turn of the

20th century. The flagship Mönk beer is the toasty-nutty **Alt** ★★☆, slightly paler than those of Düsseldorf but almost on a par; the **Kellerbier** ★★☆ is a relatively recent introduction and has a whiff of smoke; appearing several times a year is the **Bock** ★★☆, essentially a stronger *alt* in the manner of *sticke bier* but lightly smoked,

from 1830. It makes more than just *kölsch*, producing a number of beers under contract for dormant breweries located elsewhere and a Sünner brand lager and *weizen* for itself. Its **Kölsch** ★★ is very well balanced, tangier and lighter than most; and it also makes an organic, citrus-fruity *weisse* called **BioColonia** ★★.

SCHUMACHER
Düsseldorf, North Rhine-Westphalia

The oldest of Düsseldorf's traditional *altbier* producers is said to be where the term "*alt*" was first coined. In 1871 the brewery moved to its current location on the eastern edge of the old town. **Schumacher Alt** ★★★ has a roasty twang and dry, bitter finish. Its stronger malty *alt* **Latzenbier** ★★★☆ is available on the third Thursday of March, September and November.

SÜNNER
Cologne, North Rhine-Westphalia

Of the 10 breweries remaining in Cologne, this is the oldest, dating

UERIGE
Düsseldorf, North Rhine-Westphalia

Perhaps the best-known of the brewers still making *altbiers* in Düsseldorf, Uerige is unusual for actively courting an export market to the US, originally making the extraordinary DoppelSticke exclusively for the States. It produces four variations on Uerige *alt*. The regular dry and bitter **Alt** ★★★★ is occasionally available unfiltered as **Alt Nicht Filtiert** ★★★☆. The stronger *alt*, **Sticke** ★★★☆ appears on draught at its wonderful rambling old tap, one block off the Rhine, on the third Tuesday of January and October, but is more widely available bottled; as is the aforementioned **Uerige DoppelSticke** ★★★☆.

REST OF GERMANY

The image of Germany as a nation awash with breweries is only half correct. The northward spread of the *Reinheitsgebot* (*see* box, page 48) during the 19th and early 20th centuries outlawed numerous regional and local beer styles that employed alien ingredients, such as spices or salt. The physical, political and economic damage of the 1939–45 war impacted heavily on local brewing too.

German reunification after the Berlin Wall came down in 1989 prompted the re-emergence of black beers (*schwarzbier*) from the east. Production of *gose* beers around the eastern city of Leipzig recommenced, too, while light, bone-dry *Berliner weisse* has struggled to survive in authentic form.

More typical of the north are large, self-contained brewpubs or *hausbrauereien*, typically making a predictable triptych of one white, one blond and one dark, though foreign influences are creeping in slowly.

ANKERBRÄU
Steinach, Thuringia

Thuringian brewer occupying premises formerly inhabited by GESSNER. The two regular beers are the soft and grainy bittersweet **Anker Pils ★★☆**; and the deep amber, toasty, slightly sweeter **Ankerla Dunkel ★★☆**, in the Franconian style.

BAYERISCHER BAHNHOF
Leipzig, Saxony

Millennium pub brewery at Leipzig's former railway terminus for trains to the south, remarkable for focusing on beer styles with a stronger East German heritage. Speciality of the house is **Original Leipziger Gose ★★☆**, a less acidic version of this revived style when compared to some; the exceptionally tart **Brettanomyces Lambicus ★★★** is brewed with lambic yeast but in the manner of a *Berliner weisse*; while the smooth, roasted-

chocolate **Heizer Schwarzbier ★★☆** is the best of the more conventional beers.

BERGSCHLÖSSCHEN
Lieske, Saxony

Small brewery in the Missionshof Lieske, a project for disabled people near Oßling in Saxony. Four Bergschlößchen beers are made, all available in the nearby tap or from a few other outlets across the state. Go for the caramelled, bittersweet **Dunkel ★★** and citrus-grassy **Zwickel ★★☆**.

BREWBAKER
Berlin

Ambitious, experimental craft brewery that opened in 2005 under a railway arch in Berlin's Tiergarten, expanding in 2011 into its current location at the Arminus Markthalle. Fifteen other bars are supplied, most in Berlin. Owner-brewer Michael Schwab has made over 60 different beers so far in a wide variety of German and other styles. The regulars include the hoppy, aromatic and bitter **Bellevue Pils ★★☆**; and refreshing and impressive citrus pale ale **Berlin IPA ★★★**.

BRUCH
Saarbrücken, Saarland

One of only two traditional Saarland breweries to have escaped the clutches of regional giant Karlsberg. Citrus-fruity **Bruch Zwickel** ★★ has some herbal notes; while **Weizen** ★★ has a clove-citrus-banana mix of flavours.

FALLERSLEBEN, ALTES BRAUHAUS ZU
Fallersleben, Lower Saxony

Phoenix-like pub brewery that rose from the ashes of a 2007 fire. Set in the grounds of Fallersleben castle, its beers are only available there. Signature brew **Fallersleber Schlossbräu** ★★ is an unfiltered but clean, hoppy golden lager; while the well-hopped **Fallersleber Weizen** ★★ has spicy banana notes.

GESSNER
Sonneberg, Thuringia

Close to the Franconian border, this modern brewery relocated from nearby Steinach in 1997. Among the many Gessner beers, the bittersweet, roasted, dark caramel lager **Alt-Sumbarcher Dunkel** ★★☆ and the similar-tasting but stronger **Dunkler Bock** ★★☆ stand out from the crowd.

GOSLAR, BRAUHAUS
Goslar, Lower Saxony

Pub brewery in the UNESCO World Heritage Site at Goslar, on the northern edge of the Harz Mountains. This is the town where *gose*, a sour, salted wheat beer flavoured with coriander, originated. Two Brauhaus Goslar varieties of this have been revived here: the more citrus and wheat-led **Helle Gose** ★★, and the sweeter, faintly sour **Dunkle Gose** ★☆, though each can be seen as safe compared to the Leipzig area recreations.

GROHE
Darmstadt, Hesse

Small town-centre brewery. Its five Grohe beers remain remarkably local to the city and its environs. Malt and grassy hops pervade the **Pils** ★★; the **Weizen** ★★ has spicy-citrus notes; and the winter seasonal dark **Bock** ★★ has a nutty, caramel flavour.

DESTINATION **DARMSTADT-EBERSTADT**

Maruhn (174 Pfungstädter Straße) is a drinks warehouse off the A5 (E35) south of Darmstadt, with well over 1000 German beers – still only about 15% of them – probably the most in the country.

HARTMANNSDORFER BRAUHAUS
Hartmannsdorf, Saxony

This medium-sized Saxony brewery is located not far from Chemnitz. Makes several brands of beer in addition to its own. Since the closure of Leipzig's Bauer brewery it has made the incomparable **Original Ritterguts Gose** ★★★☆, a citrus-sour beer with a salty finish, a beer that was popular in the area before it was *Reinheitsgebot*-ed out in 1919.

HEIDENPETERS
Kreuzberg, Berlin

Tiny ale brewery operating since 2012 in the cellar of the gentrified Neun market hall. Little of its beer gets beyond the small bar in the hall upstairs and much is seasonal or one-off brews, but as a sign of solidarity we list two regular offerings, US-style citrus and grassy, if under-hopped pale ale **Thirsty Lady** ★★; and slightly hoppier **Pale Ale** ★★, still a bit rough around its edges.

DESTINATION
BERLIN

Ambrosetti (103 Schillerstraße) is a beer store in the Charlottenburg district stocking in the order of 300 different German beers and maybe 100 imports. By far the biggest selection in the capital. **Mommsen-Eck** (45 Mommsenstraße), in the same district, is one of Germany's few emporium beer bars, showcasing around 100 German beers, the best range in the capital.

HOMBURGER BRAUHAUS
Homburg, Saarland

The first phase of the German beer revival began in the 1980s with a rash of pub breweries spreading across the north and middle of the country. This one is found on the first floor of a shopping centre. It makes two Wirtsbräu beers all year, supplemented by several others as seasons dictate. The dry and hoppy year-round **Hell** ★★ could pass for an unfiltered pils; while best of the seasonals is the bitter-chocolate **Bock** ★★☆ that appears in winter.

HOPS & BARLEY
Friedrichshain, Berlin

A former butcher's shop, this bohemian pub brewery opened in 2008 and has already

expanded, likely for the popularity of its 20+ seasonal or occasional Friedrichshainer beers and its three regulars – fruity-hoppy-bitter **Pilsner** ★★☆; chocolate-roasted-coffee **Dunkles** ★★☆; and soft-banana-spicy **Weizen** ★★– which are well above average for a modern pub brewery.

KLOSTER MACHERN
Wehlen, Rhineland-Palatinate

Pub brewery (since 2004) in a former monastery near Bernkastel-Keus, in the Mosel valley wine country, again distinguished for the above-average quality of its standard triptych. The Kloster Machern beers are all unfiltered and include a yeasty, aromatic **Hell** ★★; banana and sharp-citrus **Weizen** ★★☆; and roasted, fruity-hoppy **Dunkel** ★★.

MEIEREI
Potsdam, Brandenburg

Visitors to Berlin increasingly spend time in Potsdam. The setting of this pub brewery in a former pumping house is superb, appreciated best when approached by boat from the city centre. Its single regular beer is the slightly sweet and gently bitter **Meierei Hell** ★★; with among a dozen seasonals the smooth, almost black, roasty and fruity autumn **Bock Sollator** ★★☆ also impressing.

METZLER
Dingsleben, Thuringia

Small brewery in southern Thuringia, not far from the Franconian border. Best of the Dingslebener bunch are the flowery **Edel-Pils** ★★, and **Lava** ★★, a strong and rich, chocolaty *schwarzbier*.

NEUSTÄDTER HAUSBRAUEREI
Dresden-Neustadt, Saxony

Small brewery producing half a dozen beers found in local bars and shops across the city. **Hecht Alt ★★** is a fruity, unfiltered *alt* that has less bitterness than the Rhineland classics; citrus and grassy **Neustadt Hell ★★** is drier than might be expected; while oddball **Lenins Hanf ★★** is a fruity, herbal beer made with hemp.

RATSHERRN
Hamburg

Revivalist brewery (since 2012) that has obtained the right to brew Ratsherrn beers, once the brand of Hamburg's Elbschloss brewery, which closed in 1997. Located in an old slaughterhouse in the city centre. The three regular beers are the crisp and dry **Pilsener ★★**; dry and bitter caramel-fruity **Rotbier ★★**; and the as yet somewhat subdued, US-inspired **Pale Ale ★☆**.

```
DESTINATION
HAMBURG

Bierland (10 Seumestraße) is
a small but impressive beer shop
near the Wandsbeker Chaussee
U- and S-bahn stations, famed for
sourcing rare and obscure German
beers, with a stock of 300+.
```

REICHENBRAND
Chemnitz, Saxony

Despite it being nearly 25 years since the Berlin Wall came down, many East German brewers are still struggling to find their voice. This small-to-medium suburban brewery at Chemnitz, also known as Bergt-Bräu, is widely seen around the city though not much yet in wider Saxony. Its Reichenbrander beers include an aromatic, dry and golden **Kellerbier ★★**; and strong, spicy, Czech style **Premium Pils ★★**.

SCHMITT
Ilmtal-Singen, Thuringia

This small brewery was one of only a handful to remain in private hands throughout the DDR period. Formally protected since 1976, there has been little significant investment here in more than a century and it is a now a working museum. This really is brewing as performed in days gone by, complete with a steam engine powering all manner of belt-driven equipment. Its sole offering, **Singer Bier ★★**, is golden, grassy, herbal and surprisingly nice.

SPECHT
Ehrenfriedersdorf, Saxony

Small brewery in the Erzgebirge ("Iron Mountains"), midway between Chemnitz and the Czech border, serving about 30 pubs in the area with six beers. The pick are the grainy and lightly bitter **Greifensteinquell Landbier ★★**; aromatic and grassy **Specht Pilsener ★★**; and **Schwarzer Specht ★★☆**, a *bock*-strength, dark-fruity *dunkel*.

ST MICHAELIS (BRAUHAUS EUTIN)
Eutin, Schleswig-Holstein

Pub brewery (since 1989) on Eutin's market square, midway between

Lübeck and Kiel, on the eastern side of Schleswig-Holstein. The three regular St Michaelis beers plus half a dozen or so seasonals include its bestseller, dry and bitter **Pils ★★**☆; and **Tafelbier ★★**, a grainy and slightly sweet unfiltered *helles*.

STÖRTEBEKER BRAUMANUFAKTUR
Stralsund, Mecklenburg-Vorpommern

Known as the Stralsunder Brauerei until 2011, this convert to craft brewing in the far northeast of mainland Mecklenburg-Vorpommern changed its name to reflect the increasing importance of its premium Störtebeker range, named after a 14th-century privateer. The fruity-sweet **Roggen-Weizen ★★** is made with rye, wheat and barley; **Atlantik-Ale ★★**☆ is a new golden, grapefruit-flavoured ale; and **Stark-Bier ★★**☆ is an almost black beer that might justify the description *schwarzbierbock*.

WATZKE
Dresden, Saxony

Lavish riverside pub brewery, converted from a ballroom. Owned by Rudi Vogel of Karlsruhe pub brewery fame (see **VOGELBRÄU**), this far-flung outpost of his empire has two regular beers: the aromatic and bitter **Das Pils ★★**☆ and fruity, bittersweet, light golden-brown **Altpieschener Spezial ★★**. There are also a dozen or more seasonal beers through the year.

WEESENSTEIN, SCHLOSSBRAUEREI
Müglitztal, Saxony

Small pub brewery within the bowels of Weesenstein Castle, in the Müglitz

valley south of Dresden. Due to the narrow lane through the castle, malt and spent grain are transported by donkey. Owner-brewer Ulrich Betsch is a keen player of the bagpipes but this does not appear to upset his beer, **Weesensteiner Schlossbräu Original ★★**☆, which is a soft and malty *vollbier* with grassy hops.

WIPPRA
Wippra, Saxony-Anhalt

This small 15th-century brewery and museum of traditional brewing is located on the southeastern edge of the Harz Mountains in Saxony-Anhalt. Its Wippraer beers are often seen in litre bottles in the region's shops, as far away as Braunschweig. The unusually dark **Pilsener ★★** has a malty, herbal flavour; while roasted coffee and caramel dominate the **Schwarzbier ★★**☆.

AUSTRIA

Austrian beer is underrated. The German purity law (see *Reinheitsgebot*, page 48) was never adopted here, though the quality of brewing in the Innviertel region, bang up against the Bavarian border, gives the neighbours a run for their money. Ruddy-brown Vienna lagers, while as distinctive as Munich's light and dark, and Pilsen's blond golden, do not share the limelight.

However, for exploration and surprise, Austria has much to offer. Its classic lagers, in all the major styles, include one of the world's best pilsners, while some newer, smaller breweries interpret foreign craft beer styles with aplomb. It even has its own Trappist abbey brewery.

1516 BREWING
Vienna

Austria's foremost US-style brewpub, in downtown Vienna since 1998. Specializes in top-fermented beers but always carries **Helles ★★** and/or **Lager ★★** on tap. Guest brewers have helped create regulars, such as the heavily hopped US-style IPA **Hop Devil ★★★☆**, with characteristic grapefruit aroma and some alcoholic warmth inspired by its US namesake from VICTORY BREWING in the US. **Eejit's Oatmeal Stout ★★☆** is a full-bodied, roasty interpretation of the style showing hints of smoke; while hazy, fruity **Grand Q ★★★☆** is a strong Belgian-style *witbier* with quince juice added during fermentation.

AUGUSTINER BRÄU (KLOSTER MÜLLN)
Salzburg

A former Augustine abbey brewery founded in 1621 just outside the centre of Salzburg. Famed for the beer halls and garden at its memorable brewery tap, where beer is still dispensed fresh from large wooden barrels. Most of its output is **Märzen ★★☆**, a dark golden, lighter-bodied Austrian interpretation of the style.

DESTINATION SALZBURG

Friesacher Einkehr (6 Brunngasse, Anif) is a large, smart, *heurige*-style restaurant in a village 5km (3 miles) south of the city, featuring a remarkable selection of perhaps 50 beers including draughts mostly from the region, a bottled selection from further afield and a collection of strong, cellar-aged stronger beers including dozens of vintage *bocks*.

BAUMGARTNER
Schärding, Upper Austria

Founded in 1609, when the Innviertel region was still part of Bavaria, the name of its very pale, full-bodied lager **Baunti 1609** ★★ reflecting this. Famed for its award-winning **Pils** ★★★, which has a flowery hoppy nose and a noble, intensely hoppy finish. A seasonal fresh hop version has a good hop aroma but seems to be a little less bitter.

BEVOG
Bad Radkersburg, Styria

State of the art microbrewery opened in 2013 near the Slovenian border to brew ales for both the Slovenian and Austrian markets, starting with an easy-drinking, medium-bodied pale ale called **Tak** ★★; then adding a more robust smoked porter, **Ond** ★★★, with distinct roasted notes, gentle smoke but a robust bitter finish.

BIERWERKSTATT WEITRA
Weitra, Lower Austria

Small brewery near the Czech border. Claims to have the oldest brewing privilege in Austria, dating back to 1321. Taken over by much larger Zwettler, from the neighbouring town, in 2002 and has since specialized in producing an organic, amber-coloured Vienna-style lager called **Hadmar** ★★☆.

EGG
Egg, Vorarlberg

Small brewery in a village in the Bregenz Forest, not to be confused with the larger Egger brewery in Lower Austria. Its beers are only generally available in the region, notably the straw-coloured, moderately hopped, yet very dry **Edel Pils** ★★; and the remarkable **Wälder Senn** ★★☆, a surprisingly flavoursome ultra-light lager brewed with whey from a local dairy.

ENGELSZELL, TRAPPISTENBIER-BRAUEREI
Engelhartszell, Upper Austria

In 2012 the small Trappist cloister in Engelhartszell, on the Danube, rebuilt the brewery that had been there until 1932. Its first beer was strong brown **Gregorius** ★★★, an improving hazy, mahogany-brown, slightly sweetish ale with a plum-like aroma, which improves in the bottle for six months. A lighter, spritzy blond ale with hints of lemon zest and a robust bitterness named **Benno** ★★★ is undergoing revision.

FORSTNER BIERE
Kalsdorf bei Graz, Styria

Tiny brewery that began in a pub in 2002 and now operates as a stand-alone brewhouse. The wide range of bottled brews includes **Styrian Ale** ★★☆, a bottle-conditioned pale ale with sulphury and roasty notes; an intensely fruity Belgian-style *tripel* called **Fünf vor 12** ★★☆; and barley wine **Bonifatius Barrique** ★★★☆, matured in wine casks, sporting aromas rich in raspberries, kiwi fruit and fresh yogurt.

GÖSS (HEINEKEN)
Göss, Styria

Large brewery in a former cloister in the hop-growing province of Styria, now part of the BrauUnion group. Gösser beers include one of Austria's most popular, a golden, medium-bodied **Märzen** ★★ characterized by a nutty flavour; fuller-bodied and slightly stronger **Spezial** ★★☆ has a robust hop bitterness; while annual **Reininghaus Jahrgangs Pils** ★★★ varies despite an identical recipe, highlighting the differences between each year's harvest of Styrian Celeja hops with which it is made, showing piney aromas.

GUSSWERK, BRAUHAUS
Hof bei Salzburg, Salzburg

All-organic small craft brewery moved from Salzburg in 2013. Regular **Edelguss** ★★ is a golden ale with medium body and bitterness; **Nicobar IPA** ★★☆ has a nutty brown colour with a lot of haze, a tobacco-like aroma and a complex bitterness; **Cerevinum** ★★ is a dry ale with little hop character that undergoes secondary fermentation with a little red grape juice; while barley wine **Dies Irae** ★★★ has a complex aroma of dried pears and plums.

HOFSTETTEN
Sankt Martin, Upper Austria

Arguably one of the oldest breweries in the country, first mentioned in 1229. Its unfiltered **Hofstettner Kübelbier** ★★ is a balanced lager with a grainy aroma; while brown **Granitbock** ★★★☆ is a *steinbier*, boiled by the immersion of

glowing hot granite stones into the wort, imbuing burnt and smoky tastes.

HUBER, FAMILIENBRAUEREI
Sankt Johann in Tirol, Tyrol

Regional brewery established in 1727, its brewery tap being atop the malt silo with impressive views of the Alpine landscape. **Meisterpils** ★★☆ has an impressive head, a herbal, almost peppery hop aroma and a dry aftertaste; **Augustinus** ★★ is a dryish dark brown *dunkel* with hints of toasted bread; and the seasonal amber **Bock** ★★★ is sweet on the palate but dry in the aftertaste.

KALTENHAUSEN, HOFBRÄU (HEINEKEN)
Hallein, Salzburg

Historic brewery, from 1475, that once supplied the court of Salzburg's archbishop. Bought and closed by Heineken, who installed a 12-hl pilot brewery to supply the former brewery tap. The regular **Kellerbier** ★☆ is disappointingly under-hopped but the Spezial series, bottled for nationwide

meine KUNST zu leben

HOFBRÄU
SPEZIALITÄTEN-MANUFAKTUR
Seit 1475
TREFFPUNKT DER BIERKULTUR
KALTENHAUSEN

KELLERBIER
Stammwürze 11,8 °P / Alk. 4,8 % vol

sale, can strike gold. Best so far is **Riesling Style ★★★☆**, from pilsner wort primed with Styrian Riesling grape juice before secondary fermentation by wine yeast, to create a refreshing, strong hybrid of great individuality.

LONCIUM, PRIVATBRAUEREI
Kötschach-Mauthen, Carinthia

Small 2007 brewery close to the Italian border making mostly bottom-fermented beers. **Austrian Amber Lager ★★☆** is currently a seasonal beer in the Vienna style, slightly hazy and moderately hopped with a touch of roasted malt; while **Schwarze Gams ★★★** is a very dark *bock* with caramel and coffee notes.

MOHRENBRAUEREI AUGUST HUBER
Dornbirn, Vorarlberg

Austria's westernmost brewery, established in 1834 not far from the Bodensee. Its Mohren beers include a stronger than average standard lager, **Spezial ★★☆**, with robust malty body and a bold bitterness; and the stronger and sweeter **Bockbier ★★**, which is rich in esters and honey-like aromas, followed by a surprisingly dry bitterness in its aftertaste.

OTTAKRINGER
Vienna

This, Vienna's only industrial-size brewery, founded in 1837, still operates in historic 19th-century buildings. A tribute to the founding period is **Rotes Zwickl ★★☆**, an unfiltered Vienna-style lager with a reddish appearance and distinctive sweet malty backtastes,

found only on draught; while golden **Goldfassl Spezial ★★** has slightly more alcohol and shows some caramel notes before finishing rather bitter.

DESTINATION VIENNA

Känguruh (20 Bürgerspitalgasse) is an evenings-only bar near the Westbahnhof with the capital's largest beer selection, mostly Germany and Belgian with US and Austria becoming more prominent. **Krah Krah** (8 Rabensteig) is the city's longest-standing speciality beer café, under the same owner since 1987, in an alley near Schwedenplatz metro, stocking a couple of dozen Austrian regionals and a growing band of others.

RIED
Ried im Innkreis, Upper Austria

Regional brewery owned by the tenants of taverns in the Innviertel beer region. The first traditional brewery in Austria to add a full-bodied **India Pale Ale ★★**, with flowery bitterness in the aftertaste, to a regular portfolio of lagers and wheat beers. Also proud of its *weizenbock*, **Rieder XXX Weisse ★★☆**, with an intense banana and not so prominent clove aroma, full, slightly sweetish body; and tart finish.

SCHLOSS EGGENBERG
Vorchdorf, Upper Austria

Regional brewery in an old palace, famous for its strong beers. Golden *doppelbock* **Urbock 23 ★★☆** has a sweet malty character, with good ageing potential at 9.9% ABV. Production of the formerly Swiss, super-strong Samichlaus brands moved here in 1999. These now come as brownish **Classic** ★★★ with chocolaty aromas; while the pale version **Hell** ★★★, for US export, is more on the sweet side, some vintages being decanted for ageing in wine casks as **Holzfass** ★★★☆, which shows distinct astringency.

STIEGLBRAUEREI ZU SALZBURG
Salzburg

Established in 1492 and now the largest independently owned brewery in Austria. Malty, somewhat nutty **Stiegl Goldbräu** ★★ is the bestselling beer in the country and style-defining for Austrian *märzen*. The brewery also makes regular seasonal beers in small runs, including a fruity **Double IPA** ★★★, some going on to become regular products such as the unfiltered, rather flat organic *zwickelbier* **Paracelsus** ★★; and medium-bodied, unfiltered *weizen* **Stiegl Weisse Naturtrüb** ★★.

TROJAN
Schrems, Lower Austria

This regional brewery can be found in Schrems, northwest of Vienna. Its **Schremser Roggen** ★★☆ is a hazy, amber-coloured ale that is brewed using organically grown ryo. It features fruity aromas, a medium-to-full body and a mild bitterness in the finish.

TRUMER PRIVATBRAUEREI JOSEF SIGL
Obertrum, Salzburg

This independent brewery, which is located north of Salzburg, was founded in 1601 and has been in the Sigl family since 1775. Josef Sigl pioneered the German style of pilsner in Austria, perfecting a straw-coloured classic of the genre, the Austrian icon, **Trumer Pils** ★★★☆, which is also brewed in Berkeley, California. Fermented in open vessels, it ends crisp with a hay-like aroma, and stands head and shoulders above most rivals. The brewery's other beers have been peripheral in comparison, although a new range of interesting seasonal beers is now starting to appear.

VITZTHUM, PRIVATBRAUEREI
Uttendorf, Salzburg

This traditional family-owned regional brewery can be found in the Innviertel region and dates back to 1600. Its straw-coloured **Uttendorfer Pils** ★★☆ has great head retention and a soft mouthfeel, despite its intense bitterness; while its **Falstaff** ★★ is a malty, Oktoberfest-style *märzen* with a sweet start and a hoppy finish.

WEISSE, DIE
Salzburg

Austria's oldest pub brewery, founded in 1901 in the part of Salzburg on the north bank of the Salzach. Focuses almost entirely on brewing wheat beers, in a wide number of styles. The regular Die Weisse beers include the original **Hell** ★★, a classic dark-blond *hefeweizen* with strong banana and a little clove aroma, low-to-medium body and a dry finish; and fuller-bodied **Dunkel** ★★☆ with hints of caramel and butterscotch. It also has a *weizenbock* and has played with making a wheat-based *märzen* and even a *doppelbock*.

ZILLERTAL BIER
Zell am Ziller, Tyrol

Small brewery dating from 1500, attached to a hotel in a remote Tyrolean valley. Brews light golden, herbal, dry and deceptively light-bodied **Gauder-Bock** ★★☆ for the Tyrol's largest folk festival each May, hiding its 7.8% ABV well. Recent addition **Weißbier Bock** ★★☆, of the same strength, is rich in banana and hazelnut aromas and dangerously easy to drink. Best consumed locally.

ZIPFER (HEINEKEN)
Zipf, Upper Austria

A sizeable brewery making the speciality beers for the (Heineken-owned) BrauUnion group. Its **Zipfer Urtyp** ★★ is a straw-coloured, crisp lager with a hoppy finish; while the **Zipfer Pils** ★★☆ shows the character of whole-leaf Tettnanger hopping; and the amber-coloured *weizen* **Edelweiss Hofbräu** ★★★ has a fruity, banana aroma and a full, but not overly sweet body.

UNITED KINGDOM

British beer has begun the second leg of its journey back to the future.

The end of the 20th century saw an unlikely revival of cask or "real" ales, limited largely to lighter draught beers (3.5 to 5% ABV), typically served in pint (57cl) measures. Local British brewers have long excelled at packing flavour into everyday "session" beers since gravities were forced down by government interference in the first half of the last century.

The revival of older, grander and more assertive British styles that have inspired modern brewers in many other countries – porters, stouts, pale ales, IPAs and others – has been less impressive, as a significant strand of public opinion expects these to be hand-drawn from open casks – which many were not in the past. As a result, British brewers underperform in export markets where they could be expected to excel.

There is some movement as newer exponents, along with older hands sensing change in the air, show a growing desire to create more challenging beers. While this has created its share of awful pastiches, the idea that Britain's brewing future somehow lies in its past is starting to be respected.

Most UK brewers have a long way to go before they become as meticulously bold as the modern beer consumer demands, but if they seek out old brewing records and blend into these the use of much-improved equipment and ingredients, plus the no-corners-cut approach adopted by the best craft brewers internationally, they will get there in the end, even if a rump of elderly protesters continues to find such beers "too fizzy".

Our UK brewery selections focus on these pioneers, alongside the best of the established family brewers and those from the wave of new brewers established in response to the "real ale" revival.

ENGLAND

It was in England, as opposed to other parts of the UK, that the revival of interest in cask-conditioned beers first flourished in the late 1970s. More than any other draught beer, cask ale demands conscientious timing and faultless hygiene to reach best condition – something that is reflected in our tasting notes below.

Locally made cask ales have made sweeping inroads into English pubs, and bottled beers into off-licences and supermarkets. Persuading hotels, restaurants and others to stock better beers has proved more difficult. Our list of featured brewers looks to the future more than the past.

ACORN BREWERY
Barnsley, South Yorkshire

Celebrated locally for slightly brackish, resinous revival of its **Barnsley Bitter** ★★ fermented by the same yeast strain as the original. Better known nationally for its series of 40-plus single-hop cask **IPAs** ★★→★★★; oily, slightly astringent **Old Moor Porter** ★★; and hopped-up Imperial stout **Gorlovka** ★★☆, full-flavoured despite modest strength.

ADNAMS
Southwold, Suffolk

Long-established, family-dominated independent brewery and wine importer on the Suffolk coast. Revered for benchmark cask ales like **Southwold Bitter** ★★★, with complex marmalade and peppery Fuggle flavours; and richer, nuttier **Broadside** ★★. Cultivating a contemporary edge with a plethora of new creations including easy-going, fragrantly grapey golden ale **Explorer** ★★ and fruity-bitter pale ale **Innovation** ★★☆. Revived, rich barley wine **Tally-Ho** ★★★ improves with ageing.

ARBOR ALES
Bristol

This inventive brewery has been winning admirers since 2007. Its beers include the chaffy and honeyed best bitter **Brigstow** ★★☆; the distinctive chocolaty, leafy **Mild West** ★★☆; and the smooth and smoky **Oyster Stout** ★★☆, for which real oysters are added to the mash. There are also numerous experimental ales, which appear under the name **Freestyle Fridays** ★★→★★★.

BATEMANS
Wainfleet All Saints, Lincolnshire

Picturesque, family-owned brewery, under a windmill. Its characterful Good Honest Ales include chewy, russet best bitter **XB** ★★; grainy and complex **Combined Harvest** ★★☆; dryly fruity and beautifully balanced dark mild **DM** ★★; and rich, fruity and stronger **Victory Ale** ★★☆.

BATHAMS
Brierley Hill, West Midlands

Tiny, traditional, family-owned independent brewery near Dudley in the Black Country, producing sweet, grainy ales. The **Mild Ale** ★★★ is classically sappy and robust with chocolate-biscuit notes; while the paler **Best Bitter** ★★☆, added in the 1950s, is full and sweetish with increased English hopping.

DESTINATION
BIRMINGHAM

The **Post Office Vaults** (84 New Street) is a relatively new beer bar next to the main station, with a wide range of contemporary British beers in cask and a wide selection of craft beers in bottles and kegs.

BEAVERTOWN BREWERY
Hackney Wick, Greater London

Originally launched by Logan Plant, son of Led Zeppelin's Robert, at his restaurant in Hackney's De Beauvoir Town in 2012, outgrowing its site and moving to dedicated premises in 2013. Decidedly contemporary beers include a beautifully smooth and perfumed black IPA **Black Betty** ★★★; citrus and pineapple packed pale ale **Gamma Ray** ★★☆; and luscious jet black Imperial stout **Heavy Water** ★★★. Already flagging multiple wild, sour and wood-aged limited edition beers.

BLACK SHEEP BREWERY
Masham, North Yorkshire

Set up in 1992 by a far-sighted wayward son of the town's THEAKSTON brewing family in Wensleydale, brewing no-nonsense ales in the traditionally dry regional style using Yorkshire Square fermenters. The **Best Bitter** ★★☆ is balanced, honeyed and slightly tannic; the **Ale** ★★★ is an understated heavier, almost austere stronger bitter; and darker stronger **Riggwelter** ★★☆ – local dialect for a sheep stranded on its back – is firm and chocolaty with burnt-fruit notes.

BRAKSPEAR BREWING (MARSTON'S)
Witney, Oxfordshire

The historic Brakspear brewery at Henley-on-Thames closed in 2002, its

brands heading upstream to Witney, on an Oxfordshire tributary, via a tortuous route. **Brakspear Bitter ★★☆** has retained its rooted, fruity, slightly sulphurous character; and powerful bottle-conditioned **Triple ★★☆** has notes of almonds and whisky.

BRISTOL BEER FACTORY
Bedminster, Bristol

Avowedly contemporary brewer in a corner of a defunct brewery at Ashton Gate. Regular beers include creditable, cloved British *weizen* **Bristol Hefe ★★**; Citra-hopped, chewy US-style pale ale **Independence ★★**; a smooth, poised and slightly smoky **Milk Stout ★★★**; and massively floral, grapefruited and bitter UK-style **Southville Hop IPA ★★★**. Annual date-stamped releases of rich, fruity and woody but not too strong barley wine **Vintage ★★★** are also worth catching.

BUTCOMBE BREWERY
Wrington, North Somerset

One of the longest-standing revivalist cask brewers, from 1978, now at Wrington in North Somerset. For two decades it

produced a single beer, a dry, generously grainy cask **Bitter ★★★** that remains a best-practice example of its style. Its appropriately well-engineered, crisp English-hopped **IPA ★★☆** shows promise too.

BUXTON BREWERY
Buxton, Derbyshire

New and keenly contemporary brewery in the eponymous spa town, within Derbyshire's Peak District National Park. Offers a sweetish, herbal, hoppy **Bitter ★★** but is better known for more adventurous bottle-conditioned beers like its curiously fruity imperial stout **Tsar ★★★**; piney and sweetish US-style IPA **Wild Boar ★★★**; and the Amarillo- and Nelson Sauvin-infused double IPA **Axe Edge ★★★**.

CAMDEN TOWN BREWERY
Kentish Town, Greater London

This hi-tech modern plant in London's Kentish Town produces technically flawless kegged and bottled beers in mainly European styles. Clean and malty **Hells** appears also in unfiltered form and occasionally a US-hopped version that challenges some German originals **★★→★★★**. **Ink ★★** is a creditable craft-brewed dry nitro stout; while well-balanced bestseller **Pale ★★** has tropical-fruit character.

CHILTERN BREWERY
Aylesbury, Buckinghamshire

Farmhouse brewery founded in 1980. Particularly adept at making stronger ales such as the outstanding long-matured **Bodgers Barley Wine ★★★**, rich with marzipan and fresh orange notes. Less hefty is the chewy chestnut- and raspberry-edged **300s Old Ale ★★☆**.

CONISTON BREWING
Coniston, Cumbria

Housed in a modest plant behind the Black Bull pub, a stone's throw from Coniston Water in the Lake District National Park. Renowned for refreshing lime- and ginger-tinged golden bitter **Bluebird**, which appears in cask, US export and bottle-conditioned versions **★★ → ★★★**. Other options include the smoky and herbal dark mild **Old Man ★★☆**; and **No 9 Barley Wine ★★★☆**, which has smooth vanilla, sherry and orange toffee tones.

CROUCH VALE BREWERY
South Woodham Ferrers, Essex

One of Britain's oldest (1981) new generation brewers. Best known of its "fine Essex ales" is multi-award-winning golden ale **Brewers Gold ★★☆**, with grape and tropical-fruit flavours. Also hop-forward and golden is stronger, apricot-tinged **Amarillo ★★☆**; while sacky, figgy **Essex Boys Bitter ★★** is flavoursome for its strength.

DARK STAR BREWING
Partridge Green, West Sussex

Former pub brewery opened near Horsham in 1995. Produces reliably outstanding beers with contemporary appeal. **Original ★★☆** is a distinctive roasty old ale; bestselling session beer **Hophead ★★☆** is fruity, citric and well balanced; **American Pale Ale ★★★** bursts with grapefruit and pineapple

flavours without excessive bitterness; while mocha flavours are well integrated into coffee stout **Espresso ★★★**.

DONNINGTON BREWERY
Stow-on-the-Wold, Gloucestershire

Small, picturesque brewery with its own trout lake, in an impossibly beautiful neck of the Cotswolds. The rarity of its beers beyond a limited estate of local pubs fuels cult status of a sort, though quality can vary. The standard bitter **BB ★★** is smooth and sweetish; darker, premium bitter **SBA ★★☆** is drier and hazier; and neglected, toffee-nosed, fruity-bodied **Double Donn ★★** is as hard to place as it is hard to find.

DURHAM BREWERY, THE
Bowburn, Durham

Reliable source of big, often bottle-conditioned beers inspired by its home city's ecclesiastical heritage, such as peach-liqueur-tinged *tripel* **Bede's Chalice ★★★**; spicily hoppy barley wine **Benedictus ★★☆**; and cakey, bitter imperial stout **Temptation ★★★** and its sour mutation **Diabolus ★★★**. Bold session casks include mineral and plum-noted golden ale **Cloister ★★☆**.

ELLAND BREWERY
Elland, West Yorkshire

Formed by a merger of two smaller concerns in 2002 and named for its location in a small market town in picturesque Calderdale. Best known for multi-award-winning cask- and bottle-conditioned **1872 Porter ★★★**, a meaty, toasty liquorice-tinged mouthful based on a historic recipe. Other beers include soft but citric-hoppy golden bitter **Beyond the Pale** ★★.

EVERARDS
Narborough, Leicestershire

Family-owned independent near Leicester, known for its much-improved dry end cask ales. Its stronger bitter **Original** ★★ is tawny, fruity and nutty; while the best bitter **Tiger** ★★☆ is subtly fruity with a burst of English hops. There are numerous seasonal beers too.

FREEDOM BREWERY
Abbots Bromley, Staffordshire

Early pioneer of newer, smaller-scale, higher spec lager brewing in UK, started in London in 1995 and transferred to new owners in rural Staffordshire. Uses *Reinheitsgebot*-compliant, vegan-friendly methods, real Burton brewing water and a minimum of four weeks' lagering. The *helles* **Organic English Lager** ★★ is full and crisp with good leafy hops; the **Organic Dark Lager**

★☆ is a light, toffee-ish and likeable *dunkel*; and the annoyingly reasonable **Pils** ★☆ makes you want them to try out 12-week lagering.

FULLER'S
Chiswick, Greater London

Long-standing, independent, family-influenced brewery producing a strong portfolio of Fuller's beers in numerous styles from a wisteria-clad riverside site in west London. Well known for cask beers like delicately hoppy and refreshing **Chiswick Bitter** ★★☆ and marmalade-tinged, style-defining **ESB** ★★★, it is gaining new respect for historical revivals like slightly smoky amber ale **1845** ★★★☆ and its annually released barley wine **Vintage Ale**, which usually becomes more complex and port-like with age ★★★→★★★★. Occasionally releases a steel-aged sourish version of the classic oak-aged barley wine **Gale's Prize Old Ale** ★★☆, which it acquired by takeover.

DESTINATION
LONDON

Craft Beer Co has pubs at 55 White Lion Street, Islington, 82 Leather Lane, Clerkenwell, 11 Brixton Station Road and 128 Clapham Manor Street, with extensive ranges of cutting-edge cask ales, and better UK and imported bottled beers. **Cask Pub & Kitchen** (6 Charlwood Street, Pimlico) is a similar establishment, or for craft beer celeb-spotting in bijou surroundings, why not try **The Rake** (14a Winchester Walk, Borough Market)?

GRAIN BREWERY
Harleston, Norfolk

Based on a farm in the Waveney Valley since 2006, with an improving portfolio of clean, competent and contemporary beers melding traditional English and international influences. Standout is the parchment pale, light but gloriously fruity refresher **3.1.6 ★★★**, brewed from pilsner malt with Amarillo hops. Others include orange-scented wheat beer **Blonde Ash ★★**; blackcurrant and smoke-tinged **Porter ★★**; and **Redwood ★★☆**, a satisfyingly earthy and toasty reddish best bitter.

GREENE KING
Bury St Edmunds, Suffolk

Once a revered regional champion this now national brewer, founded in 1799, remains committed to cask ale, though ubiquitous light bitter **Greene King IPA ★☆** is out of step with current expectations of its name. In contrast, it is the only UK brewer to continue maturing a strong stock ale in oak vats: vinous, slightly sour **Old 5X ★★★☆** makes rare solo appearances but is mostly blended with fresh ale to create

bottled classic **Strong Suffolk ★★☆**. Its old-fashioned cask dark mild **XX ★★** is only slightly less rare.

> ### DESTINATION CAMBRIDGE
>
> **The Cambridge Blue** (85 Gwydir Street) is currently the best of various beer bars off Mill Road, having expanded its cask beer interest to include 120 or so international bottled brews.

GREEN JACK BREWING
Lowestoft, Suffolk

Britain's most easterly brewer, on the Waveney coast, launched an improving range of 75cl flip-top bottled speciality beers in the late 2000s, including roasted, blackcurranty export stout **Baltic Trader ★★☆**; fruity, gracefully ageing barley wine **Ripper ★★★**; and the more sessionable, soft, chocolaty **Lurcher Stout ★★★**. Chaffy best bitter **Trawlerboys ★★** is made entirely from East Anglian ingredients.

GROWLER BREWERY
Pentlow, Essex

The former Nethergate brewery, which played a key role in the revival of porter when it produced full-flavoured, cakey and tangy **Old Growler ★★★**, still one of the best. Also reintroduced spiced beers to the UK with coriander-laced, flowery, copper **Umbel Ale ★★** and the deliciously complex, spiced porter **Umbel Magna ★★☆**. The recipe for **Augustinian ★★☆** has varied but is currently a big toasty ESB.

HAMBLETON ALES
Melmerby, North Yorkshire

Much-expanded 1991 brewery, located north of Ripon, that produces beautifully judged, consistent, tasty beers. The beer names and logo nod to a white horse figure that is carved into a nearby hillside. Best known for its dreamy, slightly pursing stout **Nightmare ★★★**, which has physalis and raisin notes; the sweetish roasted porter **Black Lightning ★★☆** and dry golden bitter **Stud ★★** are good too.

HARBOUR BREWING
Bodmin, Cornwall

Small-scale contemporary outfit that was launched in rural Cornwall in 2012 using US-designed kit. Regulars include an easy drinking **Light Ale ★★** with a tropical-fruit hop kick; and a resinous, grapefruity transatlantic-style **India Pale Ale ★★☆**. An above-average succession of specials has included several double IPAs and strong porters, and a **Chocolate Vanilla Imperial Stout ★★☆**.

HARDKNOTT
Millom, Cumbria

Creative newer brewery in south Cumbria producing boldly flavoured beers. The range includes the floral and lemony contemporary bitter **Continuum ★★☆**; the treacly but hoppy dry stout **Dark Energy ★★☆**; and extreme beers like the sherry- and mature-cheese-scented barley wine **Granite ★★★**; and the riotous strong stout **Vitesse Noir ★★☆**, which is infused with coffee, vanilla and cocoa.

HARVEYS
Lewes, East Sussex

Revered, family-dominated south coast brewer, with a classic Victorian-design tower brewery. Best known for dryish, beautifully balanced and slightly toffee-ed **Sussex Best Bitter ★★★**; and internationally for the benchmark grainy, leathery, slightly sour and long-ageing historic recreation **Imperial Extra Double Stout ★★★★**. Numerous cask and bottled specialities, often in endangered styles, include a generously malty dark **Mild ★★☆**; hoppy, woody barley wine **Elizabethan Ale ★★★**; and indulgently sweet and complex **Christmas Ale ★★★**.

HAWKSHEAD BREWERY
Staveley, Cumbria

Begun in a barn in the Lake District National Park and expanding rapidly on the strength of solid cask beers with a contemporary edge, like its appealingly creamy and astringent flagship **Bitter ★★★**; a blackberry-shaded porter called **Brodie's Prime ★★★**; fruity **Lakeland Gold ★★★**; and dark golden, grapefruity and peachy occasional cask bitter **Cumbrian Five Hop ★★★☆**, which shows a new hop-forward direction.

HEPWORTH & CO BREWERS
Horsham, West Sussex

Technically accomplished newer brewer in mid-Sussex, producing numerous bottle-conditioned ales, mostly under contract to others. Its own brands include smooth and orchard-influenced traditional bitter **Pullman ★★**; and sacky, liquoriced and comforting winter seasonal **Classic Old Ale ★★☆**.

HOBSONS BREWERY
Cleobury Mortimer, Shropshire

In a former granary in south Shropshire. Best known for its low-gravity but surprisingly flavoursome malty **Mild ★★☆** but also good for sooty double brown **Postman's Knock ★★☆** with added vanilla, and perfumed flowery bitter **Town Crier ★★☆**.

HOGGLEYS BREWERY
Litchborough, Northamptonshire

An underrated former home brewery that outgrew its garden shed to become Northamptonshire brewing's best-known "best kept secret". It's notable for bottle-conditioned beers in traditional styles. Its **Northamptonshire Bitter ★★☆** is golden with a citric floral tang; the **Mill Lane Mild ★★☆** is blackcurranty and dry; while the **Solstice Stout ★★★** is a skilful blend of roast and hop flavours.

HOOK NORTON BREWERY
Hook Norton, Oxfordshire

Established independent brewer in the eponymous Oxfordshire village, its Victorian tower brewery still partly steam-powered. Best known for its rooted, earthy ESB **Old Hooky ★★**. More interesting are **Double Stout ★★☆** with its long, roasted finish; full-bodied and chocolaty, low-gravity **Hooky Mild ★★**; and new seasonals that include the plummy and unashamedly English bottle-conditioned IPA **Flagship ★★★**.

HOP BACK BREWERY
Downton, Wiltshire

A 1980s Wiltshire brewery that outgrew its brewpub origins after changing UK drinking habits with **Summer Lightning ★★☆**, a gooseberry-tinged cracker of a golden cask ale also sold bottle-conditioned, designed to compete with premium lagers. **Entire Stout ★★☆**, its roasted coffee notes softened by malted milk ones, is at least as good.

HOPSHACKLE BREWERY
Market Deeping, Lincolnshire

One-man operation in south Lincolnshire, producing meticulously crafted historical recreations and flavoursome originals in bottle-conditioned form, such as the sternly roasted, cherry- and geranium-tinged **Historic Porter ★★★**, also found in aniseed and vanilla versions. IPA **Resination ★★★** is sherbert-like and peppery; while the **Extra Special Bitter ★★★** is complex and chewy; and vintage barley wine **Restoration ★★★** is fruity and medicinal.

HYDES BREWERY
Salford, Greater Manchester

Long considered one of the most conservative brewers in the UK, with some recipes unchanged for 50 years, this Manchester independent has rebranded its straightforward though notably dry and herbal dark mild as **1863 ★★**, and its equally old-school bitter as **Original ★★**. Its spicy, whisky-tinged, reddish-amber, stronger winter ale **XXXX ★★★** is one of several seasonals.

ILKLEY BREWERY
Ilkley, West Yorkshire

This recent set-up in the town by the eponymous moor near the Yorkshire Dales National Park is rapidly winning admirers for its contemporary session beers like the earthy but cheerily refreshing golden ale **Mary Jane** ★★★; and the caramelled mild **Black** ★★. There is US influence in brews like the eucalyptus-tinged **Lotus IPA** ★★☆; and a number of oddball specials like the lively, tart "rhubarb *saison*" **Siberia** ★★☆.

JENNINGS BREWERY (MARSTON'S)
Cockermouth, Cumbria

A classic Victorian small-town brewery that is located on the Cumbrian coast. It still uses well water for traditional ales such as its dryly malted, earthily hopped **Bitter** ★★; and its distinctive darker speciality **Sneck Lifter** ★★☆, which is rich with treacle toffee, burnt toast and tangy orange-peel flavours.

KELHAM ISLAND BREWERY
Sheffield, South Yorkshire

The seminal small brewery that brought beer-making back to Sheffield in 1990, under the stewardship of the late Dave Wickett, who was a visionary among smaller brewers. Popular light but robust golden ale **Pale Rider** ★★★ has a tropical-fruit aroma and helped steer Britain toward higher-hopped paler beers. Also noted for jet-black, fruit and chocolate stout **Bête Noire** ★★☆, and numerous specials and collaborations.

DESTINATION SHEFFIELD

The **Sheffield Tap** is the restored refreshment room on Platform 1B of Sheffield's main station, with a range of more interesting casks and a clever selection of kegged and bottled British and foreign craft beers.

KERNEL, THE
Bermondsey, Greater London

Determinedly artisanal 2009 London brewery widely lauded and awarded for authentic historic recreations and contemporary styles, mainly bottle-conditioned though occasionally in keg. The former being spiky **Export Stout London 1890** ★★★☆, with tobacco and liquorice notes; and elegant, prune-tinged **Imperial Brown Stout London 1856** ★★★★. The latter are big, hop-forward but always well-judged pale ales, IPAs and black IPAs with recipes that change from brew to brew, always worth trying: great examples have included vividly fruity **Pale Ale Centennial** ★★★ and richly piney **India Pale Ale Citra** ★★★. More sessionable but astonishingly flavourful is cheerful low-gravity golden **Table Beer** ★★★.

LEEDS BREWERY
Leeds, West Yorkshire

Highly professional and ambitious 2007 set-up in the city where Tetley was king until Carlsberg closed it down. Its calling card is the treacly, vermouth-tinged mild **Midnight Bell** ★★★; the bestseller is the grainy, easy-going **Pale** ★★☆; with the lusciously flavoursome, woody stout **Gathering Storm** ★★☆ and sweetish, lemony cask lager **Leodis** ★★ also of interest. It has a small, high-quality pub estate.

DESTINATION
LEEDS

North Bar (24 New Briggate) is a pioneering, contemporary, minimalist, right friendly beer bar with an eclectic range of British and imported beers. **Friends of Ham** (4 New Station Street) matches an attentively curated beer list to cheese and charcuterie in chichi but comfortable surroundings.

LEES, J W
Middleton, Greater Manchester

Manchester-based regional independent that supplements cask ales like classic creamy, fruity mild **Brewer's Dark** ★★★ with strong bottled specialities like caramel-smooth and persistently bitter barley wine **Moonraker** ★★★ and widely exported oak-aged barley wine **Harvest Ale** ★★★☆, this last made annually with new season's ingredients, with a nutty, sherried and slightly salty, olive-imbued complexity.

LIVERPOOL ORGANIC BREWERY
Bootle, Merseyside

Ambitious and inventive new brewer offering a diverse range including flavoured beers. Strong brews like its oily and blackcurrant-edged **Imperial Russian Stout** ★★ are light for the style. Grassy and grapefruity **Shipwreck IPA** ★★☆ appeals to contemporary craft beer fans; while orangey and mellow **24 Carat Gold** ★★☆ and the floral and biscuity revival of **Higsons Best Bitter** ★★ are more sessionable.

LOVIBONDS BREWERY
Henley-on-Thames, Oxfordshire

Keg and bottle specialist helmed by a US expat in the Thames Valley regatta town. Products include aromatic piney, US-style **69 IPA** ★★☆; fruity and chocolaty porter **Henley Dark** ★★; and tart, herbal, complex fruit beer **Sour Grapes** ★★☆, a World Beer Cup gold medallist.

MAGIC ROCK BREWING
Huddersfield, West Yorkshire

Craft brewer commanding youthful attention since 2011 with a bold, heavily US-influenced hop-forward range, including piney but rounded **Cannonball IPA** ★★☆; its intense chilli-dipped double brother **Human Cannonball** ★★☆; fruity and spicy red ale **Rapture** ★★; and a charred ooze of an Imperial stout called **Bearded Lady** ★★☆, which is also the basis for some impressive barrel-aged specials.

MARBLE BEERS
Ancoats, Greater Manchester

Originally in the Marble Arch heritage pub on the northern edge of Manchester city centre, expanding off-site in 2009 following deserved success for consistently excellent and innovative output. Fine session ales like creamy, golden, perfumed **Manchester Bitter** ★★☆, evoking once-legendary Boddingtons at its peak, and luscious, stronger, dark mild **Chocolate Marble**

★★★☆ are supplemented by big bottle-conditioned specialities like the complex and fruity Imperial stout **Decadence** ★★★★; and the delightful tea- and bergamot-infused **Earl Grey IPA** ★★☆.

DESTINATION
MANCHESTER

Port Street Beer House (39 Port Street) is a stylish specialist beer bar in the city centre's Northern Quarter with an ever-changing range of exciting brews from hand-pulled local ales to rare and exotic imports.

MARSTON'S
Burton upon Trent, Staffordshire

One of only two historic breweries left in the old brewing town of Burton. Retains a Union fermentation system of interlinked banks of wooden casks, to make the creamily dry flagship pale ale **Pedigree**, said to retain the struck match or "Burton snatch" aroma. Designed to be a cask beer edified by good keeping, it rarely is, while other formats diminish it ★→★★★. Others brews include salty, liquoriced **Oyster Stout** ★★; the apple-edged mid-Atlantic IPA, **Old Empire** ★★☆; and, for now, London's much

misunderstood, low-alcohol, sweet heritage ale, **Manns Brown** ★★.

MEANTIME BREWING
Greenwich, Greater London

Smallish brewery located near the Thames at Greenwich, exploring life beyond real ale since 1999. Good at German-style lagers such as notably nutty Vienna-style **Union** ★★☆, alongside clean and pineapple-edged **London Pale Ale** ★★☆ and outstanding historical revivals in 75cl bottles like **India Pale Ale** ★★★ and **London Porter** ★★★☆.

MIGHTY OAK BREWING
Maldon, Essex

This well-respected small Essex brewery on the Blackwater Estuary is best known for its award-winning mild **Oscar Wilde** ★★☆, which is rich, roasty and bracing for the style. Other beers include pleasantly floral and easy-drinking **Maldon Gold** ★★.

MOOR BEER
Pitney, Somerset

Small, rural Somerset brewery rejigged in 2007 by a Californian expat, retaining and improving the signature old, strong brown ale, the tart, malt-bread- and fruit-tinged **Old Freddy Walker** ★★★; and the complex and roasty Amoor, aka **Peat Porter** ★★★. Contemporary flavours were added with the nettly, chocolate black IPA **Illusion** ★★★; and the huge cracked-pepper and peach tones of US-style **JJJ IPA** ★★★☆. The brewery also makes numerous cask and unfined keg beers.

MORDUE BREWERY
North Shields, Tyne and Wear

Reviving the name of a defunct 18th-century company, this award-winning small brewery by the Tyne Tunnel flaunts Geordie character in its zesty, grapey blond bitter **Five Bridges** ★ ★ ☆; grainy, hoppy **Geordie Pride** ★★☆; and deep, peppery and deliciously autumnal flagship dark bitter **Workie Ticket** ★★☆, meaning "troublemaker" in local dialect.

OAKHAM ALES
Peterborough

A successful early adopter of light-coloured, higher hopped ales. The bestseller status of elegant, lychee-tinged, pale golden bitter **JHB** ★★☆ is now threatened by crisp and grassy US-hopped pale ale **Citra** ★★☆. Straw-coloured **Bishop's Farewell** ★★☆ has lime and passion-fruit notes; while **Green Devil IPA** ★★★ is one of the better US-influenced British IPAs.

OKELL'S
Douglas, Isle of Man

Long-established independent brewer on a semi-autonomous island in the Irish Sea that still has a local beer purity law. Cask-conditioned biscuity and complex **Okell's Bitter** ★★★ is a fine session beer; while newer brews play on Celtic and historical themes, like tarry, leathery, smoked porter **Aile** ★★☆; light and lemony **Doctor Okell's IPA** ★★; and big, burry, citrus wheat beer **Maclir** ★★☆.

PARTIZAN BREWING
Bermondsey, Greater London

Forged in the heat of London's recent brewing revival using near neighbour KERNEL BREWERY's old kit, and ploughing a similarly artisanal furrow favouring bottle-conditioned limited editions. **Saisons** are a speciality, using Belgian yeasts, fruits, spices and international hops (★★→★★★); tasty **pale ales** ★★→★★★ are also brewed. Other successes have included a forbiddingly dense but rounded **FES Stout** ★★★ and a dry, raisiny strong **Mild** ★★★.

PURITY BREWING
Great Alne, Warwickshire

Reliable, popular producer of clean-tasting, consistent, appealing and

accessible session ales, operating in rural Warwickshire since 2005. Tastiest of the regulars are perfumed and peppery but generously malty golden ale **Mad Goose** ★★☆ and nuttier, more traditional amber bitter **Pure Ubu** ★★☆.

REDEMPTION BREWING
Tottenham, Greater London

Another of the better new-wave London brewers launched since Young's departed in 2006, producing individual but approachable beers. Standout is golden ale **Trinity** ★★★, only 3% ABV but packed with floral and tropical fruits; also sappy, roasted brown mild **Urban Dusk** ★★☆ and easy-drinking, blackcurranty **Fellowship Porter** ★★☆.

REDWILLOW BREWERY
Macclesfield, Cheshire

Former home-brewer, turned pro in 2010 and already making waves with an eclectic range of flavoursome ales including one of Britain's best modern double IPAs, sesame- and lavender-scented **Ageless** ★★★☆; fruity smoked porter **Smokeless** ★★☆; aromatic US-style pale **Wreckless IPA** ★★★; and the always interesting series of **Faithless** experimental beers ★★→★★★.

RINGWOOD BREWERY (MARSTON'S)
Ringwood, Hampshire

Founded in 1977 on the edge of the New Forest by the late Peter Austin, a one-man wellspring of craft brewing, who made and sold kit that revived smaller scale commercial brewing across Britain and around the world. Best known for nutty ESB **Old Thumper** ★★☆, also

brewed by Shipyard in Portland, Maine; golden bitter **Fortyniner** ★★☆; and warming, marmalade-tinged winter warmer, **XXXX Porter** ★★★.

ROBINSONS
Stockport, Cheshire

Big regional independent, family-dominated brewery southeast of Manchester, in a town that was a former stronghold of the hat industry. The best of its cask beers is the smooth and slightly whisky-ish light mild **1892** ★★, formerly Hatters; while citric but balanced bitter **Trooper** ★☆, brewed with rock band Iron Maiden, is a more recent success. Star of the range is the deep brown barley wine **Old Tom** ★★★ with rich, coffee-ish, slightly tart flavours.

ROOSTER'S BREWING
Knaresborough, North Yorkshire

Early UK champion of US hops, under new owners since 2011. Award-winning golden ale **Yankee** ★★☆ has lime and mandarin notes; while **Wild Mule** ★★ foregrounds Nelson Sauvin hops; and citric, fruity **YPA** ★★ is more English-styled. The Outlaw brand has started to mark out numerous inventive specials.

RUDGATE BREWERY
Tockwith, North Yorkshire

Reputable small brewery on a disused airfield near York. Noted for lemony, quinine-bitter, light golden ale **Jorvik** ★★☆; and malty but bracing **Ruby Mild** ★★★. It has absorbed Marston Moor brewery but has retained the brand for pruney, woody **Matchlock Mild** ★★ and others.

ST AUSTELL BREWERY
St Austell, Cornwall

The longest-surviving independent Cornish brewery has secured national success for its lemon-pepper premium bitter **Tribute ★★☆**, made with a unique custom made malt from local Maris Otter barley; and citrus-and-strawberry, hop-led IPA **Proper Job**, made to different specs for cask **★★☆** and bottle **★★★**. Its in-house pilot brewery makes piney, nutty and complex strong IPA **Big Job ★★★**, and slightly vinous, oat-dosed historical revival **1913 Cornish Stout ★★☆**, among others.

ST PETER'S BREWERY
St Michael South Elmham, Suffolk

Small high-tech brewery in an Elizabethan manor near Bungay in north Suffolk, producing widely exported specialities in designer bottles. Its fruit and spiced beers do not always work but its stylish hoppy **Grapefruit ★★** wheat beer stands out. Better are the light but tasty **Cream Stout ★★☆**; cola- and candy-tinged **Ruby Red Ale ★★**; and toffee-ish double brown **Winter Ale ★★☆**.

SALTAIRE BREWERY
Shipley, West Yorkshire

Award-winning small brewery in a disused power station by the Saltaire UNESCO World Heritage Site . Makes citric, slightly bitter **Cascade Pale Ale ★★** and flavoured specialities such as delicate, floral **Elderflower Blonde ★★**; nutty but restrained **Hazelnut Coffee Porter ★★☆**; and cakey but tart stout **Triple Chocoholic ★★**.

SAMUEL SMITH
Tadcaster, North Yorkshire

Yorkshire's oldest brewery, founded 1758. Eccentric, taciturn, determinedly independent and successful, its single cask ale **Old Brewery Bitter ★★** and own-brewed lagers contrast with bottled specialities aimed at the US and other export markets, where they impacted decades before the rest. Get the point with the silky-smooth, sweetish, mellow **Oatmeal Stout ★★★**; rich and vinous **Nut Brown Ale ★★☆**; creamy but dryly bitter **Taddy Porter ★★★**; and oak-aged, red-fruit and spiced-toffee barley wine **Yorkshire Stingo ★★★☆**.

SARAH HUGHES
Sedgley, West Midlands

Brewing was restored at the Beacon Hotel in the Black Country near Wolverhampton in 1987 after a 30-year break, reviving recipes used by ancestral proprietor Sarah Hughes. **Dark Ruby ★★★☆** is a benchmark strong dark mild, moreishly drying with blackcurrant and ripe plum tones; while subtly citric **Sedgley Surprise ★★☆** is a more contemporary premium bitter.

SHARP'S BREWERY (MOLSON COORS)
Rock, Cornwall

Brewing under a spotlight since taken over by MoCo, this north Cornish brewer's ubiquitous sweetish bitter **Doom Bar ★☆** appears simplified, leaving the session bitter, flowery golden **Cornish Coaster ★★** superior. Bottle-conditioned wild-fennel-infused wheat beer **Chalky's Bite ★★☆** is less common but the new Connoisser's Choice range of bottled beers, starting with big and bitingly spicy **Honey Spice Tripel** ★★☆, show promise.

SHEPHERD NEAME
Faversham, Kent

Family-infused independent with a claim to be Britain's longest-established licensed brewery, founded in 1698 in the hop-growing part of Kent. Flagship premium bitter **Spitfire** ★★ has lost something while ascending to national brand status, but recent speciality launches like meaty, plummy barley wine **Generation Ale** ★★☆; and rich, honeyed English-style **India Pale Ale** ★★★ have restored respect. Sappy **Late Red** ★★ is the tastiest of the regular casks.

SUMMER WINE BREWERY
Honley, West Yorkshire

Though its name nods to a much-loved British TV sitcom about misbehaving pensioners, filmed around nearby Holmfirth, this determinedly modern

operation foregrounds bold flavoured beers like "double black Belgian rye pale ale" **Cohort** ★★ – black American, not pale Flemish; floral, grapefruity IPA **Diablo** ★★☆; berried and tropical amber ale **Rouge Hop** ★★☆; and roasted, smoky, coffee-grounds, 10-malt, Imperially stout **Teleporter** ★★☆.

THEAKSTON
Masham, North Yorkshire

This respected 19th-century brewery has been back in family hands since 2003. The once self-governing market town of Masham had a 12th-century ecclesiastical court called a Peculier, after which **Old Peculier** ★★★ is named, an old ale that turns remarkably dry after a complex, sweetish start. Slightly chalky, straightforward, tasty best bitter **XB** ★★ is worth a try. The notably malty and stronger **Masham Ale** ★★ lies somewhere between complex and uneven.

THORNBRIDGE BREWERY
Bakewell, Derbyshire

Hailed by many as Britain's leading 21st-century brewery. An offshoot of KELHAM ISLAND and originally based at a Derbyshire stately home, it now brews at Bakewell. Its flagship is the resinous but approachable **Jaipur IPA** ★★★★, perhaps the archetype for a new UK hop-forward version of a historic English style originally made down the way at Burton. An imaginative and consistently excellent range also includes lighter and more citric **Wild Swan** ★★★; toasty Vienna lager **Kill Your Darlings** ★★★; superb Imperial stout **St Petersburg** ★★★ (→★★★☆ in its whisky-cask-aged versions); and the unique dark, sweet and spicy honey beer **Bracia** ★★★.

THREE TUNS BREWERY
Bishops Castle, Shropshire

A small but classically designed tower brewery near the Welsh border, active from 1642 and holding the oldest known brewing licence in Britain, with possible interruptions. The main products are figgy, mellow bitter **Cleric's Cure** ★★☆; fruity, sticky barley wine **Old Scrooge** ★★☆; and grainy, grassy golden bitter **XXX** ★★★.

THWAITES
Blackburn, Lancashire

This family-owned regional independent plans a major downsizing of its historic 1807 site in Blackburn during 2014 despite uncertainty over redevelopment plans, retaining only the recently installed "Crafty Dan" pilot brewery, which has won accolades with innovations like rich, fruity and bready strong brown ale **Big Ben** ★★★. Other beers will be contract brewed while a new site is sought, which makes it difficult to rate previously reliable regulars like smooth, chocolaty mild Nutty Black (slightly stronger and labelled Very Nutty Black in bottles); full-bodied golden ale Wainwright, celebrating a renowned local outdoor writer; and sweetish, buttery bottle-conditioned old ale Old Dan.

TIMOTHY TAYLOR
Keighley, West Yorkshire

Recently expanded family-owned brewery in the south Pennines, making characteristically dry, chalky beers. Peppery, slightly gingery best bitter **Landlord** ★★☆ has gone a bit simple since the move but still looms large, overshadowing lower-powered but smart cask ales like the delicate and flowery light mild **Golden Best** ★★★; the nutty, substantial **Dark Mild** ★★☆; and the distinctive plum- and raisin-edged old ale **Ram Tam** ★★☆.

TITANIC BREWERY
Burslem, Stoke-on-Trent

Consistently high-achieving 1985 brewery at Stoke-on-Trent, home city of the captain of the SS *Titanic*. The intense, roasted and mocha-tinged **Stout** ★★★ is occasionally available in limited-edition fruited versions. There also is a soft, slightly appley **Mild** ★★☆; a stronger, more citric winter mild **Black Ice** ★★; and flowery US-hopped wheat beer **Iceberg** ★★.

WELLS & YOUNG'S
Bedford, Bedfordshire

Young's abandoned centuries of brewing in London by merging its brewing into Bedford-based Wells in 2006. **Young's**

INNOVATION · PASSION · KNOWLEDGE

Thornbridge

WILD SWAN

WHITE GOLD PALE ALE
3.5% ABV

500ml℮

Bitter ★★ remains distinctive and faintly winey. **Double Chocolate Stout** ★★☆ fulfils the promise of its name; while complex, liquorice-laced seasonal **Winter Warmer** ★★★ is derived from a 19th-century Burton ale. The 2011 relaunch of the legendary **Courage Imperial Russian Stout** ★★☆ needs more ageing, and courage.

WESTERHAM BREWERY
Crockham Hill, Kent

Traditionally focused 2004 brewery in a rural setting at the foot of the Greensand Ridge just south of London, working with local hops and yeast resurrected from a historic namesake closed in the 1960s. **Finchcocks Original** ★★★ is a classic, fruity, ordinary bitter with a good hop bite; grainy golden **British Bulldog** ★★ honours Winston Churchill, who lived at nearby Chartwell; and bitter orange-tinged **Audit Ale** ★★☆ recreates an extinct strong ale style.

WILD BEER
Evercreech, Somerset

Launched near Shepton Mallet in 2012 by two brewers, one an expat Californian. Caused instant excitement with a succession of confidently inventive, provocatively flavourful and attractively packaged beers, some deploying wild yeast and wood ageing. Highlights include elegantly grapefruity **Epic Saison** ★★★; **Fresh**, a pale ale brewed with a different hop blend each time (★★→★★★); plummy, vinous barrel-aged **Modus Operandi** ★★★; astonishing **Ninkasi** ★★★☆, a spicy and complex champagne beer with apple juice; and whisky-tinged Imperial coffee stout **Wildebeest** ★★☆.

WINDSOR & ETON BREWERY
Windsor, Berkshire

Accomplished new brewery, located in the shadow of Windsor Castle, Berkshire, that is steering skilfully between "real ale" and innovation. Its seductive golden ale **Windsor Knot** ★★☆ showcases fruity New Zealand hops; while its black IPA **Conqueror** and its stronger **1075** version ★★→★★★ expertly marry chocolate and resinous hops. Its pollen-dabbed, bitterish **Republika** ★★ is a pale lager that uses Czech yeast.

DESTINATION NORWICH

Norfolk's county town boasts a concentration of quality beer outlets to rival that of far larger cities. Highlights include cosy cask house the **Kings Head** (42 Magdalen Street), craft specialist **The Norwich Tap House** (8 Redwell Street) and Grain brewery tap, **The Plough** (58 St Benedicts Street).

THE **WILD BEER** CO

Epic Saison

Crisp + Zesty + Spicy

DRINK WILDLY DIFFERENT

WOODFORDE'S NORFOLK ALES
Woodbastwick, Norfolk

This award-winning 1980 regional brewery in the Norfolk Broads is best known for its cheerful, blackcurranty and slightly astringent golden bitter **Wherry ★★☆**. Also good are earthy, dark **Nelson's Revenge ★★☆** and resinous stronger ale **Headcracker ★★☆**. Bottle-conditioned heritage barley wine **Norfolk Nip ★★★** is sadly rarely seen.

DESTINATION
KINGS LYNN

Beers of Europe, at Setchey, south of Kings Lynn, is a beer warehouse in the middle of nowhere that stocks over 2000 beers from all over the world for walk-in supermarket-style purchase or delivery across the UK.

WORTHINGTON'S (MOLSON COORS)
Burton upon Trent, Staffordshire

MoCo acquired the site of the old Bass brewery at Burton in 2011 and created an impressive small brewery within the National Brewing Centre there. That most adept survivor, classically English pale ale **White Shield**, is far better bottle- than cask-conditioned **★→★★★**, and is once more nationally distributed, alongside the more floral, golden **Red Shield ★★**. Other recreations include the estery, vinous Imperial stout **P2 ★★★**; and a distinctly tea-like version of upmarket bitter **Worthington's E ★★☆**, from before the age of kegging, appear occasionally.

WYCHWOOD BREWERY (MARSTON'S)
Witney, Oxfordshire

A different plant on the same site as **BRAKSPEAR** produces cakey, dark bitter **Hobgoblin ★★**; and darker, deeper, amber-coloured **King Goblin ★★☆**, plus the Royally connected Duchy brands.

WYE VALLEY BREWERY
Stoke Lacy, Herefordshire

Reliable, well-settled 1985 brewery near Hereford, often using local hops. Crisp and grapefruity golden cask bitter **HPA ★★☆** and softer, stronger bitter **Butty Bach ★★☆** are supplemented by impressive bottle-conditioned ales fronted by fictional forces' sweetheart Dorothy Goodbody, including her generously malty and sharply roasted **Wholesome Stout ★★★☆**; and nutty, darkish pale **Country Ale ★★☆**.

SCOTLAND

In the late 19th century, sugar refining became a major industry in Scotland, fuelling a shift in the Scottish diet that remains. Around that time strong, sweet beers nicknamed and sometimes branded "wee heavy" emerged, later gifted to the world via Belgium and elsewhere as "Scotch ale". In the 20th century, the independent brewery sector fell to mergers and takeovers more swiftly in Scotland than in England, though its revival has seen determined small breweries emerge in some remarkably remote places.

BELHAVEN BREWERY (GREENE KING)
Dunbar, East Lothian

This medium-sized brewery in an ancient coastal town, east of Edinburgh, boasts a longer history of continuous brewing than any other in Scotland, beginning by 1719 and possibly earlier. Part of Greene King since 2005, it produces its own brands, notably the thick, malty and gooseberry-fruity cask **80/- ★★☆**; more berry-fruited, dry-hopped **St Andrews Ale ★★**; dry and slick but disappointingly nitro-kegged stout, **Black ★☆**; and the more interesting low-gravity "light" **60/- ★★☆**.

BREWDOG
Ellon, Aberdeenshire

The UK's most provocative and, for its size, successful brewer exports to the world from northeast Scotland. Its style vocabulary and edgy marketing are US-influenced, while its UK-wide chain of evangelical beer bars comes from a mix of business sense and passion. Its daring but finely filtered, kegged and bottled beers include flagship grapefruit-hoppy **Punk IPA ★★☆**; chewy modern amber ale **5am Saint ★★☆**; and crude

but reliable hop bomb **Hardcore IPA ★★★☆**. A large and oft-changing range also includes massive weird stuff like 18.2% ABV, viscous cranberry stout **Tokyo* ★★★**; various often complex barrel-aged strong stouts under the name **Paradox ★★→★★★☆**; and the unsteady but occasionally sublime **Abstrakt** specials **★★→★★★★★**.

┌─────────────────────────────
: DESTINATION
: **ENGLAND AND SCOTLAND**
└ ─ ─ ─ ─ ─ ─ ─ ─ ─ ─ ─ ─ ─

The growing **BrewDog** chain of beer bars has set up in a dozen UK cities, including Bristol (58 Baldwin Street), Nottingham (20 Broad Street) and Edinburgh (143 Cowgate) with its own beers on draft and international craft nobility in bottle. Specialist beer stores can be expected to follow.

CALEDONIAN BREWING (HEINEKEN)
Slateford, Edinburgh

The only brewery in Edinburgh in continuous production since the 19th century still uses direct fired coppers. New corporate owners have smoothed out the charmingly flowery, bestselling golden ale **Deuchars IPA ★★☆** and creamily malty, fruity, traditional **80/- ★★☆**, unfortunately. Numerous specials include nutty and more complex **Merman ★★★**.

FYNE ALES
Achadunan, Argyll & Bute

Farm brewery near Inverary, overlooking Loch Fyne, with a rapidly improving range that includes the outstanding zesty, lychee- and kiwi-fruit-tinged, hoppy golden cask ale, **Jarl ★★★☆**; slightly stronger, sweeter and more floral **Avalanche ★★☆**; and deeper, richer **Highlander ★★☆**, which airs aromatic specialist malt notes.

HARVIESTOUN BREWERY
Alva, Clackmannanshire

Founded in 1987, so now one of Scotland's oldest breweries, moved to east of Stirling. Pioneered lighter, hoppier styles with grassy, citric **Bitter & Twisted ★★★**; and flowery, resinous, blond lager **Schiehallion ★★**, which is better in the keg or bottle. Notable thick,

chocolaty, oated porter **Old Engine Oil ★★★** is matured in various whisky casks to produce varieties of enormously enjoyable, complex, Scotch-pepped **Ola Dubh ★★★→★★★★**.

HIGHLAND BREWING
Swannay, Orkney

Accomplished small brewery in an old cheese factory at the north of Orkney mainland. Producing nectary, citric, strong pale ale **Orkney Blast ★★**; bitterish, tasty and spicy, if underpowered **Orkney IPA ★★**; and a fruity, liquoriced, easy-drinking **Porter ★★☆**.

ORKNEY BREWERY
Quoyloo, Orkney

Longer-established of the Orkney brewers, near the neolithic village at Skara Brae, known for its malt-led, sweetish and lightly tart dark brown ale **Dark Island ★★** and its peaty, fruity, whisky-barrel-aged and massive big brother **Dark Island Reserve ★★★☆**. Slightly lighter **Skull Splitter ★★☆** is a walnut- and apple-tinged barley wine named after a former Norse ruler of the islands. Also brews the Atlas brands such as grassy and floral cask-conditioned "pilsner" **Latitude ★★**.

STEWART BREWING
Loanhead, Midlothian

Newish, highly regarded brewer near Edinburgh, making traditionally styled malty Scottish ales with contemporary flair, including comfortingly biscuity **80/- ★★★** with tobacco and dark fruit notes; olive- and toasted-coconut-tinged bitter **Embra ★★☆**; determinedly malty and cindery

St Giles ★★☆; and chaffy, plummy **Edinburgh No 3 Scotch Ale** ★★. Often even better when bottle-conditioned.

TEMPEST BREWING
Kelso, Borders

Contemporary craft brewer establishing a reputation for big flavours since launching in 2010. IPA **Brave New World** ★★☆ exudes mango, apricot and menthol; four-grain, strong stout **Double Cresta** ★★ is creamily fruity; fruit-charged golden ale **Long White Cloud** ★★☆ is oily, tropical and rich; while the porter **Red Eye Flight** ★★★ has coffee and ash.

TRAQUAIR HOUSE BREWERY
Traquair, Borders

From the oldest inhabited house in Scotland, near Innerleithen, south of Edinburgh. The late laird revived the 16th-century brewhouse in the grounds in 1965 to create the benchmark revivalist wee heavy. **Traquair House Ale** ★★★☆ is a dark delight of rich malt with tart fruit and vermouth tones; while sweetish, complex, liquoriced, coriander-

spiced **Jacobite Ale** ★★★ reflects in its name the family's historic loyalties.

TRYST BREWERY
Larbert, Falkirk

Former home brewery named after Falkirk's historic cattle market. Distinctive and reliable cask- and bottle-conditioned ales include refreshing, summery, elderflower-dosed golden **Blàthan** ★★; rare chocolaty Scottish-style mild **Brockville Dark** ★★☆; smooth but cuttingly roasted **Carron Oatmalt Stout** ★★☆; and sage-and-cinder, toffee-tinged **Drovers 80/-** ★★☆.

VALHALLA BREWERY
Haroldswick, Shetland

Small brewer at the north end of the island of Unst in Shetland, the UK's northernmost community, once part of Norway and closer to Bergen than Edinburgh. Fittingly for a remote producer, its sweet, golden brew **Island Bere** ★★☆ is unique, made from an ancient form of barley called bere, offset by Cascade hops; delicate, fruity pale ale **White Wife** ★★ is bulkier in the bottle; while easy-drinking **Sjolmet Stout** ★★ is a good all-rounder.

WEST BREWERY
Bridgeton, Glasgow

Pub brewery owned and run by a German brewster in one of Glasgow's quirkier landmarks, a former carpet factory modelled on Venice's Doge's Palace. Flagship citric-hoppy but honeyed *helles* **St Mungo** ★★☆ is one of the UK's best-tasting craft lagers. There is also the decent chewy and chocolaty

Dunkel ★★☆; and the drinkable, slightly fruity **Munich Red** ★★.

DESTINATION
GLASGOW

The **Blackfriars** (36 Bell Street) is a large pub and eating house in the fashionable Merchant City area, with Scottish cask ales and craft beers and a more eclectic range of bottles, especially from the US.

WILLIAMS BROS. BREWING
Alloa, Clackmannanshire

The only brewery left in a once great brewing town. The enterprising inventors of distinctively infused **Fraoch Heather Ale** ★★☆, which changed perceptions of Scottish brewing history when launched in 1992, have now created refreshingly tart gooseberry **Grozet** ★★; floral, firm golden ale **Seven Giraffes** ★★ with elderflower and lemon zest; and fruity, substantial and elegant **Profanity Stout** ★★☆.

WALES

Indigenous beer styles that would distinguish Welsh brewing from that of old industrial or sparsely populated rural areas in England are yet to be recognized, though localism thrives there, so something will emerge in time, no doubt.

BRAINS
Cardiff

One of only two long-established Welsh independent brewers, still under family influence. Its cask ales include the sharpish, slightly perfumed mild **Dark** ★★☆; winey, gooseberry-tinged bitter **SA** ★★★; and **SA Gold** ★★☆, with notes of apple pie and ice cream. Improving bottled, cask and keg brews in many styles, created on pilot kit for the Brains Craft Brewery brand, have thus far toned down creativity in favour of broader appeal, yielding no recurring favourites.

BRYNCELYN BREWERY
Ystradgynlais, Powys

Tiny pub brewery expanded to become a small stand-alone brewhouse on the river Tawe, upstream of Swansea. Its subtle, cheerful beers owe their names to Buddy Holly, for some reason. The soft, slightly smoky dark mild is **Buddy Marvellous** ★★☆; the flowery golden ale, **Holly Hop** ★★; and the more toffee-ish pale ale, **Oh Boy** ★★.

DESTINATION
CARDIFF

The **Urban Tap House** (25 Westgate Street) is run by **TINY REBEL** but features up to 200 other beers from the UK and elsewhere, while round the corner is traditional flagship **The City Arms** (10 Quay Street), offering an increasingly Welsh range of cask and craft beers.

CELT EXPERIENCE, THE
Caerphilly

Appealing beers, with a sharp eye for design that evokes Celtic romanticism, are the hallmarks of this 2007 start-up from Caerphilly. Early regulars included the hoppy, coffee-ish mild **Dark Age** ★★; and the fruity, zesty golden ale **Silures** ★★. The curiously spicy Belgian-Welsh *tripel* **Ogham Oak** ★★☆ laid the foundations for Belgian and US influences evident in the **Shapeshifter Series** of specials (★★☆→★★★), with much more promised.

MWS PIWS (PURPLE MOOSE BREWERY)
Porthmadog, Gwynedd

Small 2005 brewery on the coastal strip of the Snowdonia National Park. Wins accolades in particular for **Ochr Tywyll y Mŵs (Dark Side of the Moose)** ★★☆, an unusual hoppy dark ale with citrus and pineapple notes. Resinous fruit-salad-tinged bitter **Cwrw Madog (Madog's Ale)** ★★ is good too.

OTLEY BREWING
Cilfynydd, Rhondda

Originally created to supply a small family-owned pub chain in the South Wales valleys. Brewing flair and hip presentation have since driven national recognition and expansion. Beers include award-winning, tangy, lemony pale ale **O1** ★★☆; audaciously named orangey *witbier* **O-Garden** ★★, fruity, toasted, seed-toned strong IPA **mOtley Brew** ★★★; and autumnal ruddy bitter **03 BOss** ★★☆. Badly designed beers are rare here.

PEN-LON COTTAGE BREWERY
Llanarth, Ceredigion

Fine range of sporadically distributed bottle-conditioned beers from a small farmhouse in rural Ceredigion. These include a smooth, pastille-like **Chocolate Stout** ★★★; a strong ale with notes of coal tar and orchard fruit, called **Ramnesia** ★★☆; the robust and characterful pale ale **Tipsy Tup** ★★☆; and occasional specials made with local fruits, like chewy, tannic plum stout **Torwen** ★★.

TINY REBEL
Newport

A youthful contemporary craft brewery, grabbing aficionados' attention soon after opening in 2012 with bold-flavoured beers like the raspberry-ish red ale **Cwtch** ★★; the luscious but assortedly charred 10-malt stout **Dirty Stop Out** ★★☆; the grapey New Zealand-hopped pale ale **Full Nelson** ★★☆; and the flowery, thistley but lightish **Urban IPA** ★★.

NORTHERN IRELAND

The politics differ in north and south but the island of Ireland shares a common beer culture, built on the historic preference for porter and stout. Where the north differs is in having some pioneering "real ale" brewers who managed to introduce limited choice into the market 15 years ahead of their southern colleagues.

CLANCONNEL BREWING
Craigavon, County Armagh

Small brewery set up near Craigavon and making mainly bottled beers, among which **McGrath's Irish Black Stout** ★★★ is a corker of a traditional dry stout, with an earthy hop that defines its Irishness.

HILDEN BREWING
Lisburn, County Antrim

Northern Ireland's first new brewery in decades appeared in 1981 southwest of Belfast, and is still flourishing under family ownership. **Scullion's Irish Ale** ★★ is a distinctively gritty and fruity session beer; and golden, zingily citric and bitterish **Twisted Hop** ★★☆ is a recent arrival. Also brews College Green beers for Belfast, notably the light cola-tinged **Molly's Chocolate Stout** ★★.

> DESTINATION
> **BELFAST**
>
> For pure Victorian pomp at its multimillion pound greatest, the **Crown Liquor Saloon** (46 Great Victoria Street) cannot be beaten, though the triangular, one-room **Bittles Bar** (70 Upper Church Lane) perhaps shows the road ahead.

WHITEWATER BREWING
Kilkeel, County Down

Successful small brewery where the mountains of Mourne sweep down to the sea, now Northern Ireland's largest. Minerally reddish-amber **Belfast Ale** ★★☆ is substantial and distinctive; **Belfast Lager** ★☆ is grainy, floral and unusually heavy; and **Clotworthy Dobbin** ★★☆ is a very dry, tart, full-flavoured porter.

REPUBLIC OF IRELAND

Opening a new brewery in Ireland was nigh-impossible for decades, owing to the absence of genuinely independent pubs and shops where beer could be sold. As these have returned, so a new wave of entrepreneurial smaller brewers has emerged, making beer in a wide variety of styles for a new, younger audience who mistrust the shiny brands promoted by global businesses.

Historically, Ireland had made lighter end porters and stouts its own by 1800, adding salt for dryness and qualifying their strength and style with terms like "plain", "extra" and "export". Whether the current revival of such beers or the attraction of US-style craft beers will win in time may depend on the answer to one new brewer's question: "In a country covered by cloud and wet under foot 80% of the time, is porter not more comforting than a tropical hop?"

CARLOW BREWING
Bagenalstown, County Carlow

This successful family brewery was founded in 1996 and expanded in 2009, the beers bearing the family name, O'Hara. It comes into its own as a brewer of stouts like the medium-bodied, drier end, near-black **Irish**

o'hara's®

leann folláin

EXTRA IRISH STOUT

Stout ★★☆, with more coffee than chocolate; and the heavier **Leann Folláin** ★★★, which has a whiff of molasses and toasted malt, liquorice and dark fruit.

CHORCA DHUIBHNE (WEST KERRY BREWERY)
Ballyferriter, County Kerry

This tiny brewery on the Gaelic-speaking Dingle peninsula was established by a sculptress who, having mastered metalwork, moved on to crack the art of making six-week-aged strong porter. **Cúl Dorcha** ★★☆ is the result – a variable brown ale found sometimes cask-conditioned; its little sister **Béal Bán** ★★ is a fruity pale golden ale with a bitter follow-through; and **Carraig Dubh** ★★★☆ is the cleverly sculpted traditional porter with smoke, spice and bitter chocolate sat within it.

DUNGARVAN BREWING
Dungarvan, County Waterford

A neat little brewery established in 2010 on the coast, east of Cork. The year-round brews here are an interesting, floral, grassy, citrus but honeyed blond **Helvick Gold ★★☆**; a surprisingly good "Irish red" called **Copper Coast ★★☆**, which is fruity and caramelled before a hoppy finish; and a medium-bodied, roasted malt and coffee bean stout **Black Rock ★★☆**. Seasonals appear too.

EIGHT DEGREES BREWING
Mitchelstown, County Cork

This 2010 start-up, located north of Cork, is run by an Australasian duo. Its crisp, citrus-edged US-style pale **Howling Gale Ale ★★** is edgy for Ireland; the **Sunburnt Irish Red ★★** breathes life into its subject with hops from New Zealand and Australia; while its top dog **Knockmealdown Porter ★★☆** is a malt-driven, nutty, dryish beer with firm bitterness.

FRANCISCAN WELL (MOLSON COORS)
Cork City

Going since 1998 and part of Molson Coors since early 2013, who have a view to increase production massively. **Rebel Red ★★** is fruity with faint bitterness, its pale cheeks suitably rouged; roasted **Shandon Stout ★★** is creamier and more approachable than most; while the unexpected star is **Friar Weisse ★★☆**, a hazy orange, banana-laced *hefeweizen* with a touch of new-mown hay.

DESTINATION CORK

The **Abbot's Ale House** (17 Devonshire Street), bang in the centre, has likely the best selection of beer in all Ireland, with the downstairs bottle shop stocking over 500 and the bar upstairs rotating craft Irish taps, though some prefer the more international **Bierhaus** (Pope's Quay).

GALWAY BAY BREWERY
Salthill, Galway City

A 2009 pub brewery serving its own chain and other bars nationally. Early beers include typical fruit-and-nut, copper-coloured **Galway Bay Ale ★★**; surprisingly good, sweet, light milk stout **Buried at Sea ★★★**; and dryish, malt-driven toasted porter **Stormy Port ★★☆**.

DESTINATION GALWAY

The **Salt House** (4 Ravens Terrace) is a tidy little pub near the quay leading a trend in the west toward craft beer, majoring on 25+ Irish brews with a larger number of quality international ones, some of considerable note.

GALWAY HOOKER
Roscommon, County Roscommon

Careful small brewery, making its way gradually with a floral, citrus, honeyed light blond ale **Irish Pale Ale ★★☆**, made with local malt and US hops; followed by a smooth, creamy, coffee-tinged take on **Irish Stout ★★★** that is quietly excellent.

METALMAN BREWING
Waterford City

Brewing since 2010, with its own place near Waterford since 2012. Their first beer **Pale Ale ★★☆** is an improving, mostly keg, occasionally cask US-style pale ale with a touch of mandarin, which has been followed by an acceptably Belgian white beer called **Alternator ★★**; occasional NZ-hopped pale ale **Windjammer ★★☆** is only made when suitable hops are available.

PORTERHOUSE BREWING
Dublin

Dublin-based firm that restarted it all. Tried and tested range includes three cleverly measured black beers. **Plain Porter ★★★** is straightforward and unenhanced, doing simple so well that some may not get it; fuller **Oyster Stout ★★☆**, with whole oysters, seems fruitier rather than drier; while heavily roasted **Wrassler's XXXX ★★★☆** has a dab of rusty nail and dark fruit. UK-hopped citrus pale ale **Hop Head ★★☆**, revived from brewpub days, recalls its prescience.

DESTINATION
DUBLIN

Always a great place for pubs, the Irish capital is getting good at beer too. Try lived-in, foody **W J Kavanagh's** (4 Lower Dorset Street), the **Porterhouse** (16 Parliament Street) and its **Central** (45–47 Nassau Street) branch, the Buckley steakhouse chain's **Bull & Castle** (5 Lord Edward Street) and **L Mulligan Grocer** (18 Stoneybatter), all of which stock 100+ beers, a healthy share of which are new Irish.

TROUBLE BREWING
Allenwood, County Kildare

Tiny 2009 brewery at Allenwood in Kildare that pitched up with accomplished **Dark Arts Porter ★★☆**, a lighter-bodied, near black, malt-led beer with a touch of caramel, and has struggled to find it a soul mate, though fruity, golden **Ór ★★** is starting to get there.

WHITE GYPSY BREWERY
Templemore, County Tipperary

The Irish new wave's great experimentalist began in 2008 after a false start. Where others play safe, here the plan is to grow all its own ingredients and be the first Irish brewery to ferment with grape must. In the meantime, it ticks over with decent potboilers like **Ruby Irish Red Ale ★★☆** and work-out beers like the country's most assertive **American Pale Ale ★★☆**; a competent, if slightly underpowered take on a **German Doppelbock ★★**; and a **Russian Imperial Stout ★★** that is a bit small. Nonetheless, watch this space.

FRANCE

Surprisingly perhaps, the concept of a "craft beer" was most likely first established in France, where the description *bière artisanale* was in use as early as the 1970s.

Historically, it was the area between Dunkerque and Lille in the north and across Alsace-Lorraine in the east that enjoyed the strongest brewing culture, but the last fe`w years have seen a massive upsurge in new breweries – over 550 at the last count – with the heaviest concentrations in areas that have traditionally had a wine culture, such as Languedoc-Roussillon, Midi-Pyrénées and Aquitaine, the region with the most breweries now being Rhône Alpes, with almost 100.

The surviving concept most closely associated with traditional French brewing is *bière de garde,* or "stored beer", referring to ales that are cool-conditioned at or near the brewery for several months before being filtered and bottled, sometimes reseeded with yeast.

The tricolour brewing habit of producing one blond, one brown and one amber beer was also deep-rooted until recently, newer brewers preferring to develop their own range of styles from all influences and none. One theme that is emerging is the desire to close the gap between producer and consumer, an aim given a special twist in many rural areas by the re-emergence of farmers who malt their own barley and then brew beers from it.

The French public is clearly engaging with this unprecedented rise in the nation's brewing prowess and it will not be long before the tradition of exploring parts of France by travelling from one wine-maker's *cave* to another will be matched by tours of local *fermier-brasseurs.*

ALIÉNOR
Saint-Caprais-de-Bordeaux, Gironde

A 2012 start-up of great promise in an old wine store located southeast of Bordeaux, run by a young Belgian vintner turned brewer. Blond, brown and white for starters, with seasonals in development; first brew **Alienor Blanche** ★★ is a creamy *witbier* with slight sourness and, unusually, well-balanced bitterness.

AN ALARC'H
Huelgoat, Finistère

Small 1998 brewery on Brittany's Finistère peninsula, collaborating with TRI MARTOLOD to make a wide range of beers including UK-style ales and stouts. Standouts are Breton-style stout, **Hini Du ★★★**, a black ale with liquorice tastes and well-balanced bitterness; and lighter-end Imperial stout **Kerzu** with burnt malt, dark chocolate, expresso and smoky flavours, improving ★★★→★★★☆ with cellaring.

ANCELLE
Ancelle, Hautes-Alpes

Opened at the end of 2012 in a ski resort in the southern Alps by two expat Belgians, who have assembled a lot of suitably well-attired kit to make their Version Originale beers. The beautifully refined **Ambrée ★★** is at once gentle but with distinct character. Great potential.

ARTZNER
Strasbourg, Bas-Rhin

An old French brewing name revived in 2009 by the last owner's grandson, currently making distinctive beers at other craft breweries. **Perle dans les Vignes ★★** is made from malted barley and grape must, giving a highly aromatic, aged character, with melon and grape juice flavours; while **Perle des Îles ★★** sports caramel with notes of tropical fruit, citrus and vanilla.

BARON, AU
Gussignies, Nord

Charming, tiny family-run bistro brewery on the Belgian border south of Mons.

Seasonal blond *bière de garde* **Cuvée des Jonquilles ★★☆** has become year-round for its exceptional floral and citrus aroma and freshness, with less well-known **Saison St Médard ★★** worth trying too.

BRETAGNE
Kerouel, Finistère

Operates breweries at Trégunc on Brittany's south coast and Tréguier on its north, and produces over a dozen ales under the Ar-Mon, Britt, Celtika, Dremmwel and Gwiniz Du brands, as well as all-grains blond special **St Erwann ★★☆**, made with barley, wheat, buckwheat, oats, rye, spelt and millet.

CAUSSENARDE
Saint-Beaulize, Aveyron

Farmhouse brewery not far from Montpelier in southwestern France. Malts home-grown barley to make accomplished **Blonde**, **Blanche** and **Ambrée** regulars (all ★★); brown autumnal **Seiglée ★★★** with a distinctive, complex grainy and hoppy character; and winter's **Triple 4 Céréales ★★★**, which balances sweetness, strength and bitterness perfectly.

CHOULETTE, LA
Hordain, Nord

Small farmhouse brewery near Cambrai, south of Lille, making a wide range of beers. Traditional *bière de garde* **Choulette Ambrée** ★★☆, with caramel, malt and hop flavours, is perhaps the best; with safer, blond **Sans Culottes** ★★ more of a starter beer.

DESTINATION LILLE

La Capsule (25 rue des 3 Mollettes) is a slightly downmarket but atmospheric candle-lit bar located near the cathedral. It offers a world-class selection of local and international ales on tap and in bottle, welcoming all.

CORRÉZIENNE
Curemonte, Corrèze

Brilliantly experimental brewer in the upper Dordogne valley, known for his Hophophop series of folksy Imperial stouts such as fruity, port-wine-flavoured **Boris Goudenov** ★★★, powerful and creamy but with a refreshing finish; also double IPA **Dordogne Valley** ★★ in which complex caramel and fruit flavours meet on a background of resin.

DAUPHINÉ
Saint Martin d'Hères, Isère

Small brewery near Grenoble in the French Alps, making beers called La Mandrin. The summer **Blanche** ★★☆, made with seven herbs, is light, dry and herbal; **Aux Noix** ★★ has subtle flavours from walnuts; and **Au Sapin** ★★★ is a strong fruity, sweet winter beer gaining freshness from fir tree sap.

DER
Montier-en-Der, Haute-Marne

Village brewery (2006) with modern kit and local ways, northeast of Troyes. La Dervoise beers include **Mellite** ★★, a dryish golden ale with chestnut-honey aroma and slight honey aftertaste and a hoppy note at the finish; while **Nuisement** ★★☆ is an intensively roasted stout with hints of coffee and a spicy end.

DUYCK
Jenlain, Nord

This successful family-run, fourth-generation (1922) brewery southeast of Lille is better known by the name of its brand and village of origin, Jenlain. Best in 75cl bottles, **Jenlain Ambrée** ★★☆ remains a classic of its kind, though newer products seem simpler. Into canning too, an odd concept for *bière de garde*.

ENTRE 2 MONDES
Mouthier-Haute-Pierre, Doubs

Small 2008 brewery between Besançon and the Swiss border, started by an experienced craft brewer from Quebec – hence the name. Bold blond ale **Eau de Pierre** ★★☆ has a strong malt aroma and flowery notes; and reddish **Indian** ★★★ is a delightful reinterpretation of IPA, with fresh hops and piney flavour, strong bitterness and an oaky, dry finish.

ENTRE DEUX BIÈRES
Mauriac, Gironde

Tiny but interesting 2009 brewery in the Entre-Deux-Mers wine region east of Bordeaux, experimenting with local twists. **L'Entre 2** ★★☆ is an organic blond beer, bottom-fermented with some white grape juice before being lagered in wine barriques; and **La Tchanquée Brune** ★★ is a roasty light stout with oyster brine added to the brew, ending slightly acidic, with a coffee taste.

FONTAINES
Les Verchers-sur-Layon, Maine-et-Loire

Small brewery south of Angers, in the vineyards of the Loire valley. **La Fosse Blonde** ★★ is rich, with a malty, spicy character; malt-led amber ale **Diabolik** ★★☆ has a warming character; while full-bodied stout, **Sarcophagus** ★★, has a smoky finish.

FRANCHE, LA
La Ferté, Jura

Tiny brewery southeast of Dijon in Franche-Comté. **Profonde Blonde** ★★☆

has highly aromatic hops and a distinctive, fresh, long finish; while regular **Ipane Brune** ★★ becomes an intense barley wine with a unique caramelized character, in its winter version **Hivernale** ★★★.

GAILLON
Courpalay, Seine-et-Marne

The second generation of the Rabourdin family to brew on the family farm southeast of Paris, badge their ales Bière de Brie. The **Blanche** ★★ is a French interpretation of *witbier*, spicy with a lemon aroma; the tasty **Blonde** ★★ is biscuity and goes well with Brie cheese; while the **Ambrée** ★★☆ is a more malt-driven *bière de garde*.

GARLAND
Algans, Tarn

This farm brewery east of Toulouse is the longest established of the region's smaller producers. Concentrating on organic Karland beers, such as **Ambrée** ★★, which has a smoked malt, rich body and dry finish.

GARRIGUES
Sommières, Gard

Creative small brewery to the west of the southern city of Nîmes. Bottle-conditioned beers inspired by British and northern French brewers include delicate **Saison des Amours** ★★☆, with candied-fruits aroma and *faux* bitterness; NZ-hopped strongly aromatic IPA, dry-hopped **Frappadingue** ★★★ is best at room temperature; and **Nuit de Goguette**, its stout brand, now comes with either oats or rye, plus barrel-aged or smoked ★★→★★★.

JOLI ROUGE
Canals, Tarn-et-Garonne

Promising brewery with a beer shop, north of Toulouse. Its **Pils** ★★ has a herbal aroma and bittersweet profile; impressive UK-influenced **Bitter** ★★☆ is hopped with Aramis, an Alsace variety derived from Strisselspalt; **India Pale Ale** ★★ is hopped UK style; while **Amber Ale** ★★☆ is made with rosehips, giving it slight acidity.

LANCELOT
Le Roc-Saint-André, Morbihan

Pioneering and successful 1990 Breton brewery, now expanded into a disused gold mine. Best known for **Cervoise Lancelot** ★★, a pale ruddy-amber ale, flavoured with herbs said to have been used in beer brewing by the Gauls; and **Telenn Du** ★★☆, a *blé noire* beer, brewed with the blackened buckwheat used in local crêpes.

LEPERS
La Chapelle-d'Armentières, Nord

Small, century-old firm, now brewing northwest of Lille, making mainly paler

beers, both in its own name and as L'Angelus. **Lepers 6** ★★ is light golden and balanced; **Lepers 8** ★★ is stronger and dry for the style, while **L'Angelus Blonde** ★★☆ is a *bière de garde* take on wheat beer, conjuring summer fields with the aroma of fresh-cut hay, a smooth bitterness, and slight acidity.

LOIRE
Saint-Just-Saint-Rambert, Loire

One of the most talented new French brewers, established in 2003 but almost unknown outside its region. A highly personal range of permanent and seasonal creations, all organic. Peaty stout **La Gueule Noire** ★★★, entirely from brown malt, tastes of prune with a chocolate texture; autumnal **La Gruette** ★★, prepared with cocoa beans, has a subtle dark chocolate flavour; and **109** ★★ is a biscuity amber ale voluptuously flavoured with hazelnuts.

LUTINE, LA
Limeuil, Dordogne

A pocket-sized brewery, located deep in the Dordogne. The **Blonde** ★★ has a generous body, grassy with spicy notes; while occasional brew **Aux Noix** ★★ has a roasted caramel flavour, sour notes, a subtle taste of nuts and a spicy finish.

MAISON DE BRASSEUR
Pont-d'Ain, Ain

Interesting if tiny brewery northeast of Lyon, making two beers of note: pale ale **Rivière d'Ain** ★★, with wild hops; and **Bresse** ★★, a caramel-sweet amber ale with a long finish.

MATTEN
Matzenheim, Bas-Rhin

Inventive, prize-winning boutique brewery with attitude, south of Strasbourg. Its well-rounded **Red Fox IPA** ★★☆ uses mostly local Alsace hops with cooked apple aromas while **La Schwortz** ★★★ is a black stout, with a strong coffee aroma, creamy, toasty, chocolate malt flavours and a fruity finish. Expect more.

MÉLUSINE
Chambretaud, Vendée

Small brewery near Chambretaud, southeast of Nantes. **Love & Flowers** ★★ is a wheat beer aromatized and flavoured with rose petals and hop flowers; **Mélusine Bio** ★★☆ is a pretty, sweet amber ale with peach notes; and **Barbe Bleue** ★★★ is a stewed brown ale with roasted malts and a hint of liquorice.

DESTINATION
BOUGUENAIS

Bières é Chopes (2 Chemin de la Vaserie) is an amazing beer store near Nantes, with northern French specialities among 500+ bottles, high-quality advice and a small cellar café-restaurant.

MONT SALÈVE
Neydens, Haute-Savoie

Rising star from south of Geneva, creating a skilful, additive-free range of Salève beers. **Sorachi Ace Bitter** ★★★ is an amazing low-strength beer with fruity, herbal aroma and exceptional body; the **Blanche** ★★★ is a daring, citrus, hoppy take on *witbier*; Nelson Sauvin-hopped IPA **Amiral Benson** ★★★ follows intense fruit-pine aromas with a full flavour and long finish; **Mademoiselle Aramis IPA** ★★★☆ showcases Aramis hops from Alsace; and winter's **Tourbée** ★★★☆ tastes of its smoked malts with toasted peach notes.

ORGEMONT
Sommepy-Tahure, Marne

Distinctive 2001 farm brewery in the western Ardennes, surrounded by the vineyards of Champagne. Beers include a strong yellow-blond **Triple** ★★☆ full of grain, with citrus notes and cracked peppercorn; while the contract-brewed Valmy brands include **Blanche** ★★, a *witbier* with spicy aroma and grainy body.

OUTLAND
Bagnolet, Seine-Saint-Denis

One of the newest arrivals on the Parisian beer scene. Visit the US without leaving Paris. The beer range would be typical of an early-days American craft brewer, including **West Coast IPA** ★★ with woody flavours; and **American Brown Ale** ★★, straight out of the big new traditions handbook.

PARADIS, LE
Blainville-sur-l'Eau, Meurthe-et-Moselle

Punchy 2009 brewer from southeast of Nancy in Lorraine, good enough to get her beers into Brussels. Flagship UK-leaning IPA **La Sylvie'cious** ★★★ begins and ends with herbal hops, fresh fruits and flowers; **Corinne-Louise** ★★☆ is a rare

French dark mild, with subtle hops and an astonishing spicy finish; and red-amber ale **Hop'ss Marie-Magdeleine** ★★ is a good French take on an ESB. One to watch.

DESTINATION
NANCY

The wonderful **Capsule Cave à Bières** (21 avenue du Général Leclerc) shop offers direct and on-line sales (www.biere-revolution.com) of 600+ brands, with high French representation and many hard-to-source beers.

PLEINE LUNE
Chabeuil, Drôme

Inventive, eye-catching new brewery from south of Lyon. Its red-amber, grainy but grapefruity IPA **Aubeloun** ★★★ has turned heads with its measured bitterness; while altogether more traditional amber ale **Lunik** ★★☆ has toffee aromas and hints of caramel and red fruits.

RATZ
Fontanes, Lot

Small, impressively efficient 2001 brewery north of Toulouse, little-known elsewhere but achieving much in this wine-growing area. **Ratz Ambrée** ★★ is sweet and nutty, in a range that now includes organic beers and occasional specials.

ROUGET DE LISLE, LA
Bletterans, Jura

Small 1994 brewery between Dijon and Geneva, making beers that absorb regional produce. Soft wheat beer **Griottines** ★★★☆ has the juice of Franche-Comté cherries added during brewing, ending in a slightly acidic blend of malt and fruit, with a surprisingly clean finish; the grainy, nutty blond version of **La Ventre Jaune** ★★ is made with grilled cornflour; while **Perles Noires** ★★★☆, a four grain black barley wine aged in wine barriques for three years before bottling, has raised it to a new level.

SAINT LÉON
Créon, Gironde

Pub brewery and music venue, surrounded by vineyards, east of Bordeaux, likely to expand. Tasty and grainy **Saint Léon Blonde** ★★ is an aromatic, well-rounded, soft pale ale, brewed from home-made malt.

SAINTE COLOMBE
Sainte-Colombe, Ille-et-Vilaine

Gradually evolving 1996 Breton brewery, south of Rennes. Apart from a sound normal range there are also **Pie Noire** ★★★, with moderate bitterness overrun by strong flavours from rye and smoked malts; and a unique barley wine **Grand Cru** ★★★, with an amazing buttery caramel aroma, full and sweet, with caramel and hints of oak and cherry.

ST ALPHONSE
Vogelgrun, Haut-Rhin

New brewery created by a Belgian in a village near the Rhine between Strasbourg and Basle, in southern Alsace. His St Alphonse beers continue to evolve, the **Blonde** ★★ showing sharp edges; the **Ambrée ★★** flip-flopping between malt and hop dominance; while the **Brune ★★☆** goes onwards and upwards, with roasted spicy flavours partly reminiscent of a Christmas beer.

ST GERMAIN
Aix-Noulette, Pas-de-Calais

Small, active brewery southwest of Lille, making the Page 24 Réserve Hildegarde beers, the **Ambrée ★★** brewed with local hops that give strong bitterness alongside toasty notes; and the **Brune ★★** having intense aromas of roasted and chocolate malts with light liquorice. **Rhub'IPA ★★★** is a blond American IPA with rhubarb, brewed in collaboration with **NØGNE Ø** of Norway.

ST RIEUL
Trumilly, Oise

A 1998 farmhouse brewery in Picardy, named after an early Christian evangelizer, spearheading the return of craft beer to this once brewery-rich area. The range includes numerous above-average ales, among which the **Blanche ★★**, a fresh-tasting *witbier* with coriander and orange peel, a surprisingly polished but unremittingly grain **Ambrée ★★★**, and triple-fermented **Grand Cru ★★☆**, a well-rounded stronger ale with rich biscuit and vanilla flavours, stand out.

ST SYLVESTRE
Saint-Sylvestre-Cappel, Nord

Successful 150-year-old family brewery between Dunkirk and Lille, best known for instantly likeable strong blond ale **3 Monts ★★☆** and its amber equivalent

La Gavroche ★★☆. Seasonals include big, strong brown but uninspired **Bière de Noël ★★**; and the aged-over-winter Easter release, golden **Bière Nouvelle ★★☆**.

DESTINATION
CASSEL

A hill town south of Dunkirk that is blessed by the supremely authentic **Kerelshof** (31 Grand Place) and **Kasteelhof** (8 rue St Nicolas) beer cafés, the **Traditions en Nord** (32 Grand Place) beer shop and much *bière de garde*.

THEILLIER
Bavay, Nord

One-man operation in a small town near the Belgian border south of Mons, producing near-perfect beers in the *bière de garde* tradition at one of France's oldest breweries (1835), using period kit. Likely to close shortly when the owner retires, so try to source its two lagered ales, rustic **La Bavaisienne Blonde ★★★**, malt-led with fruity edges, and **Ambrée ★★★☆**, with toasted, caramel malt aroma and beautifully judged bitterness, while you still can.

THIRIEZ
Esquelbecq, Nord

Pioneering 1996 small brewery, south of Dunkirk. First brew **Blonde d'Esquelbecq ★★☆**, is a crisp, golden, modern interpretation of a traditional farmhouse ale; **Etoile du Nord ★★★** uses richer, flavourful hops to bring grapefruit notes; incredible double IPA,

Dalva ★★★☆, has intense hop, fruit and floral flavours while managing to be well rounded and refreshing too; while **Fievre de Cacao ★★☆** has cocoa beans added at the end of the fermentation, bringing a silky mouthfeel and hints of cacao on a bed of dark malt.

TRI MARTOLOD
Concarneau, Finistère

Small 1999 brewery and craft produce store on the south coast of Brittany, collaborating with AN ALARC'H since 2006 to make Tri Martolod beers like a not-too-spicy, *hefeweizen*-style **Blanche ★★**; and well-balanced smoked *dunkelweisse* **Fumée ★★**, with toasted malt.

TROIS FONTAINES
Fenay, Côte-d'Or

Early new-wave brewer in the Burgundy area, south of Dijon. Uses regional malts and French hops in its La Mandubienne beers, such as dark and rich **Brune ★★☆**, with roasted malt character and strong coffee bitterness. Also makes Téméraire brands with additives, such as **Ambrée au Cassis ★★** with blackcurrant seeds – very Dijonnais; and **Blanche au Pain d'Épices ★★**, a *witbier* with gingerbread notes.

VALLÉE DE CHEVREUSE
Bonnelles, Yvelines

Small 2008 brewery in a parkland area southwest of Paris, recently moved to organic production. Best so far of its Volcelest brands is the cloudy, fruity **Ambrée ★★**, with a malty aroma and similar fruit and malt flavours, but keep an eye out for others.

DESTINATION
PARIS

Small and cosy **La Fine Mousse** (6 avenue Jean Aicard) in the 11e arrondissement is the capital's best café for French and international ales, topping 170 varieties with 20 on draught. **La Cave à Bulles** (45 rue Quincampoix), between the Pompidou Centre and Les Halles, is France's premier beer boutique, fronting French and other craft brewing among the galleries and fashion houses, though for the best selection of experimental modern French, **Biérocratie** (32 rue de l'Espérance) in the 13e arrondissement is hard to beat.

VALLÉE DU GIFFRE
Sixt, Rhône-Alpes

In the middle of a circle of mountains near Chamonix, this well-regarded new brewery delivers an impressive array of beers in various styles, such as crisp, dry, fruity, blond, golden rye beer **Bérotte ★★**, with lots of hops; and appropriately named **Robust Porter ★★★** with cassis, nut, fruit and mocha flavours, and a beautiful dry espresso finish.

VEXIN
Théméricourt, Val-d'Oise

Low-key 1992 farm brewery in a regional park northwest of Paris. **Blonde du Vexin ★★☆** is a pale ale that looks, tastes and smells like crushed grain juice, with more bitterness than many; while **Veliocasse Ambrée ★★** is a smooth, honey-flavoured amber ale.

NETHERLANDS

By 1979 Dutch beer production consisted of two large combines, Skol and Heineken; a few mostly southern smaller breweries making safe lagers; and a single ale brewer, the Trappist abbey of Koningshoeven.

A consumer group (PINT) was formed in 1980 and a small chain of independent cafés (ABT) followed, persuading a few Dutch home-brewers to chance going into small-scale commercial production. Interest grew slowly, as quality was notoriously unpredictable. Then, in 2004 came the DE MOLEN brewery at Bodegraven, designing ever more confident beers to a high technical standard, prompting a new wave of smaller brewers to take design flair and precision as their watchwords. The result is a beer scene that is starting to buzz.

Historically, Dutch brewers have tended to ape beer styles from elsewhere, though dark autumnal "*bok*", off the same tree as German *bockbier*, has migrated far enough to be considered a Dutch speciality, and old-style "*kuit*" beers are making a comeback.

Our list of recommended brewers errs away from safety.

3 HORNE, DE
Kaatsheuvel, North Brabant

Hobby brewery (1991) that grew with improving quality. Often rented to wannabe brewers and not averse to smaller-scale contract brewing. Dark, pleasing **Horn's Bock** ★★ has marshmallow hints but avoids cloying sweetness; finely balanced bittersweet **Trippelaer** ★★ is meant to be easy-drinking; and balanced pale **Meibock** ★★ has caramel with bitterness.

7 DEUGDEN, DE
Amsterdam

Small brewery that experiments with adding stuff into established styles with interesting results. **Spring+Tijm** ★★☆ is a thyme-infused *meibok* with herbal freshness and bitter finish; intensely dark, mid-strength **Stout+Moedig** ★★☆ uses three types of malt and some coffee; **Dubbel+Dik** ★★☆ is enlivened by spices that give a rounded warmth; and **Wijs+Neuzig** ★★☆ is a *dunkelweisse* with faint clove hints.

BERGHOEVE
Den Ham, Overijssel

Tiny but impressive semi-rural brewery in rural Overijssel, occasionally brewing larger runs at DE MOLEN. **Donkerbruin Vermoeden** ★★★ is a black IPA with strong burnt coffee and subtle fruity bitterness; quaffable, hoppy blond **Khoppig** ★★☆ is a light US-style pale ale; golden ale **Vuurdoop** ★★☆ has citrus hopping and added coriander; and warming **1842 Hammer Brand** ★★☆ is a chilli-stained porter drinking well above its lowly weight.

BRAND (HEINEKEN)
Wijlre, Limburg

Solid if unspectacular smaller brewery, claiming to be the oldest in the Netherlands, with a heritage back to 1340. Best known for its impressively full-bodied, malty **UP** ★★☆, short for Urtyp ("Original") Pilsner, the best blond lager in the Heineken stable; while its seasonal **Dubbelbock** ★★ has nice caramel tinges but insufficient bitterness.

BUDELS
Budel, North Brabant

Fourth-generation family-run 1870 brewery producing standard and organic ranges with dependable results. Blond barley wine **Zware Dobbel** ★★☆ is richly warming without overbearing sweetness; above-average **Goudblond** ★★ is balanced

by a light-dry bitterness; and playful, aromatic, off-mainstream **Capucijn** *dubbel* ★★☆ has a slightly sour edge.

BUTCHER'S TEARS
Amsterdam

Small brewery with an expat Swedish brewer, which gained its own brewhouse in 2013. Beers are often superb, including the rounded hoppy blond **Green Cap** ★★★, the accomplished flagship; deliciously dry *saison* **Raggle Taggle** ★★★; and tangy black *saison* **Ex Voto** ★★☆.

DESTINATION AMSTERDAM

Proeflokaal Arendsnest (90 Herengracht) has driven the Dutch brewing revival by serving exclusively beers from the Netherlands since opening in 2000, often giving smaller brewers their first airing in the capital, while **In De Wildeman** (3 Kolksteeg), a hundred metres off the station end of Damrak, is one of the world's great beer bars – instantly impressive, its eclectic list of 150+ beers increasingly features top Dutch brewers. **The Bierkoning** (125 Paleisstraat) beer shop, off Dam Square in the bustling heart of the city, somehow packs 1100 beers into its warren, including strong ranges of Dutch, Belgian and American.

EEM, DE
Amersfoort, Utrecht

Gypsy brewer often using **PRAEL** and **PRAGHT** among others, with plans to settle down

1842 Hammer Brand
~ Chili porter ~

Berghoeve
Brouwerij

33 cl
Alc 4% vol
THT 12-2014

A pa't bier

in Amersfoort. Golden-blond **Eem Bitter** ★★ does what it says, both on the palate and in its follow-through; likeable **Tasty Lady** ★★ is a spiced blond ale with subtle bitterness; while dark, rich Christmas ale **Eem Kerst** ★★☆ tastes of toffee but with a bitter kick.

> **DESTINATION DELFT**
>
> **Trappistenlokaal 't Klooster** (2 Vlamingstraat) is a corner bar in the heart of this historic city, with a beer list of 300+ that reads like a who's who of Dutch, European and global brewing greats.

EMELISSE
Kamperland, Zeeland

Interesting and improving Zeeland brewery, now up there with the best. Accomplished **DIPA** ★★★ is a double IPA that packs a mighty bitter punch into an increasingly delicious ale; deep and rich **Rauchbier** ★★☆ is an ale made with smoked malt from Bamberg; rich, black, coffee-tinged **Espresso Stout** ★★★ is becoming a classic of its kind; while the one-off series of barley wine or Imperial stout aged in whisky cask, called **White Label** ★★☆→★★★☆, can be sensational.

FONTEIN, DE
Stein, Limburg

Semi-rural farmhouse brewery, which also brews beers to order for a wide range of regional bars and restaurants. Beers include lychee-laced amber **Cherubijn** ★★☆; lightly fruity **Limburgs Tripel** ★★☆; and summer blond **Euleteul**

Zomer ★★☆, which gains delicate floral notes from added elderflowers.

FRIESE BIERBROUWERIJ
Bolsward, Friesland

Us Heit beers are Friesland's contribution to modern Dutch beer culture, defying the sober reputation of locals since 1985. First brew, light amber **Buorren Bier** ("Local Beer") ★★ would be a *vollbier*, were it only German; richly rounded golden-blond **Dubbel Tarwe** ★★☆ is a bigger-than-average *witbier* with fulsome sweetness and citrus edges; while stronger amber **Elfstedenbier** ★★☆ has a fine bittersweet balance.

GOEYE GOET, 'T
Arnhem, Gelderland

Tiny brewery set incongruously amid heritage buildings at the national open-air museum near Arnhem. In distinctive stone bottles it sells an impressively refreshing and malty **Pilsener** ★★☆, exceptional for one so small; an abbey-style **Dubbel** ★★ with a slight sourness we hope is deliberate; and a dark autumn **Herfstbock** ★★ with unintrusive sweetness.

GULPENER
Gulpen, Limburg

1825 brewery producing a huge range of beers, from agreeable to mediocre. Crisp, malty **Château Neubourg** ★★ is a dryish and bitter pilsner; sweet 'n' sour wood-aged **Mestreechs Aajt** ★★★, once reserved to the brewery tap, is now available in Maastricht; while rock-solid, dryish *witbier* **Korenwolf** ★★☆ is a cut above many Belgian peers.

HEMEL
Nijmegen, Gelderland

Best of the Dutch pub breweries, found elsewhere in hometown Nijmegen and sometimes beyond. Makes simple beers like citrus *witbier*, **Serafijn ★★**; but more in its element with the likes of lightly smoked, deep and fruity winter ale **Moenen ★★☆**; rich, well-balanced, dark golden-blond *tripel* **Helse Engel ★★☆**; and lovable giant amber barley wine **Nieuw Ligt ★★★**, warming and soft when young and magnificent as spicy, cellar-aged **Grand Cru ★★★☆**.

IJ, 'T
Amsterdam

Amsterdam's oldest brewery, established in 1983, has a new brewhouse treble the size. Currently on a roll, its latest attractions are double-strength **IJwit ★★☆**, which leans neither to Bavaria nor Belgium; and hazy golden-blond **IPA ★★☆**, still finding its way in the bitterness stakes. Old troopers include strong *tripel*-ish, orange-amber **Columbus ★★**, a collage of clashing flavours; and seasonals like dry, rounded superior amber winter brew **IJndejaars ★★☆**.

JOPEN BIER
Haarlem, North Holland

Finally blessed with its own brewery in a former church, a well-practised range is now supplemented by one-offs, some of which stick. Dry and hoppy blond ale **Hoppen ★★☆** is starting to push its bitterness envelope; intensely hopped **Jacobus RPA ★★☆**, an IPA with rye, is ahead of its time in Europe; triple-grain **Trinitas Tripel ★★★** is gaining confidence with time; and four-grained **Bokbier ★★★** has so much bitter cocoa taste it is almost a porter.

KIEVIT, TRAPPISTENBROUWERIJ DE
Zundert, North Brabant

The Netherlands' second Trappist brewery, gaining Authentic Trappist Product status in 2013. The focus remains on a single beer while it gets established. Sweetish copper-amber **Zundert ★★** is thus far competent but needs more depth before it challenges its peers.

KLEIN DUIMPJE
Hillegom, South Holland

Tiny brewery in the bulb-growing part of South Holland. Too many beers but some

decent. Dryish **American Pale Ale** ★★ has a pleasing fruity hop; well-practised **Hazelnoot Porter** ★★☆ is less nutty than its name suggests; **Blackbird Schwarz** ★★☆ has roasted barley and bitterness to the fore with some chocolate notes; and rounded **Imperial Russian Stout** ★★☆ tastes coffee'd.

nationally. Quality varies, but new beers show more ambition, including delicately hoppy blond **IBA** ★★☆; assertively hopped **IPA** ★★☆; *dubbel* **Crom Hout** ★★☆, with dabs of cocoa painted onto a slightly sour background; and balanced, elegant barley wine **Blauwe Bijl** ★★, a high-malt beer with a gentle, bitter finish.

LA TRAPPE
Berkel-Enschot, North Brabant

The Netherlands' older Trappist brewery, known as Koningshoeven in some places. Operated by commercial brewers Bavaria of Lieshout, but brewing within the walls of Koningshoeven abbey near Tilburg and answerable to the Order. Simpler beers like pale ale **Isid'or** are better bottled than on tap ★→★★; golden-amber **Tripel** ★★ has hints of bitter orange; while its slowly evolving, year-dated barley wine Quadrupel, full of nuance, loses gooey-ness and can gain gravitas when **Oak Aged** ★★☆→★★★★.

LEIDSCH BIER
Leiden, South Holland

Accomplished brewer making some beers on a tiny scale in Leiden and commissioning larger runs from elsewhere. Own-brew standouts thus far are assertive, highly attenuated, English-hopped **Morsporter** ★★★, with chocolate and cocoa to the fore; and pine-scented, fragrant, highly spiced Christmas ale, **Kerstbomenbier** ★★☆. Its flagship US-style IPA **Leidsch Aaipiejee** ★★☆ is brewed at PROEF in Belgium.

DESTINATION
OIRSCHOT

Buitenlust (5 Spoordonkseweg) is a charming, simple, but welcoming, small-town local café northwest of Eindhoven boasting probably the longest and among the best beer lists of any in the country, totalling over 800 much of the time.

MAALLUST
Veenhuizen, Drenthe

Small brewery of promise in a converted grain mill at Veenhuizen, a former colony town for vagrants and beggars, now home to a prison. Malty, bitter **Vagebond Vienna** ★★☆ is one of very few Dutch takes on a Vienna amber lager; citrus **Kolonist Weizen** ★★ is well rounded and tangy; bittersweet **Weldoener Blond** ★★ is satisfyingly malty; and **Zware Jongen Tripel** ★★☆ has enough grass to conjure summer meadows.

LECKERE, DE
De Meern, Utrecht

Brewing in Utrecht since 1997, the first to go organic and found in health food stores

MAXIMUS
De Meern, Utrecht

New-wave Utrecht brewer, outstanding from day one. Superbly rich, fruity hoppy

Brutus ★★☆ amber lager is a real star, rich in US influence; US-style IPA **Pandora** ★★★ has a lovely floral aroma and major bitter finish; while its variant, immensely likeable golden IPA **Highhops** ★★★ is different again; and **Stout 8** ★★★, the stronger, almost Imperial stout is dry and bitter.

MOLEN, DE
Bodegraven, South Holland

For some years the guiding light of modern Dutch brewing, now a world leader in craft brewing. Experimentation, bordering on insane alchemy at times, has produced a range of 15 regular beers and upward of 200 one-off variants and collaborations. Stunningly aromatic six-hop but only modestly bitter, **Vuur & Vlam** ★★★★ is one of the world's great IPAs; equally wonderfully hopped, intensely floral double IPA **Amarillo** ★★★☆ plays the hop-monster role; varieties of **Tsarina Esra** ★★★★ Imperial stout or super-strong porter have treacly whisky tinges when oak-aged as Reserva; while bitter, coffee-tinged **Hel & Verdoemenis** ★★★☆ is another Imperial stout with an almost smoky finish. It even has the audacity to brew US-hopped British-style bitter **Op & Top** ★★★☆ better than most UK brewers could.

MOMMERIETE
Gramsbergen, Overijssel

Small canalside brewery whose outstanding beers belie its small stature. Its regular **Blond** ★★★ is an excellent example of simple done well, a pale ale that smells like a hay barn; the fragrant, malty and complex **Meibock** ★★★ is among the best in class; perfectly balanced

Rookbock ★★☆ juggles smoky notes with a fruity, bitter finish; while the two Van Gramsbergen barley wines come in her warming, bittersweet, alcoholic toffee **Vrouwe** ★★★; and his addictive rich, smoky and dry **Heer** ★★★.

MUIFELBROUWERIJ
Berghem, North Brabant

North Brabant brewer with some tiny kit, mostly brewing at PROEF in Belgium and Sint Servattumus in North Brabant. Showing potential are blond ale **Graaf Dicbier** ★★; decidedly off-centre **D'n Osse Bock** ★★; barley wine **Zuster Agatha** ★★☆; and sometimes **1851 Bik & Arnold Dubbel** ★★.

NATTE GIJT, DE
Weert, Limburg

Talented Limburg brewer renting time at Anders in Belgium or DE 3 HORNE. **Hop met de Gijt** is a US-style IPA with flowery nose, fruity, hoppy taste and a bitter finish, even better in some of its single-hop special editions ★★☆→★★★★.

OERSOEP BROUWERIJ
Nijmegen, Gelderland

Small brewer of organic beers with a growing reputation for excellence. A 2014 move to larger premises has made its beers easier to source. Brews 'lines' that vary each time but retain a theme. The **God is Goed** ★★★→★★★☆ line of sour, complex wood-aged ales and lambics are the standouts; **Bruisend en Blond** ★★★ are hoppy farmhouse IPAs; and **Donker en Diep** ★★☆→★★★ are stouts, occasionally with fruit.

PAMPUS
Amsterdam

Young brewers with links to the Arendsnest (see box, page 127) and Beer Temple beer bars, brewing at SALLANDSE. Started with dry-edged pale ale **Seeheld** ★★☆; tangy milk stout **Melkmeisje** ★★☆; and superbly bitter juniper-spiced **Drenkeling** ★★★.

PRAEL, DE
Amsterdam

Remarkable state-funded rehabilitation project, morphed into a successful small brewery that is starting to experiment. Nelis Bock now has a dry-edged smoked version **Met Pijp** ★★; blond **Johnny** ★★ is just bitter enough to work; bittersweet **Mary** ★★ is an amber *tripel* with a fruity finish; and malty, warming **Willy** ★★☆ is a spiced barley wine for winter.

PRAGHT
Dronten, Flevoland

Small brewery in the Flevoland beer void, creating above-average beers. Lovely multi-textured imperial **Extra Stout** ★★☆ is chocolaty throughout, with raspberry on the nose and a dry bitter finish; darkly complex **Blackbox** ★★★ *doppelbock* has a hint of liquorice and plenty of coffee; while rock-solid **Tripel** ★★ is dry-edged and bitter.

RAMSES BIER
Wagenberg, North Brabant

Now with its own brewhouse, a top-table place is beckoning. Superb dark amber IPA **Den Dorstige Tijger** ★★★☆ blends fruity notes with rampant bitterness; full-bodied, rounded **Mamba Porter** ★★★ has a fruity, bitter centre and coffee-cocoa edges; impressive golden **Antenne Tripel** ★★★ balances bitter and honey; while lovely rounded Imperial **Shire Stout** gains further in its barrel-aged version ★★★.

RODENBURG
Rha, Gelderland

Rural Gelderland brewery run by an expat Yorkshireman, whose Bronckhorster beers are rarely less than excellent and are gaining international renown: intensely hoppy double IPA **Hoptimist** ★★★; treacly **Night Porter** ★★☆, with a full rainbow of coffee, cocoa and dry bitterness; its sticky imperial sister **Midnight Porter** ★★★☆; and superbly rich, fruity barley wine **Terra Incognita** ★★★☆.

DESTINATION
ERMELO

Burg Bieren (45 Putterweg) is the country's largest beer retailer and within its 1000+ range has probably the best Dutch range anywhere, some way off the beaten track in the Veluwe region of western Gelderland.

ROOIE DOP
Utrecht

Utrecht brewer launched in 2012, developing mini test brews in a canalside cellar bar and brewing larger volumes at DE MOLEN. Strongly dry-hopped and aggressively bitter **Chica Americana IPA** ★★★ has 10% oats in the mash to round it out; while **Double Oatmeal Stout** ★★☆ gives off cocoa and rich chocolate.

DESTINATION
UTRECHT

De Drie Dorstige Herten (47 Lange Nieuwstraat) is a diminutive, street-corner beer café that boasts a carefully chosen list made up almost entirely of beers from small, hard-to-source local producers.

SALLANDSE LANDBIER
Raalte, Overijssel

A small-town brewery that is located beneath a local events complex and hired out to at least a dozen wannabe craft brewers currently without kit. Its own range includes malty amber **Donkere Henricus** ★★; standout flowery, hoppy blond **Novello** ★★☆; and decent autumn *bock* **Bokkige Theodorus** ★★.

SCHANS, DE
Uithoorn, North Holland

Brewery-distillery sited in North Holland eschewing commercial success to make Schans beers when it feels like it. Spiced **Saison** ★★☆ balances bitter and sweet with clove and ginger; the inky-black 7% ABV **Stout** ★★☆ is nowadays seen more commonly than its acquired historic brand, **Van Vollenhoven's Extra** ★★; while the **Imperial** ★★★ is similar with 25% less water.

TEXELSE BIERBROUWERIJ
Oudeschild, North Holland

Small 1999 brewery on the island of Texel, off the North Holland peninsula. A solid range in established styles, with no show-stoppers but beginning to accrue prizes, especially for seasonal *bocks*. **Skuumkoppe** ★★ was the first Dutch *dunkelweisse*; old trooper **Tripel** ★★☆ is growing in complexity; but for prowess try the increasingly popular **Bock Bier** ★★★ and less subtle strong *doppelbock* **StormBock** ★★☆.

VOLENDAM
Volendam, North Holland

Tiny brewery in a tourist village in North Holland, also known by its brand, 't Vølen Bier. Often favours larger bottles. Its scale promotes laterality but reduces reliability. Dark seasonal **Vølenbock** ★★ has a sharpish finish countering any sweetness; strong golden **Ootje** *tripel* ★★☆ has a touch of the barley wines to it; and hazy amber, sweetish strong ale **Øster** ★★☆ might be a great if it were more reliable.

SCANDINAVIA

Innovative microbiologists at the Carlsberg brewery helped to shape beer in the late 19th century. In the 20th, it was temperance-affecting politicians wielding punitive beer taxes who made the play. Folk traditions live on in Finnish *sahti* and others, but the modern theme is that if beer must be expensive, it should taste superb, leading to big, assertive stouts, porters and pale ales.

DENMARK

The speed with which the Danish beer scene shifted from dependably dull to near psychedelic took even ardent beer enthusiasts by surprise.

Fifteen years ago, confronted with the prospect of other global brewers coming to take slices from its home markets, the Danish giant Carlsberg bravely decided to inject a little fun into the game by enabling the growth of new small breweries. What happened next was an explosion of interest in beers of all types, old and new, taking this normally conservative but open-minded nation completely by surprise.

Some fear progress may have been so rapid that the general drinking public will not wish to keep up and the absence of brewing infrastructure and financial commitment is sometimes a worry, as the most creative exponents do not bother with the inconvenience of having their own brewery, or employees.

Yet nobody visiting the countless Copenhagen bars where the world's great beers are being matched and excelled for quality and originality by lesser-known local products, or touring the country to discover the shops and taphouses of its 150 or more new breweries can be in doubt that something remarkable has happened.

AMAGER
Copenhagen

Energetic Copenhagen craft brewer with a large but reliable range, strong local following and growing export trade.

Interesting beers include **Sloth** ★★☆, a super-dry single malt, Simcoe-only pale ale designed with US colleagues; new regular **Rugporter** ★★★ with rye to add a spicy sweetness; monstrous juicy double IPA **Gluttony** ★★☆, loaded with

C-hops; and **Hr. Frederiksen ★★★☆**, a heavily dry-hopped, massively roasted and powerful Imperial stout.

BEER HERE
Copenhagen

Revolutionary beer commissioner actively involved in designing the brews it has produced at PROEF in Belgium. Delightful sounding **Dead Cat ★★☆** is a pine and melon amber ale with Simcoe hops; **Kama Citra ★★★** is an alternative take on brown ale hopped only with Citra; super-hopped, coppery **Hopfix ★★★☆** an IPA high in alpha acids; while at the opposite end milk stout **Ammestout ★★★** brims with smooth, sweet flavours from a solid roast base.

BØGEDAL
Jerlev, Hovedstaden

Farmhouse brewery in the rolling hills outside Vejle in the south of Jutland using ancient techniques to make lost Danish beer styles. No two brews are identical but individually numbered gyles are themed. So **Lys #1 ★★☆** indicates a rustic type of IPA with citrus aroma; biggest seller **Hvede ★★** is an ultra-sweet type of *witbier*; and **Mork #8 ★★★** is a full-bodied Christmas brown ale made with muscovado and orange peel.

CROOCKED MOON
Copenhagen

One-man enterprise based at a Copenhagen pub, hiring other Danish breweries when they need to produce. Fat and moist **All Blacks ★★★** is a pale ale showcasing New Zealand hops; **Bad Karma ★★☆** is a rich, pruney

coffee stout with vanilla and overripe fruit; while IPA **Stonewall ★★★** is a no-frills, powerful hop punch-in-the-mouth.

DET LILLE BRYGGERI
Viby, Sjælland

Innovative hobby brewery southwest of Copenhagen, making an impressive range with many experimental beers and one-offs. Fairly regular are **Lakrids Porter ★★☆**, the subtle roastiness of which allows the added raw liquorice to shine; **Columbus Ale ★★★**, an IPA with eponymous hops from the US and both malt and yeast from the UK; and the ever-changing incarnations of **Barley Wine ★★★☆**, each perfectly balanced and warming.

DJÆVLEBRYG
Copenhagen

Beer commissioner contracting various brewers to make its dark, gothic-imaged beers. **Dark Beast ★★★** is a black IPA in which hops overpower the high-roasted malts; **Mareridt ★★☆** a challenging beer that combines smoked malt with brettanomyces; and **Gudeløs ★★★☆** is a pitch-black Imperial stout that balances its roasts with some light sweetness.

EBELTOFT GÅRDBRYGGERI
Ebeltoft, Midtjylland

Small farmhouse brewery in rolling countryside overlooking the sea, east of Aarhus. At the lighter end **Gårdbryg ★★☆** is a crisp Bohemian pilsner with lots of grassy hops; **Porter Special ★★★** is dark brown and strong, with sweet liquorice and dried fruit playing amid the roasted malts; while in powerful *doppelbock* **Bock No. 4** ★★☆ they are complemented by pumpernickel and burnt caramel.

EVIL TWIN BREWING
Copenhagen

Danish company fronted by New York-based Jeppe Bjergsø, twin brother to Mikkel, of **MIKKELLER**. Commissions the beers it designs from breweries in many countries to sell on to even more. **Bikini Beer** ★★☆ is a citrus, hop-forward, low-alcohol pale ale; **Soft Dookie** ★★★☆ a filling Imperial stout with a gentle edge of milk chocolate; while **Imperial Biscotti Break** ★★★ is a super-potent porter loaded with coffee and bitter dark chocolate.

FANØ
Nordby (Fanø), Syddanmark

Small brewery on the island of Fanø, off the ferry port of Esbjerg, brewing for beer commissioners but also with its own lateral-thinking clutch. Low-strength (2.7%) IPA-hopped **Havgus** ★★☆ packs lots of hop punch into not much; stronger **Vestkyst** ★★★ is a classic American pale ale with crisp and piney hop aromas; **Forår** ★★☆ is a dead straight seasonal spring pale *bock*; while massive **Imperial X-mas Porter** ★★★★ will knock out any Christmas dinner with its overload of roasted malts, spices and alcohol.

FLYING COUCH
Copenhagen

One of the brewers at **NØRREBRO**, who also freelances at **HERSLEV**, has them make respectively draught and bottled beers for him, such as so-called black

IPA **Paint It Black** ★★☆, more like a strong, roasted stout with light aromatic hops; and sweet, mellow **Phister de Noël** ★★★, a winter Imperial stout made with vanilla.

FREDERIKSODDE HAANDBRYGGERLAUG
Fredericia, Syddanmark

Two home brewers recently turned pro, commissioning a solid range of beers from the Kvajj brewery in Vejle. **6 Juli Ale** ★★ is a light, quaffable American-style pale ale loaded with Cascade; **Etlars IPA** ★★ is another beer called a black IPA but needing its stout-like hop profile tuned up; and **Lundings Porter** ★★☆ is rustic and strong with notes of tar and smoke.

GRAUBALLE
Grauballe, Midtjylland

Farmhouse brewery and 2002 pioneer of the Danish beer revolution, making solid, no-nonsense brews. **Enebær Stout** ★★☆ is a mid-strength British stout but with juniper spicing; subtle Scotch ale **Mørk Mosebryg** ★★☆ combines smoked malts with First Gold hops; and Christmas's

strong **Peters Jul** ★★ offers no spice but has a rich, warming caramel base.

HERSLEV
Herslev, Sjælland

Purpose-built farm brewery converted in 2004, due west of Copenhagen. It went green in 2013, using malted home-grown barley. **Økologisk India Dark Ale** ★★☆ is basically a strong brown ale made zippy by NZ hops; **Four Grain Stout** ★★★ comes rich and smooth with an amazing aroma; and **Mjølner** ★★☆ is a powerful seasonal barley wine with occasional consistency problems.

HORNBEER
Kirke-Hyllinge, Sjælland

Small brewery in rural Zealand that has managed to become popular with regular Danish beer lovers, despite producing some challenging beers. **Dryhop** ★★☆ is a lager that is hopped like an IPA; **Hophorn** ★★☆ is a full-throttle strong black IPA heavy on both roasted malts and aromatic hops; **Caribbean Rumstout** ★★★ is a sweet Imperial stout spiced with rum; while multiple-award-winner **The Fundamental Blackhorn** ★★★★ is an Imperial stout that has undergone dry-hopping, barrel-ageing and the addition of walnuts.

INDSLEV
Nørre Aaby, Syddanmark

Small brewery off the motorway northwest of Odense, rented much of the time to UGLY DUCK and others, but also making its own Indslev range including **Sort Hvede** ★★☆, a heavy, dark wheat

beer that looks and tastes like a Breton-style stout; and **Spelt Bock** ★★☆, a creamy *weizenbock* with dark chocolate from the roasted spelt.

DESTINATION **ODENSE**

Christian Firtal (31 Vintapperstræde) and **Carlsens Kvarter** (19 Hunderupvej) are two cosy, traditional pubs in the city centre with good selections of Danish craft beers on tap and in the bottle, each appealing to locals, beer geeks and tourists alike. More taps at the first, more bottles at the second.

KRAGELUND
Kragelund, Midtjylland

Small village brewery near Silkeborg, west of Aarhus, that is impressing some tough judges. **Steam Beer** ★★☆ is pale beer with a dry-grape character, hopped by Nelson Sauvin; **Katarinas Mild** ★★★ is an original "small beer", designed as a UK dark mild but made from the first run-off from the monstrous Imperial **Katarinas Stout** ★★★; while **Pramdrager Porter** ★★★ elegantly runs smooth vanilla into a roasted beer with a tar-like edge.

KRENKERUP
Sakskøbing, Sjælland

Small brewery in an ancient barn on the Krenkerup estate, near Sakskøbing in the south of Zealand, making mostly German-style beers. **Lolland og Falster Guld** ★★☆ emphasizes rich, clean and sweet malts balanced with flowery hops; **Rauch ★★** has just enough smoked malts to count as a subtle *rauchbier*; while the gem is **Doppel Bock ★★★☆**, rich in caramel with pumpernickel accents, an excellent example of the style.

MIDTFYNS
Årslev, Syddanmark

Recently moved and expanded 2004 brewery south of Odense, owned by an American expat, whose homeland is reflected in its range. The **Chili Tripel ★★** has more novelty value than anything else; similarly Belgian-nudged **Rough Snuff ★★☆** is dark and rich with a tobacco and molasses character; while strong black IPA **Gleipner ★★★** offers fresh citrus hops on a base of roasted malts.

MIKKELLER
Copenhagen

The world's most prolific brewer of idolized new beers runs no brewhouse. Rather Mikkel Bjergsø's aura is such that other brewers the world over will do his bidding. Occasionally makes a right dog and best left to experiment. Get the drift with super-hopped brown ale **Jackie Brown ★★★**; wittily concocted, fabulously delivered, complex coffee stout **Beer Geek Breakfast ★★★☆**, ratcheted up to the beautifully absurd Imperial stout **Beer Geek Brunch Weasel ★★★★**, flavoured with coffee beans that have passed through a civet; and voyage of discovery **Nelson Sauvignon ★★★☆**, a refined, Belgian-pointing, Bretty strong ale aged in Austrian white wine barriques.

NØRREBRO
Copenhagen

Pioneering US-style brewpub that spawned a busy production brewery. **Ravnsborg Rød ★★** is a deceptively slick, smart and easy-going red-amber ale; **La Granja Stout ★★☆** is a rich and sweet coffee stout; while **Little Korkny Ale ★★★☆** is a warming, English barley wine served from a snifter that is not far off the perfect after-dinner drink. Numerous rotating and one-off beers too, rarely dull.

DESTINATION COPENHAGEN

For smaller Danish brewers try the comfortable, relaxed **Ørsted Ølbar** (13 Nørre Farimagsgade) or pokier, more functional **Ølbaren** (2 Elmegade). To find chic-geek at its most splendidly horizontal, visit the minimalist **Mikkeller Bar** (8 Viktoriagade) or brightly sparser **Mikkeller & Friends** (35 Stefansgade), where the global elite of craft beer snuggles up with some expensive jokes. The latter has a beer shop that is complemented neatly by the delightful and better-stocked **BarleyWine** (21 Admiralgade).

OKKARA
Velbastaður, Faroe Islands

The semi-autonomous Faroe Islands, in the north Atlantic, only recently legalized stronger beers and neither of the local independent breweries has yet perfected them. **Olavur ★★** is a sweet golden ale with flowery hops, brewed for the islands' national day in July; flagship red-brown stone beer **Rinkusteinur** ★★★ is brewed by immersing glowing lava rocks into the wort, giving it burnt edges; while the stronger version of dry, deep brown **Portari** ★★☆ remains plain with a crudely roasted character.

SKAGEN
Skagen, Nordjylland

Pub brewery near the northernmost point on the Danish mainland, offering a solid range. **Skawskum** ★★ is a clean *dunkel* rich in Munich malts, with a dry and hoppy finish; **Bundgarn** ★★☆ a rugged, lightly smoked porter with English liquorice in the boil; while **Væltepeter** ★★☆ is a filling, warming *doppelbock* with a slightly salty edge.

SØGAARDS
Aalborg, Nordjylland

Pub brewery to the south of the last entry, with an extensive range of bottled beers. **Stout Noire** ★★☆ is a complex brew blending lightly smoked malts with salty liquorice; potent **Bispens Trippel** ★★☆ offers the expected yeastiness but with a note of refined almonds; and **Fort Dansborg IPA** ★★ is a well-crafted if modest example of the style.

SØKILDEGAARD
Vipperød, Sjælland

Tiny farmhouse brewery west of Copenhagen, selling its beers only on its premises. A roast coffee aroma from **Farfars Favorit** stout ★★★ preludes a smooth and sweet oatmeal follow-through; **Humleguf** ★★☆ is a far from

traditional pale ale with interwoven coriander, orange peel and American hops; while New Year beer **Nytårsøl** ★★★ is a sophisticated blend of the farm's grapes with American hops in a strong Belgian ale base.

STRONZO BREWING
Copenhagen

The new naughty boy of Danish beer may have fun with exports to Italy, even with the respectability that comes with getting your own brewhouse. **Hop Lunch** ★★☆ is a quaffable, low-alcohol IPA, dry-hopped with Cascade; simple golden ale **Proud Stronzo** ★★☆ is made enticing by loads of crispy aroma hops; quadruple-mashed, the almost vulgar **1000 EBC** ★★★ may be the world's blackest Imperial stout; while **Honey Badger** ★★★☆ is an extreme Imperial stout that manages to make honey and booze strike a balanced stand-off.

SVANEKE
Svaneke, Hovedstaden

Denmark's easternmost brewery, on the island of Bornholm, has a second

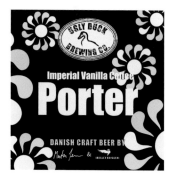

smaller brewpub plant for experimental beers. Straight, well-made **In Your Pale Face IPA** ★★★ offers an overload of resinous piney hops; **Liquorice Stout** ★★☆ comes with locally produced sweet liquorice added; super-clean and fresh **Session Pilsner** ★★☆ is rich in citrus hops; while the oddly named **Den Udødelige Hest** ("The Immortal Horse") ★★★☆ is a rugged take on Baltic porter.

TO ØL
Copenhagen

Experimental brand created by two **MIKKELLER** pupils who now commission for themselves. **Raid Beer** ★★☆ is a lager hopped as an IPA; **Ov-ral Wild Yeast IIPA** ★★☆ is what happens if you add brettanomyces into the fermentation of a double IPA; adding lactose and coffee to a strong brown ale makes **Mochaccino Messiah** ★★★; and making a super-strong milk stout then putting it in a whisky barrel creates **Sort Mælk** ★★★.

UGLY DUCK BREWING
Nørre Aaby, Syddanmark

Semi-detached from **INDSLEV**, where all its products are made, this hands-on producer has its own range of five pale ales and two porters, including **Hopfest** ★★☆, an IPA celebrating US aromatic hops; and strong **Imperial Vanilla Coffee Porter** ★★★, which keeps the hops and blends them with mocha and a layer of vanilla.

WINTERCOAT
Sabro, Midtjylland

Tiny brewery near Aarhus, brewing beers in styles imported from Britain that could usefully be exported back. **Double Hop** ★★☆ is what a British double IPA might taste like; creamy and nutty **Oatmeal Stout** ★★☆ is loaded with malts and oats; and Christmas's **Yule Ale** ★★ is a fresh and dark British strong ale with bitter orange for a citric zest.

NORWAY

Even when compared to other Scandinavian countries, the tax on beer in Norway is eye-watering. Having been the home of the Gulating code, which compelled every farmer to brew beer, Norwegian independence in 1905 was followed briefly by prohibition and then domination by ordinary lagers and *lettøl*, sweet light beer up to 2.5% ABV.

Then lateral-thinking NØGNE Ø took a risk, believing that if beer drinkers were forced to pay a shocking amount for a sawn-off glass of decent but dull light lager, they might just part with an outrageous sum for an overfull glass of heavy but superb ale made to uncompromising standards. Thus began the small miracle that brought full-on craft brewing to the fjords and fjells of the country with the world's crinkliest coastline.

7 FJELL BRYGGERI
Fana, Hordaland

One of the most experienced and respected home-brewers in Norway currently makes his hard-to-place but beautifully judged, strongish brown **Vinter** ale ★★★ at **LERVIG** but will have his own place on the outskirts of Bergen shortly. Tipped for stardom.

AASS
Drammen, Buskerud

One of three remaining older independent breweries, in the family since 1867. There is historic interest in its regular lagers, as with two dark Christmas beers, sweet and gentle **Juleøl 4.5** ★★ and the more robust **Juleøl 6.5** ★★☆. The standout is autumnal dark **Bok** ★★★☆, Norway's best in a breed similar to Dutch *bokbier*.

DESTINATION OSLO

Despite the prices, Oslo has spawned some superb beer venues recently, including the exquisitely dark and ornate **Håndverkerstuene** (7 Rozenkrantzgate), massive restaurant and terrace bar **Olympen** (15 Grønlandsleiret) and attractive brewpub **Schouskjelleren** (2 Trondheimsveien), though we cannot help returning to the elegant original, **Lorry** (12 Parkveien).

ÆGIR
Flåm, Sogn og Fjordane

Tiny brewery next to a famous end-of-fjord railhead, northeast of Bergen.

Bøyla Blonde Ale ★★☆ is the easy-drinking golden session brew; **India Pale Ale** ★★★☆ is a superb, floral, heavily hopped bitter but fruity IPA; the near-black Imperial stout **Natt Porter** ★★★☆ gains nuance and depth as **Lynchburg Natt** ★★★★, steeped in bourbon casks; while barley wine **Tors Hammer** ★★★ perhaps takes intensity too far at 13.5% ABV.

DESTINATION BERGEN

Henrik (10 Engen) is a specialist beer bar with minimalist décor, over 50 brews on tap and more in bottle, mostly Scandinavian; while old-style wooden **Bryggen Tracteursted** (2 Bryggestredet) has 30 Norwegian ales and exceptional food.

AUSTMANN
Trondheim

New brewers who started at **KINN** but now have their own place. We may be premature to include it but have a good feeling from its honest, straightforward brown ale **Northumberland** ★★☆ and well-crafted experiment, dryish **Blåbærstout** ★★, with blueberries.

BERENTSENS
Egersund, Rogaland

Interesting small brewery south of Stavanger, an offshoot from a long-established cider maker. **RAV Amber Ale ★★** is fruity and bittersweet; **Sorte Får Stout ★★☆** is dry and bitter with a taste of unsweetened prunes; and heavy-duty but mid-strength **Jules Avec ★★★☆** is one of the finest Christmas beers in Scandinavia.

HAANDBRYGGERIET
Drammen, Buskerud

Questing small brewer in the same town as AASS, making hand-crafted beers that do not always work but can be spectacular. Heavily smoked dark beer **Røyk Uten Ild ★★★** avoids being oppressive; the mid-strength **Porter ★★★☆** is robust but smooth and fruity; **Bestefar ★★★** is a hefty black winter beer; **Dark Force ★★★** is an Imperial stout with a high wheat content; and unique **Norwegian Wood ★★★☆** alludes to Gulating-type beer with smoked piney flavours.

KINN
Florø, Sogn og Fjordane

Successful small brewery, pronounced "Shin", located between Bergen and Ålesund, making mainly UK- and Belgian-inspired beers. **Pilegrim ★★** is a bottled English bitter; **Svart Hav ★★☆** is a toasted, bitterish dry lighter stout sometimes found in cask; **Bøvelen ★★☆** is a Norwegian take on a Belgian *tripel*; while **Vestkyst ★★★** more successfully resembles a US-style IPA.

LERVIG
Stavanger, Rogaland

Small, commercially driven brewery established in 2005, making a range of standard lagers as well as hoppy US pale ale **Lucky Jack ★★☆** and various Brewers Reserve beers like **Rye IPA ★★★**, a double IPA with fruity sweetness from the rye, and **Konrad's Stout ★★☆**, making Imperial approachable using oatmeal.

DESTINATION
STAVANGER

Nicely positioned just off the harbour, with the feel of a traditional 1980s London pub, the **Cardinal** (21 Skagen) is a remarkably well-stocked beer bar with over 400 mostly bottled beers, including many from the region and some real rarities.

NØGNE Ø (HANSA BORG)
Grimstad, Aust-Agder

One of the world's greatest craft breweries, pronounced "nurg-na ur", based at a former hydroelectric plant, northeast of Kristiansand. Can brew anything well but excels with its ordinary strength **Brown Ale ★★★☆**; virtually perfect, middleweight **Porter ★★★☆**; an **India Pale Ale ★★★★** that is rarely if ever bettered; an **Imperial Stout ★★★☆** with admirable restraint for a blockbuster; and **# 100 ★★★☆** super-strong IPA, created by pure self-indulgence. Taken over by the country's largest independent brewery in 2014.

SWEDEN

With the active approval of the state, mergers had, by 1985, left Sweden with just nine regular breweries, plus some old-style, low-alcohol *svagdricka* makers. Reversal of this trend was hampered initially by strict licensing laws and high taxation but new brewers now number well over 100 and in 2013 alone 40 new brewhouses were built.

Svagdricka remains the only true indigenous Swedish beer style, though *Gotlandsdricke,* a distant cousin of Finnish *sahti* and the Estonian *koduõlu*, made with malt smoked over juniper wood, continues to be found on the island of Gotland.

BREKERIET
Staffanstorp, Skåne

Early days experimental beer maker run by three brothers. Since 2012, it has been fermenting beers with *Brettanomyces*, receiving plaudits not for extreme creations but for subtle ones. **Cassis ★★★** is a sour beer in which blackcurrants are steeped during secondary fermentation; **Vieille Saison ★★★** is a light ale aged in oak; while **Brettporter ★★★** is a porter fermented entirely with *Brettanomyces*. We watch with interest.

DUGGES
Landvetter, Västra Götland

Small, prolific 2005 brewery, east of Gothenburg. **Avenyn Ale ★★☆** is a US-style pale ale with a fresh, grapefruit flavour from Chinook, Centennial and Simcoe; **Holy Cow ★★★** is a much-malted IPA, its alcohol cleverly hidden by slight sweetness and a large, lingering, five-hop bitter finish; while anything called **Idjit ★★☆→★★★☆** will be dark, generous, strong and portery.

JÄMTLANDS
Pilgrimstad, Jämtland

Small 1996 brewery near Östersund, midway up the country in the unpopulated part, winning countless national awards for beers like well-made, pleasantly balanced amber lager **Bärnsten ★★☆**; **Postiljon ★★☆**, an ESB with a fruity malt character and lingering bitterness; and deep reddish winter ale **Julöl ★★☆**, with a strong earthy hop aroma, some malt sweetness and straight bitterness.

MALMÖ BRYGGHUS
Malmö, Skåne

Pub brewery in an old chocolate factory. **Vete-öl ★★** is a refreshing *witbier* with coriander and citrus peel; **Canned Wheat ★★★** is a highly aromatic, 50% malted wheat IPA with Citra hops; **Cacao-Porter Criollo ★★☆** is robust, with real cacao punctuating a sweet, malty flavour; and occasional **Grand Crew ★★☆** is a much-praised oddball sour "lambic", aged for 14 months in Cognac barrels before bottling.

DESTINATION
MALMÖ

The 40-strong chain of **Bishops Arms** beer and whisky bars are found throughout Sweden, serving beers from mainstream industrial to rare local and international craft brews. Malmö's two, a beauty in the old town (49 Gustav Adolfs Torg) and a slick one by the main station (62 Norra Vallgatan), are typical of the breed.

MOHAWK
Täby, Stockholm

Beer commissioner north of Stockholm with its own pilot brewery. Hazy **Unfiltered Lager** ★★☆ has a Vienna-style foundation but US and NZ hopping; **Extra IPA** ★★★ is made by heavily dry-hopping an already high-hopped double IPA; and **Double Rocket** ★★☆ is a monstrous hybrid of Imperial stout and strong IPA, force-fed and aged in bourbon barrels to end at sherry strength.

NÄRKE KULTURBRYGGERI
Örebro

Small experimental brewery west of Stockholm, best known for variations on superb heavyweight stout Stormaktsporter, which has not been released since 2010. **Örebro Bitter** ★★★ is in the delicate English style, with Goldings and Cascade; **Närke Slättöl** ★★☆ is a simple, refreshing, lighter pale ale; **Black Golding Starkporter** ★★★☆ is a heavy-middleweight dark porter; while potent **Fimbulvinter** ★★★ is brewed from

smoked malt from Gotland and flavoured with honey and juniper twigs – not far of a *Gotlandsdricke*.

NILS OSCAR
Nyköping, Södermanland

Small 1996 brewery that was in Stockholm until 2006, with its own distillery and maltings. First brew **God Lager** ★★ is a Vienna lager with Spalt Select and Tettnanger imparting aroma and bitterness; **India Ale** ★★ is an IPA with Amarillo supplying impressive bitterness; **Rökporter** ★★☆ has a caramel, dried-fruit aroma and fairly slight smoky character despite 80% of its malt being beechwood-smoked; while the star is a great full-bodied **Barley Wine** with slight sweetness, which ages to perfection ★★★→★★★★.

DESTINATION
STOCKHOLM

The capital is awash with good beer bars but the two world-class established ones are within 100m (109 yards) of each other, by the Stadsmuseum and Slussen metro station. **Oliver Twist** (6 Repslagargatan) is a UK-style pub with 300+ Swedish and US beers, while **Akkurat** (18 Hornsgatan) is open-plan with a 600+ international range. Each has good food.

NYNÄSHAMNS ÅNGBRYGGERI
Nynäshamn, Stockholm

South of Stockholm since 1997, with a loyal following. Amber-coloured **Bedarö Bitter** ★★☆ is full-flavoured with English malt but US C-hops; blond **Landsort Lager** ★★☆ is the Swedish style, slightly sweet with medium bitterness from Perle, Tettnanger and Saaz; rounded **Brännskär Brown Ale** ★★☆ is US-style, brewed with four malts, honey and cane sugar; and **Mysingen Midvinterbrygd** ★★★ is a spicy winter ale with nutmeg, cumin, cloves, vanilla and fresh orange peel.

OCEANBRYGGERIET
Gothenburg, Västra Götaland

In the grounds of the old Lyckholms brewery since 2007. **Ocean India Pale Ale** ★★☆ is American, malty and rounded with a distinct hoppy finish; **Göteborgs Porter** ★★☆ is full-bodied in the London style, with blackcurrant on the nose, a hint of liquorice on the palate and chocolate throughout; and **Julöl** ★★☆ is a fussy winter ale with a grassy, blackcurrant aroma from a six-malt mash and five-hopped boil.

DESTINATION GOTHENBURG

The **Ölrepubliken** (2B Kronhusgatan) has been in Gothenburg city centre since 2009, having pioneered beer at a smaller place for a lot longer. Thirty taps and a huge bottle selection with good representation of smaller Swedish brewers, and food.

OPPIGÅRDS
Hedemora, Dalarna

Small 2004 farmhouse brewery, northwest of Uppsala, brewing some of the best beer

in Sweden. Nicely balanced **Golden Ale** ★★☆ mixes Goldings, Pacific Gem and Cascade; **Amarillo** ★★★ is a single-hopped American pale ale dry-hopped for aroma but perfectly balanced to give a full-bodied ale with lingering bitterness; and **Indian Tribute** ★★★ is an American IPA with citrus aroma, all the flavours expected from the style, a malty body and a long, fresh, bitter finish.

SIGTUNA/ST. ERIKS
Arlandastad, Stockholm

A shared rather than merged operation, St. Eriks using Sigtuna's facilities near Arlanda airport. The St. Eriks brands include surprisingly complex US-style **Pale Ale** ★★☆, with a nice citrus finish; and robust **Porter** ★★☆, with hints of coffee, chocolate and rye bread; and **#1 Enbär** ★★☆, a refreshing lager brewed with juniper and spruce tips. Sigtuna itself has roasted malt character **Prince of Darkness Black IPA** ★★★, with a hint of mocha and a smack of Cascade hops; and **Red Ale** ★★☆, an up-hopped, almost mahogany ale with Centennial and Amarillo.

SCANDINAVIA 145

SKEBO BRUKSBRYGGERI
Skebobruk, Stockholm

Anglophile institution celebrating the British beer heritage since 2006, producing UK-style session beers in cask-conditioned format for bars like Akkurat and Oliver Twist (*see* box, page 144), plus kegged and bottle-conditioned ales. Needs to focus but creates authentically English beers like **Triple Gold Bitter** ★★☆, hopped with East Kent and Styrian Goldings, and First Gold; and **Herrgårdsporter** ★★☆, a down-to-earth milder end porter.

FINLAND

Commercial beer making in Finland was rendered bizarre by well-meaning but ineffectual laws aimed at reducing alcohol misuse. Via a tortuous path this has led to the government-controlled national chain of liquor stores, Alko, discriminating against smaller Finnish brewers, and the long-established culture of inter-generational drinking in well-regulated pubs being priced out in favour of solitary consumption at home.

Meanwhile, massive volumes of cheap beer enter the country perfectly legally via the ferry from Estonia and the country's great heritage beer style, *sahti*, struggles to survive. It takes determination to make one's way as an entrepreneurial small brewer here, but a few exceptional people are doing so, the 30 or so new small breweries expanding at the rate of five or six a year. Our selection covers all sorts.

FINLANDIA SAHTI
Sastamala, Pirkanmaa

A legendary maker of traditional *sahti*, Finlandia is located to the west of the city of Tampere, and was saved from extinction in 2011 but is still very small. Two differing versions of *sahti* are made there, both of them as flat as pancakes, sweet and full of banana, allspice, juniper and bread pudding, the light brown **8% Sahti** ★★★ less so than the murkier, heavier and darker **10% Strong Sahti** ★★★☆.

LAITILAN
Laitila, Finland Proper

Beer and beverage maker that was established in 1995 and enjoying commercial success through making numerous supermarket labels. Splits its brands into simpler Kukko and more interesting Kievari beers, though even the latter are too restrained. Their best beers to sample are **Portteri** ★★☆, an upscale porter with some raisin and coffee; and seasonal *weizen*, **Vehnänen** ★★☆.

LAMMIN SAHTI
Hämeenlinna, Tavastia Proper

Small specialist brewery, set up in 1985 to make traditional *sahti* at Lammi hamlet, southeast of Tampere. Now the largest producer but still tiny. **Original Lammin Sahti** ★★★☆ is a murky brown symphony of spiced rotting fruit with super-smooth undertones, which are somewhat lost in the filtered version, **Juhlaolut** ★★☆, which appears in the national chain of liquor stores at Christmas.

MALMGÅRDIN
Malmgård, Uusimaa

Small brewery in a beautiful, old country house an hour northeast of Helsinki, brewing beers under two different brands. In the Malmgård range the standout is **Ceci n'est pas une Belge** ★★★, a strong, copper-brown beer with yeast-led spiciness and cleverly understated hopping; while the best Huvila beers are a Goldings-hopped **ESB** ★★☆ that beats what most British brewers would dare make; mid-range **X-Porter** ★★☆, which veers toward creamy and nutty; and chestnut-coloured, juniper-laced **Arctic Circle Ale** ★★★, which has a nice bitter finish.

NOKIAN
Nokia, Pirkanmaa

Commercially successful small brewery with an odd mix of dull and interesting beers, most sold under the name Keisari, often to different formats. Black lager **Året Runt 4.5%** ★★ is better at **5.7%** ★★☆; the canned version of **EloWehnä** *weizen* is dwarfed by the slightly stronger bottled version ★☆→★★☆; and dark winter brew **Talvi** ★★☆ is better when stronger.

PLEVNA
Tampere, Pirkanmaa

This pub-based brewery, which is also called Koskipanimo, is located in Finland's second city, and is regarded as the country's best craft producer. Its dozen or 30 regular Panimoravintola Pevna Tampere brands include a high-wheat *hefeweizen* called **Vehnäolut** ★★★; the soft, sweetish Czech-style dark lager, **Tumma** ★★☆; the sharply hopped US-style **Severin Extra IPA** ★★★☆; the sweet and soft German-style amber-coloured **Bock** ★★★; and the surprisingly approachable, tar-coloured, fruity, roasted **Siperia Imperial Stout** ★★★★.

DESTINATION
TAMPERE

The country's second city after Helsinki has its next-best beer crawl, and peaks with two self-styled gastropubs, **Tuulensuu** (16 Puutarhakatu) for more breadth and imports, and **Nordic** (3 Otavalankatu) for a more regional focus in both beer and food.

SINEBRYCHOFF (CARLSBERG)
Kerava, Uusimaa

Carlsberg's presence in the Finnish market is mostly mass. However, **Sinebrychoff Koff Porter ★★★** is a teaser that so bounces the palate with coffee-chocolate-prune that smaller brewers should be grateful it does not play serious in other styles; with US BROOKLYN BREWERY's Garrett Oliver, it has also co-designed **Sinebrychoff & Brooklyn Two Tree Porter ★★★** featuring syrups derived from Finnish spruce and New York maple trees.

STADIN
Helsinki, Uusimaa

Tiny brewery in the capital, so obsessed with experimentation that it has produced over 400 beers in 15 years, some more than once. The most frequent are semi-predictable **American Pale Ale ★★☆**; almost reliable **American Dark Ale ★★★**; steady but uninspiring **Weizen ★★**; and a Finnish interpretation of *doppelbock*, **Ultimator ★★☆**.

STALLHAGEN
Godby, Åland Islands

Small brewery on an island midway between Finland and Sweden. Produces some dull beers but more that are interesting and a few that reach excellent. Beers can be brewed differently for the Swedish market. Highlights include a gentle *dunkel* called **Delikat Dark Lager ★★**; much-praised American-style amber **US Red Ale ★★★**; a steady **Baltic Porter ★★☆**; and variable but never dull Easter seasonal **Påsköl ★★☆ → ★★★**.

SUOMENLINNAN
Helsinki, Uusimaa

Pub brewery on Suomenlinna, one of the islands that shelters Helsinki harbour from the Baltic. A recently installed bottling line is allowing its fame to spread. Reliable beers include copper-coloured UK-style pale **Coyet Ale ★★**; equally English in spirit, **Spithead Bitter ★★**; Bohemian-style Saaz-accented **Höpken Pils ★★**; and an homage to London porters called **Helsinki Portteri ★★**.

DESTINATION HELSINKI

The capital's best-known beer pubs are **One Pint** (2 Sinikaislankuja) and **St Uhro's** (10 Museokatu); the best for the beers of smaller Finnish breweries is **Villi Wäinö** (4 Kalevankatu); and the easiest to find, by the main railway station, is **Kaisla** (4 Vilhonkatu). The smoothest, best run and stocked, and most informative, is **Pikkulintu** (11 Klaavuntie), hidden in a dreary shopping precinct out near Puotila metro station – best of luck!

TEERENPELI
Lahti, Päijänne Tavastia

Small brewery at the southern end of Lake Vesijärvi, with franchised brewpubs at Tampere, Turku and Kamppi (Helsinki), making mostly solid beers. **Hippaheikki TESB ★★** is a reasonable bash at a stronger British bitter; *hefeweizen* **Vauhtiveikko ★★☆** is one of Finland's best; and **Pakkaspaavo ★★** is a sort of Scotch ale produced in winter.

VAKKA-SUOMEN
Uusikaupunki, Finland Proper

Small brewery making an increasingly interesting range of Prykmestar beers. The **Pils** ★★ is more German than most, with Perle hops; Finland's first *weizenbock*, **Wehnäbock** ★★☆, arrived in 2012; evolving and increasingly impressive **Double IPA** ★★★ is set to go far; and juniper-smoked heavyweight **Savu Kataja** ★★★, its stronger *rauchbier*, removed any doubt that the brewer means business.

ICELAND

Some visitors to the "land of fire and ice" conclude that it has little interest in brewing, unaware that beer was only decriminalized here in 1989, after 70 years. Iceland now has eight breweries, with several making beers fit to compete in the world, and its first speciality beer bars have arrived, suggesting healthy growth.

GÆÐINGUR ÖL
Sauðárkrókur, Skagafjarðarsýsla

Best and most authentic of the smaller producers, brewing with British equipment on the northwest coast. The clever **Pale Ale** ★★☆ is soft enough to coax a pils drinker but sharp enough to impress; a sweetish light-to-medium **Stout** ★★ can waver; and clearly accented hop-forward **Tumi Humall IPA** ★★★☆ is currently the country's best pale beer.

ÖLVISHOLT BRUGGHÚS
Selfoss, Árnessýsla

A 2007 start-up on a 1000-year-old farm in the southwest. **Skjálfti** ★★☆ is a blond lager with a nice bite; original **Móri** ★★☆ would be a great Vienna lager were it not an amber ale; grapefruit bitter **Röðull India Pale Ale** ★★★ is silky and confident; and **Lava** ★★★☆ is the much-exported, heavy, smoky Imperial stout made downwind from a real volcano.

VIKING ÖLGERÐ
Akureyri, Eyjafjarðarsýsla

The country's largest brewery, at the sheltered southern end of a north coast inlet. Firm, dryish **Íslenskur Úrvals Stout** ★★☆, also sold as Black Death, is their only 'special beer' though they brew four Einstök beers for a US-UK beer commissioner, including a pleasant enough **White Ale** ★★; restrained but interesting **Toasted Porter** ★★☆; and a ruddy-brown lightish **Doppelbock** ★★☆.

DESTINATION REYKJAVIK

The **Micro Bar** (6 Austurstræti) is a room at the back of the Central Hotel that somehow sources over 100 beers, mostly from Scandinavia, while up the way burger joint **73** (73 Laugavegur) serves most Icelandic bottled ales, and **K-bar** opposite (74 Laugavegur) about 60 others.

IBERIA

There is little brewing tradition on the Iberian peninsula beyond international-style lagers and a spat with Watneys Red and its ilk in the 1970s. Yet just as el Bulli taught Spanish chefs to cook outside the box, so the region's brewers are exploring the art of the possible, tantalizing with their potential, from plain to seismic.

SPAIN

First it was Italy that surprised the drinks world by daring to park a host of imaginative new beer makers on the wine world's front lawn. Then the beer bug swarmed across the vineyards of France. Next to fall will be Spain.

Thankfully, Iberian beer has moved on since British expats ensured the survival of Watneys Red Barrel on the Costa del Sol long after it had died off elsewhere. Today, encouraged by all they see developing in Europe and North America, young Spanish brewers are charging headlong into the craft beer mists, sometimes stumbling and occasionally running into a wall, but generally progressing at an encouraging pace.

ALES AGULLONS
Sant Joan de Mediona, Barcelona

One of the Spanish brewing pioneers, located west of Barcelona, creating ales that seem to have an English soul. The beautifully simple **Pura Ale ★★☆** might even appeal to some of those homesick ex-pat Brits when it appears cask-conditioned; the **Bruno ★★☆** is light brown from Crystal malts and aromatic from a mix of Cascade and Fuggles hops; while the well-off-beat **Setembre ★★★** is produced each year to a slightly different recipe but typically is a blend of Pura Ale and one-year-old lambic from Belgium's brewery **3 FONTEINEN**.

DESTINATION BARCELONA

Find a healthy mix of sought-after imports and local craft beers at the stylish **BierCaB** (55 Carrer de Muntaner) and older **Ale&Hop** (10 Carrer de les Basses de Sant Pere), while Catalonian beers rule at the estimable **HomoSibaris** (4 Plaça d'Osca) and backpacker-ish **Cat Bar** (17 Carrer de la Bòria), with cosy but oft-crowded **La Cerveteca** (25 Carrer d'En Gignàs) another suggested stop. For ease of Spanish beer exploration, watch out for the springtime Barcelona Beer Festival (www.barcelonabeerfestival.com).

ART CERVESERS
Canovelles, Barcelona

One of the pioneers of the Barcelona craft beer boom, its brewery and tap outside Canovelles reflecting the architectural splendour of the city itself. Of its Art beers, **Orus** ★★ is a solid *märzen*, **Flama** ★★☆ is an IPA more British than American in character, best sampled near to home; while **Coure** ★★☆ is an unhopped winter ale, spiced with nutmeg, cinnamon and sweet gale.

DOMUS
Toledo

Impressive, growing brewery with a reputation for solid and polished beers. **Aurea** ★★☆ is a highly aromatic and refreshing IPA favouring balance over bitterness, in contrast to pale ale **Europa** ★★, brewed with six kinds of European hop. Winter Scotch ale **Summa** ★★☆ is sweet and brown-sugary, while marzipan-inspired, almond-saffron-lemon-and-cinnamon-spiced **Greco** ★★★ may one day prove pivotal in the development of a Spanish approach to craft beer.

GUINEU
Valls de Torroella, Barcelona

Not a dedicated brewing company but rather the beer brand of a brewery supplies company, north of Barcelona. **Riner** ★★☆ is a well-above-average low-alcohol pale ale with a rabid hop bite giving it spirit; **Antius** ★★ is an ordinary bitter that could cope in an English pub despite American hops; and **Montserrat** ★★★ is an inspired, multi-layered stout with a surprise with almost every sip.

MILANA
Montemayor de Pililla, Valladolid

Youthful and energetic brewery located north of Madrid, with obvious potential apparent in beers like the surprisingly dry and hoppy *witbier*, **Trigo** ★★; the floral, perfumey and peppery pale ale, **Bonita** ★★☆; and the comparatively benign, toasty amber ale, **Tostada** ★☆. Best is a limited edition black IPA called **Black Feet** ★★☆, with a light sweetness giving way to burnt citrus peel and roasty bitterness.

DESTINATION MADRID

The Spanish capital is developing its entire beer scene in one very walkable district. Begin at the **Fábrica Maravillas** brewpub (29 Calle Valverde), stop to pick up a few bottles for later at **Cervezorama** (29 Calle de San Andrés) or **La Birratorium** (21 Calle de Blasco de Garay) and finish the night at **Animal** (9 Calle Hartzenbusch), being sure to save room for a sampling of the bar's impressive cuisine.

MONTSENY
Sant Miquel de Balenyà, Barcelona

The biggest and most ambitious of the Spanish newbies, north of Barcelona in northern Catalonia, aiming for a wider audience. **Lupulus** ★★ is a fresh, balanced and refreshing mainstream IPA; whereas **Malta** ★☆ is pedestrian in its raw form but interesting after a year in wine barrels as **Malta Cuveé** ★★☆, the love child of pale ale and oak-aged Chardonnay. Winter ale **HivernAle** changes recipe slightly every year but is always spice-loaded with a pinch of muscovado sugar ★☆→★★☆.

on one side, pine and herbs on the other and rock 'n' roll at its heart.

NAPARBIER
Noáin, Navarre

A cooperative located near the town of Pamplona that has quickly earned respect beyond Spain and seems to improve with every batch. **Janis Porter** ★★ is roasted, with coffee and citrus bringing some lightness; **ZZ+ ★★☆** is a refreshing, complex amber beer of contrasts, with syrup and caramel

YRIA
Toledo

Although plans are in place to open a brewery in Toledo, at present this is part of beer commissioner Yria-Guinea Pigs, both operated by the co-owners of Madrid's Cervezorama beer shop (*see* box, page 151). Named after the daughter of one of the co-owners, Yria is the more conventional label, brewing ales like the solidly malty, faintly spicy **Golden** ★★☆ and singularly rich, cocoa-ish and mildly sweet **Obscura** ★★☆.

PORTUGAL

While beer is popular in Portugal, the market is utterly dominated by two breweries: Unicer, co-owned by Portugal's Viacer Group (56%) and Carlsberg (44%) and maker of the mainstream Super Bock brands; and Heineken-owned Central de Cervejas, brewers of the equally mass-market Sagres line. Visitors confused by the repeated presence of *cervejarias* – literally "breweries" – need know that these places, though often wonderfully atmospheric and almost always fine locales in which to spend an evening, are typically beer halls or restaurants without brewing facilities, in the fashion of many French brasseries.

We know of a handful of craft brewing set-ups, most very new and centred around Porto: Os Três Cervejeiros, makers of the Sovina line of beers in the city itself; Fermentum with its Minho beers at Braga; Amphora, which opened its doors in early 2014 just north of Braga; and Vadia to the south. Closer to Lisbon is new arrival, Cerveja Toira, not far from one of the country's few brewpubs, Praxis in Coimbra.

THE BALTIC STATES

The post-Soviet Baltic pecking order sees Latvia and Lithuania normally competing for second place behind Estonia. In brewing the rule is reversed, as a countryside tradition of folk brewing from the Lithuanian highlands vies with early Latvian interest, leaving Estonia behind, though this may change soon.

ESTONIA

Well over 95% of Estonian beer is brewed by three foreign-owned companies. The largest, Saku, is part of Carlsberg; historically important A Le Coq is now owned by Olvi of Finland; and the third, Viru, by Harboe of Denmark. Recent years have seen efforts to bring new beers to the market, with most wildly off the mark, or else poorly promoted. New thinking is required and may be arriving.

ÕLLENAUT
Saue, Harjumaa

A new, small brewery located southwest of Tallinn that is the young face of modern Estonian brewing, proving that it can do a range of different styles – simple with its solid, fruity, bready amber **Kuldne Eil ★★**; bold with its **Eesti Rukki Eil ★★☆**, a rye beer that sits like pungent pumpernickel bread in a glass; or ballsy, with the deep red-brown, wood-smoked, leathery **Suitsu Porter ★★☆**.

ESTONIAN RYE ALE

Eesti
Rukki Eil
ÕLLENAUT

CERVEZA · BEER · ÕLU · BIER · OLUT

DESTINATION TALLINN

Two bars that are located in the capital's old town try hard to raise awareness of quality beers, for now relying more on imports than on beers from local producers. **Drink Baar** (8 Vaike Karja) is a nice UK-style pub that is run by an expat, while **Hell Hunt** (39 Pikk) is a youthful hang-out that nonetheless tolerates older beer travellers.

SILLIMÄE ÕLLETEHAS
Sillamäe, Ida-Virumaa

The fourth-largest Estonian brewer, this minnow was founded in 1993 in a Baltic port near the Russian border. Makes four München brand beers that include a variable blond lager called **Hele ★★**; a dark brown one called **Tume ★★**; and a stronger, copper-coloured Vienna lager, **Vaskne ★★**, with syrupy backtastes.

TAAKO
Pihtla, Saaremaa

On the western island of Saaremaa, this brewery may well be the last commercial producer of koduõlu, an Estonian type of blond *sahti*. Its **Pihtla Õlu ★★☆** is a hazy, sharpish, herbal and clove-laden ale with a taste profile somewhere between the Finnish speciality and a lambic. There are other producers on the island but we suspect they are unlicensed.

LATVIA

The Latvian beer scene is starting to germinate. Its three largest breweries, Aldaris, Cēsu and Līvu-Lāčplēša, are all part of large Scandinavian groups and historically its better-organized independents have remained conservative. However, a new clutch of brewpubs is emerging especially in the capital, Riga, and a growing band of enthusiastic and competent home-brewers are starting to brew commercially.

ABULA
Brenguļi, Vidzeme

Former farm brewery (1969) on the Abula River near Valmiera in the north, hiring a German brewer once it grew, following independence and privatization. Its two Brenguļu beers are as typical of Latvian beer as it gets, **Gaišais ★★** being a hazy, sweetish stronger pale lager; and **Tumšais ★★☆** a murky-brown country *dunkel* with sweet caramel, raisins and subtle roasting.

ALDARIS (CARLSBERG)
Riga

This, Latvia's largest brewery, makes roughly half of the nation's beer. Its

principle brands are safe and unexciting, a charge that cannot be levelled at **Porteris ★★☆**, a medium-to-full-bodied, dark ruby-brown Baltic porter with a bitter chocolate aroma and roasted malt, liquorice and molasses.

DESTINATION
RIGA

ALEhouse (12 Lāčplēša iela) is the capital's top beer bar and shop, located in the embassy district and serving a brilliant range of 200 beers to a local audience keen to learn. Food all day, every day, too.

MADONAS ALUS
Bodnieki, Vidzeme

Tiny 2009 brewery associated with an old country house near Madona, 100km (62 miles) east of Riga, producing a well-offbeat, honeyed, cloudy pale draught beer, **Madonas Bodnieku Gaišais** ★★, unfiltered, musty and medicinal. There is a stronger beer too.

MALDUGUNS
Cēsis, Vidzeme

Small brewery that opened in 2013 northeast of Riga to make UK- and US-inspired ales, starting with copper-coloured bitter full of malt and English hops, **Rudais Rudens** ★★; dry, dark-as-night porter **Pilota Nakts** ★★; and a sweet, herbal double IPA called **Lauvas Pacietība** ★★.

TĒRVETE, AGROFIRMA
Kroņauce, Zemgale

Collective farm brewery (1971) with its own maltings, near Tērvete, southwest of Riga. Generally regarded as the best of the established smaller brewers, making five different pale Tērvetes lagers. Top beer is **Oriģinālais** ★★☆, a full-bodied, deep golden, wholesome-tasting pils with a bitter finish; with the *zwickelbier*, **Nefiltrētais** ★★, also worthy.

UŽAVAS ALUS
Užava, Kurzeme

Small 1994 brewery located not far south of Latvia's largest port, Ventspils. Brews mostly two Užavas beers: the lighter, balanced and sweetish **Gaišais**; and the slightly stronger **Tumšais**, which is a chewy, toffee-laced comfort beer with mild roasty flavours and caramel, each better when unfiltered ★★→★★★☆.

VALMIERMUIŽA
Valmiera, Vidzeme

A small brewery in the same town as ABULA, established in 2009, making its regular beers more carefully than other traditional brewers leading to greater attenuation. The unfiltered draught versions of **Gaišais** ★★ and **Tumšais** ★★ are noticeably better.

LITHUANIA

Lithuania deserves a special place in the world of beer.

Most of the country enjoys a culture typical in much of Eastern Europe 25 years on from the fall of the Berlin Wall – a few larger breweries owned by foreign companies, some smaller ones seeking to expand and a growing clutch of brewpubs from which entrepreneurial craft brewers are starting to emerge, making around 80 in total.

However, in the northeastern Aukštaitija region, or Highlands, there remain two dozen breweries making *kaimiškas alus*, or "country beers", unique relics of brewing practices long-gone elsewhere.

These are run mainly by local people looking to make a living by supplying their wares to a few villages. Until recently, few were ever seen outside the region, but then a couple of beer bars in the capital, Vilnius, began to obtain supplies, and since then interest in the countryside beer culture has started to grow.

Locally honed brewing traditions include that, instead of being added to sweet wort in a separate boil, hops are stewed separately and added directly to the mash in the form of a tea. Fermentation then takes place in open vessels, sometimes kept underground, using yeast strains that have mutated without being refreshed, often over decades.

The extent to which the Soviet authorities knew about these local brewing activities is a moot point, though they had been in existence long before the 50 years of Russian rule ended in 1990. Ironically, since independence and European Union membership, the number of traditional brewhouses, some quite primitive, has dwindled as licensing regulators insist that equipment be modernized.

These are not entrepreneurial enterprises hungry for publicity and few can be visited on a whim. Rather they are run by people of modest means, survivors of a craft tradition, baffled by and wary of the renaissance of interest that is enabling them to sell their idiosyncratic products into an entirely alien market in the capital, their plastic bottles speaking of ill-preparedness.

Kaimiškas alus are not robust and should be discovered as fresh and close to source as possible. They are unlikely ever to be suitable for export, varying hugely in flavour and character, and with few reference points to compare their often raw character to more conventional types of beer. Star-rating them is thus made difficult, though we have tried.

BUTAUTŲ DVARO BRAVORAS
Biržai, Panevėžys

Traditional brewery located in an old manor close to the Latvian border, that was once used by Soviet officials to "relax". **Šviesus** ★★☆ is a quenching, mineral vehicle with toasted cereals and herbal hops; while **Tamsus** ★★☆ has earthy nuances and strays from heavy caramel to evolve bready and spicy flavours.

ČIŽO ALUS
Dusetos, Utena

This tiny brewery, which is located in a house outside the village of Dusetos, oozes local colour. This is possibly the last remaining brewer of authentic *keptinis*, a beer in which malted barley is baked into a bread before being steeped in water and then mashed with hops. The resulting unnamed beer ★★☆ is a near-flat, earthy, woody, slightly smoky, rough-and-ready time-travel brew.

DAVRA
Pakruojis, Šiauliai

Small, purpose-built brewery in the heart of the Highlands brewing region. Its stalwart, **Varniuku ★★★** is a rich, raisiny dark brew, or *tamsus*; **Daujotų ★★★** is a supremely toasty blond affair; and **Linksmieji Vyrukai ★★☆** is an equally toasty but slicker amber-hued companion. A remarkably luxurious tasting room is available if you call ahead.

JOVARU ALUS
Jovarai, Utena

An unmarked house in the hamlet of Jovarai that is the domain of the queen of Lithuanian traditional brewing, whose main beer bears her name. **Aldona Udriene ★★★** is a toasty, fruity and quenching brew that is the house beer at Šnekutis (*see* box, above right). Mashed with its hops and fermented at nearly 30°C (86°F), it ends up tasting like an ancient rustic ESB. The honey-infused bottled version, **Su Medumi ★★☆** is sweeter and smoother.

DESTINATION
VILNIUS

The capital's best outlets for draught countryside beers are the two **Šnekutis** bars. The first, like a cottage that got lost in the city, can be found at 7a Polocko gatvé; the second, smarter bar, is located more centrally at 8 Šv. Stepono gatvé. For bottled beers, the highly civilized, stone-walled cellar bar and shop **Bambalyne** (7 Stiklių gatvé) is better.

KUPIŠKIO ALUS
Kupiškis, Panevėžys

At this brewery, located inside one of the town's former food bunkers, with a tiny shop on site. **Magaryčių Alus ★★☆** is brewed with roasted hazelnuts to make a balanced marvel of local *je-ne-sais-quoi*; **Keptinis ★★☆** is a polished modern take on a forgotten smoky style; **Patulo Alus ★★☆** aligns citrus fruitiness with lightly toasted malts; while **Salaus Alus ★★** is an elegant *šviesus* containing honey and citrus accents.

KURKLIŲ BRAVORAS
Kurklių, Utena

A tiny brewery that is part of the Aukštaitijos brewing group, which tries to protect and grow the area's unique beer culture. Its only beer is the extraordinary **I O Boiko ★★★**, which adjoins rye to spicy hops, haystack and banana esters creating huge character. Some batches are also brewed and bottled at BUTAUTŲ.

MORKŪNO ALUS
Pasvalys, Panevėžys

A modest, one-man operation in an unmarked house in a small country town. His beer **Morkūno ★★☆** has typical *kaimiškas alus* earthiness with herbal elements in a faintly carbonated, highly drinkable liquid.

PINIAVOS ALUTIS
Piniava, Panevėžys

Small brewery in an apartment building outside the city that is the unofficial capital of the Highlands. **Seklyčios ★★★** is a thirst-quencher in which fresh toasted malts and elegant honeyed sweetness converge; **Laukinių Aviečių ★★☆** is the same beer filtered through raspberry bush branches; while using a bed of red clover to filter **Raudonųųų Dobilų ★★** lends it floral character.

ŠIRVĖNOS BRAVORAS
Panevėžys

Founded in 1997 in a small city in the Highlands. A mix of regular and traditional brewer, its products get better the further they veer from the Lithuanian mainstream. Best in a range of a dozen Dindulis beers are unfiltered dark rye lager **Dounkelis ★★★**, with great character for a lightish beer; **Gutstoutas ★★☆**, a relatively bitter, well-attenuated oatmeal stout; and newcomer **Dubults ★★☆**, a fragrant, sweetish double IPA.

SU PUTA
Paliūniškis, Panevėžys

In a small warehouse, with a bottle-filling shop for walk-in patrons. **Senovinis-Senolių ★★☆** is a powerful yeasty wheat beer with a potent hop character; **Sidabrinē Puta Šviesus ★★** is toasted and floral; **Paliūniškis Medutis ★★** has mild honey flavours balanced out by leafy hops; and **Stiprus Tamsus ★★☆** is a winter showcase of bready caramel and warming alcohol.

TARUŠKŲ ALAUS BRAVORAS
Trakiškio, Panevėžys

Excellent small brewery near Panevėžys, which is also part of the Aukštaitijos group. **Šviesus ★★★** delights with modest barnyard character and spicy hop bitterness; **Kanapinis Tamsus ★★** is a textbook brown ale; and **Su Kanapemis ★★** is a quaffer that is brewed with hemp seeds.

ITALY

Italy is a wine land, no doubt, but it is also very much a gastronomically inclined nation and it is this fact that has allowed the Italian craft brewing industry to develop, grow and indeed prosper in a relatively short period of time.

From almost the moment craft beer appeared on the Italian scene, its creators have made the dining table their focus, creating beers that harmonize well with the local cuisine, packaging in ornate, restaurant-friendly bottles and marketing their wares at the kind of prices that almost demand respect. It has been a successful strategy, establishing in short order Italian craft beer as a comparable alternative to wine, rather than a cheaper substitute better suited to quenching thirst than complementing dinner.

It helps, of course, that Italian craft breweries have shown a steady improvement since they came on the scene in force around the year 2000. The past several years, in particular, have seen remarkable progress in both the quality and quantity of Italian craft beers, to the point where some breweries might now be said to rival the best producers in northern Europe in terms of brewing creativity and flavour complexity.

While brewing remains still most concentrated in the north, Rome is emerging as the titular centre of Italian craft beer, with the populace growing increasingly enamoured of ales and lagers of quality and character.

32 VIA DEI BIRRAI
Pederobba, Treviso

Brilliant brewery in the Veneto region named for the Belgium telephone country code and known for its clever marketing ideas. Flagship **Oppale ★★★** is a hoppy ale with a bitter finish reminiscent of chives; cloudy, spiced **Curmi ★★☆** is brewed with spelt and barley malt;

Audace ★★ is a fruity, spicy strong golden ale; local chestnut honey flavours the full-bodied **Nectar ★★**.

ALMOND '22 BEER
Spoltore, Pescara

Brewery located in a disused almond-processing plant – hence the name –

near Pescara in coastal Abruzzo. Organic spelt and honey lend a sweet nuttiness to **Farrotta** ★★; smoky, plummy, cinnamony **Torbata** ★★★ is brewed with peated malt; and **Pink IPA** ★★★ is named after the pink peppercorns that give the beer an appealingly zippy spiciness.

AMIATA
Arcidosso, Grosseto

Small sibling-operated Tuscan brewery that has had its problems in the past, but appears more consistently reliable now. Tropical-fruit and pine flavours dominate **Contessa** ★★, billed an "Italian pale ale"; while saffron-spiced **Crocus** ★★ combines fruitiness with a spicy floral character. Best is the chestnut beer, **Vecchia Bastarda** ★★★, aged in wine barrels for a sweet and vanilla-accented nutty fruitiness.

B94
Lecce

Worthy brewery located in southern Puglia, a region known as "the heel of the boot". Deep amber **Terrarossa** ★★★ is a well-balanced ESB with nutty, toffee flavours and a dry, hoppy finish; **Porteresa** ★★ is a robust porter brewed from six kinds of barley malt and Fairtrade cane sugar; sweet and fruity **Malagrika** ★★☆, brewed with significant amounts of local quince jelly, is perfect to pair with matured cheeses.

BALADIN, LE
Piozzo, Cuneo

Italy's most famous craft brewery, founded in mid-1990s by creative innovator Teo Musso in Piedmont. **Isaac** ★★☆ is a pioneering Belgian-style wheat beer, rich in exotic fruit flavours; **Wayan** ★★☆ is a zesty, fruity *saison*; ancient Egypt-inspired **Nora** ★★★ is spiced with ginger and myrrh; former flagship brand, the warming, nutty **Super** ★★★, was designed to pair with food; targeted oxidization give sherry flavours to the still, intense and already classic **Xyauyù** ★★★★.

BARLEY
Maracalagonis, Cagliari

South Sardinia brewery that began the Italian trend of using wine must in brewing. **Friska** ★★☆ is a characterful, quenching wheat ale; local orange-blossom honey makes **Zagara** ★★☆ a pleasant, refreshing session beer; amber, malty **Sella del Diavolo** ★★☆ is an Italian take on the French *bière de garde*; **Toccadibò** ★★★ is a warming golden ale with dryly bitter and amaretto-ish finish; strong and vinous **BB10** ★★★☆ is an astonishing barley wine made with local Cannonau grapes.

BI-DU
Olgiate Comasco, Como

Located near Lake Como, this brewery is best known for its bravely hoppy beers. The **Rodersch** ★★☆ is a flowery, herbal, hoppy take on a *kölsch*; the **ArtigianAle** ★★★ is well balanced and strong; generously hoppy **Confine** ★★☆ is a coffee-ish and smoky porter; the **H10op5** ★★☆ is highly hopped with 10 varieties added in five stages; while quenching, dry, flowery **Saaz of Anarchy** ★★ is a tribute to Saaz hops and anarchist ideology.

BIRRONE
Isola Vicentina, Vicenza

Recently expanded brewery with a taproom in the Veneto region, brewing a wide range of lagers and a few ales. Clean, elegant **Brusca ★★★** is dry, bitter, traditional pils; the use of Vienna malt and Cascade hops combines German and American brewing influences, producing the unique beer **Gerica ★★**; and the sweet, malty amber *bock* gets the mischevious name of **Punto G ★★**, Italian for G-spot.

BORGO, BIRRA DEL
Borgorose, Rieti

Successful brewery located northeast of Rome, specializing in interesting seasonals and experimental brews. Citrus-fruity and piney flagship **Re Ale ★★★** pioneered the US-style pale ale in Italy; refreshingly sweet and mellow **Duchessa ★★☆** uses local spelt; strong and hoppy pilsner **My Antonia ★★★** is a collaboration with the US's DOGFISH HEAD BREWING; smoky, roasted **KeTo RePorter ★★☆** is well balanced despite being infused with tobacco leaves from Kentucky.

GERmania-amerICA (6.0)

DESTINATION
ROME

Once a beer desert, the Italian capital is now also the nation's craft beer capital. Not to be missed is **Ma Che Siete Venuti a Fà** (25 via Benedetta), with a clever rotation of classics and rarities on tap. Across the street is **Bir&Fud** (23 via Benedetta) with excellent food and a wide, varying selection of Italian craft beers, while not far away is **Open Baladin Roma** (5–6 via degli Specchi) with 100+ bottles of Italian craft beers and an impressive 40 taps.

BREWFIST
Codogno, Lodi

Young brewery taking southern Italy by storm from its base in Lombardy. **24K Golden Ale ★★☆** shows citrus and peach notes when bottled but is more best bitter-like on cask; a perfumey start to **Spaceman India Pale Ale ★★** is obliterated by mid-palate hoppiness; **Burocracy India Pale Ale ★★☆** fares better with caramel maltiness and herbal, citrus hops; **Fear Milk Chocolate Stout ★★☆** delivers on its name with a creamy, roasty character.

BRÙTON
San Cassiano di Moriano, Lucca

Export-minded brewery and restaurant offshoot of a successful Tuscan winery, located near Pisa. **Flagship Brùton ★★** is light and fragrantly spicy; **Stoner ★★☆** is loaded with tropical-fruit notes balanced by hop and rye spiciness;

pale ale **Lilith ★★** has a restrained hoppiness and lots of yeasty character; the spelt, wheat and barley brew **Bianca ★★☆** is floral and quenching.

CARROBIOLO, BIRRA DEL CONVENTO
Monza, Milan

Milan-area brewery that unusually names all its beers after their original gravity (OG). **O.G. 1045 ★★★** is a *kölsch*-style ale with pineapple and gooseberry notes from New Zealand hops; **O.G. 1043 ★★** is a fragrant and floral wheat beer that finishes citrus and off-dry; **O.G. 1056 ★★** is a dryly spicy pils; and ultra-strong **O.G. 1111 ★★★** is a barely carbonated, peaty warmer loaded with flavours of raisin and date.

CITABIUNDA
Neive, Cuneo

Belgian-influenced brewpub housed in an old school building in the heart of the vineyards of Piedmont. Strongly spiced *witbier* **Biancaneive ★★★** is refermented with Champagne yeast; **Black Rebel ★☆** is an unusual dry

stout brewed with locally made cocoa-mint cream; dangerous quaffable **Serpica ★★☆** is a Belgian-style strong golden ale brewed with lime zest, becoming **Serpicata ★★★** when blended and aged in oak barrels with *Brettanomyces*.

CIVALE
Spinetta Marengo, Alessandria

Rapidly improving craft brewery near Alessandria. Quaffable **Alica ★☆** is a blond ale with bready and malty flavours; flagship **Lùmina ★★★** is an irresistible pale ale with a clean, dry finish; amber ale **Ulula ★★** is the brewery's most bitter beer, with aggressive citrus and exotic-fruit flavours.

CROCE DI MALTO
Trecate, Novara

Brewery touting itself as "the evolution of tradition", situated between Milan and Turin. Orange-hued **Temporis ★★** is a spiced ale with lovely bitter and peppery notes; **Magnus ★★** is a dark and strong ale, spicy and roasty with dried-fruit flavours; flagship **Triplexxx ★★★** is a sweet and fruity, internationally awarded strong golden ale.

DESTINATION
NICORVO

Sherwood Music Pub (7 via Giarone) is a temple for beer enthusiasts near Milan, featuring tasty pizzas, Italian craft beers and many rare selections from Belgium and Germany collected by the passionate owner-traveller.

DADA
Correggio, Reggio Emilia

Young, enterprising craft brewery in Emilia-Romagna, named after the avant-garde art movement. **Tzara** ★★ is a fresh wheat ale with exotic-fruit flavours; **Lop Lop** ★★ is a peppery, gently hoppy IPA; **Gattomao** ★★☆ is a fruity, hoppy amber ale take on the French *bière de garde*; **Rrose Sélavy** ★★★, named for one of artist Marcel Duchamp's pseudonyms, is a peppery, zesty and yeasty *saison*.

DEL DUCATO
Roncole Verdi di Busseto, Parma

From the Parma village where Verdi was born comes this much-awarded brewery. **Verdi Imperial Stout** ★★★ is a lovely mix of peppery spice and espresso, better still in barrel-aged **Black Jack** ★★★ version; **Chimera** ★★★☆ is warming, faintly cinnamony and spicy, evoking thoughts of a fine Barolo wine; flagship **VIÆMILIA** ★★★ is a crisp and ideally balanced lager; and seasonal **Winterlude** ★★★ is tropical-fruity and herbal, with a more bitter and warming finish.

DOPPIO MALTO BREWING
Erba, Como

Brewery located in Lombardy and attached to an American-style restaurant. **Bitterland** ★★☆ is a dry, crisp golden ale made with five different American hops; **Mahogany IPA** ★★ is as dark, citrus and hoppy as its name suggests; liquorice and coffee notes are obvious in the chocolate stout, **Old Jack** ★★.

EXTRAOMNES
Marnate, Varese

Belgian-inspired Lombardy brewery with a taste for experimental brewing. **Blond** ★★☆ is a light golden ale with impressive complexity; special offering **Zest** ★★ is similar, but more peppery and lemony thanks to the use of Citra hops; **Tripel** ★★★ is sweetish with preserved lemon notes and a warming finish; **Donker** ★★☆ has a sweet espresso flavour accented by chocolate-raisin notes.

FOGLIE D'ERBA
Forni di Sopra, Udine

Much-awarded brewpub in the Dolomites, focused on brewing with local and Fairtrade spices. **Babél** ★★☆ is a pale ale with a bitter, long finish; **Hopfelia** ★★★ is a strong IPA spiced with local mugo pine to a fresh and resiny bitterness; black IPA **Ulysses** ★★☆ is a successful mix of roasted wheat and barley malts and with ample hoppiness; **Song from the Wood** ★★☆ is a strong, coffee-ish Imperial stout.

FORTE, DEL
Pietrasanta, Lucca

Young and dynamic craft brewery in touristy Versilia coast area. Thirst-quenching, zesty, dry **Gassa d'Amante** ★★☆ is the house session beer; **2 Cilindri** ★★★ is a coffee-ish and roasty porter with a slightly smoky finish; ripe fruit notes are detectable in the golden strong ale **La Mancina** ★★★, which becomes **La Mancina XL** ★★☆ in its stronger and spiced version.

GECO
Milan

An interesting and promising small brewery located near Milan. Seven different malts make their flagship **Pecora Nera ★★★** a very quaffable milk stout with tobacco and liquorice notes; the **Barabba ★★** is a strong dark ale with a bitter, citrusy and piney finish; and a blend of four different local cherries is added to the fruity, woody **Scarfiun ★★☆**, oak-barrel-aged for eight months.

GRADO PLATO
Chieri, Turin

Pub and brewery located near Turin in Piedmont, with brands instantly recognizable thanks to its elegant swing-top bottle. **Strada S. Felice ★★★** is a nutty, toffee and orange brandy-ish chestnut ale; unusual **Weizentea ★★☆** combines wheat with green tea and American hops, and successfully so; **Sveva ★★☆** is a quaffable homage to Bavarian *helles*.

DESTINATION
MILAN

New arrival **Lambiczoon** (46 via Friuli) places its focus upon sour beers, while another new entry, **Baladin Milano** (56 via Solferino), offers a wide selection from Italy's most recognized craft brewery. Beer store **Bere Buona Birra** (13 via Adige) offers three taps, one handpump and numerous bottles from local small breweries, and pioneering brewpub, **Birrificio Lambrate**, now boasts two locations, the tiny original (5 via Adelchi) and the large and modern taproom (60 via Golgi).

ITALIANO
Lurago Marinone, Como

Technically focused brewery midway between Milan and the Swiss border. **Tipopils ★★★** drinks like an homage to the best of Czech brewing, with marvellous balance and structure; **Extra Hop ★★☆** is similarly German pils inspired; **Bi-Weizen ★★** is a malty,

slightly heavy *hefeweizen*; **Bibock** ★★☆ offers toffee-ish malt with a drying finish; **Vùdù** ★★★ is a delicious clove and cocoa take on a slightly potent *dunkelweisse*.

KAMUN
Predosa, Alessandria

Young, lower Piedmont craft brewery making promising ales. **Prima Lux** ★★★ is a crisp, dry-hopped session beer; much-awarded oatmeal stout **Nocturna** ★★★ is soft, velvety and silky on the palate; **Occasum** ★★ is a surprisingly balanced amber ale generously spiced with hibiscus flowers, orange peel, ginger and cinnamon.

KARMA
Alvignano, Caserta

Located near Naples, this brewery emphasizes local ingredients and spices. **Cubulteria** ★★ is a full-bodied, malty and strong wheat ale; reddish **Carminia** ★★ is a sessionable English-style IPA with a herbal and bitter finish; **Lemon Ale** ★★☆ is a refreshing, zesty wheat and rye ale with coriander and local lemon peel; **Centesimale** ★★☆ is a warming and vinous strong ale made with grape must and local apple jam.

LARIANO
Dolzago, Lecco

Creative and versatile brewery in Lombardy. English-style bitter, **Miloud** ★★, is well balanced between malt and hops; **Aura** ★☆ is a sweet blond ale spiced with coriander and orange peel; strong golden ale **Tripè** ★★ is malty, fruity and warming; the addition of salt

and coriander make **Salada** ★★ a citric wheat ale take on a Leipziger *gose*.

DESTINATION
NEMBRO

Birroteca The Dome (15 via Case Sparse Europa) is a large pub deserving of more success than yet realized, with an extensive rotating selection of taps and bottles emphasizing emerging craft breweries, especially local ones.

LOVERBEER
Marentino, Turin

Punning on his own name, home-brewer Valter Loverier went pro with this exceptional enterprise near Turin. The best brands are barrel-aged, like the tart, sour cherry-ish, appetizing **Dama Brun-a** ★★★, the spontaneously fermented **BeerBera** ★★★, fermented with Barbera grapes; and the plummy, sweet-and-sour **BeerBrugna** ★★★. Fresher, grapey and cinnamon-ish **D'uuvaBeer** ★★ is lovely, as well.

MAIELLA
Casoli, Chieti

Central Italian (Abruzzo region) brewery using local ingredients also prized by area's renowned pasta makers. Durum wheat and lavender flowers are used in refreshing, herbal, bitter **Noviluna** ★★☆; **Cluviae** ★★ is a fruity, flowery, green-apple-flavoured golden ale; acacia honey makes amber ale **Matthias** ★★★ sweet, soft and fruity; **Bucefalo** ★★☆ is an elegant foreign extra stout with roasty, balsamic flavours.

MALTOVIVO
Capriglia Irpina, Avellino

Experienced craft brewery in the Campania region. Fresh, flowery, dry **Tschö!** ★★ is an interpretation of the *kölsch* style; coppery **Noscia** ★★☆ is a well-balanced US-style IPA with resinous herbal notes; robust **Black Lizard** ★★ is a coffee-ish, roasty and slightly smoked porter; and vinous, warming **Memoriae** ★★★ is a dark strong ale successfully aged in oak barrels that previously held local Taurasi wine.

MALTUS FABER
Genoa

Environmentally aware brewery focused on interpretations of Belgian styles. **Bianca** ★★ is a refreshing, unspiced Belgian-style wheat beer; **Blonde** ★★☆ is herbal and hoppy; well-balanced **Ambrata** ★★☆ has biscuity and nutty flavours; **Triple** ★★☆ is a dangerous, quaffable, strong and fruity ale; Belgian-inspired **Extra Brune** ★★★ is soft, dark and warming.

MANEBA
Striano, Naples

Promising operation near Naples brewing interpretations of classic styles. Blond ale **L'Oro Di Napoli** ★★ is malty and zesty with a dry finish; **Clelia** ★☆ is a peppery and lemony take on a Belgian-style wheat beer; **Vesuvia** ★★ is a fruity, warming amber ale spiced with coriander; fruity flavours and a bitter finish place **Masaniello** ★★☆ somewhere between an IPA and a dark strong ale.

MANERBA BREWERY
Manerba del Garda, Brescia

Manerba is Garda's lakefront brewery and restaurant. **La Bionda** ★★ is a classic *helles*, malty with gentle hop flavours; a hoppier, unfiltered lager simply called **Pils** ★★★ is dry and crisp; **Route 66** ★★ is a clean, dry-hopped US-style pale ale with grapefruit flavours; while **Rebuffone** ★☆ is a roasty, fruity brown ale close to a Belgian *dubbel*.

MENARESTA
Carate Brianza, Monza and Brianza

Gastronomically inclined brewery located near Milan. Bread yeast-fermented **Birra Madre** ★★☆ has a gently tangy, pear-ish fruitiness; quaffable **Bevara** ★★ is dry with peppery peach-pie notes; elderflower-flavoured **Flora Sambuco** ★★☆ recalls elderflower cordial with a peppery finish; **22 La Verguenza** ★★☆ is a strong IPA with piney, almost garlicky hoppiness, which drinks better in its lighter **La Verguenza Summer IPA** ★★★ edition.

MISTER DRINK
Cervia, Ravenna

The town of Cervia on the Adriatic Riviera is best known for its salt, which appears in everything from chocolate to beauty products to a beer called **Salinae** ★★★. Light in alcohol content and colour, it has a minerally aroma, a gentle body with lemony, salty notes and a sustained minerality that gives the impression of a health drink as much as a beer.

MONTEGIOCO
Montegioco, Alessandria

Named for the Alessandrian town in which it is based, this impressive brewery makes excellent use of wine barrels, as per its star, **La Mummia** ★★★★, a spicy-tart, vanilla-accented golden ale aged in Barbera barrels. Montegioco also brews the mildly fruity **Runa** ★★★, a golden ale used as a base beer for other brands; **Tentatripel** ★★★, a spicy, candied-pear nightcap; and **Tibir** ★★☆, a peachy, passionfruity ale.

OLMAIA, L'
Sant'Albino di Montepulciano, Siena

Tuscan wine country brewery. Their hoppy, quaffable **La 5** ★★☆ is a basic blond ale; local grains are the secret of the dry and thirst-quenching **PVK** ★★★; **La 9** ★★ is a strong, complex amber ale with caramel and dried-fruit flavours; **BK** ★★ is a gentle dry stout with liquorice and coffee flavours and a dry finish.

OLMO
Arsego di San Giorgio delle Pertiche, Padua

Young craft brewery in Padua area, aspiring to become the Italian version of Scottish iconoclasts, BREWDOG. Hops from US, New Zealand and Japan make **Mundaka** ★★, a light, refreshing summer ale; **White Rabbit** ★★ is a spiced, peppery wheat ale brewed with unmalted spelt; golden ale **Butterfly** ★☆ reveals citrus and exotic fruit flavours; **Guerrilla IPA** ★★ is an aggressively hoppy pale ale.

OPPERBACCO
Notaresco, Teramo

Enterprising craft brewery in Abruzzo region, using pure water from Gran Sasso mountain. Fresh and tangy wheat ale **Bianca Piperita** ★★ is unusually spiced with peppermint; roasty, coffee-ish **10 e Lode** ★★★ is a strong dark ale that turns smoky when infused with tobacco to become **Extra Vecchio** ★★☆, and vinous when barrel-aged for **Barricata 050** ★★☆ and **Sour 050** ★★☆.

ORSO VERDE, L'
Busto Arsizio, Varese

Lombardy brewery that produces uncompromising ales. Golden ale **Wabi** ★★★ is irresistibly flowery, fruity and extremely dry; **Back Door Bitter** ★★☆ is rich in caramel, citrus-fruit flavours with a long and dryly bitter finish; robust porter **Nubia** ★★☆ features roasty, liquorice and coffee flavours; **Rebelde** ★★ is a strong amber ale made sweet with Belgian malts and bitter with American hops.

PANIL (BIRRIFICIO TORRECHIARA)
Torrechiara, Parma

Craft brewery near Parma, pioneering in spontaneous fermentation. Former flagship **Panil Ambrè** ★★ is a fruity, roasty amber ale; flat lambic-like **Divina** ★★★ is spontaneously fermented by local bacteria and wild yeasts; brown ale **Panil Barriquée** ★★★ is fermented 15 days in stainless steel, then 90 days in oak and 30 days in the bottle; sour version **Panil Barriquée Sour** ★★★☆ has lactic, vinegary flavours.

PASTURANA
Pasturana, Alessandria

Lower Piedmont craft brewery, museum and brewing school. **Filo d'Arianna** ★★ is a fresh, fruity, sessionable pale ale; **Filo di Fumo** ★★ is an elegant, gently smoked ale; **Fil Rouge** ★★☆ is a slightly sour ale brewed with lees from Brachetto wine; the vinous flavours and warming mouthfeel of **Filo Forte Oro** ★★☆ come from the addition of Muscat grape must.

PAUSA CAFÈ
Turin

A "social cooperative" café dedicated to assisting producers in the developing world, and crafting some decent beers as well, the brewing of which takes place off-site. Most successful include **Tosta** ★★★, made with Costa Rican chocolate and evocative of a fruity chocolate liqueur; **Chicca** ★★, brewed with Huehuetenango coffee and full-bodied but subtle and balanced in its coffee flavour; and a very floral, herbal, hoppy pils called **P.I.L.S** ★★☆.

PETROGNOLA, LA
Piazza al Serchio, Lucca

A Tuscan craft brewery using locally grown spelt in all of its beers. Unique **Farro** ★★★, brewed from 100% malted spelt, is fruity and spicy; the flagship **La Petrognola** ★★☆ is a flowery, roasty amber ale that also has a lighter version called **Mezza Petrognola** ★★; **Petrognola Nera** ★★☆ is a coffe-ish, black ale; and **Sandy** ★★ is a reddish, nutty ale named after brewer's daughter.

RETORTO (BIRRA PIACENZA DI CERESA MARCELLO)
Podenzano, Piacenza

Open since only the spring of 2012, this brewery midway between Parma and Milan made an almost immediate impact on the Rome beer scene. The four regular brands include **Morning Glory** ★★, a fragrant but light-bodied pale ale; a highly aromatic IPA with soft citrus notes and a dryish finish, called **Krakatoa** ★★☆; and a plummy, lightly peaty Scotch ale, **Daughter of Autumn** ★★★.

ROCCA DEI CONTI
Modica, Ragusa

Sicilian brewery located in a beautiful, historic baroque town, brewing both distinctive interpretations of foreign beer styles and ales made with local ingredients. **Tarì Frumì** ★★☆ is a fruity, quenching *hefeweizen* ideal for the Sicilian summer; **Tarì Wit** ★★☆ is a local take on the *witbier* using Sicilian-grown lemon peel, basil, ginger and coriander; and deep dark full-bodied **Tarì Qirat** ★★★ is an innovative ale using fruit of the local carob tree.

RURALE
Vigevano, Pavia

Lombard farmhouse brewery founded by a group of home-brewers in 2009. Basic brands include a most refreshing and orange blossom-accented Belgian-style wheat beer, **Seta** ★★☆; the beautifully reserved, perfumey **Terzo Miglio** ★★☆, fashioned as a US-style pale ale; and **Blackout** ★★★, a dryly roasty stout that tastes more Irish than many Irish stouts.

SAN PAOLO
Turin

Brewery in San Paolo district of Turin specializing in bottle-conditioned beers. **Fraké** ★★☆ is a caramelly, citrus amber lager; **Pecan** ★★ is *kölsch*-inspired and authentically balanced; flagship IPA **Ipè** ★★★ is American-inspired with caramel malt contrasting citrus and piney hops; golden ale **Robinia** ★★ is sweetened with organic dandelion honey and bittered by aromatic American hops.

DESTINATION
TURIN

Another Italian city in the midst of a beer renaissance, featuring: **Black Barrels** (98/e via Principessa Clotilde), with a beer shop upstairs and downstairs a pub focused on spontaneously fermented beers; **BSP Pub** (11/b via Airasca), with a special focus on seasonal beers; **Piazza dei Mestieri** (13 via Jacopo Durandi), a brewpub where challenged youth are given a second chance through brewing; and ground-breaking brewpub **Birrificio Torino** (30 via Parma).

TOCCALMATTO
Fidenza, Parma

Parma-area brewery with a passion for bottle-fermentation and hops. Pale ale **Re Hop** ★★☆ offers soft citrus hoppiness on appley malt; **Skizoid** ★★☆ is a subdued and amber-hued, nutty IPA; **Zona Cesarini** ★★☆ uses Pacific hops to create big, fruity-spicy, food-friendly flavours; **Dudes Barley Wine** ★★★ shows brandy-ish, almondy complexity, and turns phenolic and smoky when aged in whisky barrels to become **Salty Dog** ★★☆.

TROLL
Vernante, Cuneo

Nestled in the mountains of Piedmont, this brewpub has gained so much popularity that it now bottles its products. **Daü** ★★☆ is a low-alcohol summer seasonal beer with peppery spice; **Shangrila** ★★☆ is brewed with a kitchen full of spices, emerging complex and warming; **Dorina** ★★ is lavender-spiced and suitably floral; while **Febbre Alta** ★★★ is a herbed *gruit* with hops that manages vaguely to resemble an amaro.

LUXEMBOURG

One of the few countries in Europe to have a stagnant beer culture, despite being, or perhaps because it is, surrounded by countries that do it far better.

SIMON
Wiltz

Family-run brewery in the north. Its Okult range was originally from the former Redange brewery and includes **No 1 Blanche ★★**, a *witbier* with obvious orange peel; while simple but satisfying **Quaffit Stout ★★☆** needs more oomph. Simon brands include fresh-tasting golden-blond spelt beer **Dinkel ★★**, with a light, bitter finish; and **Noël ★★☆**, the slightly too sweet Christmas ale.

SWITZERLAND

In the latter half of the 20th century Switzerland mimicked the pan-European taste for variants on blond lager and came late to craft brewing. However, progress is now strong, with over 100 new breweries either up and running or in the works, prompting some longer-established independents to brush up their act. As one would expect, the best of the new breed are starting to register their presence.

BFM
Saignelégier, Jura

BFM (Brasserie des Franches-Montagnes) is the brewery that put Switzerland on the craft beer map of the world. Its flagship brew, the vinous, fruity, sour dark red **Abbaye de St Bon-Chien** ★★★☆ is a blend of oak-aged beers, while its one-off **Grand Cru** varieties ★★★→★★★★★ usually come from a single cask. Offbeat spicy, warming Imperial stout **Cuvée Alex le Rouge** ★★☆ is worth a try, as is sage-infused, funky blond **La Meule** ★★★.

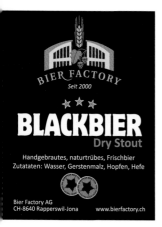

BIER FACTORY
Seit 2000

★ ★ ★

BLACKBIER
Dry Stout

Handgebrautes, naturtrübes, Frischbier
Zutataten: Wasser, Gerstenmalz, Hopfen, Hefe

Bier Factory AG
CH-8640 Rapperswil-Jona   www.bierfactory.ch

BIER FACTORY
Rapperswil, St Gallen

Promising newish small brewery at the southernmost tip of Lake Zurich, formerly known as Rappi. Its smooth **Blackbier** ★★ is a good, dry session-strength stout, while peppery, earthy UK-style **XXA India Pale Ale** ★★☆ delivers just what is expected.

FELSENAU
Bern

Small independent brewery in the northern suburbs of the capital and ubiquitous in and around the city. Smooth, roasty, toffee-ish **Bärni** ★★ is a good example of a Swiss *dunkel*, while fragrant, crisp **Junkerbier** ★★☆ is an excellent pilsner, especially when on draught.

LOCHER
Appenzell, Appenzell Innerhoden

Medium-sized, independent, family-dominated brewery, southeast of Zurich. Its Appenzeller brands include soft, unfiltered pale lager **Naturperle** ★☆, the first organic Swiss beer; vanilla-edged, woody, oak-aged amber lager

Holzfassbier ★★; and **Schwarzer Kristall** ★★★, a rounded, roasted, smoky, chocolaty and rich *schwarzbier*, far above the usual standard for beers of this type.

OFFICINA DELLA BIRRA
Bioggio, Ticino

Pioneering brewpub not far from Lugano, in the mountainous north of Ticino, founded in 1999. Its bottled output now regularly appears in specialist beer shops across the country, highlights being dry, dark, chestnut and honey strong ale **Oroincenso** ★★☆; and pale, fragrant and fruity IPA-like **Lisbeth** ★★☆.

SCHÜTZENGARTEN
St Gallen

St Gallen, famous for its medieval abbey, is also home to the oldest (1779) and largest remaining independent Swiss brewery. Soft, fragrant, flowery **Klosterbräu** ★★ is one of the country's best unfiltered bottled lagers; while light brown, fruity, dry, spicy, juniper-infused **Gallus 612 Old-Style Ale** ★★ is a bold recent departure for a normally reserved company.

STILLMAN'S, THE
Gurmels, Fribourg

Some way west of Bern, this small spirits importer matures a brown ale brewed by Fleisch & Brau at Alterswil, in hogsheads used to import single malt whiskies. The **Darach Mòr** series necessarily varies depending on both cask and beer, but is an intriguing if sometimes slightly over-the-top contribution to Swiss beer diversity ★★→★★★.

DESTINATION
BERN (AND ELSEWHERE)

In the southwest of the capital, between Köniz and Liebefeld railway stations, **Erzbierschof** (276 Könizstrasse) began life as the shop of a beer importer. They added a cellar bar and it is now the country's top outlet of any description. In all, 300+ hand-picked Swiss and imported beers are stocked, with a dozen on tap. The owners have created a second, similar outlet, at Winterthur near Zurich, called **Punkt** (53 Stadthausstrasse).

STORM & ANCHOR
Kyburg, Zurich

A rising star of Swiss craft brewing, decidedly refusing to dumb down its crisp and clean UK-US-influenced range of brews to accommodate delicate eastern palates. Famous locally for note-perfect, massive beers such as **Beast Double IPA** ★★★ and **Kodiak Imperial Stout** ★★☆, as well as for a solid range of impressively fragrant **Single Hop IPAs** ★★☆→★★★, the recipes for which change with the brewer's inspiration and sourcing ability.

SUDWERK
Pfäffikon, Zurich

Newer craft brewery east of Zurich, making US-influenced beers toned down for local palates, such as the crisp, peppery, golden bitter **Gold Miner** ★★; occasional roasty, rounded mid-strength

Liborator Stout ★★; and easy-drinking, smooth, chocolaty, treacly **Pacific Pioneer Porter ★★**.

TICINO BREWING
Stabio, Ticino

Small brewery at the southernmost tip of Tessin, also known as Birrificio Ticinese, producing the UK-US-Italian-influenced range of Bad Attitude beers, far removed from the Germanic beer traditions of the area. These include dry, fragrant and fruity golden session bitter **Kurt ★★☆**; earthy-citrus, fruity rye **IPA Hobo ★★**; and rounded, rich, warming, treacly, roasted **Two Penny ★★☆** strong porter.

TROIS DAMES
Ste-Croix, Vaud

Small brewery in the Jura mountains, at the northern end of Vaud, the first to introduce true-to-style Anglo-US-Belgo ales to Swiss palates. Its bready, smooth, nutty Irish red ale **Rivale ★★** is complex but light; citrus, peppery, earthy **India Pale Ale ★★★** has become a Swiss classic; fruity, spicy **Fraîcheur du Soir ★★** is a lush, double-strength *witbier*; and unique, heretical **Grande Dame Oud Bruin ★★★☆** is made from a blend of strong stout with fermented apricots but ends stunningly close to a Belgian sour brown ale.

EASTERN EUROPE & THE BALKANS

In Soviet times, Czechoslovakian beers were delicious while those of the occupiers were not. After they left, it took Czech brewers two decades to muster the confidence and influence to invest in new brewing talent, followed recently by Poland. Progress elsewhere is patchy but several countries now have hero innovators and the signs are that several – starting with Hungary – are about to have their own little counter-revolutions.

CZECH REPUBLIC

Beer in Bohemia is entitled to obey different rules. This is the place where in the 7th century hops were first cultivated and that first began using them routinely in brewing, that by the 11th century had established a network of town breweries to supplement home brewing and that in 1842 at Plzeň, known by its German inhabitants as Pilsen, first trumpeted a blond lager.

Ironically, the preservation of small regional breweries making beers to careful standards long into the 20th century owes more to neglect than anything. Failure to invest after 1945 by the occupying Soviets forced brewers into a make-do-and-mend mentality, though as many foreign investors learned to their cost after the Russian occupation ended in 1989, the beer-obsessed Czechs had come to appreciate the slow and careful methods this preserved.

The post-war legacy of sometimes decrepit or dilapidated local breweries was put up for sale to the highest bidders. Many closed, while others were taught glitzy, corner-cutting ways to make beer, to the disdain of local drinkers.

Two decades on, numerous smaller companies started to use the older ways once more and a few new brewers have arrived who take a broader vision. Yet even now, few if any Czech brewers seek to set the world on fire by making swaggering, assertive or shocking beers. Rather they concentrate on making relatively light beers, perfectly.

Pale (*světlý*) and dark (*tmavý*) Bohemian lagers typically use hops from around Žatec (Saaz in German) and malt from the Haná valley in Moravia, to make decoction-mashed, bottom-fermented, 8- to 12-week lagered beers, classified by degrees Plato, 8° signifying light, 10° standard and 12° premium.

ANTOŠ
Slaný, Central Bohemia

Small pub brewery in the heart of the hop-growing region around Žatec, making excellent traditional lagers and newer creations for its taphouse. Bottles and kegs can land as far away as Prague. **Antošův Ležák ★★★** is a Bohemian pale lager with a pronounced hop bite; hefeweizen **Slánská Pšenka ★★☆** presents a classic Bavarian clove and banana slate; while **Tlustý Netopýr Rye IPA ★★☆** melds US hops with peppery rye.

BERNARD
Humpolec, Vysočina

Neglected old brewery midway between Prague and Brno, declared bankrupt in 1991 and bought by the Bernard family. It has since become a national exemplar, with hands-off Belgian co-owners **DUVEL MOORTGAT** investing in 2001. Biscuity, malt-focused pale **Sváteční Ležák ★★☆** is now the brewery flagship; food-friendly **Černý Ležák ★★☆** is one of the best wider-distribution dark lagers, with chocolate and cola notes; and amber lager **Polotmavý Ležák 11° ★★** can impress too.

BŘEVNOVSKÝ
Prague

On the site of a long-past 10th-century brewery at Prague's Břevnov Monastery, where a new facility opened in 2012, creating an instant classic in **Benedict**

Světlý Ležák ★★★☆, the unusually minty, vegetal hop flavours deriving from an old-growth Saaz strain; while imported traditional styles have thus far included a spiced *dubbel*, **Abbey Ale ★★**, and a deceptively easy-drinking pale strong lager, **Imperial Pilsner ★★☆**.

BŘEZŇÁK (HEINEKEN)
Velké Březno, Ústí nad Labem

Long-established brewery in northern Bohemia, now owned by Heineken but still remarkable for its continued use of traditional open fermenters. **Březňák Světlý Ležák ★★**, the flagship pale lager, remains unusually fragrant and peppery when fresh.

BROUMOV
Broumov, Hradec Králové

Regional brewer in northern Bohemia, exporting significant volumes across the nearby Polish border. Beers bear the brand name Olivětinský Opat, with favourites being the up-hopped **Bitter ★★☆**, with pronounced Saaz cedar notes; and the holiday seasonal **Sváteční Speciál 17° ★★★**, a stronger amber lager with rich stewed-plum and gingerbread flavours.

BUDWEISER BUDVAR
České Budějovice, South Bohemia

The Budějovický Budvar brewery in České Budějovice, or Budweis in German, has become well known for its long-running trademark battle with a large American brewer that leads to its flagship beer **Budvar** being called **Czechvar** in the US. Formally **Budějovický Světlý Ležák ★★★**, it is a well-attenuated pale lager with crisp, crackery malt and well-rounded bitterness that maintains excellence by cutting no corners; less well-known **Budvar Dark**, or **Tmavý Ležák ★★★** is a classic dark lager with deep toffee and coffee notes.

DALEŠICE
Dalešice, Vysočina

Once-shuttered Moravian brewery where the pre-revolutionary cult film comedy *Postřižiny* (*Cutting it Short*) was shot. Reopened in 2002 with a few star beers like **Dalešická 11° ★★☆**, a pale lager with a berries-and-cream flavour; amber **Dalešické Májové 13° ★★☆**, which starts malty but finishes with prickly hops; and dark lager **Fledermaus 13° ★★**, which typically emphasizes bitterness over sweetness.

FALKON
Žatec, Ústí nad Labem

Beer commissioner in Bohemian hop country run by one of the brewers at **ANTOŠ**, creating beers for his own label. Beyond common-or-garden craft fare like US-inspired bittersweet **Stalker IPA ★★☆** are experiments in alien and overlooked styles like the sweet and roasty **Milk Stout ★★☆**.

HEROLD
Březnice, Central Bohemia

Solid regional brewery in the grounds of a castle, south of Prague. Still has its own

floor maltings, balancing tradition and innovation. Classically **Czech Premium Lager ★★☆** emphasizes malt over hops, as also in roasty and bitter **Bohemian Black Lager ★★★** and sweetly malty **Bohemian Wheat Lager ★★☆**.

JIHLAVSKÝ RADNIČNÍ
Jihlava, Vysočina

New small brewery and restaurant in the Moravian Highlands making a number of unusual brews, including its Post Apocalyptic Ale series of single-hopped pale brews, each with different recipes. The best of the series is **Kazbek ★★☆** employing the new Czech hop; while the brewery's gingery, well-balanced **Pumpkin Ale ★★★** is likely Central Europe's best – and possibly only – example of this US style.

JIHOMĚSTSKÝ
Prague

Stylish František Richter brewpub (*see* **U BULOVKY**) set incongruously among the *paneláky* housing estates of south Prague. Its specials bring in the curious, while locals stick to standards like house lager **Jihoměšťan ★★**, with a spicy

Saaz nose; the clove-scented *hefeweizen*
Weissbier ★★☆; and stout-like dark
lager **Tmavý Speciál ★★★**.

KOCOUR
Varnsdorf, Ústí nad Labem

New-school brewery near the German
border, making largely top-fermented
beers, including many collaboration
brews. High points include **Samuraj
★★☆**, an aggressive, US-style IPA
brewed with Toshi Ishii from Guam
(*see* Ishii Brewing, page 301); **Gypsy
Porter ★★☆**, a citrus-inflected Baltic
porter produced with UK brewer, Steel
City; and low-octane pale ale **Sumeček
★★☆**, with plenty of (mostly US) hops.

KOUT NA ŠUMAVĚ
Kout na Šumavě, Plzeň

Cult favourite from a renovated small
town brewery in western Bohemia,
making four obsessively fine lagers – two
pale, two dark. **Punchy Kout 10° ★★★**
has more Saaz character than many 12°
premiums; the sharply bittersweet **Kout
12° ★★★★** balances spicy hops with a
rich, caramel body; while the two darks,
Kout 14° ★★★ and **Kout 18°, ★★★☆**
share the same grain bill, each offering
similar gingery spice and cola notes.

DESTINATION
PLZEŇ

Klub Malých Pivovarů (16
Nádražní) is a grungy, grimy beer bar
with a "Small Breweries Club" that
delights in serving unknown Czech
and Bavarian beers, just a few steps
from behemoth **PILSNER URQUELL**.

KRAKONOŠ
Trutnov, Hradec Králové

Solid regional brewer a stone's throw
from the Polish border, named after the
legendary giant of the Krkonoše, or Giant
Mountains. The premium pale lager,
Světlý Ležák 12° ★★☆, remains an
easy-drinking favourite for its full malt
body and delicate finishing hop aroma.

KRUŠOVICE (HEINEKEN)
Krušovice, Central Bohemia

Before 1989, the hop-popping pale lager
from Krušovice, west of Prague, was a
high spot of any Prague beer hunt. The
brewery, once owned by King Rudolf II,
currently uses its renowned soft water
supply to make solid but frustratingly
unexciting beers, none better than
Krušovice Černé ★☆, a dark lager
balancing sugary malt with a gently spicy
hop note. Needs radical de-renovation.

LOBKOWICZ
Protivín, South Bohemia

A small but important new brewing
group has gained the rights to the name
Lobkowicz, for beers from southern
Bohemia. Its flagship pale lager,
Premium ★★, offers round, almost
buttery malt sweetness finishing with
a whiff of noble hop aroma.

LUCKY BASTARD
Brno, South Moravia

New nanobrewery in the Moravian capital
run by local beer writer Jan Grmela with
a focus on top-fermented craft styles, the
best of which is his American-hopped

Black ★★, a brown ale with pronounced coffee and caramel notes.

DESTINATION
BRNO

U Modrého (19 Česká) is a neat, modern beer shop near the city centre with over 200 Czech and foreign beers, mostly chosen for interest.

MATUŠKA
Broumy, Central Bohemia

Small family brewery west of Prague, run by father-and-son master brewers, producing classic beers from across the continent and beyond. Citrus, well-balanced **Pšeničné Pivo 13° ★★★** is perhaps the country's best *hefeweizen*; while **Weizenbock ★★★** is plummy and fruity. Modern craft styles include crisp, US-style pale ale **California ★★☆**; and pugnacious, bittersweet IPA, **Raptor ★★☆**.

NA RYCHTĚ
Ústí nad Labem

A new pub brewery in industrial northern Bohemia, founded by former employees

of nearby Heineken-owned Zlatopramen, making beers that hark back to the heyday of classic lager brewing. The pilsner-style **Mazel ★★★☆** pushes Saaz bite into C-hop territory; while pale, caramel and Munich malts make up the rich backbone for the sugary dark lager **Vojtěch ★★☆**.

NOMÁD
Prague

Prague-based beer commissioner run by the former prime mover at KOCOUR. Innovative beers include all-Czech IPA, **Karel ★★☆**, which showcases lemony, raspberry-scented, Saaz-related Kazbek hops; **Black Hawk ★★☆**, which pairs various American C-hops with Moravian dark malts; and **Pelikán ★★★**, a peppery double IPA that cuts Kazbek and Czech Agnus hops with US Chinook and Cascade.

PERNŠTEJN
Pardubice

Regional brewer in the steeplechase town of Pardubice, east of Prague, with a stable of solid but standard brews and one eye-catching special, a Baltic porter washed up many miles inland. First brewed for a Prague exhibition in 1891, **Pardubický Porter ★★☆** is full of butterscotch and treacly malt, like a Christmas pudding with a shot of brandy on top.

PILSNER URQUELL (SABMILLER)
Plzeň

Modern descendant of the first pale lager and original role model for the style. Still malt-driven and fairly well-hopped, bittersweet, with floral, citrus-scented Saaz notes, flagship **Pilsner Urquell ★★★** is superior when served fresh and unpasteurized, as it is in numerous, mostly Czech pubs.

PIVOVARSKÝ DŮM
Prague

Small Prague pub brewery making Czech classics as well as German, American and UK styles, some of which arrive hand-pulled. House pale lager **Štěpán Světlý Ležák ★★★** is a riot of Saaz fireworks over pure pilsner malt; dark-lager variation **Štěpán Tmavý Ležák ★★☆** tastes of café au lait and gingerbread; and **Pšeničné Pivo ★★☆** is a banana-scented German *hefeweizen*.

DESTINATION
PRAGUE

Pivovarský Klub (17 Křižíkova) is a well-lit beer bar and hearty-fare restaurant, just off the centre, with six independent Czech breweries on tap and 200 local and foreign brews in the bottle, while **Zlý Časy** (5 Čestmírova) has an airy street-level bar and atmospheric cellar offering 30+ draught beers from rural producers, plus international and rare local beers in bottle, also in its shop.

POLIČCE, MĚŠŤANSKÝ PIVOVAR V
Polička, Pardubice

The old brewery of this ancient walled town in the Moravian Highlands was founded in 1517 and has quietly flourished under the direction of hippie-

era rock guitarist Karel Witz. The malting of classic dark lager, **Hradební Tmavé Pivo 10° ★★☆**, is spicy and ginger; while in highly traditional pale lager **Záviš 12° ★★☆** it is biscuit-inflected.

PRIMÁTOR
Náchod, Hradec Králuvé

Regional brewery in eastern Bohemia, with a diverse line of specialities that included the first widely available **Czech Stout ★★☆**, with smoky malt roastiness and a lightly sweet body; the best of the country's industrial pale lagers, Saaz-scented **Premium ★★☆**; the Bavarian-style **Weizenbier**, a treat of doughy wheat and spicy yeast when fresh **★★→★★★**; and the sharply bitter but sugary golden bock **Exkluziv 16° ★★**.

PURKMISTR
Plzeň

Pub brewery named for a brand that echoes a long-gone local brew. Exemplary pale lager **Purkmistr Světlý Ležák ★★★** caps honey-scented malt with a bitter bite; **Tmavý Ležák ★★☆** is a rich and sugary dark beer; while *hefeweizen*-style **Písař Pšeničné Pivo ★★☆** marries yeasty spice with crisp wheat body. The associated upmarket hotel offers a beer spa – tub and all.

RAMBOUSEK
Hradec Králové

Well-regarded small brewery in eastern Bohemia, best known for its **Eliščino Královské Kaštanomedový Speciál 13° ★★☆**, a sweetly aromatic amber lager with a dose of chestnut honey in the mash, a mouthful in both name and deed, named after medieval queen Elizabeth Richeza.

ROHOZEC
Malý Rohozec, Liberec

A small regional brewer located in the the rolling hills of Český Raj, or the Bohemian Paradise. Its beers are popular locally but are rarely seen elsewhere. **Skalák Světlý Ležák 12° ★★** is the premium pale lager, with crackery malt and a moderate noble hop aroma; while **Skalák Tmavý 13° ★★☆** is a cola-sweet dark lager with loads of roasted malt flavours.

RYCHTÁŘ (LOBKOWICZ)
Hlinsko ve Čechách, Pardubice

Small brewery in the central highlands, halfway between the hop-growing region of northern Bohemia and the barley fields of the Haná Valley in southern Moravia, now part of the LOBKOWICZ group. Unfiltered flagship pale lager **Rychtář Natur ★★☆** splits the geographical difference too, balancing Saaz hop perfumes with toasty malt flavours, elevating both with a rich dose of bready yeast.

STRAHOV, KLÁŠTERNÍ PIVOVAR
Prague

Renovated brewpub at a hilltop monastery near Prague Castle, making both traditional and contemporary brews in the name of Sv. ("St") Norbert. **Antidepressant ★★☆** is a dark bock brightened by freshly harvested Saaz hops; **India Pale Ale ★★☆** leans on imported US hops; while Vienna-style **Amber Lager ★★★** and *tmavé* **Dark Lager ★★★** stick with Moravian malt and regular Bohemian hops.

ŠTRAMBERK
Štramberk, Moravia-Silesia

Pub brewery in the hilltop citadel, south of Ostrava, taking the brand name Trubač from the medieval watchtower across the town square. Well-made, sweetish **Světlý Ležák ★★☆** travels more than **Tmavý Ležák ★★★**, one of the Czech Republic's best darks, with a Java nose and bitter-sugary coffee in the mouth.

SVIJANY
Svijany, Liberec

Successful regional brewer from north Bohemia, the first to connect craft beer appeal to traditional techniques. The bready malt of pale lager **Svijanský Rytíř ★★** is balanced by grassy hops, while slightly turbid **Kvasničák ★★☆** brightens noble-hop bite with a dose of fresh yeast.

U BULOVKY
Prague

Brewing entrepreneur František Richter's beachhead brewpub sits 200m (656ft) from the end of the E55 motorway in the north of Prague. Sugary malt meets peppery Saaz in house pale lager, **Ležák** ★★☆; the Czech take on an **Alt** ★★ is brave, hoppy and estery; and the **Weizenbock** ★★☆ is a winter cocktail of boozy stewed-fruit flavours.

U FLEKŮ
Prague

This 500-year-old brewery attached to a huge, touristy pub near the centre of Prague makes just one beer. Only available on draught, bar the odd souvenir bottle, unaltered for 40 years and likely much longer, the fruity, roasty, rich, chocolaty dark lager known as **Flekovský Tmavý Ležák** ★★★★ gains a fourth star for being an icon rather than a stunner. An essential line on any beer-drinking CV.

UHERSKÝ BROD (LOBKOWICZ)
Uherský Brod, Zlín

Regional brewer not far from the Slovak border, now part of the LOBKOWICZ group.

Most of its brews are solid, but the stronger pale lager, **Comenius Speciál 14°** ★★☆, stands out, with loads of toffee malt balanced by bright, fragrant hop aroma.

ÚNĚTICE
Únětice, Central Bohemia

Renewed brewery just outside Prague, mainly producing two traditional Czech pale lagers. The basic model, **Únětice 10°** ★★★, is surprisingly bitter for a session beer; while highly hopped flagship **Únětice 12°** ★★★☆ resembles pale ale as much as pils. Seasonal specials, like malty, amber **Vánoční Speciál 13°** ★★, offer variety but feel less self-assured.

VALÁŠEK
Vsetín, Zlín

Way out in Moravia's Beskydy Mountains, this long-overlooked brewpub has been quietly turning out great beers since 2002, a fact only noticed when bottles started showing up in Prague. Sweet, full-bodied yeast beer, **Kvasnicový Ležák Světlý** ★★★, tops sugary Haná malt with an earthy hop finish; while newcomer **IPA Saison** ★★★ shows off peppery Belgian yeast notes and citrusy American hops.

VYŠKOV
Vyškov, South Moravia

Regional brewer in southern Moravia. Its unusual range of Vyškovské Pivo brews are often overlooked. Pale *bock*-like **Jubiler 16,80** ★★☆ is a strong lager with unusually pronounced Saaz aroma; super-hoppy pale lager **Generál** ★★☆ has won prizes as an IPA (!); and dark lager **Tmavý Džbán** ★★☆ dabs hoppy spice on molasses-like malt.

ZEMSKÝ
Prague

New beer commissioner currently having beers made to order at Chotěboř, with plans afoot to open its own brewery in Prague. **Světlé Výčepní ★★★** blends grassy and cedar Saaz notes and chewy malt into a graceful everyday pilsner; while sweet caramel and citrus notes are the strong suits of the premium **Světlý Ležák ★★☆**.

ZHŮŘÁK
Zhůř, Plzeň

Tiny American-owned and -styled brewery in the West Bohemian hinterlands, turning out ales inspired by the owner's time at Sacramento's Hoppy Brewing Co, including a local version of **Hoppy Face Amber Ale ★★☆**; and **Total Eclipse Black Ale ★★☆**, marrying evergreen US C-hop character with a roasty, chocolate-inflected porter.

SLOVAK REPUBLIC

Before their amicable divorce in 1993, the two halves of the former Czechoslovakia had only been together for 75 years and had different traditions of beer making, the fanatical pivophiles being found more in the western side that became the Czech Republic.

As of 2014 the country has only one established top-quality craft brewery, though a few smaller ones are emerging and there remains a slender collection of better regional producers.

KALTENECKER
Rožňava, Košice

The country's most interesting brewery, founded in 1997 near the Hungarian border, with an exceptional range of products, from simpler blond and brown lagers to reliable, spicy **Weizen ★★**; American-inspired ones, such as its Imperial stout **Archa ★★☆** and **Atlantis IPA ★★☆**; and the country's strongest beer, **B27 ★★★**, an old ale matured in Tokaji wine casks. It also take commissions for numerous beers that have won national home-brewing prizes here and in Hungary.

DESTINATION BRATISLAVA

The Slovak capital now has seven brewpubs. One, **Richtár Jakub** (16 Moskovská), experiments with its own beers and gets in quite a few from other small brewers.

ŠARIŠ (SABMILLER)
Veľký Šariš, Prešov

Although its pale lagers are the big sellers it is the dark beers from the Šariš (or Topvar) brewery in the east of the country that are of more interest. **Šariš Tmavé 11° ★★** is an easy-drinking *dunkel*; **Topvar 11° Tmavý Výčapný Ležiak ★★** is a more aromatic variant; and **Topvar Marina ★★☆** has sufficient complexity to be an altogether more serious proposition.

SESSLER
Trnava

Small pub brewery near Bratislava, re-founded in 2004, producing decent regular lagers like **Svetlý Ležiak 11.5° ★★** and its bready, caramelled, dark equivalent **Tmavý Ležiak 11.5° ★★**;

plus frequent limited-edition heavier brown **Tmavý Špeciál** brews between **13°** and **21° ★★→★★★**.

URPINER
Banská Bystrica

Officially the Banskobystrický brewery but known by its brand name, this well-organized firm produces a workmanlike range of pale and dark lagers including reliable but unexciting blond **Ležiak Svetlý 12° ★★**, also called Premium; and the instantly appealing "draught" dark lager **Ležiak Výčapný Tmavý 11° ★★☆**, more often found bottled, and full of dried fruit, rich malt, chocolate and other flavours.

POLAND

Some 80–85% of Polish beer is produced by subsidiaries of three global giants. SABMiller runs brands like Tyskie, Żubr, Lech, Dębowe, Książęce, Redd's and Gingers; Heineken has Żywiec, Warka, Tatra, Specjal and Leżajsk; and Carlsberg makes Okocim, Harnaś, Kasztelan and Karmi.

The rest is shared between 80 or so regional and smaller brewers, including over 30 pub breweries. Many older breweries remain conservative but there is a growing trend for home brewers to turn pro, opening small craft breweries, many brewing for others under contract, such as PINTA and ALEBROWAR.

After a slow start, the last couple of years have seen rapidly expanding awareness of better-quality beers, especially among young Poles, with pride in local products also noticeably increasing.

ALEBROWAR
Lebork, Pomerania

Beer seller commissioning craft beers from Browar Gościszewo, near Gdańsk.

Mostly American styles thus far, like the bittersweet, citrus and piney **Rowing Jack ★★★**, the best US-style IPA in Poland; the American-hopped pale ale **Amber Boy ★★**; and Poland's first black IPA, with an intense hop aroma and roasted flavour, **Black Hope** ★★☆. In contrast, **Sweet Cow** ★★ is a soft milk stout that would pass for British.

DESTINATION
GDAŃSK

In the history-steeped Baltic port city, **Degustatornia** (16 Grodzka) and its associated **Dom Piwa** bottle-shop serve 150 mainly Polish and Czech beers, as does its eponymous sister bar and shop up the coast at Gdynia (130 Świętojańska).

AMBER BROWAR
Bielkówko, Pomerania

A medium-sized, modern brewery located near Gdańsk. Its sweet flagship **Żywe** ★☆ began the trend towards unpasteurized and unfiltered beers; **Grand** ★★ is a lighter weight, chocolate-malty Baltic porter; and **Koźlak** ★★ is a *bock*, complete with a painted goat's head on the bottle. Bottles of *hefeweizen*-style **Pszeniczniak** ★★ are similarly adorned.

ARTEZAN
Natolin, Masovia

Poland's first brewery to specialize in making Belgian and British styles of beer, created by home brewers southeast of Warsaw. The quality and accuracy of its product can vary. Its first beer, **Wit** ★★☆, was based on Pierre Celis's original recipe for his Hoegaarden beer; **Dubbel** ★★☆ ends up more a regular brown ale than in the fuller abbey style; its **India Pale Ale** ★★, fruity, slightly caramelized and of modest bitterness is English-style; with the best effort so far being a balanced but potent first Polish example of **Imperial Stout** ★★★.

BRACKI BROWAR ZAMKOWY (HEINEKEN)
Cieszyn, Silesia

A small traditional brewery within the Heineken-controlled Żywiec group, located near the Czech border, southwest of Kraków. Its distinctly bitter *helles* lager **Brackie** ★★ is only available locally, while the dry, bitter and potent Baltic-style **Żywiec Porter** ★★☆ can be found throughout the country in better beer shops. This might one day happen for malty and lightly smoked **Bracki Rauch Bock** ★★☆, the 2012 winner of the national Festiwal Birofilia home-brewing competition, rewarded with a one-off commercialization as Bracki Grand Champion beer, launched on 6 December each year.

DESTINATION
KRAKÓW

The unofficial capital of the south is home to four fine beer bars. In Kazimierz, the old Jewish quarter, cool **Omerta** (3 Kupa) divides itself into Polish and international halves, and plainer **Strefa Piwa** (6 Józefa) concentrates on regional revivalists; while in the centre, **Dominikańska** (3 Ul. Dominikańska Ul.) and **House of Beer** (35 Ul. Św. Tomaszka) both chalk up 100+ brews.

CIECHAN
Ciechanów, Masovia

Small traditional brewery north of Warsaw, with good distribution in and around the capital. Flagship honeyed lager **Miodowe** ★★☆ is golden and honey-sweet; *weizen* **Pszeniczne** ★★ has an intense aroma of clove and banana; blond **Marcowe** ★★ is a *märzen*; and its traditional, rich, malted and roasted Baltic porter is called simply **Porter 22** ★★★.

FORTUNA
Miłosław, Greater Poland

Small traditional brewery near Poznań. Best known for **Fortuna Czarne** ★★, an extremely sweet *dunkel* brewed with kola nuts, though its soothing dark and rich Baltic-style **Komes Porter** ★★★ is far more interesting. The Komes brand has recently been expanded to include a couple of evolving bottle-conditioned beers, a *dubbel* called **Podwójny** ★★☆ and *tripel* called **Potrójny** ★★.

KONSTANCIN
Konstancin-Jeziorna, Masovia

Small brewery located to the south of Warsaw, responsible for the production of **Żytnie** ★★☆, Poland's first, rather promising, rye beer; and the odd but interesting dark, sweet, chicory-laced **Czarny Dąb** ★★.

KORMORAN
Olsztyn, Warmia-Masuria

Medium-sized independent brewery in the picturesque northeast, achieving a national reputation following awards for its rich, roasted Baltic porter **Warmiński** ★★★☆ and light lager **Orkiszowe z Miodem** ★★☆, made with spelt and honey. Its weirdest concoction thus far has been **Orkiszowe z Czosnkiem** ★☆, a spelt beer with garlic.

LWÓWEK ŚLĄSKI
Lwówek Śląski, Lower Silesia

Small traditional brewery named after its home town, west of Wrocław, owned by the same people as CIECHAN. Although it claims an ancient heritage, its range points to the future, with a pleasant *helles* lager **Lwówek Książęce** ★★; and a caramelled pale ale named **Belg** ★★ but tasting rather more Brit.

PINTA
Wrocław, Lower Silesia

Beer commissioners formed in 2011, who use Browar na Jurze at Zawiercie, near Katowice to create beers in styles unfamiliar to older Poles. These go as far off piste as the improving, muddy and yeasty, near-flat *sahti*-style **Koniec Świata** ★★; the first Polish-made US-style IPA, **Atak Chmielu** ★★, with more caramel than most; the amazing **Viva la Wita** ★★★☆ US-hopped, heavy *witbier*; and much-praised Baltic porter **Imperator Baltycki** ★★☆.

WIDAWA
Chrząstawa Mała, Lower Silesia

Pub brewery and restaurant, located east of Wrocław, collaborating with a home-brewer to produce beers that get into the best multi-tap pubs in the country. **Czarny Kur** ★★ is a well-roasted *schwarzbier*; better are **Kruk** ★★★, an American dry stout heavily hopped with Simcoe; US-style pale ale **Shark** ★★★, extremely bitter with a citrus aroma and currently the most highly hopped beer in Poland, just shy of 100 IBU; and **Kawka** ★★☆, a stout flavoured with coffee grounds.

WITNICA
Witnica, Lubuskie

Independent commercial brewery in the northwest near the German border, making a wide range of standard beers

under the Lubuskie brand but famed in export markets for its treacly dark **Black Boss Porter** that comes in 7% ★★, 8.5% ★★☆ and 9.4% ★★★.

```
DESTINATION
OTHER CITIES

Beer cafés are cropping up all over
Poland. In Wrocław try Zakład
Usług Piwnych (34 Ruska); in
Poznań extraordinary Setka (8 Ul.
Św. Marcin); and in Łódź Piwoteka
Narodowa (1–3 Ul. 6 Sierpnia).
```

SLOVENIA

The northernmost province of former Yugoslavia, now an independent EU state, has over 20 pub-based breweries, most supplying a single outlet. The number of new small breweries has risen to five, the others being Vizir, Carniola and Pelican.

HUMANFISH BREWERY
Vrhnika

The country's premier craft brewer (2008), run by an expat Australian, is named after a local amphibian. Now southwest of Ljubljana, it makes an excellent, US-UK, crisp, aromatic **Pale Ale** ★★★; an unusually fresh-hoppy but enticing oatmeal **Stout** ★★☆; and a hoppy amber-coloured Slovenian IPA or **SIPA** ★★☆.

KRATOCHWILL
Ljubljana

Small, Czech-influenced family brewery operating in the capital since 1992, with three pubs. Its standard unfiltered,

bottle-fermented lagers include pilsner-style **Svetlo** ★★; strongish Baltic porter **Temno** ★★☆; and sweet, golden honey beer **Medeno** ★★, all found also in 75cl format, which adds further to the quality.

```
DESTINATION
LJUBLJANA

Two bars in the capital, a couple
of blocks apart — Patrick's
Irish Pub (6 Prečna Ul.) and
Sir William's Pub (8a Tavčarjeva
Ul.) — accrue better beers from
round the country and abroad to
offer around 100 in all. For take-
home, try Za Popen't Pivoteka
(5 Stari Trg), which tops 150.
```

HUNGARY

In the 20th century, Hungary was more associated with wine than beer, brewing being largely restricted to restrained, mostly industrial lagers until 1993. In that year a loophole in brewery licensing laws led to an explosion of smaller brewers making mostly cheap, folksy – for which read unpleasant – brews. The loophole and most of the breweries it spawned were closed within a few years but enough interest was sparked to encourage some altogether better brewers to stay in business.

The last few years has seen a surge in enthusiam for unusual beers and an almost limitless desire to experiment, catalysed by Budapest's well-attended annual Főzdefeszt of Hungarian craft beers each May.

ARMANDO OTCHOA
Budapest

The pseudonym of one-man national beer improvement campaigner Gergely Kővári, who commissions beers from Brandecker, near Budapest airport. They include medium-bodied US-style **Grabanc IPA ★★★**, with tropical-fruit aroma and earthy resinous flavours in its aftertaste; **Freaky Wheaty Grabanc ★★★**, an IPA fermented with Weihenstephaner yeast; and experimental US-hopped ruddy Christmas beer **Hangover Santa ★★★**.

BANDUSZ
Tárnok, Pest

Beer commissioner formed in 2008 to revive the Hungarian folk tradition of brewing with millet. Amber-coloured **Köleses ★★** has a malty sweetness and herbal hoppy notes; newer, sweeter **Zümi ★★** is brewed with honey; while **Dupla Köleses ★★☆** has twice the millet, giving it a fuller body, specific sweetness and spicy earthy notes.

BÉKÉSSZENTANDRÁSI
Békésszentandrás, Békés

Hungary's original *kézműves sörfőzde*, or "craft brewery", back in 1993, in the southeast of the country. After a shaky start it now makes the best Hungarian pilsner, **Ogre Söre ★★☆**; an outstanding strong, plummy *doppelbock*, **Black Rose ★★★**, fermented by Champagne yeast and showcasing chocolate malt; absurdly strong reddish-brown lager, **Pöröly ★★**; and enjoyable light plum beer, **Szilvás ★★☆**.

BORS
Győrzámoly, Győr-Moson-Sopron

Early 1990s brewery in the northwest, near the Austrian border. Switched from lagers to ales in 2012. **Marian Maid** 6% **★★** is a wheat beer brewed with honey, sporting fruity esters and some hop; **Sherwood** 6.5% **★★★** is a robust porter with an earthy aroma and leathery, smoky, complex body plus a hint of fruitiness; and Belgian *dubbel*-style

Tuck Barát ★★☆ has fruity and earthy aromas, candy sugar and malty flavours plus a hoppy finish.

FÓTI
Fót, Pest

Another pioneer, northeast of Budapest, since 1994. Pale-ale-inspired but bottom-fermented **Keserű Méz ★★★** is unfiltered and golden, with biscuity malt and a pronounced grassy aroma of Spalt, mirrored in its stronger, spicier winter version, **Winternacht ★★★**; while its two strong brown *doppelbocks*, **Barcagi Dupla Bak ★★☆** and winter's **Hammurapi +21 ★★☆**, get an edge from Champagne yeast.

HOPFANATIC
Kiskunhalas, Bács-Kiskun

Champion home-brewers who got their own place in the rural south of the country in 2013. Overwhemingly citrus-bitter **Bitterfly ★★☆** is a US-style hop-forward IPA fermented with Belgian yeast; **NoHopLimit ★★★☆** is a double IPA with complex, layered hop presence, a firm, rich malty background and tastable alcohol; and **Angry Beast ★★★** is a strong, complex brew with roasted coffee, oatiness and hops lingering in the aftertaste.

RIZMAJER
Budapest

Another 1994 start-up that is veering away from the mainstream with beers like not-quite-Baltic, sweet, caramelled **Cingulus Fekete Sör ★★**; the home-smoked newer porter **424 ★★★☆**; the neatly named beefy *hefeweizen* **Búza ★★★**; and seasonal brands like its acclaimed **Maibock ★★★☆**.

DESTINATION BUDAPEST

For Hungarian brews and the best international range head for **Csak a Jó Sör!** (42 Kertész Utca), aka Only Good Beer, a tightly packed beer shop with a convivial small tasting area.

ZIP'S BREWHOUSE
Miskolc, Borsod-Abaúj-Zemplen

State-of-the-art brewpub-restaurant showing off the wares of a brewery manufacturer in the country's fourth largest city. Demonstrates the potential with a reliable, firm golden Czech Saaz-hopped **Pilsner ★★☆**; Hungary's first and remarkably accomplished **Saison ★★★**, with peppery and spicy yeast notes, and malt-accented and fruity flavours; spicy strong **Golden Ale ★★☆** with sweet malt and alcohol notes; and a nicely roasted, chocolaty **Stout ★★☆**.

UKRAINE

The beer culture of the western part of Ukraine is in some ways a continuum of that of its western neighbour, Poland, but without the burgeoning craft brewing scene. There are early hopeful signs, with local tourist authorities in the regional capital Lviv promoting a five-brewery tour of the city, with tastings.

LVIVSKE (CARLSBERG)
Lviv

The largest brewery in Ukraine's beeriest city. Its mainstream beers are better balanced than some but do not survive export well; *witbier* **Bilyi Lev** ★★ is malt-accented with a big vanilla finish; and the strong **Porter** ★★☆, intended to be Baltic but with German *dunkel* leanings, is another example of a Carlsberg local blockbuster.

MIKULINETSKY
Mykulyntsi, Ternopil

Forward-thinking independent brewery in western Ukraine tracing its origins to 1457. Has a link with König Ludwig in Germany. Produces 17 mostly well-balanced and unpasteurized lagers, at the last count, among which the pilsner **Koruna Česka** ★★☆ has a rich Saaz aroma and hearty bitterness; lighter, more basic **Mikulin Svitle** ★★ has a bitter, mineral character; **Ukrainske Dark** ★★☆ is complex with lots of toffee and bread crust; and pale **Troyan** ★★ has a herbal, bitter character, underpinned by sweet malt.

GREECE

Something about craft beer seems to make it resilient in the face of hard economic times. Witness Greece, where a new clutch of small brewers are making gradual progress in a country unused to the joys of tasty beer.

Corfu Beer opened on the well-known holiday island in 2006 to make UK-style pale ales like darker toasty, nutty **Real Ale Bitter** ★★; grainy lagers like **Royal Ionian Pilsner** ★★ with a sweet malt finish; and a winter-only barley wine, **Ionian Epos** ★★☆.

Newer breweries on the rise include the Santorini Brewing Company, set up on that island in 2011 by a mixed bag of expats, whose brews thus far have included a blond **Yellow Donkey** ★★☆, a brown **Red Donkey** ★★☆ and Greece's first IPA, **Crazy Donkey** ★★★, all featuring US and New Zealand hops. Also Septem, on the near-island of Euboea, north of Athens, which names its beers by day of the week and has earned praise for **Friday's Pale Ale ★★**, **Sunday's Honey Golden Ale ★★☆** and **Seasonal Winter's Day Porter ★★**.

On the island of Chios, just off the Turkish coast, Chios Micro makes a single bottled hazy blond **Fresh Chios Beer ★★☆**, which is getting about, as is the unpasteurized bottled version of **Zeos Pilsner ★★☆** from Zeos Brewing Co at Argos on the Peloponnese.

Currently we know of a dozen others who are either dipping a toe in the water in German *hausbrauerei* style or else contemplating creating their own US-style craft beers.

DESTINATION
ATHENS

The Local Pub (25 Chaimanta, Chalandri) in the north of Athens, off the beaten track but two minutes from Xaimanta tram/bus stop, has the best range of craft beers in the capital, with 120+, including a dozen from Greek brewers.

DESTINATION
THESSALONIKI

Cafeneio Prigipos (22 Apostolou Pavlou) is a traditional-style northern Greek drinks café in the centre with a dozen or so Greek craft beers in a range of 100+, while out near the airport in the village of Trilofos the evenings-only **Ipanema Beer Bar** (Perikleous) does even more despite its obscure location.

RUSSIAN FEDERATION

Gathering information about brewing in the old Soviet Union was nigh on impossible, a situation that continued in the first two decades after its break-up. In *The World Atlas of Beer* we acknowledged these difficulties at the same time as recognizing that Russia, as consumer or producer, will feature strongly in the future of beer worldwide.

Carlsberg, Heineken and AB InBev all have clutches of breweries here but with the exception of the first, make no beers of interest.

The current crucible of craft beer revival is Saint Petersburg, home to an increasingly interesting variety of pub breweries, some of which are starting to sell their beers elsewhere. But as more young Russians take an interest in quality beers from the West, information is starting to flow about brewers in far-flung corners that are cranking up after decades of poor investment. Watch this (massive) space.

AFANASIUS
Tver, Tver Oblast

Regional brewer since 1887 and in its current form since 1976, northwest of Moscow on the road to Saint Petersburg. The Afanasius brands include numerous local brews such as the two unfiltered ones in stoppered bottles: a safe-ish, mid-strength **Porter** ★★☆; and unusual, fruity dark **Temnoe** ★★.

BALTIKA (CARLSBERG)
Saint Petersburg

Russia's largest brewery company, formed by the merger and takeover of three large plants in 2006, now with production facilities all over the country and in Azerbaijan. Most beers are instantly forgettable but there are exceptions –

DESTINATION
SAINT PETERSBURG

Perhaps the first bar anywhere to showcase modern Russian beer is the amazing **Bier Cafe Craft** (6 ul. Gagarinskaya), with some dozens. There are now around 20 brewpubs in the city, too: the best for beer is the spectacular and beautiful **Metropole** (22/2 ul. Sadovaya); the flashiest is **Baltika Brew** (3 ul. Bol'shaya Morskaya), owned by BALTIKA; and the best positioned, with full Bavarian kitsch, is the **Karl and Friedrich** (15 dor. Yuzhnaya) out in the island park.

No 8 Pschenichnoye ★★ is a dryish, balanced and refreshing *weizen*; **No 6 Porter** ★★ is treacly, vinous and dark brown; and **Žatecký Gus Černý** ★★☆ is an oddly charming, low-strength dark lager that resembles an English dark mild.

BIER HAUS
Ulan-Ude, Buryatia

This hotel and beer garden southeast of Irkutsk, not far from the Mongolian border in southern Siberia, proves that a German pub brewery can be constructed anywhere. It makes one of Asia's better stouts, chocolaty **Bagheera** ★★☆, with a roast fudge character and full body. Its other beers are less successful, though pale **Hans** ★☆ has a quirky mid-strength style that is becoming an Eastern staple.

JOKER BAR
Kazan, Tatarstan

Brewpub at the Mirage Hotel in Kazan, a long way east of Moscow, with an excellent view of the Kazan Kremlin UNESCO World Heritage site. Its **Helles** ★★☆ is fresh-tasting, with fruity hop notes and a bready peach finish; the **Dunkel** ★★☆ has a hearty bread-crust character with cocoa notes; and the **Märzen** ★★ is caramelly, nutty and slightly toasty in the finish.

TOMSKOE
Tomsk, Tomsk Oblast

A regional brewer in southwestern Siberia that is making the Saaz-rich **Český Džbánek** ★★, one of Russia's more credible pilsners; **Krüger** ★★☆, named for the brewery's founder, with a rich molasses character; the soft and sweet **Barkhatnoe** ★★☆ with pleasing roast in the finish; and **Zhigulyovskoe** ★★, a surprisingly beer-like take on the Soviet-era standard, with a herbal-spicy hop character and bready malt sugars.

NORTH AMERICA & THE CARIBBEAN

UNITED STATES

Once upon a time, a mention of American beer would elicit nought but ridicule around the world. For although US breweries counted among the world's largest throughout most of the 20th century, or perhaps at least partially because of that fact, the nation's lagers had gone from light to lighter and even "lite", reaching their nadir when the Monty Python comedy troupe famously and with some justification compared them to "making love in a canoe".

But then, as the century drew to a close, entrepreneurial Americans did what they have always done best and began to transform the beer market not just in their own backyard, but also around the globe.

First, so-called "microbreweries" were unleashed, then they increased steadily in number, and once they grew too large for the "micro" label, they became craft breweries. Then they began to influence others to follow their lead, inspiring craft brewers near and far, in Canada and Japan, Brazil and Sweden.

By the dawn of the new millennium, the proverbial craft brewing "tail" had started to wag the brewing industry "dog". Making matters even worse for the big brewers, not only were they losing market share to the smaller guys, they were also losing national control of their own companies, with takeovers and mergers soon limiting domestic ownership of the now Big Two breweries to a mere 25% stake in one of the two.

Meanwhile, craft brewing continues to grow at a rapacious rate, escalating in number of breweries – in excess of 2,500 in operation at time of writing, with hundreds more in development – increasing in both volume and dollar market share and generally dominating the social beer consciousness. And with a brewery-to-population ratio well below that of countries like Belgium and the United Kingdom, there would seem to be still ample room for market growth in the immediate, perhaps even long-term future.

CALIFORNIA

By almost any measure, whether by Fritz Maytag's famous resuscitation of San Francisco's ANCHOR BREWING or Jack McAuliffe's ultimately unsuccessful founding of New Albion Brewing, modern American craft beer got its start in California. It is also in that state, particularly the north, that it first thrived.

Brewpubs were legalized in California in 1982 and shortly thereafter they proliferated across the state, notably so around the San Francisco Bay area, but also further north and, at the dawning of the 21st century, in the southern reaches around San Diego and Los Angeles, as well. Today, the state remains a craft beer leader, not only in terms of total number of breweries, with more than twice as many as the next most brewery-populated state, but also, and perhaps more importantly, as the enduring source of inspiration for others.

21ST AMENDMENT BREWERY
San Francisco, California

Brewpub in the shadow of the baseball stadium, now contract-brewing its major brands for canning. Seasonal **Hell or High Watermelon** ★★☆ is softly sweet with flavours of fresh watermelon; **Bitter American** ★★☆ is a quaffably light pale ale; piney and herbal **Brew Free! or Die IPA** ★★☆ is slightly sharp on the finish; **Back in Black** ★★★ is a not-quite black IPA with a roasty body and hoppy finish.

ALESMITH BREWING
San Diego, California

Fiercely local San Diego brewery only recently stretching sales beyond city

borders. February seasonal **Bloody Valentine** ★★★ combines assertive hoppiness with red apple flavours, deliciously; pale ale **X** ★★☆ is fragrant and very dry and quaffable; complex **Grand Cru** ★★★ uses Belgian yeast to coax flavours of dried fruit and spice; flagship **Horny Devil** ★★★☆ tweaks maltiness with peppery, citrus spice; **Old Numbskull** ★★★ barley wine is intense and warming.

ALPINE BEER
Alpine, California

This San Diego area brewery is justly well known for extremely hoppy beers like **Pure Hoppiness** ★★★☆, a classic double IPA with fruity mango/pineapple aromas and sticky pine character; and

Exponential Hoppiness ★★★☆
another double that's dry-hopped twice,
the second time with oak chips, for
extreme hop character that's surprisingly
well balanced. **Nelson** ★★☆ is a rye
IPA that's spicy with Sauvignon Blanc
flavours; and **Duet** ★★★ is a nicely
balanced IPA with grassy, pineapple,
mango notes.

ANCHOR BREWING
San Francisco, California

Prohibition-era San Francisco brewery
revived by Fritz Maytag in the 1970s to
become craft beer vanguard. Flagship
Steam Beer ★★★★ mixes ale and
lager characteristics in a most refreshing
fashion; moderately strong and crisply
hopped **Liberty Ale** ★★★ arguably set
the stage for IPAs to come; mellow and
warming **Old Foghorn Barley Wine**
★★★☆ pioneered the style in the US
and remains maltier than most; newer
Humming Ale ★★☆ screams hoppy
freshness; and spiced **Christmas Ale**
★★★ changes annually, but remains
reliably balanced.

ANDERSON VALLEY BREWING
Boonville, California

Stalwart northern California brewery,
delighting in the use of local dialect
"Boontling" on its labels. **Hop Ottin' IPA**
★★★ is an ale that mixes well bitter
hop and sweet, fruity malt; **Barney Flats
Oatmeal Stout** ★★★☆ is a smooth,
silky, lightly sweet black ale with mild
roastiness; **Brother David's Double**
★★★, brewed in cooperation with San
Francisco's Toronado bar, is rich with
raisin and other dried-fruit flavours;
Poleeko Gold Pale Ale ★★☆ is
peachy and quaffable.

BALLAST POINT BREWING
San Diego, California

A San Diego brewery born out of a
home-brew shop. Fish-named ales
include the highly regarded, grapefruity
Fish Eye IPA ★★★; and more roundly
fruity, lighter-tasting **Sculpin IPA**
★★☆. Simply named **Pale Ale** ★★☆
pleases with easy quaffability; while
food-friendly **Marlin Porter** ★★★
is mocha-ish and drying.

DESTINATION
SAN DIEGO

San Diego boasts a number of
great beer destinations, including
Hamilton's (1521 30th Street) and
the **Toronado San Diego** (4026
30th Street), two great multi-taps
on the same street a couple of
miles apart. Around the city and
county, there's also **O'Brien's**
(4646 Convoy Street), **Churchill's**
(887 W San Marcos Boulevard,
San Marcos) and the new **Stone
Brewing World Bistro and
Gardens** complex at Liberty Station
(2816 Historic Decatur Road).

BEACHWOOD BBQ & BREWING
Seal Beach, California

One of the bright spots in beer-starved
LA, two years ago the restaurant added
a brewery when award-winning home-
brewer Julian Shrago became a co-
owner and started producing beers like
Tovarish ★★★, a decadent Imperial
stout bursting with creamy espresso and
sweet molasses; **Amalgamator IPA**
★★☆, a tropical mélange with mango

and guava notes; and **Hop Vader ★★**, a roasty, cocoa-ish black IPA balanced by bright, spicy hops.

BEAR REPUBLIC BREWING
Healdsburg, California

Father-and-son brewery long a staple of California wine country. Flagship **Racer 5 IPA ★★★☆** is a testament to US hops in its citrus appeal; **Hop Rod Rye ★★★** was one of the first US beers successfully to combine the spiciness of rye with strength and hoppiness; seasonal **Racer X ★★★** is a superbly balanced double IPA.

BRUERY, THE
Placentia, California

Brewer Patrick Rue punned on his name to create his brewery's moniker and quickly earned a devoted following for his oft-quirky ales. Spicy-yeasty and faintly tart **Saison Rue ★★☆**; and peppery, pear-ish **Mischief ★★☆** headline the core beers; while **Autumn Maple ★★★**; brewed with yams and complex with sweet maple, spice and yam flavours, and lightish, quenching, dryly tart **Saison de Lente ★★☆** highlight seasonal offerings.

CRAFTSMAN BREWING
Pasadena, California

Under-the-radar brewery brewing a wide range of mostly draught-only ales. Unusual offerings include the herbaceous **Triple White Sage ★★★**; seasoned with wild white sage, and the suitably orangey **Orange Grove Ale ★★☆**.

DESTINATION
PASADENA

Lucky Baldwin's Pub (17 S Raymond Avenue), now with two sister bars, is a pioneering southern Californian beer bar opened by the late David Farnworth, offering a mix of British pub tradition and local and Belgian beers.

DEVIL'S CANYON BREWING
Belmont, California

Long-time brewery-for-hire in the San Francisco area, now making more of an effort with its own brands, including the variably peaty **Full Boar Scotch Ale ★★**, best when its smokiness is restrained; **Deadicated Amber ★★☆**, a caramelly, nutty session ale; the surprisingly soft and inviting **California Sunshine IPA ★★**, with only a moderate citrus hop character; and work-in-progress **Belle ★☆**, a Champagne-esque *bière brut* that has real potential.

FIFTYFIFTY BREWING
Truckee, California

Nestled in the mountain town of Truckee, near the Nevada border, award-winning brewer Todd Ashman creates snow-friendly beers like **Imperial Eclipse Stout ★★★**, with barrel-aged versions matured in different used bourbon barrels; the **Pappy Van Winkle ★★★☆** and **Elijah Craig ★★★☆** versions are particularly complex and delicious. Others include **RyePA ★★☆**, with floral, citrus notes; rich, bittersweet chocolate **Totality Imperial Stout ★★☆**; and **Donner Party Porter ★★☆**, a molasses, espresso delight.

FIRESTONE WALKER BREWING
Paso Robles, California

Extraordinary Paso Robles brewery specializing in all things barrel- and blending-related. Flagship **DBA ★★★☆** is remarkably rich for its modest strength and arguably the most British beer brewed in America; **Union Jack IPA ★★★** blends juicy malt and orange marmalade flavours with citrus hop; and **Pale 31 ★★★** is light, mellow and fruity. Proprietor's Reserve line includes **Double Jack ★★★**, with resinous hops and overripe fruit; and always interesting, differently blended **Anniversary Series** of ales, usually stunning **★★★→★★★★★**.

GREEN FLASH BREWING
San Diego, California

San Diego brewery expanding at a record pace. Known for prodigiously hoppy ales like the intensely piney **West Coast IPA ★★★**; the more intense but complex **Palate Wrecker ★★★**; and the Belgian *tripel*-American IPA mash-up known as **Le Freak ★★★☆**. For all that bombast, it can still be nuanced in beers like **Fizzy Yellow Beer ★★☆**, a crisp and floral

pilsner; and seasonal **Summer Saison ★★**, with honey-ish malt and spice.

HERETIC BREWING
Pittsburg, California

Suitably unorthodox brewery located midway between San Francisco and Sacramento. Rye beer **Gramarye ★★☆** combines bold hoppiness with rye spiciness and session beer strength; **Evil Twin Red Ale ★★★** surprises with a richly hoppy aroma but maltier, fruity body; massive **Evil Cousin ★★☆** is a hugely herbaceous, almost oily double IPA that's not dominatingly bitter; marvellously named **Shallow Grave ★★★** is a porter with roasted fruit notes and well-disguised strength.

HIGH WATER BREWING
San Leandro, California

Veteran Californian brewer Steve Altimari's first self-run effort, contract-brewed at Drakes Brewing in San Leandro. Spiced winter ale **Blind Spot ★★★** is gingerbready without being confectionary; tropical-fruity **No Boundary IPA ★★★** uses New Zealand hops to glorious effect; **Hop Riot IPA ★★★** is strongly grapefruit but also oddly mellow; **Retribution ★★★**is a fruity-hoppy double IPA swat at Altimari's former employers.

KARL STRAUSS BREWING
San Diego, California

Pioneering brewery producing southern California craft beer long before it was cool. Basic brands seem produced with mass market in mind, as with the sweetish, caramelly and slightly nutty

Karl Straus Amber ★★. Speciality brands get more interesting: **Two Tortugas ★★★**, a spicy, toffee-ish fruitcake of an ale; spicy, tropical fruit and citrus **Blackball Belgian IPA ★★☆**; and various barrel-aged anniversary beers – including the bourbony **23rd Anniversary Old Ale ★★★** – among them.

LAGUNITAS BREWING
Petaluma, California

Brewery north of San Francisco with a second facility in construction in Chicago. Usually irreverent attitude held in check for **Pils ★★★**, a distinctly crisp yet floral lager, but in full evidence in potent **Hairy Eyeball ★★☆**, a malty, toffee-ish ale that stops just short of sweet. Chocolate and port-wine notes define dessert-like **Imperial Stout ★★★**; while basic **IPA ★★★** is dryly fruity and herbal; and **Brown Shugga ★★★** is a hoppy fruitcake of a beer.

LINDEN STREET BREWERY
Oakland, California

Draught-only brewery that is housed in an historic warehouse in Oakland.

Black Lager ★★★ is not a *schwarzbier*, but a crisp, tobacco-ish and lightly fruity cross of porter and *helles*; the flagship **Urban People's Common Lager ★★☆** is a gently fruity brew in the steam beer style; while **Deep Roots Red Lager ★★★** is a toasty, almost smoky lager with a refreshingly dry finish.

LOST ABBEY/PORT BREWING
San Marcos, California

Two storied breweries in one location, just north of San Diego. The Port line is more American in approach, evidenced by the strong, forcefully roasty and complex **Old Viscosity ★★★**; and the perennially award-winning **Shark Attack★★★**, a "double red ale" of prodigious hoppiness. Belgian-inspired Lost Abbey brews include the spiced and strong, but quenching, **Red Barn Ale ★★★**; the barrel-aged, vanilla-streaked, complex and warming **Angel's Share ★★★★**; and the bold, lightly tart and deeply nuanced, although occasionally variable, **Cuvée de Tomme, ★★★☆** when it is as at its best.

MAD RIVER BREWING
Blue Lake, California

Brewery hidden behind the Redwood Curtain in Humboldt County, about five hours north of San Francisco, in the tiny town of Blue Lake. Standouts include the barley wine **John Barleycorn ★★☆**, which is caramel-sweet with tons of US hops; **Serious Madness ★★☆**, a nutty, coffee-infused black ale; **Jamaica Red ★★** with toffee maltiness and spicy hopping; and **Steelhead Extra Stout ★★★**, a thick, creamy, chocolate delight.

MAGNOLIA GASTROPUB & BREWERY
San Francisco, California

This Haight/Ashbury brewpub recently opened a second brewery in the Dogpatch district, specializing in barbecues. It brews English-style ales, including **Old Thunderpussy ★★★**, a barley wine highlighting the restrained bitterness of English hop alongside rich toffee and candied fruit flavours; **Proving Ground IPA ★★☆**, a balanced blend of spicy and citrus flavours; and **Sara's Ruby Mild ★★**, a rich, malty ale with caramel and raisin notes.

MOONLIGHT BREWING
Santa Rosa, California

Santa Rosa draught-only, one-man operation is a true undiscovered gem of the San Francisco Bay area, with the toasty, complex **Death & Taxes ★★★☆** black lager a standout. **Reality Czeck ★★★** is a soft, floral/grassy pilsner; and **Bombay by Boat ★★☆** a worthy West Coast IPA with grapefruit notes. **Working For Tips** *gruut* **★★☆** features spicy redwood tips. New growler-filling station in downtown offers refills.

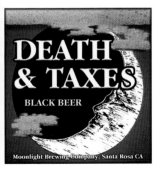

Moonlight Brewing Company, Santa Rosa CA

NORTH COAST BREWING
Fort Bragg, California

Long-standing brewery in far northern California. Best known for big beers, but excellent also when greater subtlety is called for, as in **Scrimshaw Pilsner ★★★**, a highly crisp and quaffable lager; and **Red Seal Ale ★★★☆**, a medium-bodied pale ale with a spicy hop kick. Bolder offerings include the liquorice-accented, sweetly malty **Brother Thelonious ★★★**; Belgian-inspired **PranQster ★★★**, with dry fruitiness and a spicy finish; and **Old Rasputin Russian Imperial Stout ★★★☆**, with lusciously sweet and complex roastiness.

RIP CURRENT BREWING
San Marcos, California

Founded by a pair of local home-brewing legends, it was named one of San Diego's top 10 breweries after being open for less than one year, thanks to such hop-centric offerings as **In the Curl IIPA ★★★**, which is loaded with passionfruit and pine aromas, finishing dry; and **Caught in a Rip ★★☆**, an 11.2% triple IPA with magnificent tropical citrus character.

RUSSIAN RIVER BREWING
Santa Rosa, California

Much-lauded Santa Rosa brewery headed by Vinnie Cilurzo, presumed inventor of the double IPA, perhaps perfected in **Pliny the Elder ★★★★**, a startlingly hoppy beer with wondrous malty balance. Barrel-ageing produces many ales in the "-tion" line, such as the earthy, sour cherry-ish, almost Burgundian **Supplication ★★★**; and subtly winey, tart and complex blond ale **Temptation** ★★★. **Redemption** ★★★ eschews both barrel and strength for quaffability; while **Pliny the Younger** ★★★ raises the bar in strength, hoppiness and cult appeal.

SANTE ADAIRIUS RUSTIC ALES
Capitola, California

Nestled in an almost hidden corner near Santa Cruz, former home-brew shop co-owner Tim Clifford produces a bewildering array of beers, many bottled, like **Saison Bernice** ★★★, a tart and funky farmhouse ale; **West Ashley** ★★☆, a sour ale redolent with tart apricots and oak character; and **Maiden Fields** ★★, a tart and fruity take on a *Berliner weisse* with funky lemon-zest notes.

SIERRA NEVADA BREWING
Chico, California

Pioneering craft brewery located in the California interior. Flagship **Pale Ale** ★★★★ arguably defined the American style; piney recent arrival **Torpedo** ★★★ aims to do same to the IPA; **Stout** ★★☆ balances sweet and bitter nicely; seasonal **Celebration** ★★☆ remains a holiday landmark of hoppy aggression; **Bigfoot** ★★★★ is a seminal hop-forward barley wine; new "Ovila" line of abbey ales shows promise.

SOCIETE BREWING
San Diego, California

Young San Diego brewery by veteran brewer Travis Smith, formerly with RUSSIAN RIVER and THE BRUERY, offering a trio of beer types: hoppy, Belgian-inspired and barrel-aged sour ales. Beers named for society's occupations, with the **Harlot**

★★★ a pale ale showing nice spicing and floral notes; **Pupil IPA** ★★☆ grassy and grapefruity dry; and **Everyman's IPA** ★★☆ a seriously complex, strong IPA with piney, tropical-fruit aromas.

SPEAKEASY ALES & LAGERS
San Francisco, California

This San Francisco institution now calls the Hunter's Point neighbourhood its home and recently opened a taproom hidden in the cellar of the brewery, where you can drink its **Payback Porter** ★★★, showcasing liquorice and chocolate flavours with spicy hops; flagship **Big Daddy** ★★☆, a crisp, spicy and complex IPA; and double IPA **Double Daddy** ★★, a zesty punching bag of hops.

DESTINATION
SAN FRANCISCO

Toronado (547 Haight Street) is your first stop for both Belgian and local hoppy beers, but there's also **La Trappe Cafe** (800 Greenwich Street) and **The Monk's Kettle** (3141 16th Street) for Belgian-style food and beer, **Zeitgeist** (199 Valencia Street) for local ambience and the new **Mikkeller Bar** (34 Mason Street) for a great mix of everything. Stop by **City Beer** (1168 Folsom Street) on your way home for an extensive assortment of bottles.

STONE BREWING
Escondido, California

Mini-empire of craft brewing located in southern California, built in part on the back of an unlikely flagship ale, **Arrogant Bastard ★★★**, which combines hops, malt and alcohol in delicious near-balance; but better still in its **Oaked Arrogant Bastard ★★★☆** version. The **IPA ★★★** provides a lean, piney contrast; while **Ruination IPA ★★☆** challenges with strongly assertive bitterness. Low-alcohol **Levitation Ale ★★★** offers relative subtlety with characteristic Stone hoppiness, and numerous special releases and collaborations offer extreme variety.

TRUMER BRAUEREI (GAMBRINUS COMPANY)
Berkeley, California

This Berkeley brewery makes only one beer, based on German-style pilsner from sister brewery outside Salzburg, Austria. Since 2003, **Trumer Pils ★★★☆**, with beautiful golden colour, sweet, biscuity aromas and signature Saaz hop character, has won countless deserved awards, and is best on draught rather than in the green bottles.

PACIFIC NORTHWEST

Despite California's claim to have the most breweries of any state, even it cannot boast the ubiquity of craft beer that is the reality in the Pacific Northwest, more specifically Washington and Oregon. Visit almost any town in either state, north or south, inland or coastal, and chances are high you will find a brewery. In all of the region, this commitment to craft beer is perhaps nowhere more in evidence than in Portland, OR, where it is estimated that nearly one out of every three beers consumed is craft.

Washington, home to the country's most prolific hop-growing region, the Yakima Valley, trails Oregon's mania for craft beer only slightly, and Alaska, for all its remoteness and transportation challenges, is not that far behind, with a brewery for roughly every 35,000 residents. Even Hawaii, included here but really standing alone geographically, has caught the craft brewery bug, with ten breweries of its own at the time of writing.

10 BARREL BREWING
Bend, Oregon

Home to several award-winning brewers in beer-centric Bend. Toasted malt restrains abundant tropical fruit-grapefruit in **Apocalypse IPA ★★★**; India-style **Session Ale (ISA) ★★☆** deploys a blast of orange with grassy-lemon zest; rotating selection **Oregon Brown Ale ★★☆**, with a heavy dose of citrus, is not your grandfather's brown; winter's seasonal **Pray For Snow ★★★** is resplendent with dark fruits.

ALASKAN BREWING
Juneau, Alaska

Long-standing craft brewery in Juneau, perhaps most famous for its caramelly, smoky – although not intrusively so – and darkly fruity **Smoked Porter ★★★☆**. Year-round brews include **Amber ★★★**, meant to resemble an *altbier*, successfully so, with a faintly raisiny earthiness; a mildly fruity, slightly thin **Pale Ale ★★☆**; and a sweetish, mildly creamy **Stout ★★☆**. Occasional Pilot Series beers encourage creativity.

BARLEY BROWN'S BREWPUB
Baker City, Oregon

Multiple-award-winning brewery, with draught-only beers available mostly at the brewpub in Baker City and occasionally in Portland or Bend. Look for assertive yet deftly balanced **Turmoil Black IPA ★★★☆**, revealing hints of pine resin, grapefruit, roasted coffee, chocolate; effervescent, refreshing, citrus **Shredder's Wheat ★★★**, a multiple-award-winning American-style wheat beer; and citrus-dominant, slightly resinous **Pallet Jack IPA ★★☆**.

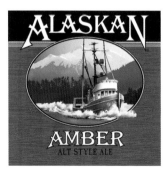

BEND BREWING
Bend, Oregon

A standout in this Oregon city of notable breweries, thanks to stellar seasonals. Locals' favourite **Hop Head Imperial IPA ★★★** is a resin bomb with citrus rind. Fruity, caramel-rich **Outback X Old Ale ★★★**; and pink-lemonade-meets-grapefruit **Ching Ching Berliner Weiss ★★☆** are two award-winning seasonals. Standards **Elk Lake IPA ★★**, grapefruity with hints of mango and orange marmalade; and caramel-nutty **Outback Old Ale ★★** don't disappoint.

BLOCK 15 BREWERY & RESTAURANT
Corvallis, Oregon

Innovative brewery with strong barrel-ageing programme. Most beers are draught-only, some bottled. **Figgy Pudding ★★★☆**, a strong ale aged in brandy barrels, is a mouthful of figs, cinnamon, nutmeg; **Pappy's Dark ★★★** is a strong ale replete with bourbon, baked bread, caramel; **Super Nebula Imperial Stout ★★★** is aged on different origin-specific cocoa nibs each year, giving each version a slightly distinctive flavour.

BONEYARD BEER
Bend, Oregon

Draught-only brewery cranking out exceptional beers in Central Oregon. Many offerings are hop-heavy: **Hop Venom Double IPA ★★★**, a spicy-yet-resinous grapefruit bomb; and pineapple-citrus **RPM IPA ★★★☆**. Originally a THREE FLOYDS BREWING collaboration, **Armored Fist Imperial CDA ★★★** keeps the citrus hops and deftly adds roasty depth. Tamer palates would enjoy **Diablo Rojo ★★☆**, an easy-going, slightly bready red ale.

BOUNDARY BAY BREWERY & BISTRO
Bellingham, Washington

Bellingham's oldest brewpub is still a locals' favourite known for assertive but balanced beers. Standouts include **Imperial IPA ★★★**, a hop bomb that sweetens up right before hitting the hop wall; **Oatmeal Stout ★★☆** and the fruitier **Imperial Oatmeal Stout ★★☆**, both of which offer dark chocolate, espresso qualities with a silky backbone; and **ESB ★★☆**, a subtly hoppy brew with toasted nut notes.

BREAKSIDE BREWING
Portland, Oregon

Up-and-coming brewery celebrated for its one-offs and seasonals, also offering solid year-round beers. Multiple-award-winning **Dry Stout ★★☆**, with hints of Dutch-processed cocoa powder, could redefine the style; while Mexican-chocolaty **Aztec Ale ★★★** could arguably define a new one. **English Session Brown ★★★**, with deep chocolate notes, proves brown doesn't mean boring; another seasonal, **Coconut Pumpkin Sweet Stout ★★★**, is very nearly a milkshake.

BRIDGEPORT BREWING (GAMBRINUS COMPANY)
Portland, Oregon

One of the Pacific Northwest's original breweries, now housed in a renovated Portland complex that includes a bakery and restaurant. **India Pale Ale ★★★**

might seem tame by today's standards, but remains a classic; **Blue Heron Pale Ale ★★** is lightish and a bit too fruity for some; annual **Ebenezer Ale ★★☆** is a restrained model of maltiness; while **Old Knucklehead ★★★** is a warming, raisiny barley wine.

CASCADE BREWING BARREL HOUSE
Portland, Oregon

Spin-off from Portland beer veteran Art Larrance's Raccoon Lodge, specializing in barrel-conditioned ales. Beers are ever changing, but more regular offerings include tart and funky, apricot-almond **Apricot ★★★**; a **Kriek ★★★** that begins with cherry pie and grows progressively more tart to a spicy-dry finish; grapey, vanilla-accented **The Vine ★★★**, aged on Muscat grapes; and complex, peppery-fruity **Strawberry ★★★**.

CHUCKANUT BREWERY & KITCHEN
Bellingham, Washington

State-of-the-art craft brewery with roots in German lager styles located in northern Washington's college town of Bellingham. Only available on draught, award-winning beers include nearly flawless, clean-finishing **Vienna ★★★** with toffee and caramel notes; crisp, slightly grassy German-style **Pilsner ★★★**; and softly subtle, fruity yet refreshing **Kölsch ★★★**. Intermittently brewed, smooth-as-silk and toffee-ish **Bock ★★☆** is a delightful winter seasonal.

COMMONS BREWERY
Portland, Oregon

Small and ambitious new Portland brewery, focused mostly on draught sales. Early flagship is **Urban Farmhouse Ale ★★**, a spicy-sweet ale that may be a bit too much of the latter; irregularly released **Golden Harvest ★★☆** is given an unusual floral jolt by the addition of lemon balm; *saison*-ish **Haver Bier ★★★** is creamy with pronounced hop and a spicy finish; and **Flemish Kiss ★★☆** is mildly tart and appley.

DESTINATION PORTLAND

Deciding which beer bars to visit in a city nicknamed "Beervana" can be tough, but start with **Bailey's Taproom** (213 SW Broadway), a chic downtown beer mecca, before turning to the **Horse Brass** (4534 SE Belmont Street), an iconic beer bar with British charm and 50+ taps. **APEX** (1216 SE Division Street) also sports 50+ taps and a huge outdoor seating area, while local beer store **Belmont Station** (4500 SE Stark Street) touts 1300+ local-to-international bottled beers and 23 rotating taps -- you can sip while you shop.

CRUX
Bend, Oregon

Founded by former DESCHUTES BREWING brewmaster Larry Sidor, this up-and-comer is gaining attention with ales like the citrusy, pineappley **Outcast IPA ★★☆**; the rich, chocolaty, barrel-aged **Tough Love Imperial Stout ★★★**; **Impasse Saison ★★☆**, a refreshingly spicy and citrusy brew; and **Off Leash ★★☆**, a 4.5% alcohol session IPA that surprises with bright bursts of citrus and a dry finish.

DESCHUTES BREWING
Bend, Oregon

Tremendously accomplished brewery in Bend. So many beers that a flagship is hard to identify, but perhaps it's the floral, lemony-spicy **Mirror Pond Pale Ale ★★☆**; or the mocha-ish **Black Butte Porter ★★★☆**, surely an American classic; or the newer, Meyer lemony **Red Chair NWPA ★★★**. Fans anxiously await the annual return of fruity-tart **The Dissident, ★★☆** at release and improving with age; and the stunning, multi-layered, high-strength anniversary edition of **Black Butte ★★★☆**.

DOUBLE MOUNTAIN BREWERY
Hood River, Oregon

Hood River brewery perhaps better known for creative seasonal offerings than its solid standards. Piney-citrus **Hop Lava IPA ★★☆**; Northwest-hoppy **Kölsch ★★☆**; and lemon-zesty **The Vaporizor Pale Ale ★★☆** are notable year-round beers. Winter favourite **Fa La La La ★★★** offers plenty of piney hop, but on a prodigiously malty base. A variety of seasonals like tart **Devil's Kriek ★★★** reveals a flair with fruit.

ELYSIAN BREWING
Seattle, Washington

Long-time Seattle brewer Dick Cantwell and partners spun a single brewpub into a mini-empire that includes a production association with NEW BELGIUM BREWING. Beers at the pubs are many and diverse, but bottled line-up always includes floral-spicy **Avatar Jasmine IPA ★★★**; assertively hoppy but balanced **Immortal IPA ★★★**; and **Bête Blanche ★★★**, a *tripel* that progresses smoothly from sweet pear to dry, bittering hop.

DESTINATION SEATTLE

Despite numerous brewpubs, Seattle is a taproom town, with ample choices beginning at Belgian-accented **Brouwer's Cafe** (400 N 35th Street), which boasts one of the most impressive draught systems in the US. Dog-friendly **Beveridge Place Pub** (6413 California Avenue SW) offers 36 taps and 150+ bottles, while upscale **Collins Pub** (526 2nd Avenue) features 20 taps focused mostly on local and regional beers.

FORT GEORGE BREWERY
Astoria, Oregon

Situated on the exact location of the first American-owned settlement on the Pacific coast. Assertive, grapefruity **Vortex IPA ★★★** is named after a tornado the owners encountered when hauling their brewery cross-country. Crisp, grassy **1811 Pre-Prohibition Lager ★★☆** honours the year Astoria was founded. Dark-chocolaty **Cavatica Imperial Stout ★★☆** lends itself to many draught-only iterations; **Sunrise Oatmeal Pale Ale ★★★** frames grapefruit-grassy hops with silky smoothness.

HAIR OF THE DOG BREWING
Portland, Oregon

Born in a Portland industrial park, this small brewery that bats way above its weight is now located closer to downtown. Flagship strong ale **Adam ★★★☆** takes a gingerbready start through roasted apple and raisin to a long, warming finish; earthy-spicy **Greg ★★☆** is fortified with squash; golden **Fred ★★★** offers sweet yellow fruit tempered by growing hoppiness; and seasonal barley wine **Doggie Claws ★★★** is a liquid fruitcake with bite.

HOPWORKS URBAN BREWERY
Portland, Oregon

Certified organic brewery with two locations. Intensely resinous-orange **Hopworks IPA ★★★** is a local favourite; while citrus **Lager ★★☆** fits the bill for gentler palates. Highly anticipated seasonals include piney, grapefruity **Abominable Winter Ale ★★★**; **Secession Cascadian Dark Ale ★★★**, which balances roastiness and grapefruit bitterness with supportive malts; and fiercely orange-hopped, sticky-malt **Ace of Spades Imperial IPA ★★★**.

LAURELWOOD PUBLIC HOUSE & BREWERY
Portland, Oregon

A mini-empire with several different locations, including two at Portland's airport. Flagship **Workhorse IPA** ★★★☆, classically Northwestern with grapefruit and pine notes, continues to draw fans; seasonals **Organic Deranger Imperial Red** ★★★, with toffee backbone and citrus-pine highlights; and floral-grapefruit **Green Elephant IPA** ★★★ showcase how well made organics can be. Softer **Hooligan Brown Ale** ★★☆ offers chocolate-nutty notes.

LOGSDON FARMHOUSE ALES
Hood River, Oregon

Overseen by the founder of Wyeast Laboratories, producer of pure liquid yeast cultures and fermentation products, this young brewery is already shaping directions for farmhouse-style beers. Complex, fruity, spicy **Seizoen** ★★★ balances hop character with malt; **Seizoen Bretta** ★★★ offers a crisper, drier finish; seasonal **Peche 'n' Brett** ★★★ features lightly acidic peach flavours; lemongrass-herbal **Kili Wit** ★★☆ is an interesting example of a Belgian-style wheat beer.

MAUI BREWING
Lahaina, Hawaii

An award-winning brewery located on Hawaii's second-largest island. Tropical-fruity, floral **Big Swell IPA** ★★☆ is what an exotic island brewery's IPA should be. Coriander-heavy **Le Perouse White** ★★☆ uses local mandarin oranges. Robust, dessert-in-a-glass **CoCoNut PorTer** ★★★ focuses on toasted coconut and chocolate; and draught-only, caramel-rich **Hawaii 90 Wee Heavy** ★★☆ proves the brewery makes some heavy-hitters despite the heat.

MIDNIGHT SUN BREWING
Anchorage, Alaska

Anchorage-based brewery steeped in the frontier spirit of Alaska. Winter is embraced through **Arctic Devil Barley Wine** ★★★, a malt-forward and age-worthy brew; while **Sockeye Red IPA** ★★☆ offers a year-round, hoppy yin to the barley wine's yang. The new addition of canned beer to the portfolio assures that beer quality remains in the lower 48.

NINKASI BREWING
Eugene, Oregon

Eugene's largest brewery keeps on growing, thanks to popular, hop-heavy standards **Total Domination IPA** ★★☆; and **Tricerahops** ★★☆. Also garnering praise are special releases like refreshing, citrusy **Maiden the Shade IPA** ★★★; and rich, warming **Sleigh'r** ★★☆, a double *altbier*. The Prismatic Lager Series, which encourages each brewer in turn to design their own limited-release beer, has so far produced such outstanding results as **Pravda Bohemian Pils** ★★★.

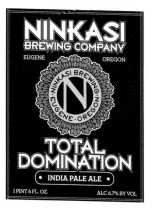

NO-LI BREWHOUSE
Spokane, Washington

Known as Northern Lights Brewing until a threatened copyright infringement lawsuit hastened a name change, this operation is definitely one to watch. Recently retooled ales include the faintly woodsy **Silent Treatment Pale Ale** ★★☆; the citrus, almost oily **Born & Raised IPA** ★★☆; the quaffable, fruity **Crystal Bitter Ale** ★★; and the pine-forest and toasted lemon peel **Jet Star Imperial IPA** ★★★.

OAKSHIRE BREWING
Eugene, Oregon

Home-brewing brothers Jeff and Chris Althouse who have turned community-minded professional brewers located in Eugene. The brands that are available year-round include a dry and toasty **Amber** ★★☆, with both nutty and citrus hop notes; and a predominantly citrus **Watershed IPA** ★★★. The seasonal **O'Dark:30** ★★★ is a sweet-to-bitter, chocolaty black IPA.

OLD SCHOOLHOUSE BREWERY
Winthrop, Washington

Although it is relatively inaccessible, it's worth the visit to Winthrop to experience this brewery's touristy location, which is reminiscent of an old Western movie set. Belly up to the bar (or find bottled versions) and try the herbal, grapefruity **Ruud Awakening IPA** ★★☆; or the rich and smooth **Hooligan Stout** ★★☆, with hints of espresso and baker's chocolate. The roasty **Rendezvous Porter** ★★☆ offers coffee, earthy notes.

PELICAN PUB & BREWERY
Pacific City, Oregon

Thrice "brewery of the year" at the Great American Beer Festival, this coastal Oregon brewery offers an **Imperial Pelican Ale** ★★★ that smacks the senses with citrus and pine while maintaining a surprising balance. Also available bottled: seasonal **Mother of All Storms** ★★★☆, a barley wine bundle of bourbon-barrel influence; year-round **Tsunami Stout** ★★★, offering dark chocolate-cream notes; and bready, fruity **Kiwanda Cream Ale** ★★☆.

PFRIEM
Hood River, Oregon

A family affair with a gorgeous view of the Columbia River, Pfriem (pronounced "freem") focuses on Belgian-inspired beers with a Northwest slant. **Belgian Strong Dark Ale** ★★☆, with hints of dark fruit and spices, is among the more Belgian-esque; while the tropical-fruity **Belgian IPA** ★★☆ crosses both worlds beautifully. Roasty, piney **Cascadian Dark Ale** ★★☆; and herbal, citrusy **Mosaic Pale Ale** ★★☆ lean decidedly toward the Northwest.

PIKE BREWING
Seattle, Washington

Teaching lab for many accomplished Pacific Northwest brewers, this Seattle brewpub has gone through many guises en route to its present and somewhat iconic status. Classic Pike brews include the nutty-fruity-floral **Pale** ★★; the rich and robust **Extra Stout** (formerly XXXXX Stout) ★★★; and the malt-intense **Old Bawdy Barley Wine** ★★★. Newer are the sessionable **Naughty Nellie ★★☆**; and fruity, perhaps overly roasty **Tandem Double Ale ★★☆**.

ROGUE ALES
Newport, Oregon

Remarkably prolific brewery on the Oregon coast, known for big beers and silk-screened labels. **Juniper Pale Ale ★★★** fuses gin-like spice with spicy hop; **Mocha Porter ★★☆** is creamy and well named; **Morimoto Soba Ale ★★☆** is toasty with buckwheat and curiously savoury. Its farm provides ingredients for **Rogue Farms OREgasmic Ale ★★☆**, grapefruity and biscuity; and the roasty but medium-bodied **Rogue Farms Dirtoir Black Lager ★★★**.

SILVER CITY BREWING
Bremerton, Washington

Relatively unknown gem opposite Puget Sound from Seattle continues to gain accolades without fanfare.

Flagship **Fat Scotch Ale ★★☆** offers molasses notes with a touch of peat; newcomer **St Florian IPA ★★☆** balances malt with pine and citrus; the resinous, intensely hoppy **Whoop Pass DIPA ★★★** is locals' favourite; polar opposites **Ziggy Zoggy Summer Lager ★★☆**, a honey-like *kellerbier*; and limited-release **Imperial Stout ★★★** showcase brewery's breadth.

UPRIGHT BREWING
Portland, Oregon

Portland brewery that combines an admiration of French and Belgian farmhouse brewing with an appreciation of jazz great Charles Mingus (really). Upright beers are named in reference to their starting gravities. The light-bodied **Four ★★** is citrus and peppery, with a tangy finish; the herbal, hoppy **Five ★★★** is dryly appetizing; the rye-based **Six ★★☆** is toasty and suitably spicy from the rye; and the highly fruity **Seven ★★★** is both eye-opening and warming.

ROCKY MOUNTAINS & THE MIDWEST

Without doubt, the heart and soul of Rocky Mountain craft brewing is Colorado. One of the country's earliest breweries (BOULDER BEER) was founded there; the craft beer trade group, the Brewers Association, is based there; the state ranks third and fifth respectively in total number of breweries and breweries per population; and the country's most important beer event, the Great American Beer Festival, is held in Denver every autumn. Outside Colorado, the more sparsely populated mountain states might boast correspondingly fewer breweries – 15 in Wyoming, for instance – but when weighted on a population basis prove that interest in craft brewing is practically a mountain region trait.

The Midwestern equivalent of Colorado is perhaps Michigan, home to well over 100 breweries, although residents of Illinois, Wisconsin and Missouri might wish to take issue with that characterization. While the region was slow to take to craft beer – the city of Chicago, for example, was famously resistant to anything other than the familiar big brewery labels throughout most of the 1980s and 1990s – the Midwest has since the start of the new century made up for lost time to become, as it was once in the early and mid-20th century, an important centre of brewing in the United States.

3 SHEEPS BREWING
Sheboygan, Wisconsin

A young and promising brewery, mixing fringe beer styles with great names. **Rebel Kent the First Amber Ale ★★★** is a spicy and very dry mix of sessionable Belgian (*enkel*) and British (bitter) styles; **Really Cool Waterslides IPA ★★☆** is a piney but mellow take on the India Pale Ale style; and the inevitable **Baaad Boy Black Wheat Ale ★★** is mocha-ish and lightly fruity. The brewery is draught-only.

4 HANDS BREWING
St. Louis, Missouri

Brewery, and tasting room, located short walk from Busch Stadium in St. Louis. Hop-centric beers like the fruity and floral

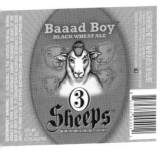

Reprise Centennial Red Ale ★★☆ are most popular; but diverse offerings include **Smoked Pigasus ★★☆**, a seamless smoked rye maple porter; **Cuvee Ange ★★★**, fermented with wild yeast, raspberries and blackberries in wine barrels; refreshing **Prussia Berliner Weiss ★★★**; and chocolate-rich **Cast Iron Oatmeal Brown ★★**.

5 RABBIT BREWING
Bedford Park, Illinois

Brewed in suburban Chicago, beers from the first Latin American-inspired brewery in the US reflect the flavours of that culture. **5 Lizard Latin-Style Witbier ★★★☆** is made with lime peel, passion-fruit and spices, with New Zealand hops accentuating tropical flavours. Ancho chillies add a smoky twist to **5 Vulture Oaxacan-Style Dark Ale ★★★**; and hibiscus and ginger keep the warming **Huitzi Midwinter Ale ★★★** floral and refreshing. Dulce de leche and various spices make **Vide y Muerte ★★** a most unusual Oktoberfest.

ALE ASYLUM
Madison, Wisconsin

Given beer names like **Ambergeddon ★★☆**, a hopped-up amber ale, it's easy to believe that the brewery's motto – "Fermented in Sanity" – is probably most accurate spoken quickly. American pale ale **Hopalicious ★★★**, rich in grapefruit and tangerine, is most widely available; but **Bedlam! ★★★**, a seasonal IPA fermented with Belgian yeast; and the fruity **Ballistic IPA ★★☆** are both worth the hunt.

ARCADIA BREWING
Battle Creek, Michigan

British-inspired brewery in Battle Creek, a town better known as the home of Kellogg's cereals. Year-round picks include **Loch Down Scotch Ale ★★★**, raisiny, rich and roasty; the dry, peppery-earthy **Sky High Rye ★★☆**; and the pine-needles and caramel-apples **Hopmouth Double IPA ★★☆**. Irregular standouts are the liquorice and dark chocolaty **Imperial Stout ★★☆**; and outstanding, vanilla-chocolate-spicy-raisin **Barrel Aged Shipwreck Porter ★★★☆**.

AUGUST SCHELL BREWING
New Ulm, Minnesota

Venerable brewery dating from 1860. Produces large quantities of forgettable, adjunct-y "Grain Belt" beers, but also legitimate craft offerings like the crisply malty **Pils ★★★**; the bready and surprisingly well-bodied, 150th anniversary brew, **Hopfenmalz ★★☆**; and the seasonal, perhaps overly full and malty **Schmaltz's Alt ★★**.

AVERY BREWING
Boulder, Colorado

Colorado brewery founded in 1993. First known for hoppy ales like still-popular, grapefruity **India Pale Ale ★★★**; but the years have seen a branching out to beers like the bold, hop-forward **Hog Heaven ★★★** barley wine; the molasses and plum **The Reverend ★★★**; and the variable-by-vintage Imperial stout **The Czar ★★☆**. Barrel-Aged series beers like the peppery, grapey, cinnamon **Dépuceleuse ★★★★** are cause for excitement.

BAYERN BREWING
Missoula, Montana

Bavarian born and trained brewmaster/owner Jürgen Knöller has focused on German-style beers since the brewery's opening in 1987. They include **Pilsener ★★☆**, bready with lingering spicy hops; the lightly fruity **St. Wilbur Weizen ★★**; and **Schwarzbier ★★☆**, chocolaty and nutty. A notable departure from the theme is **Killarney ★★**, a creamy, caramelly Irish red ale with a hint of chocolate, brewed for St Patrick's Day.

BELL'S BREWERY
Kalamazoo, Michigan

Instigator of the Michigan craft beer explosion, based in Kalamazoo. Wide range of beers from the apricoty, herbal **Amber Ale ★★★**; to the hops-and-honey **Hopslam ★★★**. Perhaps best known, however, for an almost endless

parade of black ales, from the **Porter** ★★★, chocolaty and sessionable; to the bigger, roast-and-coffee **Kalamazoo Stout** ★★★; to the potent, intense and darkly fruity **Expedition Stout** ★★★☆.

BIG SKY BREWING
Missoula, Montana

Moose Drool Brown Ale ★★★, malt-rich and balanced, offers more than just a memorable name used to sell tee-shirts in nearby Montana national parks. Other equally solid brews include: **Big Sky IPA** ★★☆, caramelly-sweet upfront, then piney and floral; the chewy **Ivan the Terrible Imperial Stout** ★★★; **Bobo's Robust Porter** ★★☆, dark, roasty and dessert-like; and **Cowboy Coffee Porter** ★★☆, espresso-like but restrained.

BOULDER BEER
Boulder, Colorado

Colorado's original craft brewery, founded in a goat shed in Boulder. Psychedelic designs adorn the labels of beers like the grapefruity, piney **Mojo IPA** ★★☆; the dry-hopped and fragrant **Hazed & Infused** ★★☆; and the seasonal, thinly malty double IPA **Mojo Risin'** ★★.

BOULEVARD BREWING (DUVEL MOORTGAT)
Kansas City, Missouri

The little Kansas City brewery that could is now part of one of the largest craft brewing operations in the States. Regular brands include the accurately named **80-Acre Hoppy Wheat Beer** ★★☆; and citrus, six-hop **Single-Wide IPA** ★★☆; but it's the Smokestack series

beers that attract most attention, like the lemony spice of **Tank 7 Farmhouse Ale** ★★★; the peppery, tangy **Saison Brett** ★★★; and the warming but not weighty **Harvest Dance Wheat Wine** ★★★☆.

BREWERY VIVANT
Grand Rapids, Michigan

Young brewery and pub in Grand Rapids, fearlessly canning Belgian and northern French farmhouse-style ales. Brands include the hoppy, spicy orange-apple **Triomphe** ★★★, billed a "Belgian IPA"; the honey-ish **Contemplation** ★★, brewed with Michigan honey; the mildly barnyardy, citrus-fruit-salad **Zaison** ★★☆; and the dry, supremely quenching **Farm Hand** ★★★.

CAPITAL BREWERY
Middleton, Wisconsin

Early Wisconsin craft brewery, located just outside the state capital, Madison. Best when brewing German-influenced beers like the slightly grainy, dryish **Pilsner** ★★; or the faintly roasty, toasted malt **Dark** ★★★. Special edition beers like **Autumnal Fire** ★★★, a *doppelbock* with toffee-like maltiness and vague spicy-mocha notes, provide variety and excitement.

CROOKED STAVE BREWING
Denver, Colorado

Founder Chad Yakobson wrote his master's dissertation on *Brettanomyces*, and different species of that "wild" yeast are a part of every beer at this Denver brewery, most the result of blending beers aged in wood barrels. They are generally tart, untamed and refreshingly dry, such as the tropical-fruity (tangerine, pineapple) **St Bretta ★★★**; and hazy golden **L'Brett d'Or ★★★**; or two *saisons*, **Saison Vielle Artisanal ★★☆**, low in alcohol and rustic; and **Surette ★★★**, fruity, earthy and acidic.

DESTINATION
DENVER

Beer aficionados flock to **Falling Rock Tap House** (1919 Blake Street), offering the broadest range of special and well-kept beers, while emphasis on both food and beer is found at nearby **Euclid Hall** (1317 14th Street). Artisan pizza pairs with beer at **Hops & Pie** (3920 Tennyson Street), and fine beer and spirits coexist at **Rackhouse Pub** (208 S Kalamath Street).

DARK HORSE BREWING
Marshall, Michigan

Brewer/owner Aaron Morse turned down an opportunity for his Michigan brewery to appear in a Nickelback music video, simply because he doesn't like their music. His assertive beers reflect similar conviction: bestselling **Crooked Tree IPA ★★★**, resinous and hauntingly herbal; seasonal **4 Elf Winter Warmer Ale ★★☆**, full of nutmeg and other spices; and richly roasted **Reserve Special Black Ale ★★☆**.

DRY DOCK BREWING
Aurora, Colorado

Fast-growing brewery that was founded in 2005 in Aurora next door to a suburban Denver homebrew shop. Excels at traditional European styles such as the light yet spicy **Hefeweizen ★★★**; and toasty **HMS Victory Amber ★★☆**, rather like a strong American take on a best bitter. **Vanilla Porter ★★**, mixing chocolate with prominent vanilla flavours; and **Paragon Apricot Blonde ★★☆**, crisp and fruity, find their own way.

EPIC BREWING
Salt Lake City, Utah

Unlike Utah's other breweries that make low-alcohol beer to serve in their brewpubs, EPIC brews only strong and stronger beers. **Hopulent IPA ★★★** has an immense citrus character with bracing bitterness; **Brainless on Peaches ★★★** is peachy, with Champagne-like notes; **Big Bad Baptist Imperial Stout ★★☆**, infused with coffee, gets aged in bourbon barrels; while **825 State Stout ★★★** is a mocha delight; and **Utah Sage Saison ★★★** offers tropical-fruit and peppery notes.

FAT HEAD'S BREWERY
Middleburg Heights, Ohio

Fathead's Saloon in Pittsburgh spawned first a brewpub in Ohio, then a production facility. Hop-centric and "absolutely uncivilized" beers include **Head Hunter India Pale Ale ★★★☆**, reeking of citrus tropical fruit; and **Hop Juju Imperial IPA ★★★**, bolder still and thick with piney resin. The range also includes spicy-bitter **Güdenhoppy Pils ★★☆**; chocolate-rich **Battle Axe Baltic Porter ★★★**; and campfire-flavoured **Up In Smoke Smoked Porter ★★★**.

FOUNDERS BREWING
Grand Rapids, Michigan

Stubbornly enduring Michigan brewery with a growing international reputation. Seamless **Centennial IPA ★★★☆** is both complex and quaffable; speciality **Curmudgeon Old Ale ★★★☆** is decadent in its youthful maltiness and built for ageing; **Red's Rye PA ★★★** balances citrus, spice and peppery accents; **Breakfast Stout ★★☆** is soothing and warming, and outstanding in its stronger, barrel-aged **KBS ★★★☆**; and **CBS ★★★★** versions.

FOUR PEAKS BREWING
Tempe, Arizona

Across a broad range, the core beers exhibit the balance you'd expect from recipes co-concocted by a British expat brewer. Flagship **Kilt Lifter Scottish-Style Ale ★★★** is rich and a touch smoky; **8 Street Ale ★★** is a mellow best bitter; **Oatmeal Stout ★★☆** offers roasty malt and layered complexity; and **Hop Knot IPA ★★☆** is floral with lingering fruity flavours.

FUNKWERKS
Fort Collins, Colorado

One of the smallest of numerous Fort Collins breweries, Funkwerks is best known for *saisons*, but offers other Belgian-influenced beers like the golden **Deceit ★★☆**, a powerful combination of fruits and spices. Straightahead **Saison ★★★** is earthy and complex, but delicate; the more robust **Tropic King ★★★**, described as Imperial, is intense, filled with tropical-fruit aromas and flavours.

GOOSE ISLAND BEER (ANHEUSER-BUSCH INBEV)
Chicago, Illinois

Chicago brewpub expanded to two pubs plus a production brewery, then sold in 2011. Certain brands such as the mildly fruity **Honkers ★☆**; now being brewed at other ABI facilities, but not (so far) Vintage Ales series beers like the (Belgian) ORVAL-inspired **Matilda ★★☆**; or the sparkling, somewhat winey **Sophie ★★☆**. Pioneering bourbon-barrel-aged brew, **Bourbon County Stout ★★★☆**, now part of a line of Bourbon County beers.

DESTINATION CHICAGO

Those focused primarily on beer may gravitate to the **Map Room** (1949 N Hoyne Avenue), a "Traveller's Tavern" masterfully mixing local and international choices, or to **Owen & Engine** (2700 N Western Avenue) for English-style cask-conditioned ales. Food and beer are equals at **Hopleaf** (5148 N Clark Street), a Belgian-esque brasserie, **Fountainhead** (1970 W Montrose Avenue), featuring comfort food with a gourmet twist, and **The Publican** (837 W Fulton Market), a spacious, upscale beer hall.

GRAND TETON BREWING
Victor, Idaho

An Idaho brewer that is based at the foot of the Teton Mountains, near Yellowstone National Park. Signature beers include the **Bitch Creek ESB** ★★☆, which stands for Extra Special Brown, rather than Bitter, and is not American-hop-shy; and the **Teton Ale** ★★☆, with toffee malt and spicy hoppiness. Brewers' Series ales include the nutty, softly spicy **Pursuit of Hoppiness** ★★☆, an Imperial red ale; and the coffee-ish, herbal **Black Cauldron Imperial Stout** ★★☆.

GREAT DIVIDE BREWING
Denver, Colorado

Downtown Denver brewery that was established in 1994, now with a tasting room attached. It is perhaps best known for the powerful yet approachable **Yeti Imperial Stout** ★★★; and all its many variations, including the whisky-accented **Oak Aged Yeti** ★★★☆. **Denver Pale Ale** ★★☆ provides a sessionable, perfumey contrast to the monster stout; as does the even lighter, delicate **Samurai** ★★★. **Titan IPA** ★★★ provides the obligatory wallop of hops.

GREAT LAKES BREWING
Cleveland, Ohio

Brewpub and production brewery that played a large part in the revival of Cleveland's Ohio City neighbourhood. **Dortmunder Gold Lager** ★★★☆ is an exceptional example of a style rarely brewed even in Germany; **Elliot Ness Amber Lager** ★★★ balances sweet and bitter and strength wonderfully; **Burning River Pale Ale** ★★☆ is a citrus quaffer; and perennial award-winner **Edmund Fitzgerald Porter** ★★★ is mocha-ish and satisfying.

GREAT NORTHERN BREWING
Whitefish, Montana

Montana brewery founded by the great-great grandson of Pacific Northwest brewing legend, Henry Weinhard. Flagship brand is **Black Star Double Hopped Lager** ★★☆, curiously reserved for a beer so described; while winter seasonal **Snow Ghost Winter Lager** ★★★ draws attention with its drying, roasty-nutty character and big malt-derived flavours.

HALF ACRE BEER
Chicago, Illinois

Largest of a new wave of Chicago breweries, sales fuelled by success of 16-oz "tallboy" cans, starting with **Daisy Cutter** ★★★☆, a pale ale brimming with grapefruit and pine; **Over Ale** ★★☆, a nutty chocolate brown ale; and crisp **Gossamer** ★★☆, a golden ale. Many specialities, like spicy rye stout, **Baumé** ★★★; and **Ambrosia** ★★, a wheat ale laced with oranges and hibiscus.

JOLLY PUMPKIN ARTISAN ALES
Dexter, Michigan

Idiosyncratic brewery near Detroit dedicated to oak-ageing and bottle-conditioning its beers. Stylistically unclassifiable beers include **La Roja** ★★★, a spicy mix of berry and vanilla notes with warming strength; fragrant and pineappley **Oro de Calabaza** ★★☆; cocoa, cinnamon and dried fruit **Maracaibo Especial** ★★★; and **Bam Bière** ★★★, a dry, tart and refreshing session beer that has spawned a line of similar "Bam" beers.

KUHNHENN BREWING
Warren, Michigan

Family-owned, Detroit-area hardware store that adjusted to the arrival of a "big box" store by transforming into a highly regarded brewery. Perhaps most famous for potent and densely fruity **Raspberry Eisbock** ★★★☆; but worth noting, too, for similarly powerful **Fourth Dementia Olde Ale** ★★★, caramelly and cherry-ish; and highly hoppy, not-quite-balanced **American IPA** ★★☆.

Maracaibo Especial

Special Brown Ale

LA CUMBRE BREWING
Albuquerque, New Mexico

Husband-and-wife brewery founded in 2009 in Albuquerque, New Mexico. Core brands include the piney and faintly nutty **Elevated IPA** ★★☆; the dry, Germanic **South Peak Pilsner** ★★☆; and the roasty, raisin-and-spice **Malpais Stout** ★★★. Limited release **Fievre d'Abricot** ("Apricot Fever") ★★☆ shows skill in complex, non-sweet fruit beer.

LAKEFRONT BREWING
Milwaukee, Wisconsin

Early Milwaukee brewery offering excellent core beers and what may be the best brewery tour in the business. Lagers are a strength: **Riverwest Stein Beer** ★★★ is teasing with malty sweetness before finishing dry; seasonal **Pumpkin Lager** ★★★ is spicy but never overly so; and perfumey **Oktoberfest** ★★★ is an off-dry mix of toffee and spice. The nutmeg and muddled fruit notes of **Bridge Burner Special Reserve Ale** ★★★ show skill at the top of the fermenter.

LEFT HAND BREWING
Longmont, Colorado

The red left hand on its labels is one of the most distinctive symbols in craft beer, the brewery's name taken from Arapahoe Chief Niwot or "Left Hand". Deep line-up from Longmont, Colorado includes **Sawtooth Ale** ★★★, a soft but assertive special bitter; **SmokeJumper** ★★☆, a powerful smoked porter; **Milk Stout** ★★★, creamy in both regular and nitro versions; and the chocolaty **Black Jack Porter** ★★☆. Intriguing Fade to Black series highlights limited edition black beers.

MARBLE BREWERY
Albuquerque, New Mexico

A young brewery that was founded by a trio of brewpub veterans, Ted Rice, Jeff Jinnett and John Gozigian. Their **Red Ale ★★** is replete with rooty and resinous herbs and citrus oils – almost an IPA in red ale form; while their **India Pale Ale ★★★** is spicy, juicy in its fruitiness and admirably restrained in bitterness. This promise shows much promise for the future.

NEBRASKA BREWING
Papillion, Nebraska

Brewery located outside Omaha that makes a solid range of beers, such as the peppery **Infinite Wit ★★**, but grabs attention with **Hop God ★★☆**, a double IPA fermented with Belgian yeast, peachy, citrus and bitter; **Melange A Trois ★★★**, a strong Belgian-inspired blond that spends six months in Chardonnay barrels; and barrel-aged **Apricot Au Poivre Saison ★★**, earthy and peppery.

NEW BELGIUM BREWING
Fort Collins, Colorado

Sustainability-obsessed (in a good way) brewery based in Colorado and building in North Carolina. Basic amber ale **Fat Tire ★★** pays many of the bills; but newer **Ranger IPA ★★★** is building fans with its fruity, piney hop character. **Trippel ★★★**, with its tangerine, spice and warming alcohol; and chocolaty, apricot **Abbey ★★☆** fly the Belgian flag; while Lips of Faith beers like the tart, dryly fruity **La Folie ★★★☆** excite experiential drinkers.

NEW GLARUS BREWING
New Glarus, Wisconsin

Famed brewery near Madison, frustrating aficionados everywhere by distributing only within the state. Light ale **Spotted Cow ★☆** pays the bills; but allows for delights like the intensely fruity **Wisconsin Belgian Red ★★★★**; the fruity-tart-tangy **Strawberry Rhubarb ★★★★**; the pleasantly restrained black IPA **Black Top ★★☆**; and seasonals such as the almost Scotch-whisky-esque **Winter Warmer ★★★**.

NEW HOLLAND BREWING
Holland, Michigan

Brewery and distillery on the shores of Lake Michigan, in the small town of Holland. Flagship is the dried-peach and citrus **Mad Hatter IPA ★★★**; now the heart of a whole Hatter line of brands, including the spicy-fruity, almost brandy-ish **Imperial Hatter ★★★**. Other ales include the plummy, bracing **Dragon's Milk Ale ★★☆**; **Black Tulip Tripel ★★★**, which begins fruity and sweet but ends with a hoppy statement; and the light and *kölsch*-like **Full Circle ★★☆**.

ODELL BREWING
Fort Collins, Colorado

Family-founded brewery in Colorado, the second to open in the state. Original draught-only focus was dropped to bottle brews like earthy, citrus and apple **5 Barrel Ale ★★★**; the rich, sweet but never overbearing **90 Shilling ★★★**; the lightly creamy, mocha-ish **Cutthroat Porter ★★☆**; and the lime- and grapefruit-accented **IPA ★★☆**. The 4 Pack series beers up the ante in strength and body.

O'FALLON BREWERY
O'Fallon, Missouri

Brewery outside of St. Louis survived near-death experience, and briefly idled until a former Anheuser-Busch marketing exec bought it. Now **Wheach ★★☆**, a wheat beer infused with peach flavour, is served at Busch Stadium baseball games. Citrusy, floral **5-Day IPA ★★☆** shows restraint; while **Smoked Porter ★★★** is rich and bacon-laden; **Hemp Hop Rye ★★** is spicy and herbal; and **Pumpkin Beer ★★** is a local favourite.

OSKAR BLUES BREWERY
Longmont, Colorado

Orchestrator of the "canned beer apocalypse", pioneering the canning of craft beer in Longmont. First in the can was **Dale's Pale Ale ★★★**, a balanced, toasty-citrus ale, followed by the toffee maltiness of **Old Chub Scotch Ale ★★★**; **Ten Fidy ★★☆**, a bold and brash Imperial stout; the rather straightforward, sweetish **Mama's Little Yella Pils ★★**; and the herbaceous, almost chewy **Gubna Imperial IPA ★★☆**.

PERENNIAL ARTISAN ALES
St. Louis, Missouri

Southside St. Louis brewery often uses yeasts from Belgium and locally sourced ingredients such as rhubarb and squash, resulting in beers like summer seasonal **Peach Berliner Weisse ★★☆**, fermented on local peaches. Dizzying range: delightfully dry and Belgian-esque **Hommel Bier ★★★**; **Abraxas ★★★**, an Imperial stout packed with spices and Ancho chillies; **Fantastic Voyage ★★★**, an Imperial milk stout aged on coconut flakes; **Black Walnut Dunkel ★★☆**, a *dunkelweisse* made with Missouri walnuts.

DESTINATION
ST. LOUIS

Bridge (1004 Locust Street) blends sophisticated surroundings with 55 taps, a couple of hundred bottled beers and a fine selection of charcuterie and cheese, plus 20 wines by the glass for the beer-phobic.

REVOLUTION BREWING
Chicago, Illinois

Brewpub in Chicago's Logan Square neighbourhood opened a production facility a short distance away in 2012. As adept at bold beers like **Anti-Hero IPA ★★☆**, a resiny, fruity/pine punch; and the husky **Eugene ★★★**, a robust porter; as it is with lower-alcohol offerings such as **Cross of Gold ★★☆**, a floral and crisp golden ale; and the toffee-like, nutty **Workingman Mild ★★★**.

SAINT LOUIS BREWERY
St. Louis, Missouri

The downtown taproom, a brewpub, and a production brewery at close-in suburb Maplewood make about 50 varieties of Schlafly beer a year, including three rotating and distinct IPAs, the **Tasmanian India Pale Ale ★★★**, showcasing Australian hops rich with melon and passion-fruit, being one. Wide range, from coffee-and-cream **Oatmeal Stout ★★★**; and delicate **Kölsch ★★☆**; to popular spiced seasonals **Pumpkin Ale ★★☆**; and **Christmas Ale ★★☆**.

SANTA FE BREWING
Santa Fe, New Mexico

Began operations in a horse barn south of Santa Fe with a square brewing kettle originally used by Boulder Beer during its early days. **State Pen Porter ★★** offers toffee notes balanced by a properly roasty character; colourfully named **Chicken Killer Barley Wine ★★** can be reminiscent of fruitcake when aged; while **Imperial Java Stout ★★☆** is suitably coffee-dominated and rich.

SANTAN BREWING
Chandler, Arizona

Brewpub-spawned canning brewery producing beers suitable for hotter-than-a-furnace-fan Arizona, such as sweetish, grainy **Sunspot Gold ★★**; banana-dominated **HefeWeizen ★★**; and also more assertive **Devil's Ale ★★☆**, full of juicy orange and pine; and the more piney **HopShock IPA ★★**. Interesting seasonals include **Mr. Pineapple ★★☆**, a pineapple-infused wheat beer.

SHORT'S BREWING
Elk Rapids, Michigan

The original northern Michigan brewpub still operates, but a separate brewery has grown into a buzz-worthy regional producer. Numerous strong, uniquely flavoured beers like **Peaches & Crème ★★★**, peachy and tart; a true to its name **Key Lime Pie ★★★**; and molasses-rich Imperial-sized **Publican Porter ★★☆**. More traditional offerings include **Huma Lupa Licious IPA ★★☆**, packed with pine and grapefruit hoppiness; and **Local's Light Beer ★★☆**, a crisp light lager.

SKA BREWING
Durango, Colorado

The founders labelled their home-brewed beer as being from Ska Brewing because they played ska while brewing in the San Juan Mountains. Chequerboard labels still adorn beers: **Modus Hoperandi IPA ★★★**, full of pine and grapefruit; **Autumnal Mole Stout ★★★**, a balanced blend of cocoa and three kinds of peppers; the spicy **Euphoria Pale Ale ★★**; and appropriately milky **Steel Toe Stout ★★☆**.

SNAKE RIVER BREWING
Jackson, Wyoming

Brewpub that also packages several beers, in the tourist destination of Jackson. **Zonker Stout ★★★** offers intense roasty notes balanced by chocolate sweetness; **Vienna Lager ★★★** is soft and faintly nutty; **Dortmunder ★★☆** is a bready and spicy lager; barrel-aged **Le Serpent Cerise ★★★☆** is cherry-laced and tart; and **Pako's Eye P-A ★★** is floral and juicy.

SPRECHER BREWING
Milwaukee, Wisconsin

Eponymous brewery founded in Milwaukee by former Pabst brewer Randy Sprecher in 1985. Classic **Black Bavarian ★★★** is the picture of balance in a black lager; special edition **Doppel Bock ★★★** is a full-bodied, malty delight; **Hefe Weiss ★★☆** tends toward the lighter side of the style; and decidedly unGermanic **IPA2 ★★☆** segues nicely from a sweet entry to a bitter but not aggressive finish.

Sugar Maple (441 E Lincoln Avenue) is a neighbourhood local that just also happens to be an outstanding beer bar pouring possibly the best selection in the region on 60 taps, with space always reserved for up-and-coming local brewers.

SQUATTERS PUBS & BEERS
Salt Lake City, Utah

Long-established Salt Lake City brewpub, now with three locations and bottling through the Utah Brewers Cooperative. Crisp and moderately bitter **Provo Girl Pilsner ★★★** refreshes with low strength; as does the peppery, nutty **Full Suspension Pale Ale ★★☆**. Stronger brews include the indulgent **Hop Rising** double IPA **★★★**; the dense, anise-accented Imperial stout **Outer Darkness ★★★**; and the sweet, tart and funky spice of oak-conditioned **529 ★★★☆**.

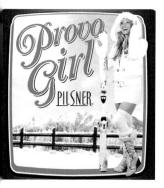

SUMMIT BREWING
Saint Paul, Minnesota

Focused on the Minnesota Twin Cities market from the outset in 1986, with a core of well-made beers, recently augmented by an Unchained series and excellent seasonals such as the restrained **Maibock ★★☆**. Core brands include **Great Northern Porter ★★★**, roasty but soft; creamy **Oatmeal Stout ★★☆**; and **Extra Pale Ale ★★☆**, with citrus/lemon notes leading to a dry finish.

SUN KING BREWING
Indianapolis, Indiana

Indianapolis brewery with acclaim disproportional to the short time it has been open (since 2009). A long list of specialities and one-offs keep the beer raters active, but regular brands are fine on their own, such as the floral, citrus **Sunlight Cream Ale ★★☆**; the admirably restrained **Osiris Pale Ale ★★★**; and the toffee and raisin, brown-spice-accented **Wee Mac Scottish-Style Ale ★★★**.

SURLY BREWING
Minneapolis, Minnesota

After opening in 2006, this Minnesota brewery quickly grabbed attention for its often "extreme" beers. Fans of **Darkness ★★★☆**, a chocolate-layered, dark-fruit Imperial stout, travel hundreds of miles to buy it on "Darkness Day". Piney IPA **Furious ★★☆** is equally intense. More nuanced offerings include the creamy oatmeal brown ale **Bender ★★☆**; an unfiltered *helles* called **Hell ★★★**; and a malty **Mild ★★☆**.

TALLGRASS BREWING
Manhattan, Kansas

Young brewery focused on draught, cans and community, near Topeka, Kansas. Main brands include the citrus and refreshing **Halcyon Wheat ★★**; the improbably named **Buffalo Sweat ★★**, a sweet and chocolaty brown ale; and **Oasis ★★☆**, a fruity, vaguely grassy strong ale best described as an amped-up ESB.

THREE FLOYDS BREWING
Munster, Indiana

This Munster brewery was founded by, you guessed it, three guys named Floyd – a father and two sons. Best known for their once pre-eminent hop bomb, **Alpha King ★★★**, still a solid illustration of the beauty of American hops. **Robert the Bruce ★★☆** is a strong and sweetly caramelly Scotch ale; **Dreadnaught ★★★** is their chewy-hoppy, tropical-fruity double IPA; and **Gumballhead ★★☆** is a love-or-hate wheat beer with a sharp shot of hoppiness.

TWO BROTHERS BREWING
Warrenville, Illinois

Like many in the 1990s, Jason and Jim Ebel started their brewery in suburban Chicago with a combination of new equipment and repurposed dairy tanks, designing it with **Ebel's Weiss ★★☆**, a soft, almost fluffy, *hefeweizen*, in mind. Diverse portfolio includes **Domaine DuPage ★★**, a sweetish *bière de garde*; roasty **Reprieve Schwarzbier Lager ★★☆**; and **Cane and Ebel ★★★**, a strong, spicy rye beer.

UINTA BREWING
Salt Lake City, Utah

Adept at low-alcohol beers, this wind-powered brewery produces three lines: Organic, Classic and Crooked, the last the strongest. **Organic Baba Black Lager ★★☆**, a chocolaty *schwarzbier*, typifies the first; while well-balanced **Cutthroat Pale Ale ★★** highlights the Classic category. Crooked includes **Anniversary Barley Wine ★★☆**, redolent of chewy caramel and citrus hops; and **Hop Notch IPA ★★**, leaner of body, floral and bitter.

UPSLOPE BREWING
Boulder, Colorado

Company expanded six times in five years after opening in 2008, first selling just two brands in cans and emphasizing that its beers are filtered. Core offerings are not flashy: **Pale Ale ★★**, brightly hoppy and balanced; **Brown Ale ★★☆**, roasty, smooth, nutty and seamless; and **Craft Lager ★★**, grainy and crisp. Seasonals, like **Foreign Style Stout ★★★**, with dark fruitiness and roasted malts prominent, tend to be more assertive.

URBAN CHESTNUT BREWING
St. Louis, Missouri

Founded in by two former Anheuser-Busch employees, who preach "beer divergency" through Reverence and Revolution series. Former features **Zwickel ★★★**, a bready *helles*; and **Schnickelfritz ★★★**, a *weissbier* brimming with vanilla, banana and clove. Revolution includes **Hopfen ★★★☆**, a floral, grassy "Bavarian IPA"; **Winged Nut ★★☆**, a roasty *weissbier* infused with chestnuts; and **STLIPA ★★**, a double IPA laced with citrus notes.

EAST COAST

Craft brewing was born in California and brewpubs got their start in the Pacific Northwest, but the successful commercialization of craft beer began in the East, specifically in Boston, home to the Boston Beer Company. Originally a beer commissioned at other breweries, SAMUEL ADAMS Boston Lager was the first craft beer to break down barriers and begin appearing on draught taps and in beer fridges across the nation, from sports bars to white-tablecloth restaurants.

It didn't take long for the idea to catch on. From Maine to Maryland, the northeast soon became a hotbed of craft brewing, oddly taking root last – but now quite solidly – in its most populated jurisdiction, New York City. And likely the hottest place in the region is Philadelphia, which along with Boston, Baltimore and Portland is without question a hub of both modern American craft brewing and the beer bar movement.

508 GASTROBREWERY
New York City

Located in Manhattan's SoHo neighborhood, this relative newcomer is turning out flavourful brews in a tiny system in a restaurant's basement, and even more amazingly, bottling for retail sale. Thick and boozy **Montezuma Imperial Stout** ★★☆; funky yet bracing, lambic-inspired **Greenwich Gueuze** ★★★; fruity-spicy **Belgian-Style Golden Strong Ale** ★★☆; balanced and dry **Smoked Rye IPA** ★★☆; and chewy, nutty **American Strong Ale** ★★ are just a few of dozens released.

ALCHEMIST, THE
Waterbury, Vermont

Brewery currently producing just one beer year-round. The double IPA **Heady Topper** ★★★☆ is not so much a hoppy punch, like some others, but more of an unfolding dance with hops, with notes of pineapple, tropical fruit, lemon and citrus, and even a little alcoholic warmth.

ALLAGASH BREWING
Portland, Maine

A brewery that is so preoccupied with Belgian beers that the founder Rob

Todd built a lambic-style coolship for spontaneous fermentation. The Belgian-style wheat beer **White** ★★★ has a great balance of citrus and peppery herbals; the **Tripel** ★★★☆ segues nicely from perfumey fruit to drying hops, and when oak-aged becomes the bizarrely attractive **Curieux** ★★★☆; the **Coolship Red** ★★★☆ is a model of dryly fruity complexity; and the **Coolship Cerise** ★★★ offers white peppery fruitiness and a dry finish.

BAXTER BREWING
Lewiston, Maine

Canning brewery located due north of Portland. Strong seasonal focus emphasizes beers like the citrus and lemongrass **Summer Swelter** ★★, with its profoundly lemony character; and mildly peppery and oak-sweetened **Hayride Autumn Ale** ★★☆; although year-rounders like the lightly fruity, nutty-citrus **Pamola Xtra Pale Ale** ★★; and wonderfully balanced, faintly roasty **Amber Road** ★★★ are worthy of exploration.

BERKSHIRE BREWING
South Deerfield, Massachusetts

Nestled in the western mountains of Massachusetts, this brewery has garnered a reputation for its uncompromised recipes and quality control. Its brands include the bready and slightly hoppy **Steel Rail Extra Pale Ale** ★★★; the roasty, caffeinated **Dean's Beans Coffeehouse Porter** ★★☆; and the hoppy/malty **Shabadoo Black & Tan Ale** ★★☆; along with the summer perennial, crisp and biscuity-spicy **Czech Style Pilsner** ★★★.

BREWER'S ART, THE
Baltimore, Maryland

European-influenced brewpub now canning several brands. **La Pétroleuse** ★★☆ is a *bière de garde* with aromas and flavours of lemon, white pepper and honey; **Ozzy** ★★★ is a take on Belgian devil beers with a spicy hop aroma and bright apricot and doughy malt flavours; and **Resurrection** ★★☆ is a *dubbel* with caramel and raisin aromas, slight alcohol heat, yeasty flavour and a dry finish.

BROOKLYN BREWERY
New York City

New York brewery fronted by well-known brewer and sometimes author Garrett Oliver. Stalwarts include the **Lager** ★★☆, toasty and somewhat Vienna-like; **Brown Ale** ★★★, bold with nutty hoppiness; and **East India Pale Ale** ★★★, which skilfully mixes British influence with American hopheadedness. Seasonal **Black Chocolate Stout** ★★★☆ is wonderfully chocolaty without the addition of chocolate; while **Local 1** ★★★ is a spicy, all-bottle-fermented restorative.

DESTINATION
NEW YORK

In recent years, the Big Apple has blossomed with beer destinations, from the pioneering **d.b.a.** (41 1st Avenue) with its apt motto, "drink good stuff," to newer arrivals like the homage to all things beer, **Rattle N Hum** (14 E 33rd Street), beer shop **Good Beer** (422 E 9th Street), craft beer standard-bearer **Blind Tiger** (281 Bleecker Street) and Brooklyn's sometimes pricey but always excellent **Spuyten Duyvil** (359 Metropolitan Avenue).

CAMBRIDGE BREWING
Cambridge, Massachusetts

A small-production brewery and pub located among Boston's college districts. The house beers brewed by brewmaster Will Meyers include the mocha-ish, dryly bitter **Charles River Porter** ★★☆; and the dry-hopped, sessionable **Tall Tale Pale Ale** ★★☆. But the brewery's strength is in its occasional releases like the **Cerise Cassée** ★★★☆, barrel-aged and loaded with tart cherry fruitiness, among others. Local draught and limited bottle distribution.

CAPTAIN LAWRENCE BREWING
Elmsford, New York

Westchester brewery known for flavourful beers that often mask high strength. Regular offerings include the clovey, banana-ish and mildly funky **Liquid Gold** ★★☆; the massively piney and slightly citrus **Captain's Reserve Imperial IPA** ★★★; and the bonfire-like **Smoked**

Porter ★★☆. Popular speciality releases include the funky **Cuvee de Castleton** ★★★☆, with pleasant notes of sour grapes; and **Nor'Easter: Winter Warmer** ★★★, brewed with elderberries and aged in bourbon barrels.

DOGFISH HEAD BREWING
Milton, Delaware

This Delaware brewery is known for its experimentation and "extreme" brewing. Its year-round brews include the continuously hopped, aggressive yet balanced **90 Minute IPA** ★★★; the raisiny and soothing **Raison d'Etre** ★★★☆; and the complex, luxurious, Paraguayan-wood-aged **Palo Santo Maron** ★★★★. Its irregular releases are highly sought-after, but less reliable, save for its **Immort Ale** ★★★, a strong, faintly smoky beast; and the outrageous and potent fruit beer, **Black & Blue** ★★★.

GEARY BREWING
(DL GEARY BREWING)
Portland, Maine

Early northeast brewery, established 1983 in Portland. **Pale Ale** ★★☆ was an early standard by which others were judged, although UK rather than US in style; **Hampshire Ale** ★★★ was born a winter warmer and is still best "when the weather sucks"; while the **IPA** ★★☆ is arguably the British-leaning brewery's most American-style ale.

HE'BREW (SHMALTZ BREWING)
Clifton Park, New York

Beer commissioner turned upstate New York brewer, mixing good-natured fun with respect for the Jewish religion. "Chosen beers" include the pomegranate-juice-fuelled **Origin** ★★★☆, a strong ale of powerful complexity; hazelnutty, burnt citrus **Messiah Nut Brown Ale ★★★**; and tamer, ESB-like **Genesis Dry Hopped Session Ale ★★☆**. Newer arrivals include the resinous and roasty **Death of a Contract Brewer Black IPA ★★**; and **Hop Manna IPA ★★★**, an orangey ale with some finesse.

HEAVY SEAS BEER
Baltimore, Maryland

A pioneering mid-Atlantic brewery which was formerly known as Clipper City Brewing. Flagship **Loose Cannon IPA ★★☆** is grapefruit and pine forward; the seasonal bourbon barrel-aged **Siren Noire Imperial Stout ★★★** is brimming with deep Belgian chocolate and fresh vanilla; and **Winter Storm ★★☆**, an "Imperial" ESB, boasts a mix of nut and melon flavours and a spicy hop finish.

DESTINATION
WASHINGTON DC

The beer scene in the US capital begins at **ChurchKey/Birch & Barley** (1337 14th Street NW), a dynamic upstairs-downstairs duo of beer bar-restaurants. Other highlights include **RFD** (810 7th Street NW), with 36 taps and a monstrous bottle list, the comfortable, low-key and two-level **Meridian Pint** (3400 11th Street NW) and Arlington's stylish **Rustico** (4075 Wilson Boulevard), with over 300 varieties of beer and cider.

HIGH POINT BREWING (RAMSTEIN BEER)
Butler, New Jersey

Brewery making Ramstein beers from all-German ingredients at a New Jersey location chosen for its pristine water source. The **Blonde Wheat Beer ★★☆** is a floral, hazy year-round bestseller; while the **Classic Wheat Beer ★★★** is a dark marvel of sweet and creamy roasted malt flavour. Traditional German seasonals include the hazy, toasted caramel-like *märzen* **Oktoberfest ★★☆**; lightly hoppy and sweetly mellow **Mai Bock ★★☆**; and the lusciously boozy **Winter Wheat ★★★**.

HILL FARMSTEAD BREWERY
Greensboro, Vermont

Known for a skilful use of hops, this Vermont brewery has a near-cult-like following. Diverse offerings include the balanced, citrus-spicy pale ale **Edward ★★★**; chewy and tropical-fruity **Abner Double IPA ★★★☆**; the strongly roasty and dark chocolaty **Everett Porter ★★★**; the grapefruity and strong **Susan IPA ★★★**; and the gorgeous **Anna ★★★★**, a *saison* that blends flavours of honey, oak, acidic citrus, vanilla and white wine.

JACK'S ABBY BREWING
Framingham, Massachusetts

Lager specialist named for the wife (Abby) of one of the brewery's trio of fraternal founders (Jack). Flagships include **Jabby Brau Session Lager ★★☆**, light and mildly bitter; **Hoponius Union ★★★**, hoppy as an IPA but with a lean, refreshing crispness; and the smoked *schwarzbier*,

Smoke & Dagger ★★★, with an aroma reminiscent of smouldering balsawood. A second anniversary lager morphed into the seasonal **Mass Rising** ★★★, strong, bitter and curiously refreshing.

MAINE BEER
Freeport, Maine

Sparse bottle labels understate the elegant flavours within. **Peeper** ★★★, a balanced, citrusy golden ale; and the thin but smooth **Mean Old Tom** ★★☆, a stout aged on vanilla beans, put spins on established styles. **Zoe** ★★☆, a hoppy, zesty and aromatic amber ale; **Lunch** ★★★, a tropical-fruity and piney IPA; and the chocolaty, hoppy porter **King Titus** ★★☆ round out offerings from this small brewery with a big buzz.

NARRAGANSETT BREWING
Providence, Rhode Island

Circa 1890 brewery on Rhode Island, closed and demolished in the 1990s but reopened in 2005 as a beer commissioner. Only year-round brand of note is the fruity **Cream Ale** ★★, quenching and off-dry; but seasonals like the dark-chocolaty, pumpernickel-ish **Porter** ★★☆; caramelly **Fest Lager** ★★; and the slightly honey-ish, mildly bitter **Summer Ale** ★★ keep the portfolio interesting.

OMMEGANG (DUVEL MOORTGAT)
Cooperstown, New York

Near the Baseball Hall of Fame, this brewery was founded by a beer importer in collaboration with three Belgian breweries, including now-sole owner Duvel. Flagship **Abbey Ale** ★★☆ is perhaps not as malty-spicy as it once was; while **Rare Vos** ★★★ remains a mellow, fruity sipper; and the dryly spicy, crisp-finishing **Hennepin** ★★★ continues to please. Newer **BPA** ★★☆, billed a Belgian-style pale ale, seems to fall just short of the mark.

PRETTY THINGS BEER & ALE PROJECT
Westport, Massachusetts

Husband-and-wife team with "visiting brewer" status at Buzzards Bay Brewing. Despite having to adapt their schedules to the brewery's non-operating times, they produce impressive brews, including a superb brown ale with a dry, rustic maltiness, **Saint Botolph's Town** ★★★☆; the almost textbook US-style **Meadowlark IPA** ★★★; **Jack D'Or** ★★★, a *saison* with a bitter-spicy US twist; the fruity-to-spicy-to-bitter **Fluffy White Rabbits Triple** ★★★; and magnificently quenching **American Darling Good Time Lager** ★★☆.

SAMUEL ADAMS (BOSTON BEER COMPANY)
Boston, Massachusetts

Pioneering beer commissioning company, now largest craft brewery in the US. Flagship **Boston Lager** ★★★ is the dry, toasty meeting place of *dunkel* and pilsner; while new arrival **Rebel IPA** ★★ is an easy piney and malty drinker. Special editions and seasonals are many, including: masterfully aromatic **Noble Pils** ★★★; the winey, barrel-aged *tripel*, **New World** ★★★; and the world's strongest fully fermented beer, the hugely complex **Utopias** ★★★★, varying year-to-year, but always an intense blend of of new and aged beers with cocoa, dark fruit and sherry-like flavours.

SARANAC BEER (MATT BREWING)
Utica, New York

An upstate New York family brewery that has been in business since before Prohibition times. It has rebranded with the craft-like Saranac line, including the newer **White IPA ★★☆**, a curious mix of IPA and Belgian-style wheat beer; the dry and biscuity, only gently hoppy **Pale Ale ★★**; and the slightly unbalanced (on the hoppy side) **India Pale Ale ★★**. High Peak series beers bring something extra to the table.

SLY FOX BREWING
Pottstown, Pennsylvania

A Philadelphia-area brewery and pub that is experiencing great local success with its canned beers. The crisply flavourful, German-inspired **Pikeland Pils ★★★** is a warm-weather treat; while the citrus **Phoenix Pale Ale ★★☆** quenches a cool-weather thirst. Large-format bottled brews include the peppery-fruity **Saison Vos ★★★**; and the quite sweet, darkly fruity and strong **Ichor ★★☆**.

SMUTTYNOSE BREWING
Portsmouth, New Hampshire

Named for an island off the coast of New Hampshire, this Portsmouth brewery was founded in 1994. Regular brands include the hugely popular **Old Brown Dog ★★★**, a brown ale with a dry, mildly bitter caramel character; **Star Island Single ★★★**, with mild sweetness balanced by spicy, citrus hop; and aptly named, chocolate-toffee **Robust Porter ★★☆**. Occasional Big Beer series fuels creativity.

SOUTHAMPTON PUBLICK HOUSE
Southampton, New York

Acclaimed Long Island brewpub turned beer commissioner, fronted for 15 years by acclaimed brewer Phil Markowski, who left in 2012. Year-round brands include the **Double White Ale ★★☆**, orangey up front, big, spicy and sweet in the finish; and the sweetish, borderline fruity **Altbier ★★☆**. Excellence is reserved for farmhouse beers like the enticingly floral **Cuvée des Fleurs ★★★☆**; and spicy, cooked caramel **Grand Cru ★★★**.

SOUTHERN TIER BREWING
Lakewood, New York

Upper New York State brewery with a solid regular line-up and sometimes inspired seasonals, including the dessert-like **Crème Brûlée Imperial Milk Stout ★★**, a vanilla and butterscotch love-it-or-hate-it ale; and the pumpkin-pie-in-a-glass spiced **Pumking ★★**. Regulars include **Iniquity ★★★**, a biscuity, toasted-orange-ish strong black ale; **Hop Sun ★★☆**, a full-bodied yet quaffable wheat; and the slightly sweet and peppery **UnEarthly IPA ★★☆**.

STOUDT'S BREWING
Adamstown, Pennsylvania

Carol Stoudt fronts this family-owned brewery in Pennsylvania Dutch Country, and the softly perfumey **Scarlet Lady Ale ★★** exists to remind anyone who forgets that fact. Other brands include the *helles*-like **Gold Lager ★★☆**, with a kiss of malty sweetness; the snappy, dry, quenching **Pils ★★★**; and the fruity, caramelly **Triple ★★☆**.

TRINITY BREWHOUSE
Providence, Rhode Island

A mainstay in Rhode Island's capital city, the brewery offers a diverse, mostly draught-only selection from its pub. Kegs are available, but one beer, the citrus hoppy **Trinity IPA ★★** is sold in bottles. It's one of the largest breweries in the small state.

TRÖEGS BREWING
Hershey, Pennsylvania

Long a well-kept Pennsylvania secret, this central state brewery is now becoming better known up and down the east coast. Beers like the winter seasonal **Mad Elf ★★★☆**, with its fruit-derived complexity and well-contained strength; the dryly malty, almost bready **Troegenator Double Bock ★★★**; and the intensely hoppy, resiny **Nugget Nectar ★★☆** help spread the word.

VICTORY BREWING
Downingtown, Pennsylvania

A versatile Philadelphia-area producer of many beer styles, including ales and lagers of both session-strength and considerable potency. Its several brands include the crisp and fragrant, Bohemian-style **Prima Pils ★★★**; the **HopDevil ★★★**, an assertive US-style India Pale Ale; the rich and oily **Storm King ★★★☆**, which is a roasty, almost chewy Imperial stout of strong character; the luxuriant **St Victorious Doppelbock ★★★☆**; and, lastly, the **Golden Monkey ★★★**, which is a strong and spicy Belgian-inspired golden ale.

DESTINATION
PHILADELPHIA

The self-proclaimed "America's best beer-drinking city" has many outstanding beer bars, from iconic, Belgian-esque **Monk's Cafe** (264 S 16th Street) to local-brewers only **Standard Tap** (901 N 2nd Street), three-outlet temple of beer, wine and cheese, **Tria** (original at 123 S 18th Street), and old school **Grey Lodge** (6235 Frankford Avenue), home of the cask ale extravaganzas, "Friday the Firkinteenth."

WHITE BIRCH BREWING
Hooksett, New Hampshire

Located between Concord and Manchester, this small, Belgian-inspired brewery boasts a growing profile. Three flagship beers are pear-ish and yeasty **Belgian Style Pale Ale ★★**; citrus and toffee-ish **Hooksett Ale ★★☆**; and resinous **Hop Session Ale ★★☆**. It also brews three seasonals, notably tangy summer **Berliner Weiss ★★**; and winter barley wine **Ol'Cattywhompus ★★★**, with dominant brown sugar and toffee flavours and earthy hops in the background.

DESTINATIONS **PENNSYLVANIA, NEW JERSEY AND DELAWARE**

Iron Hill Brewery (147 E Main Street, Newark) is a group of 10 award-winning brewpubs spanning three states: Delaware, New Jersey and Pennsylvania. Always creative, seasonally adjusted draught choices are supplemented by an impressive "Bottled Reserve" programme.

UNITED STATES

SOUTH

Time was that the American south would be referred to by beer aficionados as a craft-brewing wasteland, and small wonder, when even today southern states like Mississippi, Alabama and Georgia remain mired at the bottom of the chart in terms of both the breweries-to-population ratio and the total number of breweries.

Still, it's not all bad beer news in the south. Following successful challenges to trade-constraining alcohol laws, states like North Carolina have blossomed as craft brewing hotbeds, while Texas and Florida have witnessed the rise of significant brewing centres within their borders. Aiding the development of craft beer across the south are the efforts of a breed of impressive southern beer bars, led by the 16-outlet Flying Saucer Chain and proud independents such as Georgia's Brick Store.

512 BREWING
Austin, Texas

Largest of the new wave of breweries in Austin, minimizing its environmental footprint by using mostly organic ingredients and selling only draught beer. Uses local pecans in its unique **Pecan Porter ★★★**, the nutty notes complementing a rich coffee flavour; offers Old World floral notes and New World citrus aromas in its **IPA ★★☆**; grapefruit peel provides a bright twist to **Wit ★★☆**; while **Bruin ★★☆**, a "double brown ale", is malty and dangerously smooth.

ABITA BREWING
Abita Springs, Louisiana

Early southern craft brewery based outside New Orleans. Flagship **Amber ★☆** enjoyed up and down Bourbon Street; but more savvy locals reach for **Turbodog ★★**, a darker, slightly stronger and maltier brew; the beautifully aromatic **Restoration Pale Ale ★★☆**; or the firmly bitter **Jockomo IPA ★★☆**. Brewed for the 25th anniversary, it is to be hoped that the intense, chocolate-fruity **Double Dog ★★★** continues.

BIG BOSS BREWING
Raleigh, North Carolina

Brewery and taproom whose core range of five brands is best at the lighter-hued end, as with the *kölsch*-like **Angry Angel ★★★**, which hints at fruitiness without ever being fruity; and **Hell's Belle ★★★**, with initial candied pear notes drying to a spicy, slightly boozy finish. The brown ale **Bad Penny ★★☆** slightly misses the mark with too much toffee-ish sweetness.

CIGAR CITY BREWING
Tampa, Florida

Floridian cult favourite, located near the Tampa Bay airport. Regular brands include **Maduro Brown Ale** ★★★, rich and creamy thanks to the use of oats in the mash; and **Jai Alai IPA** ★★★, smooth with soft fruitiness and measured bitterness. Big-bottle seasonals include **Big Sound Scotch Ale** ★★☆, port-wine-ish with plum and brown-spice flavours; and **Marshal Zhukov's Imperial Stout** ★★★☆, with lashings of liquorice, roasted spice, coffee and warming alcohol.

COMMUNITY BEER

Dallas, Texas

Young, centrally located brewery with a suitably community-minded spirit. Firmly malty **Public Ale** ★★★ is a fitting homage to Fuller's ESB; much-awarded **Vienna Lager** ★★★ is toasty and crisp; **Mosaic IPA** ★★☆, named for its principal hop, submerges berry fruitiness beneath spicy, citrusy hop; and strong **Trinity Tripel** ★★★ gets its uniquely perfumey fruit character from a judicious blend of hops.

COOP ALE WORKS

Oklahoma City

Craft breweries are a bit of a rarity in Oklahoma, which left ample room for this draught-focused operation to open in Oklahoma City in late 2008. **Horny Toad Cerveza** ★★☆ might sound like a simple light lager, but its gentle fruitiness and integrated hop says otherwise; while the chocolate-caramelly **Native Amber** ★★☆ boasts drying, moderately bitter hoppiness. Territorial Reserve series beers allow the brewery to push the envelope.

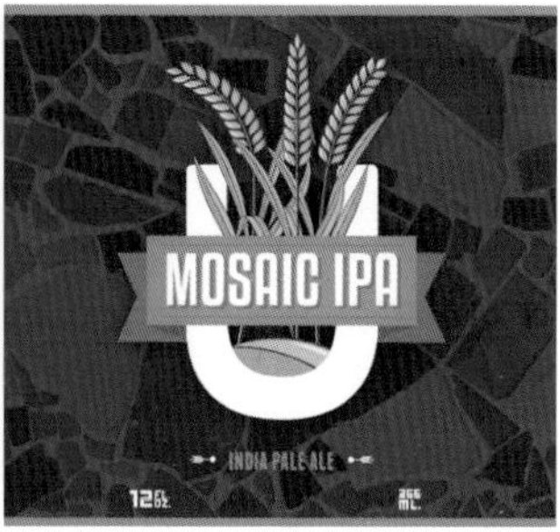

DEVILS BACKBONE BREWING

Roseland, Virginia

A newcomer that opened as a brewpub in only 2008, establishing a reputation for German-inspired beers that are brewed with continental precision. A separate production facility was added in 2012, also in central Virginia. The seamless and slightly nutty **Vienna Lager** ★★★; and the citrus-laden **Eight Point IPA** ★★☆ are most widely available. **Danzig** ★★★☆, a silky Baltic porter; **Dark Abby** ★★☆, a delicate and complex dubbel; and the grainy **Gold Leaf Lager** ★★ illustrate the brewery's diversity.

DESTINATION
HENRICO, VIRGINIA

Mekong Restaurant (6004 W Broad Street) may appear an ordinary Vietnamese restaurant, but owner An "Mekong" Bui's passion for beer has transformed it into a true destination for the craft beer aficionado.

DUCK-RABBIT CRAFT BREWERY

Farmville, North Carolina

Calling itself a "dark beer specialist", this east North Carolina brewery is likely best known for its rounded, mocha-ish **Milk Stout ★★☆**. Other brands include a sweet-starting, dryly bitter-finishing **Brown Ale ★★★**; and a slightly winey, milk-chocolaty **Porter ★★☆**.

FUNKY BUDDHA BREWERY
Oakland Park, Florida

Maple Bacon Coffee Porter ★★★, a beer with a tasting note as its name, gave what was a tiny, quirky brewpub instant fame, and a production facility quickly followed. Unusual beers like **No Crusts ★★**, tasting like a peanut butter and jam sandwich; join others better suited to south Florida's hot climate, like **Floridian Hefeweizen ★★☆**, with prominent banana and citrus notes; and **Passionfruit Berliner Weisse ★★☆**, tropical-fruit-infused and tart.

GREEN MAN BREWING
Asheville, North Carolina

Born in the mid-1990s, this draught-only brewery is both one of North Carolina's oldest and a cornerstone of the burgeoning Asheville craft beer scene. The tangerine and grapefruit flavours of

its **IPA ★★☆** fuels hophead joy; while the more restrained **Pale Ale ★★☆** blends both malty and hoppy fruitiness. The midpoint is the **ESB★★★**, which combines biscuity British maltiness with spicy-fruity American hoppiness.

HIGHLAND BREWING
Asheville, North Carolina

This brewery is an almost-two-decade-old stalwart of the Asheville craft beer scene. Its flagship beer, **Gaelic Ale ★★★**, starts fruity, then turns toasty, then becomes mildly bitter and finally finishes softly roasty and dry; the light-hued **St Terese's Pale Ale ★★☆** layers spicy hop on top of nutty maltiness; and the unusual **Oatmeal Porter ★★** combines prune and plum notes with roasted malt and not quite enough silky smoothness.

JESTER KING
Austin, Texas

Young Austin-area brewery overcoming adversity – including drought – to forge some outstanding beers. Known for big beers, but best might be a little one, **Le Petit Prince ★★★☆**, dry, peppery and quenching at less than 3% ABV. Others include the fruity-bitter **Noble King ★★☆**; a delicious mild aged on oak to a very gently smokiness, **Commercial Suicide ★★★**; and the hoppy but otherwise *bière de garde*-like **Mad Meg ★★☆**.

KARBACH BREWING
Houston, Texas

The former CEO of Flying Dog Brewing, Eric Warner, left that company to co-found this Houston brewery in 2011. The canned beers produced thus far validate the move, with the floral, hoppy **Sympathy for the Lager ★★**; leading the way for such bigger beers as the **Hopadillo IPA ★★☆**, with peachy fruit matched by citrus hop; and the **Rodeo Clown Double IPA ★★★**, an ale that highlights fruity malt over aggressive hop. Seasonal **Karbachtoberfest ★★★** showcases Warner's German brewing roots.

KREBS BREWING
Krebs, Oklahoma

If America has a living indigenous beer it is Choc, brewed in eastern Oklahoma since before Prohibition from a recipe said to have come from Choctaw Nation Indians. The Krebs range goes beyond the **1919 Choc Beer ★☆**, a somewhat fruity wheat beer; to a Brewmaster Signature series that includes the tart, salty **Gose ★★**; and **Grätzer ★★☆**, a relatively bitter beer in the style known as *grodziskie*, made with smoked wheat and fermented with Polish yeast.

LIVE OAK BREWING
Austin, Texas

Rare survivor from an original round of breweries that opened in Austin in the mid-1990s, and still draught-only. Czech immigrants who settled the region in the late 19th century would easily recognize the bready but crisp and spicy **Pilz ★★★☆**. Other brands include **Big Bark ★★**, a food-friendly amber lager; **HefeWeizen ★★★**, complex beneath its typical banana and clove flavours; and **Primus ★★**, an intense, spicy *weizenbock*.

DESTINATION
AUSTIN

Craft Pride (61 Rainey Street) showcases the city's booming beer scene, serving only Texas beers from 54 taps and two casks, while newcomer **Hopfields** (3110 Guadalupe Street) and venerable **Gingerman** (301 Lavaca Street) offer a mix of imports and locals. Newish **Pinthouse Pizza** (4729 Burnet Road), with its hop-forward beers, and **Draught House Pub & Brewery** (4112 Medical Parkway), a multi-tap and brewpub, underline Austin's affection for local.

NOLA BREWING (NEW ORLEANS LAGER & ALE BREWING)
New Orleans, Louisiana

Young brewery bringing the brewing tradition back to the Big Easy. Launched in 2008 with two ales: a lightly fruity, faintly toasty **Blonde ★★☆**; and a roasty, southern US take on a mild, the light-bodied **Brown ★★**. The duo were joined later by **Hopitoulas IPA ★★☆**, with assertive citrus-spicy-fruity hoppiness.

AUSTIN, TEXAS

Craft beer has a better presence outside the French Quarter, although on its edge **d.b.a.** (618 Frenchmen Street) mixes excellent live music and beer. Best in town for beer selection is **The Avenue Pub** (1732 St Charles Avenue), open at all hours and all days, although also worthy of a visit are **Cooter Brown's** (509 S Carrollton Avenue) and both outlets of **The Bulldog** (3236 Magazine Street and 5135 Canal Boulevard).

PRAIRIE ARTISAN ALES
Tulsa, Oklahoma

Two brothers leveraged contract brewing and Kickstarter to open their own small brewery, with beers reflecting a rustic, Belgian farmhouse-inspired vision. **Prairie Ale** ★★☆ is a bold *saison*; **Birra** ★★ a lighter version, both pleasantly combining ripe fruit, a hay-like aroma and pepper finish; with **Gold** ★★☆ the wild take on *saison*, grapey and tart. Altogether different, Imperial stout **Bomb!** ★★★ balances rich coffee flavours with cacao nibs and chilli peppers.

RAHR & SON BREWING
Fort Worth, Texas

The roof literally fell in on this brewery in 2010 after a record snowfall, which knocked it out of business for a period of time. But it came back with a line-up of mostly lagers and adventurous seasonals, including **Ugly Pug** ★★☆, a chocolaty

schwarzbier with coffee bitterness; the *weizenbock* **Angry Goat** ★★☆, which offers rich and deep banana flavours; the subtly smoky Scotch ale, **Iron Thistle** ★★★; and the suitably strong and warming **Winter Warmer** ★★.

REAL ALE BREWING
Blanco, Texas

Real Ale Brewing long ago outgrew the Texas Hill Country antique-store basement that first housed it. The golden **Fireman's #4** ★★, which is light and floral, has driven growth, but the brewery's line-up is diverse: **Full Moon Pale Rye Ale** ★★★ is spicy and well suited to local barbecues; **Sisyphus** ★★☆ is a rich, but balanced barley wine; **Hans Pils** ★★★ is floral and unapologetically bitter; while the *tripel* **Devil's Backbone** ★★ is lightly fruity.

The Meddlesome Moth (1621 Oak Lawn Avenue) is the "gastropub" spin-off of the multi-location chain of Flying Saucer beer bars. Unlike the tavern-like Saucers – also recommended – the Moth is more casual chic bistro, featuring creative cuisine and a carefully curated list of draught and bottled beers.

SAINT ARNOLD BREWING
Houston, Texas

Named after a brewing saint and founded by two former investment bankers. Grew into the largest brewery in Texas opened since Prohibition, crafting a wide range that includes the perfectly rounded **Oktoberfest** ★★☆; the *kölsch*-inspired **Fancy Lawnmower Ale** ★★, an ideal refresher for hot and humid Houston; **Weedwacker** ★★, in which Bavarian yeast turns Lawnmower base recipe into a *weissbier*; and hop-forward but sensibly balanced **Elissa IPA** ★★☆.

ST SOMEWHERE BREWING
Tarpon Springs, Florida

Clearwater-area brewery that was one of the first to bring creative craft brewing to the state. Large format, cork-finished bottles adorned with ornate, art nouveau labels hold Belgian-inspired ales like the perfumey, herbal-spicy **Saison Athene** ★★☆; and the tart, sweet peach- and apricot-accented **Lectio Divina** ★★☆.

SWEETWATER BREWING
Atlanta, Georgia

Inspired by the Atlanta Olympics, two former college roommates founded this early southern brewery on Atlanta's west side. A half-dozen regulars include the nutty, drying **Georgia Brown** ★★☆; an **IPA** ★★☆ that balances citrus hoppiness atop peachy malt; the bready,

caraway-ish and peppery **LowRYEder IPA** ★★★; and the chocolate and prune **Exodus Porter** ★★. Catch & Release seasonals include the almost mincemeat-like seasonal **Festive Ale** ★★☆.

DESTINATION DECATUR

The Brick Store (125 E Court Square) is a neighbourhood pub located a short transit ride from downtown Atlanta. It has a community feel and offers an impressive selection of draught and bottled beers.

TERRAPIN BEER
Athens, Georgia

Iconoclastic brewery opened over a decade ago with a mission to do things differently. Which it did, launching with a spicy, hop-accented **Rye Pale Ale** ★★☆, a beer few were brewing at the time. Other brands include the spicier, grapefruity **Hopsecutioner** ★★, an IPA not shy in its hoppiness; and seasonal **Hop Karma** ★★☆, a brown ale with IPA-like hoppiness.

CANADA

Although it seldom receives the recognition that is accorded to its neighbour to the south, Canada's craft brewing industry has been around for almost as long and has marked almost as many significant continental craft beer milestones, including first brewpub (the now-defunct Horseshoe Bay Brewing in British Columbia); first brewery specializing in cask-conditioned ale (Ontario's WELLINGTON COUNTY BREWERY) and first *eisbock* brewed outside Europe (Eisbock from the former Niagara Falls Brewing Company).

Born in the west, nurtured in major cities from Vancouver to Calgary to Toronto to Halifax, and best known internationally for its creative brewing forces clustered around Montréal, Canadian craft beer is today vibrant and expanding. A change to the taxation structure in Québec around the turn of the century caused a rapid increase in the number of breweries in that province – estimated at time of writing to be somewhere in excess of 100 – while recent growth in local craft beer markets has caused new breweries to pop up with astonishing regularity in southern Ontario and the lower mainland of British Columbia, and to a lesser degree in Nova Scotia and Alberta.

Long self-identifying as a nation of beer drinkers, Canadians now seem prepared to embrace craft beer with the same enthusiasm they usually reserve for hockey or complaining about the weather.

WESTERN CANADA

Canadian craft brewing got its start in and around Vancouver, but it took some time for it to thrive anywhere in British Columbia outside of south Vancouver Island, remaining through most of the 1990s broadly defined by timid blond ales and hemp beers. Thankfully, all that changed with the dawn of the new millennium, as an emerging wave of craft brewers arrived on the scene, producing all manner of new and assertive styles of ale and lager.

Elsewhere in western Canada, however, progress was not nearly so swift. Although it remains the only province in Canada with fully privatized beer sales, Alberta has not yet witnessed a significant expansion in the number of craft breweries it boasts, while both Saskatchewan and Manitoba remain largely craft beer-challenged, save for the odd oasis of characterful beer in Regina, Saskatoon and Winnipeg.

33 ACRES BREWING
Vancouver, British Columbia

Centrally located, family-owned brewery with both an artistic and a community bent. Emphasis on sessionable beers has produced **Life** ★★☆, a faintly fruity and dry, spicy finishing amber ale; and **Ocean** ★★☆, a pale ale with IPA aspirations and quaffable dryness.

DESTINATION
VANCOUVER

Alibi Room (157 Alexander Street) is Vancouver's go-to place for craft beer, with two smallish floors of mostly communal seating, 50 taps and a menu that sits somewhere between "pub" and "restaurant".

ALLEY KAT BREWING
Edmonton, Alberta

For close to two decades the craft beer standard-bearer in northern Alberta, this Edmonton stalwart seems to have found new creativity in recent years. Long-time brands like the appetizingly dry **Full Moon Pale Ale** ★★☆; and rich and complex **Old Deuteronomy Barley Wine** ★★★; have been joined by seasonals like the plummy, boozy, cellarable **Belgian Style Quad** ★★☆ and an impressive Dragon series of single-hop double IPAs, some of which merit greater regularity.

CENTRAL CITY BREWING
Surrey, British Columbia

Suburban Surrey is a beloved butt of Vancouver jokes, but this expanding brewery can add a note of envy. **Red Racer ESB** ★★☆ is a piney but subtly fruity quaff; dry, grassy and citrus **Red Racer Pale Ale** ★★★☆ might be the best of its type in Canada; bigger **Red Racer IPA** ★★★ is more aggressive in its herbal-citrus hop bitterness; complex **Thor's Hammer Barley Wine** ★★★ hits the palate with spice, grows fruity then finishes off-dry and warming.

CRANNÓG ALES
Sorrento, British Columbia

Based on an operational farm in the BC interior, this all-organic brewery produces Irish-inspired, draught-only ales that are distributed only so far as the brewery truck can be driven in a day. Best bets are the wonderfully named **Back Hand of God Stout** ★★☆, roasty with a hint of tobacco leaf; and the unusual, deeply malty **Gael's Blood Potato Ale** ★★☆. Cask-conditioned specialities are usually worth a detour.

DRIFTWOOD BREWING
Victoria, British Columbia

Fast-expanding brewery serving Vancouver Island and the lower mainland of BC. Brands include the perfumey and peppery **Farmhand Ale** ★★☆; fruity and herbal, almost lavender-evoking **White Bark Wit** ★★☆, a highly aromatic Belgian-style wheat beer; and foresty, almost oily **Fat Tug IPA** ★★☆. **Old Cellar Dweller** ★★☆ is a darkly fruity and vanilla-ish barley wine that improves with ageing.

HALF PINTS BREWING
Winnipeg, Manitoba

Manitoba was a bit of a craft beer wasteland until this brewery came along, headed by a former brewer at Regina's Bushwakker Brewpub (*see* box, right). Highlights include the chocolate-cinnamon-cherry **Pothole Porter** ★★☆; the citrus-spicy **Little Scrapper IPA** ★★☆; a cellar-worthy barley wine called **Burly Wine** ★★☆; and an ale that promises "ludicrous" hoppiness, but delivers something far more balanced, **Humulus Ludicrous** ★★★.

HOWE SOUND BREWING
Squamish, British Columbia

This brewpub-turned-production brewery displays a deft hand with strong ales packaged in large bottles. One that perhaps shouldn't work, but does, is the

strong, fruity-sweet and spicy **King Heffy Imperial Hefeweizen** ★★★; the more conventional **Pothole Filler Imperial Stout** ★★☆ doesn't disappoint with dried-fruit and espresso flavours; fresh pumpkin notes add to the pleasure of the almost bourbon-ish **Pumpkineater** ★★☆; while **Woolly Bugger Barley Wine** ★★★ balances rich and earthy malt with toasted spiciness and dried fruit notes.

DESTINATION
REGINA

Bushwakker (2206 Dewdney Avenue) was a pioneering brewpub on the Prairies and remains a craft beer oasis in a region mostly devoid of attractive beer-drinking options.

LONGWOOD BREWERY
Nanaimo, British Columbia

Central Vancouver Island brewpub-spawned brewery with many brands in distinctive, Imperial pint cans. Although brewed with wheat, **SteamPunk Dunkel** ★★☆ is a slightly sweet, mildly roasty quencher that's neither *dunkel* nor *weizen*; blond **Extra Ale** ★★☆ is a faintly sweet and creamy pale ale with a bone dry finish; more assertive, **The Big One IPA** ★★★ features local hops and a woodsy, spicy bitterness; and **Berried Alive** ★★☆ is a natural-tasting raspberry ale for hopheads.

PADDOCK WOOD
Saskatoon, Saskatchewan

One of Saskatchewan's few and true home-grown craft beer options. Regulars include the nutty, toasted malt and apple-ish **Red Hammer ★★★**; and **Loki IPA ★★**, once intense in its citrus hop but now more malt-driven. When barrel-aged, Loki becomes the more rounded, hazelnutty **Oaky Loki ★★☆**; while other seasonals include the warming, sweet, vanilla-ish **Barrel Full of Monkeys Imperial Stout ★★**.

PARALLEL 49 BREWING
Vancouver, British Columbia

Born of a craft beer-friendly restaurant partnership, this east Vancouver brewery earned local attention from almost day one. Cartoon labels adorn beers like **Hoparazzi ★★☆**, an off-dry, spicy-fruity IPA; **Old Boy ★★☆**, a nutty, lightly tannic ale that seems to grow drier with every sip; and **Gypsy Tears Ruby Ale ★★☆**, a robust brew with plum fruitiness hidden behind walnutty, citrus, spicy hoppiness.

PHILLIPS BREWING
Victoria, British Columbia

From shoestring beginnings, Matt Phillips has built his namesake brewery into one of the more influential on Canada's west coast. Flagship is the floral, peachy **Blue Buck ★☆**; but enthusiasts opt instead for the **Amnesiac Double IPA ★★☆**; an ale of spicy, grapefruity hoppiness atop a soft, fruity malt backbone. Other beers of note include a more assertive, herbal-citrus **Hop Circle IPA ★★**; and gingery but mellow **Ginger Beer ★★☆**.

SPINNAKERS GASTRO BREWPUB & GUESTHOUSES
Victoria, British Columbia

Victoria is a hotbed of craft brewing at least in part thanks to Spinnakers,

Canada's longest-surviving brewpub. Bottling and distribution now allows others to try pub favourites like full and floral-fruity **Mitchell's Extra Special Bitter ★★★**; the mildly nutty and sessionable **Nut Brown Ale ★★☆**; and newer **Blue Bridge Double Pale Ale ★★**, which is a surprisingly gentle and approachable take on what's usually an aggressive style. The pub beers offer greater variety.

DESTINATION
VICTORIA

A good beer crawl in the provincial capital is not much more than an easy stroll, beginning at the elegant waterfront **Canoe Brewpub** (450 Swift Street), ambling along to the brewery-cum-boutique hotel, **Swans** (506 Pandora Avenue), stopping in at the recently renovated multi-tap, the **Garrick's Head Pub** (69 Bastion Square) and ending a water-taxi ride away at **Spinnakers** (308 Catherine Street), which is Canada's first in-house brewpub.

TOFINO BREWING
Tofino, British Columbia

Environmentally aware Vancouver Island brewery that is located almost as far west as is possible in Canada. The flagship **Tuff Session Ale ★★★** leads with an orange-peach fruitiness but softens and dries in the toasted malt finish; while the stronger **Hop Cretin IPA ★★☆** packs a piney, grapefruity hop punch, then grows more floral in the dry finish.

TOWNSITE BREWING
Powell River, British Columbia

Young but immediately impressive brewery on BC's "Sunshine Coast". **Pow Town Porter** ★★ is a mocha-ish, nutty and lightly sweet brew; strong **Charleston** ★★ is a malty powerhouse wrapped in the guise of a *tripel*; and **Zunga** ★★☆ is a peaches-and-cream golden ale that proves blond need not be boring. Summer seasonal **Blackberry Festive Ale** ★★★ evokes thoughts of sparkling rosé wine in its floral, off-dry fruitiness.

TREE BREWING
Kelowna, British Columbia

Once BC's most shape-shifting brewery, Tree has settled down of late into a comfortable guise. Best when embracing hops, as with the highly aromatic, tangerine-herbal **Hop Head IPA** ★★★; and caramel-chocolaty, bitterly roasty **Hop Head Black IPA** ★★☆; with the rather heavy-handed **Hop Head Double IPA** ★★ less successful. Greater subtlety is shown by the summer seasonal **Hefeweizen** ★★☆, a distinctly lemony interpretation of the style.

YUKON BREWING
Whitehorse, Yukon

The sole brewery in Canada's far northern territories. Beers tend toward the conventional, as with the soft, dryish and mildly bitter **Yukon Gold** ★★; and fruity, modestly warming **Yukon Red** ★★. Of greater interest to aficionados is the winter seasonal **Lead Dog Ale** ★★☆, with raisin and plum notes backed by cinnamon spice and a suggestion of hop.

EASTERN CANADA

It may have lagged behind much of the rest of the country in jumping on the craft beer bandwagon – the city didn't get a brewery of its own until 1987 – but Montréal has since leapfrogged Toronto, Halifax and other eastern cities to become the heart of creative Canadian craft brewing. Best known both domestically and abroad for their Belgian-influenced brews, Québec brewers have more lately embraced a spirit of unbridled creativity, brewing beers made with all manner of ingredients, aged in all sorts of barrels and fermented in any number of ways.

And the creativity is catching. Having been mired for years in conservative brewing traditions, brewers in southern Ontario and the Maritimes are branching finally into big beers, bold hoppiness, Belgian influences and unusual expressions of the brewing arts. Coupled with the recent growth in both size and numbers of craft breweries, it portends a rosy future for craft brewing in eastern Canada.

À LA FÛT
Saint-Tite, Québec

A small-town Québec brewery and pub that was thrust into the limelight by winning Beer of the Year at the 2012 Canadian Brewing Awards with its **Co-Hop V ★★★**, a wonderfully balanced sweet-tart cherry beer. Others in the stable include **La British ★★★☆**, a very nutty brown ale with supreme sessionability; the spicy-hop, dry finishing **À la Belge Saison ★★★**; the citrus hop, peachy malt of **Cuvée Houblonnée IPA ★★★**; and the grassy, quenching **Ma Première Blonde Pilsner ★★☆**.

AMSTERDAM BREWING
Toronto, Ontario

The city's original brewpub-turned-production brewery with a new waterfront brewpub. The highlight of the mainstays is definitely the **Boneshaker IPA ★★☆**, with a firm malty fruitness balancing ample hops; while special editions provide excitement, including the **Tempest Imperial Stout ★★★**, cocoa-y, rich and rewarding; and better still when amped up as **Double Tempest ★★★☆**. Other beers of note are the fruity, grapefruity **Fracture Double IPA ★★☆**; and almost mincemeat-esque **Vicar's Vice Olde Ale ★★☆**.

BEAU'S ALL NATURAL BREWING
Vankleek Hill, Ontario

A family operation based in eastern Ontario close to the Québec border. Excels at the Germanic approach to brewing, as with its homage to *kölsch*, the lightly fruity, suitably crisp **Lug-Tread Lagered Ale ★★☆**; the outstanding, toasted caramelly **Night Märzen ★★★**; and the leafy-nutty, malt-driven and *altbier*-inspired **FestiveAle ★★☆**. Numerous seasonals and one-offs abound, including a **Screamin' Beaver Oak Aged Double IPA ★★☆**, rich with alcoholic warmth and flavours of stewed fruit and hoppy herbals.

BELLWOODS BREWERY
Toronto, Ontario

Funky and highly experimental brewery, which took Toronto by storm when it opened in 2012, producing a wider range of styles than the city had previously seen. Seasonal and limited bottled beers are sold from the on-site store, perhaps including the liquoricy **Lost River Baltic Porter ★★★**; gently fruity, off-dry **Fortune Cookie Tripel ★★☆**; herbal and almost sticky Imperial stout, **Hellwoods ★★☆**; and unexpectedly impressive smoked *Berliner weisse* **Mash Pipe ★★★**.

DESTINATION
TORONTO

Canada's beer bar capital offers something for everyone, from the pioneering, locals- and cask-centric **C'est What** (67 Front Street East) to the eclectic oasis that is **Bar Volo** (587 Yonge Street), justly celebrated newcomer **Bar Hop** (391 King Street West), rough-at-the-edges **Rhino** (1249 Queen Street West) and stylish beer cuisine innovator **beerbistro** (18 King Street East).

BLACK OAK BREWING
Toronto, Ontario

Originally from the suburbs, this now west-Toronto-based brewery produces a handful of regular and seasonal brands. Flagship offerings are a light and fruity **Pale Ale** ★★; and an appropriately nutty, mildly roasty **Nut Brown Ale** ★★★. Well-received seasonals include **10 Bitter Years** ★★★, a boozy cocktail of a double IPA, with peachy malt and herbaceous hoppiness; **Nutcracker** ★★☆, a cinnamony spiced porter; and **Oaktoberfest** ★★☆, a hoppy and malt-heavy take on a *märzen*.

BRASSEURS DU TEMPS, LES
Gatineau, Québec

Atmospheric brewery-restaurant located just across the border from Ottawa, distributing mostly stronger ales on a limited basis. Summery **La Saison**

Haute ★★★ pleases with peppery citrus and a dry finish; while **La Messe de Minuit** ★★☆ is a gingerbready ode to Christmas. In between come the flamed orange zest and hop resin of **Diable au Corps** ★★★, a double IPA; and **Obscur Désir** ★★★, an inky and warming Imperial stout that is aged in bourbon barrels.

CHARLEVOIX
Baie-Saint-Paul, Québec

Québec-City-region brewery offering two lines: Belgium-inspired Dominus Vobiscum and broadly British-influenced Vache Folle. Of the former, **Triple** ★★★ impresses with tropical-fruit flavours and spicy alcohol notes; **Saison** ★★★ offers citrus and grapey notes atop more spice; the hoppy **Lupulus** ★★★ is yeasty, peppery and refreshing despite its strength; and the Champagne-esque **Brut** ★★★☆ is subtle and dryly fruity. Best of the Mad Cow line is a complex, intensely flavourful and surprisingly strong **Imperial Milk Stout** ★★★.

DIEU DU CIEL!
Montréal, Québec

Stunningly innovative (and successfully so) Montréal brewpub-spawned brewery. Wide range of impressive brands, including black pepper and rye beer that balances the spiciness with precision, **Route des Épices** ★★★; hibiscus-flower-flavoured and summery **Rosée d'Hibiscus** ★★★; coffee-accented and deliciously intense **Péché Mortel** ★★★; Belgian-inspired, fruity **Dernière Volonté** ★★☆, which finishes with a decidedly bitter twist; and the cocoa-and-vanilla masterpiece, **Aphrodisiaque** ★★★.

DUNHAM (BRASSERIE DUNHAM)
Dunham, Quebec

An up-and-coming brewery born south of Montréal near the US border. Tongue-in-cheek **Leo's Early Breakfast IPA ★★☆**, made with tea and guava, is tropical fruity, citrusy and spicy; **Saison Framboise Zinfandel ★★★** is a sweet-to-dry, funky-fruity-nutty delight; **IPA Belge ★★☆** is almost chartreuse-like in its herbal character; and **Black Imperial IPA ★★☆** is neither hoppy porter nor roasty IPA, but something in between.

GARRISON BREWING
Halifax, Nova Scotia

Sometimes locally polarizing brewery established in 1997, but only really hitting its stride a few years into the new century. Brews the lemony and herbal **Hop Yard Pale Ale ★★☆**; roundly fruity, bitter-finishing **Imperial IPA ★★★**; molasses- and liquorice-accented **Grand Baltic Porter ★★★**; toffee-ish but bitter-finishing **Ol' Fog Burner Barley Wine ★★★**; plus occasional specialities, like the unlikely sounding but excellent 15th Anniversary Hops, **Mango & Ginger ★★★**.

DESTINATION
HALIFAX

Rogue's Roost (5435 Spring Garden Road), established in 1999, is the good beer anchor on Halifax's main shopping street, with traditional and creative beers crafted by the only brewer the brewpub has ever known, Lorne Romano.

GLUTENBERG (BRASSEURS SANS GLUTEN)
Montréal, Québec

Though a young brewery, this exclusively gluten-free brewing operation has impressed greatly. Hopheads like the intensely bitter **Pale Ale Américaine ★★**; more balanced and measured is the dryly citrus **Blonde ★★☆**; while a buckwheat character is apparent in **Red Ale ★★☆**. Seasonals have included a perfumey, lemony, lightly spicy **Belge de Saison ★★★**.

GRANITE BREWERY
Toronto, Ontario

Granite is a long-established and growing midtown-Toronto brewpub-turned-brewery. Growing interest in experimental and US-influenced beers, but still at its best with the dry and leafy **Best Bitter ★★☆**, which becomes still better as the dry-hopped and cask-conditioned **Best Bitter Special ★★★☆**. Also impressive are the nitro-poured and roasty-creamy **Keefe's Irish Stout ★★★**; and boldly hoppy but British-inspired **IPA ★★★**.

GREAT LAKES BREWING
Toronto, Ontario

Born a malt extract brewery in suburban Toronto, this brewery moved downtown to evolve into a more serious craft-driven operation, balanced fruity-citrusy-caramelly-floral **Crazy Canuck Pale Ale ★★★** being emblematic of this shift. The brewery's 25th anniversary spawned a Tank Ten series of experimental ales, including **My Bitter Wife IPA ★★☆**, leafy and resinous; **Lake Effect IPA**

★★☆, big, fruity and warming; and bourbon barrel-aged **Beard of Zeus Barley Wine ★★**, heady and overly oaky when young.

HELL BAY BREWING
Cherry Hill, Nova Scotia

Promising young brewery making primarily English-inspired ales with a New World attitude. Cocoa-ish and roasty **Brown Ale ★★☆** is a seasonal beer that is expected to go year-round; while ballsy **English Ale ★★☆** applies aggressive hopping techniques to the best bitter style. Quaffable but slightly thin seasonal **Oatmeal Stout ★★☆**; and experimental, campfire-and-spice **Smoked Rye Beer ★★☆** show potential.

HOPFENSTARK
L'Assomption, Québec

While best known for its multiple interpretations of the *saison* style, this small brewery and pub east of Montréal displays admirable breadth with such ales as caramel-citrus **Post-Colonial IPA ★★☆**; rich, creamy and almost port-like **Greg American Foreign Stout ★★★**; the stylistic mash-up of *rauchbier*, *saison* and *Berliner weisse* known as **Boson de Higgs ★★☆**; and the dry, spicy and pear-ish **Saison Station 55 ★★★**.

JUNCTION CRAFT BREWING
Toronto, Ontario

Neighbourhood brewery perhaps hampered by stylistic ambitions. Flagship **Conductor's Craft Ale ★★☆** is a firmly malty reminder of the Canadian ales of old, with an extra hop bite; while brewery-only brands include **Stationmaster Stout ★★☆**, with a coffee-accented nose and roasted nuttiness; **Extra Pale Ale ★★☆**, with reserved bitterness and a high degree of quaffability; and a solid but underconditioned **Kölsch ★★**.

KICHESIPPI BEER
Ottawa, Ontario

This once-contract brewery got off to a rough start, but a purchase of the brewery

it was contracting and the importation of a seasoned western Canadian brewer has done wonders. **Heller High Water** ★★☆ is a seasonal *helles* with a crisp palate and mildly bitter finish; **Blonde** ★★☆ is a mildly fruity, slightly herbal and quaffable ale; and another summer seasonal, **Uncle Mark's Hopfen Weisse** ★★☆, combines a banana-intense front with a more hoppy middle and a dry and fast finish.

KING BREWERY
Nobleton, Ontario

North of Toronto brewery specializing in spot-on interpretation of European lager styles. Flagship **Pilsner** ★★★ is strongly Czech in character, with a slight butteriness and firm hop finish; second brand **Dark Lager** ★★☆ speaks strongly to Bavarian *dunkel* traditions with an earthy, cocoa-ish taste; and **Vienna Lager** ★★★ begins with malty sweetness but ends refreshingly dry and softly bitter.

MCAUSLAN BREWING (BRASSERIE MCAUSLAN)
Montréal, Québec

Over-two-decades-old company produces two lines of beer – St Ambroise and Griffon – the more successful named after the working class district in which the brewery was founded. Flagship **St Ambroise Pale Ale** ★★☆ inspires memories of the Québécois ales of the 1950s; **St Ambroise Oatmeal Stout** ★★★☆ is a silken, roasty, mocha-ish delight; **St Ambroise Vintage Ale** ★★★ benefits well from several years of age; and **St Ambroise Imperial Stout** ★★★ solidifies the brewery's stout credentials with a complex, winey character.

DESTINATION MONTRÉAL

Québec's largest city boasts a multiplicity of excellent brewpubs, beginning with the original, **Le Cheval Blanc** (809 rue Ontario est), a classic Québécois tavern that added a brewery in 1988. Perhaps more celebrated these days, though, are the likes of the always intriguing **Dieu du Ciel!** (29 Avenue Laurier ouest), creative and industrial-esque **Brasserie Benelux** (245 rue Sherbrooke ouest) and lager haven **l'Amère à Boire** (2049 rue St- Denis).

MILL STREET BREWING
Toronto, Ontario

Brewery founded in historic Distillery District, turned brewpub with separate production facility in city's east end. Flagship **Tankhouse Ale** ★★☆ layers lightly citrus hop on a firm malt base; nitro-canned **Cobblestone Stout** ★★★ mixes dark chocolate with appetizing roastiness; and *helles*-esque **Organic Lager** ★★☆ serves as a dryish quaffer. More variety available at the brewpub:

MUSKOKA BREWERY
Bracebridge, Ontario

Based in Toronto's northern "Cottage Country", this operation went from humdrum to impressive in a short time, spearheaded by the wonderfully fragrant, refreshingly hoppy **Mad Tom IPA** ★★★; and a reworking of core brands such as the slightly winey, raisiny **Dark Ale** ★★☆. Later releases include the bigger, burnt-orangey **Twice as Mad Tom** ★★☆; and seasonals like the judiciously spiced, Belgian-esque **Spring Oddity** ★★★; and autumnal, earthy **Harvest Ale** ★★☆.

PEI BREWING/THE GAHAN HOUSE
Charlottetown, Prince Edward Island

Working in a tough market, PEI Brewing has successfully transitioned from tiny brewpub to larger brewery-restaurant to packaging brewery. Brands include the overtly gimmicky, but genuinely *helles*-esque **Beach Chair Lager** ★★; the apple-nutty **Island Red** ★★☆, reminiscent of Irish red ales of old; and the yeasty, nutty-citrus **1772 India Pale Ale** ★★.

PICAROONS BREWING
Fredericton, New Brunswick

Stalwart Maritime brewery that's been through its ups and downs, although quite stable and reliable for the last several years, even winning Brewery of the Year honours at the Canadian Brewing Awards in 2011. Brews ales mostly in the English tradition, such as the dry, biscuity **Best Bitter** ★★☆, imbued with leafy hop notes; but can deviate at times, as with the fragrant and citrusy **Yippee IPA** ★★☆.

PROPELLER BREWING
Halifax, Nova Scotia

Once unapologetically British in inspiration, this long-standing craft brewery has more recently branched into diverse styles, largely in support of a successful growler-filling programme at the brewery. Still, English styles remain the forte, such as the raw cocoa- and chocolate-accented **London-Style Porter** ★★★; appley **ESB** ★★, especially good on tap; and the more New World-styled, floral-fruity **IPA** ★★. A notable diversion is the impressive, mango-ish, nutty **Double IPA** ★★☆.

STEAM WHISTLE BREWING
Toronto, Ontario

Housed in the shadow of Toronto's CN Tower, the motto of this fast-growing brewery is "Do one thing really, really well", and it does. The lone beer is labelled a **Pilsner** ★★★, but is more akin to a Bavarian *helles*, fragrant and floral in its aroma, with a softly sweet graininess tempered by a moderately bitter, drying hoppiness.

TROIS MOUSQUETAIRES, LES
Brossard, Québec

Highly regarded for its cork-finished, large-bottle speciality beers, this brewery founded by a trio of friends maintains a fascination with lagers in general and German brewing traditions in particular. Great success has been experienced with the floral, chocolaty **Rauchbier** ★★★; the spicy and dryly fruity **Hopfenweisse** ★★☆; and the outstanding, chocolate-raisin-cinnamon **Porter Baltique** ★★★☆.

TROU DU DIABLE
Shawinigan, Québec

Experimental and graphically inclined brewery midway between Montréal and Québec City, ageing ales in oak, naming beers after political in-jokes and generally having a good time. Successes include the appealingly sweet and sour **La Buteuse ★★★**, strong and matured in apple brandy barrels; the snappy, slightly grapey **Dulcis Succubus ★★★**; a hybrid pale ale/*hefeweizen* called **Shawinigan Handshake ★★☆**, dedicated to a former Canadian prime minister; and the deceptively light-tasting and fruity **Saison du Tracteur ★★**.

UNIBROUE (SAPPORO)
Chambly, Québec

Now owned by Japan's Sapporo, this Montréal-area brewery has been a leader in both Belgian-inspired brewing and export development. Flagships are a coriander-ish, quenching **Blanche de Chambly ★★**; and spicy, dark and food-friendly **Maudite ★★☆**, which might have lost a bit of character through the years. Also fruity *tripel*, **Fin du Monde ★★★**; dark, rich and slightly cloying **Trois Pistoles ★★☆**; and humorously named **Terrible ★★★☆**, a strong ale that drinks like a fine brandy.

WELLINGTON COUNTY BREWERY
Guelph, Ontario

Conceived as a producer of cask-conditioned ale, Ontario's third craft brewery (opened in 1985) adjusted quickly to the hard realities of the market. **Arkell Best Bitter ★★**, softly fruity and gently bitter, remains best on cask **★★☆**; while co-flagship **County Dark Ale ★★☆** is nutty and faintly minerally in the finish. Local aficionados highlight the winey, dark plum flavours of the **Imperial Stout ★★☆**.

THE CARIBBEAN

With its extensive and commercially important tourism industry, one could be forgiven for expecting the islands of the Caribbean to be at least a viable, if not vibrant craft brewing market. But for whatever reason, that has not proved to be the case, at least so far.

Almost anywhere you care to visit in the Caribbean, you will find the market dominated utterly by light lagers, either brewed by one of a handful of regional brewing powers or a local brewery most likely aligned in some fashion with a brewing multinational. Independent craft brewers do exist, but unless you know specifically where to look, finding the beers can be akin to the proverbial search for a needle in the haystack, and sometimes a needle not necessarily worth the hunt.

If the beer is not golden and light-tasting, it almost certainly will be dark and sugary and potent. A legacy of the so-called "export strength" black ales brought to the islands over a century ago, strong and sweet, usually bottom-fermented stouts remain popular across the Caribbean, often marketed through innuendo-filled ads alluding to the beer's reputed aphrodisiacal properties.

The three powers of Caribbean beer are Jamaica's Desnoes & Geddes, owned by Diageo; Trinidad and Tobago's Carib; and the Guyana-headquartered brewery of Barbados, Banks.

The best-known beer of Desnoes & Geddes, and likely the best known of all West Indies beers internationally, is Red Stripe ★, a slightly grainy lager refreshing when served very cold. Better by a very small measure is the slightly spicy Carib ★☆; while Banks Caribbean Lager ★ tends toward the sweeter side in taste.

On the stout side of the ledger, Desnoes & Geddes leads with Dragon Stout ★★ lightly roasty and thinnish with a hint of anise; while Royal Extra Stout ★★ from Carib offers a sweetness that is light yet silky on the palate. A newer entry from Banks is Banks Amber Ale, as yet untasted.

What can appear to be craft brewing in the Caribbean can be misleading. Once independent Big City Brewing of Kingston, Jamaica, is now owned by a local businessman with no brewing experience and an alliance with the world's largest brewer, Anheuser-Busch InBev. The St Vincent Brewery in tiny St Vincent & the Grenadines is owned by Denmark's Royal Unibrew, as is the Antigua Brewery. Trinidad's Samba Brewing and the Bahamian Brewery of the Bahamas are each truly independent, but with little in apparent brewing ambition beyond the light lager/strong stout standard.

One of the few successful craft beer concerns in the Caribbean is St John Brewers in the US Virgin Islands. Although the bulk of its beer is contract-brewed in Maine, and available in bottled form in the northeastern United States, the partners maintain a small Tap House bar on the island where they are able to test new recipes out on willing customers. Among its brands is one of the few IPAs sold in the West Indies, Island Hoppin' IPA ★★, a British-influenced brew with fruity and nutty flavours.

LATIN AMERICA

MEXICO

Mexico gets its modern brewing traditions from Germany, thanks to the Germans and Swiss who set up post-independence commercial breweries in the 19th century. By the mid-to-late 20th century, the country was known for golden, *helles*-esque lagers, amber beers that resembled Vienna lagers and the occasional *Münchener* style dark beer, known locally as *cerveza obscura*.

Then came Corona.

The light lager in the clear bottle, back then sometimes served with a squeeze of lime and a dash of salt or hot pepper sauce, had existed in Mexico for decades, but when it arrived as an import to the Texas and California markets in the 1980s, it became a cultural phenomenon. From thence forward, Mexican beer was known by the lightness of its taste, the clarity of its container and the ubiquity of the slice of lime wedged into the bottle.

Against this backdrop are several emerging craft breweries, each struggling to introduce more characterful ales and lagers to Mexico. Standing in their way is not only a public conditioned to light-tasting lagers served ice-cold, but also a retail and distribution system that favours the oligarchs to a tremendous degree.

Progress has been slow but steady, with greatest access to the new craft beers being in the capital of Mexico City, the Baja California peninsula and Guadalajara. Should gains in availability be made, and quality continue to improve, there may yet be a day when the country's brewers are known more for spicy Mexican Imperial stout than bland golden lager.

CAMARADA
Oaxaca

This young Oaxacan brewery got off to a shaky start with a trio of mostly pedestrian beers, including a decidedly unBavarian **Weissbier** ★. Experimental and one-off brews, however, such as an off-dry and compellingly spicy **Red Ale** ★★, infused with local *rosita de cacao*; and a captivating and sweet corn beer called **Santería** ★★, hint at possible successes to come.

DESTINATION
RIVIERA MAYA

Fairmont Mayakoba (298 Playa del Carmen) distinguishes itself by being one of the very few Mexican resorts to feature local craft beer, even hosting regular beer tastings with complementary food pairings.

CHINGONERÍA, LA
Mexico City

Home-brewer from Mexico City who developed his passion into a business. Oddly compelling golden pilsner **Chekate Esta** ★★ is spicy-herbal and curiously lemony; **Házmela Rusa** ★★★ is a lovely, plummy Mexican Imperial stout that warms beyond its strength; and **Amargator IPA** ★★ is a double IPA with a pleasing fruitiness interrupted by a sharp, hoppy bitterness and hit of alcohol.

CUCAPÁ
Mexicali, Baja California

Almost as well known in the US as in Mexico, this northern Baja California brewery produces flagship **Cucapá Clásica** ★★, which is off-dry and mildly bitter, with citrusy notes; and **Lowrider Ale** ★★☆, which is spicy from the use of rye and warming with orange toffee flavours on the finish. **Chupacabras** ★★★ is a herbaceous midpoint between pale ale and IPA.

GOURMET CALAVERA
Mexico City

This is a creative, experimental and gastronomically influenced brewery in Mexico City. Belgian styles an obvious interest, as shown by the slightly thin, chocolaty **Dubbel** ★★; and faintly candied **Tripel** ★★☆. An **American Pale Ale** ★★☆ is fruity and quaffable; **Mexican Imperial Stout** ★★★ has wonderful dark chocolaty dryness; and special **Lovecraft Beer** ★★★ is spicy and molé-esque.

DESTINATION
MEXICO CITY

Pujol (254 Francisco Petrarca) is not just one of Mexico's most highly acclaimed restaurants, it is also a place where the gastronomic possibilities presented by craft beer are recognized through a rather extensive list of local labels.

JACK
Mexico City

Mexico City brewery branching out from its British-brewing-inspired roots with **Alebrije** ★★☆, an unusual take on a *weissbier* with strong mango and peach

MEXICO

flavours. More typical are **Jack Stout** ★★, black, sweet and rounded; **Jack Chocolate Sweet Stout** ★★☆, strong and massively chocolaty with notes of cinnamon and allspice; and **Jack Clown Smile** ★★☆, a slightly roasty Scotch ale with flavours of toffee and plum and a hint of nutmeg.

MINERVA
Guadalajara, Jalisco

Relatively high-profile brewery in Guadalajara. **Pale Ale** ★★ is malty upfront, hoppier in back; **Viena** ★★★ is a toasty, drying lager true to its style; **Imperial Stout** ★★☆ is light for its billing but roasty and coffee-ish; tequila barrel-aged **Imperial Tequila Ale** ★★☆ derives peppery spiciness from its maturing process.

DESTINATION
GUADALAJARA

The Tap Room (1533 López Cotilla), a "Pastrami-Beer-Store", stands out as among the better beer bars in one of the few Mexican cities where a relatively large number of such places exist.

PRIMUS
Mexico City

México City brewery known better by the Tempus name it gives its beers. **Tempus Dorada** ★★☆ offers aromas and rounded, sweetish flavours of canned peach and apricot leading to an off-dry finish; **Tempus Doble Malta** ★★★ is raisiny in its strength, with clove-edged spice showing toward the peppery finish.

PÚBLICA CONDESA
Mexico City

Mexico City brewery producing a single beer, but a good one. **Poe Brown Ale** ★★☆ is sweetly roasty on the nose and offers a creamy body with notes of dark chocolate and dried fruit.

RÁMURI
Tijuana, Baja California

Tijuana brewery on its way to mastering classic beer styles. Best so far are **Lágrimas Negras** ★★★, an intensely chocolaty oatmeal stout at a strength 10% more akin to an Imperial, and **Bucéfalo** ★★, a mildly herbaceous and curiously low-key Imperial stout. Experimental brews show some promise.

TIJUANA BEER
Tijuana, Baja California

Known informally as TJ Beer, this Baja California brewery produces clean, conventional brews such as **Rosarito Beach** ★☆, a dryish alternative to Corona; and **Güera** ★★☆, a floral pilsner evocative of the Czech Republic. More boundary-stretching are **Morena** ★★, a dark and sweetish *dunkel* with tobacco leaf notes; and **Bufadora** ★★★, a full and toffee-ish lager identified as a *maibock*.

BRAZIL

Brazil is the fourth-largest beer-producing nation in the world. Yet all but a very small minority of that beer is light lager brewed from a minimum of barley malt by one of three companies: Anheuser-Busch InBev, with an estimated 70% market share; Kirin Brazil; and Heineken-owned Kaiser.

This leaves some 200 Brazilian craft brewers grappling for roughly 1% of the beer market, while hamstrung by tax laws that treat them the same as the big brewers!

Still, there is hope for the Brazilian craft beer future. A growing middle class in the country is actively seeking to upgrade its eating and drinking experiences, and upcoming Olympics in Rio in 2016 will surely shine a light on at least some of the country's small breweries, as the World Cup did in 2014. Additionally, over the last few years, many Brazilian brewers have shown vast improvement in the quality, originality and consistency of their beers.

If the government ever decides to follow the lead of developed nations across the west and introduces a graduated system of taxation based on brewery size and output, the future of craft brewing in Brazil might become very bright indeed.

ABADESSA
Porto Alegre, Rio Grande do Sul

Located in Rio Grande do Sul, this brewery doesn't pasteurize or filter any of its beers (unusual for Brazil, even in craft beer circles). **Slava Pilsen ★★** is a refreshing, yeasty and flowery lager; **Export ★★** has a biscuit-like aroma and nutty maltiness balanced with discreet bitterness; **Helles ★☆** offers an evident breadiness in the body and a yeasty finish; and **Dunkles Nektar ★★** starts with intensely caramelly aromatics and finishes with a slight spiciness.

AMAZON BEER
Belém, Pará

Based in a tourism and cultural centre in Belém, this innovative brewery tweaks beer styles through the addition of different Amazonian fruits. Examples include the **Witbier Taperebá ★★**, which is flavoured with *taperebá* fruit, also known as *cajá*, for a highly perfumey aroma and citrus, zesty, plummy body; and the **Forest Bacuri ★★★**, a pilsner with a sweet yet crisp, pineappley flavour thanks to the use of the *bacuri* fruit.

BACKER/3 LOBOS
Belo Horizonte, Minas Gerais

Belo Horizonte operation producing two line-ups of beer, plus a stand-alone ale called **Medieval ★★**, with a bottle more striking than its spiced mandarin orange flavours. Of the two lines, Backer and 3 Lobos, the latter is more interesting, with a crisp, light and mildly spicy wheat ale called **Exterminador ★★**; and the spicy-vanilla **Bravo American Imperial Porter ★★★**, aged in Amazonian wood. Best of the Backer line is the thinly chocolaty **Brown ★★**.

BAMBERG BIER
Sorocaba, São Paulo

Highly regarded, much lauded and perhaps predictably German-influenced brewery situated not far from São Paulo. Beers include a light-tasting but decidedly *dunkel*-ish **München ★★**; a most credible **Alt ★★**, with off-dry caramel notes and a dry finish; a toffee-ish **Bock ★★☆**; the gently smoky, appley **Rauchbier ★★★**; and a surprising paean to Belgium, **Due ★★★**, a toffee, pomegranate and chocolate delight brewed for the Melograno Restaurant in São Paulo.

BIERLAND
Blumenau, Santa Catarina

Blumenau brewery producing some of the most awarded beers in the country. **Vienna ★★☆** has a gentle citrus hop aroma balanced with smooth caramel malt flavours; **Pale Ale ★★★** satisfies hopheads with an abundance of passionfruity hoppiness and a lingering, dryly bitter finish; **Weizen ★★** is quite lively, smooth and predominantly clovey; **Bock ★★★** offers nutty, brandy-ish flavours and a warming finish; and a very rich, syrupy **Imperial Stout ★★★☆** attempts to redefine the style with chocolate liqueur, coffee and liquorice notes.

BODEBROWN
Curitiba, Paraná

Refreshingly irreverent brewer/teacher leading the drive to make Curitiba Brazil's craft beer capital. Style-bending brews include **Cerveja do Amor ★★☆**, a berry *hefeweizen* that morphed into a stronger, mildly peppery, berry-flavoured *tripel*, while the more conventional **Wee Heavy ★★★** is a very rich, warming and fudge-evoking Scotch ale. Improbable flagship is the strong, orangey and passionfruity **Perigosa ★★★**, developed as Brazil's first double IPA.

DESTINATION
CURITIBA

Cervejaria da Vila (2631 Rua Mateus Leme), open since 2004 in the city and fast becoming the heart of Brazilian craft brewing, is one of the region's most impressive beer bars, often featuring hard-to-find American and Belgian beers.

COLORADO
Ribeirão Preto, São Paulo

Pioneer of the Brazilian craft beer movement. Local ingredients feature in beers like the honey-ish, lemony **Appia ★★**, brewed with honey; the gently bitter IPA, **Indica ★★☆**, fortified with a hard sugar called *rapadura* and better on tap than bottled; and the coffee porter **Demoiselle** ★★, an intense, espresso-ish jolt of flavour. Newer is the very successful **Vixnu** ★★★, a firmly bitter, apricot-and-allspice double IPA.

DESTINATION
SÃO PAULO

Brazil's largest city is also big on good beer options. **FrangÓ** (168 Largo da Matriz de Nossa Senhora do Ó), founded in 1987, is the oldest and most traditional beer bar, while the bar and beer store **Empório Alto dos Pinheiros** (305 Rua Vupabussu) is celebrated today for its more than 30 taps and multitude of bottles. **Aconchego Carioca** (379 Rua Barão de Iguatemi) is another excellent local, with creative cuisine and over 200 beers.

CORUJA
Porto Alegre, Rio Grande do Sul

Marketing-conscious brewery packaging some beers in eye-catching 1l (1¾ pint) bottles. Brews a sweet, biscuity and warming **Strix Extra** ★☆; the unusual, softly smoky and robustly clovey **Alba Weizen** ★★; and **Labareda** ★★, a chilli-spiced *kellerbier*-style lager with hints of smoke in the body and a gentle burn on the finish.

DAMA BIER
Piracicaba, São Paulo

Modern, well-organized, three-year-old brewery northwest of São Paulo. Brews a malty and slightly spicy *dunkel*, **Amber Lady** ★★; **Indian Lady IPA** ★★, with robust balance between intense, resiny hop bitterness and caramel malt flavours; **Summer Lady** ★☆, with a rich sweetness and evident banana-like fruitiness on the palate; and a sociable, smooth, cocoa-and-coffee-tasting **Dark Lady** ★★☆.

DUM CERVEJARIA
Curitiba, Paraná

Founded by three amateur brewers in 2010, this beer commissioner expanded in scale in 2013. Intense beers include **Petroleum** ★★★☆ a silken and chocolaty powerhouse of an oatmeal stout, 12% alcohol and brewed with Belgian cocoa; and **Jan Kubis** ★★☆, a hoppy-fruity and dry-finishing "American pale lager".

EISENBAHN (KIRIN BRAZIL)
Blumenau, Santa Catarina

Early Blumenau-based brewer and exporter of Brazilian craft beer, sold in 2008. Flavours seem slightly lessened of late, as with the more malty than hoppy **Pale Ale** ★☆ and the modestly fruity **Golden Ale** ★★. (The latter is

355ml CERVEJA FORTE ESCURA 12%vol

given traditional-method sparkling wine treatment to become the effervescent yet somewhat dull-tasting **Lust ★★**.) Better are more traditionally German brands such as the satisfyingly roasty, yet light on the palate **Dunkel ★★☆**.

FALKE BIER
Ribeirão das Neves, Minas Gerais

Belo Horizonte brewery founded by three brothers, producing a wide range of styles. **Ouro Preto ★★☆** is a *schwarzbier* offering pumpernickel aromas and dry molasses and mocha notes in the body; **ER India Pale Ale ★★☆** is more ESB than IPA, with notes of apple and fig; **Monasterium ★★☆** is a spicy ale billed a *tripel* but really more a dryish *dubbel*; while **Vivre Pour Vivre ★★★** is an outstanding, tartly spicy fruit beer using native *jabuticaba* fruit.

INVICTA
Ribeirão Preto, São Paulo

This recent brewery arrival honours city monuments on its labels. Its beers include a traditional, floral **German Pils ★★**; a roasty and citrusy **India Black**

INVICTA
IMPERIAL INDIA PALE ALE

1000 IBU

8% VOL 500 ML
CERVEJA FORTE ESCURA

Ale ★★☆; an assertively hoppy and bitter **Imperial IPA ★★**; and a lovely, spicy-citrusy and tart **Saison À Trois ★★★**, brewed in partnership with Cervejaria 2cabeças.

JÚPITER
São Paulo

This newly arrived beer commissioner was born of the recent growth in Brazilian home-brewing. First beer, and the brewery's flagship, is a light, mellow and passionfruity **American Pale Ale ★★☆**; while the more recent **American India Pale Ale ★★☆** is surprisingly fruity in aroma and light-bodied.

DESTINATION
RIO DE JANEIRO

Hot, beach-centric Rio demands good, refreshing beers, supplied by **Boteco Colarinho** (100 Rua Nelson Mandela) with multiple taps and impressive finger foods. **Botto Bar do Mestre Cervejeiro** (205 Rua Barão de Iguatemi) combines good beer with live music, while the local branch of the **Delirium Café** (183 Rua Barão da Torre) offers a Belgian emphasis and excellent beer cuisine.

KLEIN BIER
Campo Largo, Paraná

Created in 2009 close to Curitiba, this brewery focuses on classic beer styles. **Brown Ale ★☆** combines caramel, medium-low roastiness and some fruitiness to a refreshing end; **Stout ★★** has bitter chocolate and coffee notes in the body and a roasty dryness on the finish; and the use of Saaz hops in **Tchec** ★★☆ imparts a flowery aroma and bitter finish.

OPA BIER (JOINVILLE)
Joinville, Santa Catarina

Coastal, historically minded brewery near Curitiba. *Reinheitsgebot*-adhering beers include a mocha-ish and plummy, but oddly thin **Porter** ★★; and a sweetish, lively **Weizen** ★☆. Better are the twin Göttlich Divina! beers brewed with *guaraná*, including an attractively floral and mildly fruity **Pilsner** ★★☆. The other Göttlich beer is a *weisse*, not yet tasted.

SEASONS
Porto Alegre, Rio Grande do Sul

Creative and innovative brewery, focused on intensity and balance. Beers include **Wallace Amber** ★★★, a balance of herbal hop freshness with biscuit-like flavours; **Green Cow IPA** ★★☆, offering a citrus hop aroma and assertive bitterness; **Cirilo Coffee Stout** ★★★, pungent with green coffee bean aromas and flavours; and **Bigfoot Russian Imperial Stout** ★★☆, partially oak-aged to a rich, vanilla-accented, chocolaty and woody aroma and a flavour approaching that of a liqueur.

WÄLS
Belo Horizonte, Minas Gerais

Prolific brewery that produces some lagers, but is at its best with ales like the mocha, raisin and liquorice **Dubbel** ★★☆; the fruity-spicy, herbaceous (lemon balm, rosemary) **Trippel** ★★★; the dried fruit and brandy-ish

Quadruppel ★★★; and the complex, delicate, Champagne-style **Brut** ★★★, with a sparkling effervescence and notes of soft fruit and citrus.

WAY BEER
Pinhais, Paraná

Flashy brewery located near the growing Brazilian craft beer hub of Curitiba. Early proponent of the use of Amazonian woods for the ageing of beer, as with its faintly smoky, spicy chocolate **Amburana Lager** ★★★, aged in the wood for which it is named. Other beers include a nutty, lightly toffee-ish **Irish Red Ale** ★★☆; and a balanced, toasty, dry-finishing **American Pale Ale** ★★☆.

WENSKY BEER
Araucária, Paraná

A family of Polish descent opened this brewery in the southeast in 2009. Brands include the dry-hopped, earthy **Vienna Lager** ★★; **Chopin Tripel** ★★, with a remarkably lemony aroma and malty body; the clean, nutty and toffee-ish **Munich Dunkel** ★★☆; a fine **Baltic Porter** ★★★ with cocoa, raisin and coffee in both aroma and body; and a superb **Dreu'na Piva Old Ale** ★★★☆, matured in French oak to an elegant vanilla and coconut character.

ARGENTINA

Argentinians are mostly descended from European settlers, so it makes sense that since the late 1980s roughly 500 new small breweries have been opened. Unfortunately, roughly half that number have also closed, though not for lack of enthusiasm.

On the upside, it is not unusual even in provincial towns to find a couple of local beers on the menu of any respectable dining or drinking establishment. On the downside, the absence of an independently owned, quality network of wholesalers with refrigerated local depots means that beer quality can suffer away from its locality.

A typical Argentine brewer makes three beers – one gold, one red and one black. The interesting part is that gold can mean anything from a light lager to a Belgian-style *tripel*, red could encompass anything from a pale ale or IPA to a Vienna lager, and black might vary from *schwarzbier* to Imperial stout.

While craft beer is still quite a rare thing in the hectic, sprawling city of Buenos Aires, the area around Río Negro, the Patagonian Lake District (including Bariloche), Llao-Llao and the hop-growing area of El Bolsón constitutes one of the most spectacular brewery crawls in the world.

ANTARES
Mar del Plata, Buenos Aires

The country's leading craft brewer since 1998, brewing at various locales for both on- and off-premises trade. Main brands include a true-to-style, thirst-quenching **Kölsch** ★★; a lightish **Porter** ★★☆, with sweet chestnut notes; a chocolaty, nutty and warming **Cream Stout** ★★☆; a boozy, tropical fruit and rounded malt **Barley Wine** ★★☆; and an oddly refreshing but strong **Wee Heavy** ★★.

DESTINATION
BUENOS AIRES

The **Buena Birra Social Club** (www.buenabirrasocialclub.com) is certainly one of the world's more unusual brewpubs, operating speakeasy-style with an address that is revealed only after a reservation is made by telephone (+ 54-911-6428-3457) or email (buenabirra@gmail.com).

BEAGLE
Ushuaia, Tierra del Fuego

Included for location rather than excellence, as it is currently the world's southernmost brewery, in the port town on Tierra del Fuego, the southern tip of Patagonia. **Rubia Ale** ★☆ is a safe blond ale; **Roja India Pale Ale** ★★ is more amber ale than IPA; and the **Negra Stout** ★★ is the biggest and boldest of the trio.

BERLINA
San Carlos de Bariloche, Río Negro

One of Bariloche's better established pub breweries, occasionally making cask ales. Best of the regular beers are **Patagonia Golden Ale** ★★, an intense golden ale with mild flowery bitterness balanced by a dab of caramel; and **Patagonia Foreign Stout** ★★☆, a moderately warming, mocha-ish ale with dark fruit notes and a long, ultra-dry finish.

DESTINATION
EL BOLSÓN

The **Fiesta Nacional del Lúpulo** (www.patagonia.com.ar), or National Hops Festival, is one of numerous festivals held throughout the year in this beautiful town that is also the heart of Argentina's hop-growing region.

BLEST
San Carlos de Bariloche, Río Negro

Established in 1989 within walking distance of **BERLINA**, Blest is said to be the first of the area's 20+ brewpubs.

Among its regulars, **Pilsen** ★★☆ is considered among the best blond beers in the country; **Scotch Ale** ★★ is a good example of a staple style in the Argentinian craft landscape; and the prize-winning **Bock** ★★☆ is a classically malt-forward beer. Seasonal **Frambuesa** ★★☆, with local raspberries, is easy-drinking despite 7.5% ABV.

BULLER
Buenos Aires

Started as a brewpub in Buenos Aires' fanciest neighbourhood, Recoleta, and now branching out as a franchise, following **ANTARES**' example on consistent quality. Reliable performers include **Oktoberfest** ★★, similar in character to a märzen but low in bitterness; and a by-the-numbers **IPA** ★★☆ that ticks all the right boxes.

DESTINATION
BUENOS AIRES

Cruzat Beer House (1617 Sarmiento) is a rarity in Argentina: a single bar carrying a wide variety of beers, both local and imported, from a multiplicity of breweries, located in the capital's San Nicolás neighbourhood.

GAMBRINUS
Zárate, Buenos Aires

Small, reclusive brewery upstream from Buenos Aires, making some impressive beers that find their way into a number of the capital's specialist bars. **Celtic Stout** ★★☆ is lighter than it seems, tasting creamy and roasted with touches of vanilla and chocolate; while **Gaelic Pale Ale** ★★☆, although stronger, is more quaffable with a good balance of malt, fruit and bitterness.

GÜLMEN
Viedma, Río Negro

Brewery with strong ties to the region. Like ANTARES, its intention is to grow smartly, expanding a network of reliable distributors in a way that retains quality. **Lager Ahumada** ★★ is a mildly smoked amber beer with balancing bitterness; and **Trigo** ★★ has clove and vanilla in the nose, mild bitterness and a smooth finish, with a deliberate but subtle sour touch.

JEROME
Mendoza

In Mendoza, Argentina's most famous winemaking area, national music legend and Oscar-winner Gustavo Santaolalla got together with this local craft brewery to make a few seriously interesting beers. **Negra** ★★, a dry mid-weight stout, is the best of the standard beers; **Diablo**

★★☆ is a pale ale with a whisky kick; and complex, daring **Grosa** ★★★ is a grapey, spicy-finishing strong ale that spends 18 months in Malbec barrels.

KRAKEN
Buenos Aires

Young brewery in Buenos Aires with much-praised beers that are favourites in the local beer community. **Red Ale** ★★☆ has handsome copper tones reflecting a solid mix of caramel and dried-fruit maltiness that barely holds its sharp bitterness; and **Stout** ★★☆ is a highly approachable, quaffable beer that hides its 6% ABV dangerously well.

OTRO MUNDO
San Carlos Sud, Santa Fe

Ambitious company that brought the old San Carlos brewery back to life, with the help of its part-owner, the Chilean brewing giant CCU. Most beer is bottled and widely available, including the aromatic, nicely balanced and refreshing **Golden Ale** ★★; and no-style **Strong Red Ale** ★★, which is both intense and confident.

PATAGONIA (AB INBEV)
Quilmes, Buenos Aires

Argentina's largest brewery by far is Quilmes, part of AB InBev, with Patagonia being its craft beer wing. In contrast to beers like **Quilmes Cristal** ★, **Patagonia's Bohemian Pilsner** ★☆ nudges above the industrial standard; **Amber Lager** ★☆ is more malt-forward, though unpretentious; and **Weisse** ★★ manages to balance between German and Belgian wheat beer styles.

CHILE

In the pecking order of Latin American craft beer, Chile sits somewhere after leader Brazil and number two Argentina, perhaps tied for third with Mexico. But as the country's growing number of craft brewers shake off their minor obsession with the *rubia, roja y negra* triptych of Central and South American beer styles/colours and start to follow in the more experimental footsteps of breweries like SZOT and ROTHHAMMER, progress could come very quickly.

CERVEZA DE AUTOR
Valparaíso

Brewery operated by chef and British-trained brewer, Ricardo Solis. Its most interesting beers arrive at the darker end of the colour spectrum, with the **Brown Ale ★★** being slightly toffee-ish, raisiny and moderately bitter; and the **Stout ★★** being milk chocolaty, creamy from the use of oats in the mash and dry on the finish.

GUAYACAN
Elqui Valley, Valparaíso

Brewery located in one of Chile's most popular tourist regions. Brands include the sweet and fruity **Pale Ale ★**, but also more robust offerings like the dryly malty **Golden Ale ★★☆**; the vanilla and mocha **Stout ★★**; and the light, citrus-spicy **Uno ★★**, with tropical-fruit notes and delicate hoppiness.

> ## DESTINATION
> ## VALPARAÍSO
>
> **El Irlandés** (Blanco 1279) might sound like a faux Irish pub, but it is in fact Chile's finest beer bar.

KROSS CERVEZA INDEPENDIENTE
Santiago

Founded by a German in search of brewing freedom, this may be Chile's most awarded brewery, now partly owned by Concha y Toro. Beers include perfumey **Pilsner ★★**; slightly sweet and chocolaty, dry-finishing **Stout ★★☆**; and a beer brewed for the brewery's fifth anniversary, **Kross 5 ★★★**, with an oaky vanilla nose and a flavour of sweet malt, berry fruit and tobacco.

MESTIZA CERVEZA GOURMET
Valparaíso

Located close to where the first Chilean beer was brewed in 1825, this brewery focuses on beers that pair well with the local cuisine, including a hoppy, herbal **American Pale Ale ★★☆** to match spicy food; a copper-coloured, bittersweet **Deutsches Altbier ★★** for grilled meat; and a roasty, coffee-ish **Irish Dry Stout ★★** for lamb or pork.

RAPA NUI
Hanga Roa, Rapa Nui

The most remote craft brewery in the world, at Hanga Roa, the only town on

Rapa Nui (or Easter Island), 3200km (1988 miles) off the Chilean coast, from where currently it imports the ingredients for its two Mahina beers, though barley cultivation is being tried on the island. Surprisingly perhaps its lightish, gently hopped US-style **Pale Ale ★★**; and middleweight dryish, less extensively hopped **Stout ★★** warrant trying on merit alone.

ROTHHAMMER
Pudahel, Santiago

Young brewery started by two brothers with a deep affection for hops. **Meantime ★★** is a dry and citrus blond ale; **Bones of Oak Stout ★★** is a lightly cocoa-ish stout; strong IPA **Brutal Hops ★★★** is extremely floral and well balanced; **Cosmos ★★☆** is a sweetly aromatic and full-bodied barley wine and the star of the brewery.

SOMA
San Bernado, Maipo

Brewery near Santiago producing only bottle-conditioned beers. **Gama Pale Ale ★★** is floral and off-dry, meant to resemble a sparkling wine; **Alfa Brown Ale ★★★** is sweet and fruity with bitterness rising on the finish; and **Beta Sweet Stout ★★** is chocolaty and full-bodied.

SZOT
Santiago

Boundary-stretching brewery founded and run by an expat Californian and his Chilean wife. Caramelly **Amber Ale ★★**; and lightly spicy **Rubia al Vapor ★★** are among the more accessible

brews; while the darkly fruity, port-wine-ish **Barley Wine ★★☆**; and densely fruity, intensely malty **Strong Ale ★★★** are among the best.

DESTINATION
SANTIAGO (AND ELSEWHERE)

Although it might seem odd, the supermarket chain **Jumbo**, with 13 outlets in Santiago and 15 elsewhere in the country, is likely the best bet for buying a variety of Chilean craft beers.

TÜBINGER
Santiago

Brewery led by a Brazilian-born brewer of German descent, somewhat surprisingly producing a variety of ales rather than lagers. Brands include: the off-dry and toasty **Red Ale ★★**; a **Pale Ale ★★** that is really more a sweetish best bitter in character; the nutty, slightly chocolaty-sweet **Brown Ale ★★☆**; and the strong, wildly successful **Tübinator ★★☆**, a roasty, raisiny ale with an off-dry finish.

REST OF LATIN AMERICA

Blond, red and black, the *tricolores* have been for years a running gag in Latin American *cerveza artesanal*. Roughly analogous to the pale ales, ambers and stouts that dominated North American craft in the early days, one measure of maturity is when breweries start to break the moulds and try new things. It's happening, even as the scattered brewpubs that came and went over the past two decades find more permanent footing and multiply. Genuine production breweries, small as they may be, are appearing with more frequency.

Colombia is beginning to show its neighbours what's possible. More than 30 new breweries have appeared since 2009, most of them shop-kit obscurities that announce themselves slightly more often than they disappear. Ambitious ones manage to stick around a while. Security has improved, and with it the beer.

Bogotá Beer Company was one of the first, overcoming a guerrilla's grenade attack in 2003 to become a thriving chain of 19 BBC pubs. Bogotá ★ is the safe lager, while the balanced Chapinero Porter ★★ is liked by craft-conscious visitors. Colón started in 1997, and while co-founder Berny Silberwasser left to start the BBC, the company followed the predictable path, making safe beers in atmospheric Palos de Moguer pubs: Roja, Rubia, Negra, and so on. Meanwhile, 3 Cordilleras in Medellín, launched in 2008, is a proper production brewery with a line-up more interesting than most in the region, made up of the citrus pale ale Mestizo and seasonals that include an IPA and a *saison*.

Uruguay has a few splashes of *cerveza artesanal*. Mastra is perhaps the most visible, with clever packaging of its gold, red and black ales, while Davok, born of the Shannon Irish Pub in Montevideo, offers a wider range of styles and has won awards in Argentina and Brazil. Cabesas Bier is a brewpub that bottles in Tacuarembó, with Trigo ★★☆, a seductively sweet Belgian-style wheat beer, and the chocolaty, brown ale-like Brown Porter ★★ among its better beers.

In Paraguay, Asunción has a German-style brewpub called Astoria that appears to promote its sangria as much as the house lager.

Bolivia's Saya Beer has been around since 1997, with a brewery in Cochabamba and popular sales outlet at the Adventure Brew Hostel in La Paz. Peru's Cebi-Chela in Lima specializes in ceviche and house-made beer, including a disturbingly green Cerveza de Menta, or "mint beer". Also in the capital, Barbarian appeared in 2013 fully formed, with an 8% alcohol IPA served in snifters. Sierra Andina in Huaraz looks like the real thing, too, playing with Andean ingredients. In Cusco, long-established backpacker bar Norton Rat has turned brewpub, providing pale ale and porter at altitude.

There are stirrings in Ecuador. The tiny Umiña brewery is putting blackberries in a *tripel* and passion-fruit in an IPA. Cuenca has the Compañia brewpub, with three main beers named after the usual colours. In Baños, a mini-brewery called Cascada is making beer for the owners of the Posada del Arte hotel and their son's Stray Dog pub.

Venezuela is not the most hospitable of places these days for entrepreneurs with capital, but Destilo brews an eponymous, slickly marketed amber ale, while Tovar makes a German-style pils in the "Germany of the Caribbean".

Central America presents some interesting cases, including a few brewpubs in Panama.

Istmo opened in 2005 in Panama City's Cangrejo neighbourhood. The best there is the dark Coclé ★☆, with dryish roasted malt helping to balance its residual sugar, while Veraguas ★ is an amber blend of Coclé and the sweet blond Colon, and better than the latter because of it.

Rana Dorada is newer to the capital, having opened in the historic Casco Viejo in February 2012. Ambition is present; the founders include Silberwasser of the BBC above. There is a bitterish Pils ★☆ and a distinctly US-style Pale Ale ★☆, besides a smooth Porter and the spicy Blanche wheat beer.

Costa Rica's Craft Brewing Company (CRCB) is Central America's most successful microbrewery to date, with dozens of draught and bottle accounts dotted around the country. The one to convert lifelong lager drinkers is the crisp blond Libertas ★★; the challenging one is the bitter and fruity red-amber Segua ★★☆; and the stable's newer member is sweet and malty Malacrianza ★☆. Seasonals have appeared on draught only, the most distinctive and impressive being the Trigo con Cas ★★★, a refreshingly acidic wheat beer made with sour guava.

Newly rebadged Lake Arenal Brewery is in Guanacaste, across the lake from Costa Rica's most photogenic cone volcano, in the Hotel Minoa. Its previous owners took boards and wax and returned to the Pacific Coast to open Tamarindo Brewing Company, bringing citrus-hopped Witch's Rock Pale Ale ★☆ and the brown Gato Malo ★ along with them. In San José, cultish Treintaycinco appears in a growing number of bars and restaurants with its hop-forward brews, led by robust barley wine Maldita Vida ★☆ and roundly fruity amber Malportada ★★.

A couple of brewpubs in Honduras meet the needs of adventure travellers, both removed from the bustle of Tegucigalpa. D&D is a secluded and rustic hotel-brewpub on Lake Yojoa, in central Honduras. Sol de Copán, near the Copán ruins, is where German expat Thomas Wagner sticks to traditional German styles, served with equally loyal dishes like sausage and *spätzle*.

El Salvador's growing economy has allowed some beery happenings. Brew Revolution, in the surf town of El Tunco, is a Pacific beach brewpub that distributes bottles to a few shops and bars in San Salvador. The enthusiastic American owner is openly learning on the job, sometimes putting out well-received IPAs like Mercurio, other times brewing with seawater. In the capital, the Cadejo microbrewery opened in 2013, fronted by a Salvadoran brewer/co-owner who studied engineering at Cornell. Its two main beers are citrus-hopped wheat beer Wapa ★★ and spicy-hopped Roja ★★.

ASIA & THE MIDDLE EAST

JAPAN

Beer brewing did not arrive in Japan until 1869 and through much of the 20th century was subject to peculiar legislative measures. These had the effect of creating a market that would be dominated by a small number of large, indigenous companies, which came to be Asahi, Kirin, Sapporo and Suntory.

In the mid-1990s smaller breweries were enabled to set up. Since then, entrepreneurs and industrialists, home-brewers and idealists, established brewers of traditional sake and existing national brewers keen to experiment have established more than 200 functioning small breweries, in every prefecture from Hokkaido to Nagasaki.

That Japan should become an important world centre of craft brewing is even more remarkable considering that *jibiiru* (locally made beers of interest) can cost two or three times as much as regular beers.

In the early days new brewhouses were influenced strongly by German practices in particular, though with British, Czech or American influences too, often employing expat brewing staff to aid authenticity.

The spread of specialist beer bars and the direct sale of beer via the internet has led to steady year-on-year growth despite an economy in constant struggle, showing that *jibiiru* is no fad. This in turn has led the second generation of Japanese craft brewers to find its own way, including creating some indigenous Japanese beer styles.

Rice, particularly the highly polished preparations used in sake production, or else in its red and heirloom varieties, is finding its way into Japanese interpretations of foreign styles. Japanese hop strains are being developed and exotic local ingredients appear as flavourings. There are even beers featuring slow fermentation in cedar sake casks or by yeast gathered from wild cherry blossom.

AKASHI
Akashi, Hyōgo

Small brewery in a museum of sake cups, at Akashi, west of Kobe. Better at lagers than ales thus far. **Kaigan Beer ★★** is a clean German-style pilsner with bitter hopping; appearing richer and unfiltered as **Meriken Beer ★★☆**; while **Yukyu no Toki ★★★** is a creamy, chocolaty *schwarzbier*.

AQULA
Akita

Small brewery on the northwest coast of Honshu. Regular line-up includes rich, moderately strong dark *bock*, **Namahage ★★☆**; mildly tart, cherry-blossom-yeast beer **Sakura Kobo ★★**; entertaining and hoppier wheat beer **Citra Weisse ★★☆**; and experimental **Kiwi IPA ★★☆**, which highlights Nelson Sauvin.

BAEREN
Morioka, Iwate

In Iwate in the north of Honshu, Baeren avoided major earthquake damage in 2011 to continue producing its solid German-influenced range of beers, like the summer seasonal **Weizen ★★**; year-round flagship **Schwarz ★★**; and hoppy, stronger blond lager **Classic ★★☆**, the cult version of which, the unfiltered **Kellerbier ★★★**, might be Japan's best simple beer.

BAIRD BREWING
Numazu, Shizuoka

American expat Bryan Baird's brewery, a couple of hours south of Tokyo on the way to Nagoya, is a leader in the business for both the consistent quality of its beers and its perpetual experimentation. Nearly 300 beers have been produced since 2000, with regulars including **Angry Boy Brown Ale ★★☆**; the up-hopped and strong **Suruga Bay Imperial IPA ★★☆**; springtime's tart, other-worldly **Yuzu Garden Temple Ale ★★★** infused with citrus yuzu, also used to perfume winter baths; and the more occasional, elusive, just plain clever **Brewer's Secret Handshake ★★★**, an impressively Düsseldorfer *alt*.

BRIMMER
Kawasaki, Kanagawa

Start-up established in 2012 by a former Sierra Nevada brewer who had been brewing at a golf resort near Mount Fuji before moving to Kawasaki, between Tokyo and Yokohama. His clean **Pale Ale ★★☆** shows balance and moderate bitterness; while the off-dry, nutty **Porter ★★☆** has excellent depth. Thus far, seasonals have included a leafy **Strong Pale Ale ★★**; and the softer, gentler **English IPA ★★☆** that stays true to its British influences.

CHATEAU KAMIYA
Ushiku, Ibaraki

Japan's oldest winery, northeast of Tokyo, has produced beer since the 1990s. Its **Helles ★★☆** is a well-balanced exemplar of the Munich original; spring brings **Sakura Kobo ★★★**, a cherry-blossom-yeast beer that could only be Japanese; autumn prefers a UK-inspired **Brown Ale ★★☆**, which could pass as native; while winter's heavy, succulent, dark **Christmas Bock ★★★** is a kind of pan-European winter warmer.

DESTINATION
TOKYO

In the enormous, sprawling capital, international beers of quality are now commonplace but the go-to bar for draught Japanese craft beers, some cask-conditioned, is **Popeye** (2–18–7 Ryōgoku) near Ryōgoku railway station, with **Ushi-Tora** (2–9–3 Kitazawa) near Shimo-Kitazawa station not far behind.

DAISEN G BEER
Tottori

Small brewery on the slopes of deceased volcano Daisen making great beers that sometimes travel poorly. Regular **Weizen ★★☆** was voted the world's best in a London competition; though fruity, rich and complex **Wheat Wine ★★★☆** has a more legitimate shout; and malt-led, UK-style **Barley Wine ★★★** impresses too. Spicy, innovative **Yago ★★☆** is what happens when the grain bill contains home-grown sake rice and fermentation is seeded with a spicy Belgian yeast.

FUJIZAKURA HEIGHTS BEER
Kawaguchiko, Yamanashi

Masterful, expanding brewery at the foot of Mount Fuji, setting the standard for German beer styles in Japan. Its **Weizen ★★★** is sweet, malty and as good as they come; relatively restrained **Rauch ★★★** is Japan's finest smoked beer; **Rauchbock ★★★** is more full-on, with chocolate malts; and winter's sweet, spicy **Weizenbock ★★☆** is a perfect dessert.

HARVESTMOON
Maihama, Chiba

In a suburban shopping centre, a stone's throw from Tokyo Disneyland, the regular line-up includes a dry, roasty **Schwarz ★★☆**; and easy-drinking **Wit ★★**; while winter sees a rich, sweet **Barley Wine ★★☆**; and big roasted **Imperial Stout ★★★** that are more captivating.

HIDA TAKAYAMA BEER
Takayama, Gifu

Impressive small brewery in the mountains of Gifu, deserving of greater renown. Its **Weizen ★★☆** is sweet and estery; the complex **Stout ★★★** is rich, chewy and slightly vinous; lighter, UK-leaning **Dark Ale ★★☆** has rich, nutty cereals and chocolate; while strong, dark and handsome **Karumina ★★★** is a barley wine spiced by Belgian yeast.

HIDEJI BEER
Nobeoka, Miyazaki

Creative brewery on the east side of Kyushu, often employing local fruits and distillates. Nicely hopped **Taiyo no Lager**

★★☆ tops a seasonal list of characterful pale lagers; **Natsumikan Lager ★★** uses local tangerines; export-strength **Kemurihige Stout ★★★** is creamy and nutty; and **White Weizen ★★** falls between Belgium and Germany.

ISE KADOYA
Ise, Mie

Small brewery within a 450-year-old family business at the pilgrimage centre of Ise. Makes 40+ beers every year, including US-style, light and fruity **Pale Ale ★★**, sometimes found dry-hopped in the cask; strong, hoppy, amber **Imperial Red Ale ★★☆** tasting of cherries and caramel; and gentle **Smoked Porter ★★☆**, which has coffee and chocolate flavours.

IWATE KURA
Ichinoseki, Iwate

One of the first Japanese craft breweries, (1995), an early leader with a background in sake brewing. Its **IPA ★★☆** shows restraint, though soft hops are elegantly balanced; the off-dry **Stout ★★** has a lot of chocolaty character, but subdued roastiness; while autumn's heavier, roasty **Oyster Stout ★★★** is briny to the palate or perhaps the imagination, accompanying the season's fresh oysters swimmingly.

KIUCHI
Naka, Ibaraki

Some brewers have two lives. What to the Japanese is the Kiuchi sake brewery's 1996 beer-brewing arm is, to the rest of the world, rock-star Nippon craft brewer Hitachino Nest, its beers easier to find abroad than at home. Blond, bottom-fermented **Ancient Nipponia ★★★**

is made from Kanego Golden barley malt with Japanese Sorachi Ace hops; its **Espresso Coffee Stout ★★★** is famously full-on; ginger and coriander-tipped **White Ale ★★★** goes well with sushi; while imaginative **Japanese Classic Ale ★★☆** is a UK-edged American IPA aged in cedar casks.

MINOH BEER
Osaka

Innovative small brewery run by three sisters who experiment in creating beers in many international styles. Excellent pale ales and stouts peak with **W-IPA ★★★**, a US-style double IPA with an immaculate malt body behind the hop hit; and brawny yet smooth **Imperial Stout ★★★**, with chocolate and café-au-lait aromas. In contrast, **Yuzu White ★★★** is a dry, tangy *witbier* with dried citrus peel.

DESTINATION
OSAKA

Q-Brick (4–6–12 Hirano-machi) is a small, friendly café near the Goryō Shrine in the north of the centre, with a fine range of Japanese beers on draught and 200+ mainly imported bottles, while near Nakamozu station to the south **Eni-Bru** (Kita-ku, 2–71 Nakamozu) is building a range of hard-to-find *jibiiru* with nearly 30 taps between itself and its sister bar upstairs.

MOJIKO RETRO BEER
Kitakyushu, Fukuoka

Pub brewery in the north of Kyushu, specializing in top-quality beers in German-derived styles. A biscuity, fruity **Pilsner** comes filtered or not ★★→★★☆; the classy **Weizen** ★★☆ balances banana, clove and citrus flavours perfectly; its **Rauch** ★★★ is almost black with big smoke and rich chocolate; and **Weizen Strong** ★★★ is a unique take on a wheat *bock* with mango and cherry alongside banana and clove flavours.

DESTINATION
NATIONAL

Many Japanese craft beers can be purchased online, with many if not most *jibiiru* brewers offering direct sale, sometimes for export too, though carriage is expensive. In Japan, to source the best range of imports easily, go to www.ezo-beer.com.

MOKU MOKU
Iga, Mie

The brewing wing of an agricultural park east of the ancient capital, Nara. High quality but hard to find, even locally. The crisp, hoppy **Golden Pilsner** ★★☆ is very German; US-nudged *weizen* **Haru Urara** ★★☆ gives spicy wheat and citrus hops; **Smoke Ale** ★★★ has sweet chocolate, caramel and big smoke flavours; and the **Barley Wine** ★★★ is a malt-driven, UK-style winter warmer.

NORTH ISLAND BEER
Sapporo, Hokkaido

Adventurous small brewery in a famous brewing town, prone to add stuff to its beers. Hence its stronger-end **India Pale Ale** ★★☆; sometimes comes out as bracingly bitter **Grapefruit IPA** ★★☆;

herbaceous **Coriander Black** ★★☆ is always that way; while the slightly tart **Stout** ★★ achieves it notes of cacao and espresso unaided, we think.

OH! LA! HO BEER
Tōmi, Nagano

Constantly improving small brewery on an agricultural park south of Nagano. **Bossa Nova** ★★☆ is the latest name for its single but evolving lower-strength IPA; winter-released **Porter** ★★★ is fruity and hoppy; **White Ale** ★★☆ has citrus hops and light banana flavours; while **Amber Ale** ★★☆ balances earthy hopping with rich caramel malt.

OKU NOTO BEER
Noto, Ishikawa

Small brewery on the north coast Noto peninsula, employing Czech brewers and taking its brand, Nihonkai Club, from its base. The **Pilsner** ★★ is sweet and malty, with Saaz hops; **Dark Lager** ★★ is also Bohemian in style but dry and bready; while the **IPA** may be unique in being offered as bespoke sub-brands, dry-hopped on a scale of 1 to 10 ★★→★★★.

OTARU BREWING
Otaru, Hokkaido

Brewery (1995) on Hokkaido, staring across the ocean at Russia but thinking of Germany. Its conventional line-up includes an off-dry organic **Dunkel** ★★; and pleasantly smooth and cloved **Weisse** ★★; though the fireworks are reserved for its *doppelbock*-strength, four-month seasoned **Dunkel Bock** ★★★; baby brother of wooden-casked

New Year treat, the seven-month, matured at low temperature, 13.5% ABV, heavy, malty **Eisbock ★★★☆**.

OUTSIDER BREWING
Kofu, Yamanashi

New brewery a couple of hours west of Tokyo, guided by imagination. Wild yeast fermentation gives its **Belgian White ★★** dry citrus flavours; **Plum Ale ★★☆** is made with Japanese apricot (*Prunus mume*) fruits, dry and tangy; the **Pale Ale ★★☆** matches rich caramel malts with Styrian Goldings; **Innkeeper Bitter Lager ★★☆** is full of prickly hops; and rich, meaty **Hamaguri Stout ★★☆** uses clams in place of oysters.

SANKT GALLEN
Atsugi, Kanagawa

Pioneer craft brewer an hour or two west of Yokohama, focusing heavily on the sweeter, darker side, a tendency seen at its best in the rich and hefty **Imperial Chocolate Stout ★★★**; more modestly in **Sweet Vanilla Stout ★★☆**; and **Kokutou Sweet Stout**, **★★**, which contains locally created brown sugar.

SHIGA KOGEN BEER
Yamanouchi, Nagano

The ale-brewing wing of the Tamamura-Honten sake brewery, in the mountains of northern Nagano. Its ever-evolving, coyly named **House IPA ★★★** is always at least double strength and with lovely hop aromas; **African Pale Ale ★★★** is dry, hoppy and US-style; while its range of Japanese-tweaked *saison* beers include home-grown sake rice and heavy hop-loading, seen simply in **Saison One ★★☆**; and most assertively in **Isseki Nicho ★★★**, a strong black variant that could pass as a heavy stout with Belgian spiciness.

SHIMANE
Matsue, Shimane

Small brewery, sometimes called Hearn Beer, near southwestern Japan's north coast. Its **Pilsner ★★** is nicely hopped and balanced; cocoa-infused **Chocolat No 7 ★★** goes well with dessert but is otherwise unfashionably sweet; a quality that summer-seasonal pick of the bunch **Honey Weizen Bock ★★☆** carries off with great refinement.

SHONAN
Chigasaki, Kanagawa

Original 1990s *jibiiru* brewery in a popular beach area south of Tokyo. Now expanded to include two taprooms, the brewers are making experimental beers that push it up to Japan's top flight. Numerous excellent IPAs have been joined by a clean, metallic **Alt ★★**; an **Imperial Stout ★★★** that has the smell of the sea over roasted malt flavours on a background of liquorice;

SanktGallen®
SWEETS BEER

KOKUTOU
SWEET STOUT

沖縄産黒糖使用

Valentine's Day chocolate beer **Shonan's Chocolate Porter ★★★**; and rich, hefty, malt-led **Belgian Stout ★★★** with amazing depth and character.

SWAN LAKE BEER
Agano, Niigata

Consistent 1997 brewery attached to a lovely old hotel-restaurant located west of Niigata, producing some of the country's finest brews. **Amber Ale ★★★☆**; and **Porter ★★★** are international medal-winning exemplars of their styles; the autumnal **IPA ★★★** is floral, fruity and balanced; while winter's **B-IPA ★★★☆**, using Belgian yeast, is even better. Relative newcomer **Imperial Stout ★★★** is tangy, spicy and highly complex.

TAZAWAKO
Senboku, Akita

Based at a hotel and hot springs near Japan's deepest lake, Tawaka, in the north of Honshu. Highlight of the regular line-up is **Dark Lager ★★☆**, showing deep roasted malts and caramel with moderate bitterness; the dry, slightly fruity **Alt ★★** is more restrained; while the highlight is a silky smooth **Rauch ★★★** – imagine meat dipped in molasses cooking on a campfire – aged versions of which show even more depth.

THRASH ZONE LABO
Yokohama, Kanagawa

A cultural phenomenon of sorts, set up in 2012 to produce only kegged IPAs, a task from which it has not shirked. Production is increasing rapidly thanks to some surprisingly approachable heavyweights of the style such as double IPA, **Hopslave**

★★☆; and an equally enjoyable regular IPA called **Hama-Cisco ★★☆**.

YO-HO BREWING
Karuizawa, Nagano

Pioneer of the Japanese craft brewing scene, losing its way for a time but now back on track. Canned US-style pale **Yona Yona Ale ★★** is the best-known craft beer in the land; though hoppy, American-style porter **Tokyo Black ★★★** is far better; the IPA, **Aooni ★★**, is reliable rather than memorable; while its ever-changing, year-dated **Barley Wine ★★☆→★★★** is invariably as English as it is good.

YOKOHAMA
Yokohama, Kanagawa

Pub brewery at a central Yokohama restaurant, initially Czech-influenced but become more eclectic. Deep golden **Yokohama Lager ★★☆** shines with New Zealand hops; solidly Bohemian mainstay **Pilsner ★★☆** has biscuit malt and Saaz; while stronger *witbier* **White Joker ★★☆** is its best Belgian effort so far, using citrus hops as spicing.

ZAKKOKU KOBO
Ogawa, Saitama

Small brewery northwest of Tokyo, experimenting with alternative grains, many of which it grows. **Zakkoku Weizen ★★☆** includes rye and two kinds of millet; spicy **Sansho Porter ★★☆** uses Szechuan pepper for a citrus nuance; tart, lambic-like **Yamamomo Ale ★★☆** uses Japanese bayberry fruits; while more standard **Akane Red Ale ★★** blends earthy hops with bready malt.

CHINA

Although China has a history of alcohol consumption dating back thousands of years, it is a drinking culture quite different from that of the West. In general, the Chinese drink less for the pleasures of the glass and more for the role the act plays within their social structure, creating an atmosphere, expressing a mood or bestowing an honour.

As a result, per capita beer consumption in China remains quite low compared to the majority of Western nations, as little as one-quarter to one-third that of the world's most prodigious beer-drinking lands. Yet despite this fact, the country has in recent years become by a considerable margin the largest producer and consumer of beer in the world, as well as an increasingly important grower of hops. And these numbers are highly volatile – if each adult Chinese drinks two or three bottles more per year, the amount consumed would roughly equal the entire production of the American craft brewing industry.

There are hundreds of breweries scattered throughout China, with the bulk being local or regional operations. As in the West, the few large national brands, including Tsingtao, Harbin, Snow and Yanjing, are light-hued and light-tasting lagers, well-suited to the typical Chinese toast, *ganbei*, meaning bottoms up.

Following several aborted and failed attempts in the 20th century, almost all of the major international breweries are now active in China, with partial or complete ownership of national or significant regional brewing interests: Anheuser-Busch InBev claims full ownership of Harbin; the globally recognized QINGDAO (TSINGTAO) is partially owned by Asahi; SABMiller co-owns CR Snow, makers of Snow Beer, the bestselling beer brand in China and the world; and the waning days of 2013 saw Carlsberg finalize the purchase of 100% of Chongqing Beer Group, operator of eight breweries in China.

Amid all of this international consolidation, however, craft beer appreciation has seen rapid advancement since 2010. At the first Shanghai Craft Beer Festival, for instance, fewer than 100 people were in attendance, whereas more than 10,000 consumers attended the third annual edition of the fest in 2013. This burgeoning popularity has led to the creation of a further two beer festivals in the city and others elsewhere, including in the capital of Beijing.

Additionally, home-brewing associations – historically, pivotal players in the development of craft beer cultures around the world – have grown in both number and size over the last two years, with some 15 such organizations operating in China today. In some cases, this has led to the development of brewpubs, particularly in China's first- and second-tier cities.

Old traditions die hard, though, and rural China remains dotted with roadside stands selling cheap beer, the poor quality of which is legendary. A single mash may be used to make six or seven run-offs, the later ones creating a drink so watery that it is humiliating to call it beer at all. Many Chinese say that they "drink beer instead of water because at least it is sanitized".

Fortunately for those who prefer good beer, brewmasters from the New World, and increasingly from China itself, are busy transforming the Chinese beer landscape, most noticeably in major cities. Of particular interest are those brewers intent on finding ways in which to employ typically Chinese ingredients, such as Sichuan peppers, *dianhong* and *wulong* teas, and other indigenous flavourings.

While still but in its infancy, this trend clearly demonstrates that not only is craft brewing on the rise in China, but also the country's brewers are on their way to developing a singularly Chinese approach to beer and brewing.

BOXING CAT BREWERY
Shanghai

Long-standing leader of the Shanghai craft beer scene with two locations offering a variety of beers and American food. **Standing 8 Pilsner** ★★☆ is a well-conditioned blond lager beer; and

TKO India Pale Ale ★★☆ is a US-style IPA with citrus and piney flavours. Seasonals include **Southpaw Winter Warme**r ★★★, an English brown ale spiced with star anise and others. Impressive **Yunnan Amber Ale** ★★☆ marked a first collaboration, with GREAT LEAP BREWING.

BREW, THE
Shanghai

Australian-designed pub brewery housed in an upscale hotel. Award-winning range includes crisp and fragrant **Skinny Green Lager** ★★☆, with assertive bitterness; Australasian-style India Pale Ale ★★☆ has bold, fresh tropical-fruit flavours; **White Ant** ★★☆ *witbier* is gently spiced with house-dried orange peel; and the massively chocolaty, vanilla-accented **Killani Russian Imperial Stout** ★★★, aged 11 months with the last three in Chinese oak barrels.

DR. BEER
Shanghai

Trendy Shanghai brewpub known for serving fresh beer, direct from tank to tap. Its six permanent beers include German-style **Wheat** ★★, with a bubblegum flavour; sweet and fuller-bodied **Pilsner** ★★; and the easy-drinking **Pale Ale** ★★.

GREAT LEAP BREWING
Beijing

Beijing's first pub brewery, a defining pioneer among new-generation Chinese brewers. Uses mainly locally sourced ingredients for a wide range that includes the distinctive standout **Iron Buddha Blonde** ★★★☆, infused with the famous Chinese tea; **Little General IPA** ★★★, which uses only Chinese hops and no dry-hopping to create a clean, crisp and distinctive bitterness; **Honey Ma Gold** ★★, with dried Szechuan peppercorns and Shandon honey, gentle but full of surprise; and a big but workaday **Imperial Stout** ★★.

NBEER PUB
Beijing

New brewpub founded in 2013. **Coffee Rye Stout** ★★ is brewed with gesha coffee and a unique hull-less barley called black qingke, discovered by one of the founders during a cycling trip to Tibet, which give the beer a distinctive cereal note and coffee flavours. Hoppy and well-balanced **Black IPA** ★★ is one of the strongest beers served from the pub's 22 taps.

QINGDAO (TSINGTAO)
Qingdao, Shandong

Globally, the most famous Chinese beer is brewed in the coastal city for which it is named, Qingdao in Chinese and, more famously, Tsingtao in English. The flagship **Tsingtao Lager** ★ is crisp and slightly hoppier than the standard Chinese lager; and gains depth and character when purchased directly from the brewery unpasteurized and unfiltered as **Yuan Jiang** ★☆, often carried home by locals in plastic bags.

REBERG
Shanghai

The offerings of this small brewery, which is *Reinheitsgebot*-obsessed. are packaged in sophisticated aluminium bottles and marketed with a declared shelf life of only one month. **Hefeweizen ★★** has a fresh citrus aroma and subtle notes of banana; **Pilsner ★★** has a light body with a crisp and dry finish; and the dark ale, **Dunkel ★★**, offers flavours of coffee and caramel.

SLOW BOAT BREWERY
Beijing

A versatile small brewery that is making an international range of craft beers, among which are the Australasian-style **Monkey's Mango First IPA ★★☆**, with pungent mango but tender bitterness; a **Porter ★★** with a fine coffee edge; and the **Safe Harbour Christmas Ale ★★☆**, a light-bodied amber ale that is flattered by spices. At the brewery's taproom the draught beers are unfiltered.

STRONG ALE WORKS
Qingdao, Shandong

A fervent home-brewer based at Qingdao, where the world-famous QINGDAO (TSINGTAO) brands are also produced. His surprisingly good bottled beers are made in 100-litre runs, currently in a choice of five different varieties, among which are **Bitter Ale ★★☆**, with a creamy mouthfeel and nice bitterness; and **Smoky Dark Beer ★★**, which has a smoky bacon flavour and fruit candy finish.

TYPHOON BREWERY
Lantau, Hong Kong

A small brewery located in Hong Kong, the first to attempt to brew English-style cask ales in China. No taproom but the beer is distributed to a few pubs in the former British colony. **T8 English Bitter ★★** is the flagship product, with a mellow but traditional character; while **Eastern Lightning ★★☆** is a US-influenced IPA with a pleasant bittersweet balance.

SOUTHEAST ASIA

Let's get this much straight right away: craft beer has indeed arrived in Southeast Asia. In some areas, like Singapore, it is even showing signs of beginning to thrive.

However, as there is no real tradition of brewing in this part of the world, save for what largely German breweries brought to the region, development of a craft brewing culture has been slow, sometimes glacially so. Part of this is due to bureaucratic constraints, but the majority, to our minds, is cultural. Simply, in nations with relatively low per capita beer consumption, the impetus to shake up the large-brewery-dominated state of affairs is minimal.

Still, there are bright spots here and there, with potential as yet unrealized in Singapore, South Korea and Thailand, in particular. Within a matter of a few years, we suspect the beer picture in Southeast Asia could be very different indeed.

SOUTH KOREA

It's not easy being a Korean craft brewer. By most estimates, within the last decade as many as 100 or more craft breweries have ceased operation, most of them brewpubs. This leaves fewer than 40 remaining craft breweries today, battling for a small fraction of a market controlled by two major brewing concerns, Hite Jinro and the Anheuser-Busch InBev-owned Oriental Brewery, known as OB.

Complicating matters further, a third large and well-financed corporation, the consumer goods company Lotte, is expected to open a large-scale brewery in 2015.

On the craft side, however, optimism still abounds, at least in part because of a recent restructuring of Korea's formerly arcane brewing laws, which now require a distributing brewery to have fermentation and storage capacity equalling or exceeding 5000 litres, as opposed to the former 150,000 litres. Such smaller breweries also qualify for a revised and slightly lower tax rate.

This very significant change, coupled with an imported beer market that grew over 25% in 2013, will certainly lead to the opening of several new breweries in the years to come, including a much-anticipated joint venture involving the BROOKLYN BREWERY of the US, Jeju Brewing, expected to open in late 2014. They will join recent arrival Platinum Brewing, based in mainland China but with a speciality beer pub in their main target market of Korea, and the only two companies to have been previously licensed to brew and distribute beer, 7 Brau and Ka-Brew.

A small handful of beers are produced by 7 Brau, including a canned IPA, of which local beer aficionados speak without enthusiasm. Ka-Brew, sometimes known as the Kapa Brewery, serves primarily as a contract brewery for three beer commissioning agents, all based in Seoul and all favoured by the expat community, with growing interest among native Koreans: Reilly's Brewing, an offshoot of Reilly's Taphouse & Gastropub; Magpie Brewing; and Korea's best-known beer outlet, Craftworks Taphouse and Bistro.

TAIWAN, CHINA

In brewing terms the island of Taiwan is a place to watch. The burgeoning interest in beers that differ from the industrial norm is reflected in the growth of organized and collaborative home-brewing, and expansion of the commercial craft brewing scene is expected with at least one US-inspired supply brewery in the works.

BLÉ D'OR, LE
Taipei City

Despite the French name, this is a chain of German-style pub breweries appearing across Taiwan – seven at the last count – with one also at Suchou on mainland China. All make and serve an easy-drinking **Dunkel** ★★ that is said to contain some smoked logan wood; **Hell** ★☆, a *helles*-style beer that impresses expats; a banana-imbued *weizen* called **Weiss** ★★ that impresses ex-pats; and a more distinctive **Honey Beer** ★★☆, which is nicely infused with local logan honey.

JOLLY
Taipei City

Pioneering pub brewery in the capital, with a long history of producing safer beers in a variety of styles to accompany its Thai cuisine. The **Pilsner** ★☆ is rounded; the **Pale Ale** ★☆ is a smooth but unsurprising amber ale; and the stronger **Scotch Ale** ★★ uses understated peat-baked malt; though best by far is the unsweetened **Witbier** ★★☆, with a whiff of freshness and an appetizing underlay from the infusion of passion-fruit.

NORTH TAIWAN
Taoyuan, Taoyuan County

New small brewery, with close links to the Taiwanese craft beer movement. Creates bottled beers based on Belgian styles, which appear in local supermarkets. Its

Weizen ★★ is a mutation of Belgian and German wheat beer styles, with clove, spice and yeasty flavours; popular **Lychee Beer** ★★ is fruity and sweetened; **Melon Beer** ★☆ similarly; while **6** ★★ is an attempt at a *dubbel* but with pronounced fruit flavours.

VIETNAM

Despite two millennia of Chinese rule, two centuries of French and two decades of American, the dominant influence in modern Vietnamese brewing is Czech, many Vietnamese having emigrated to Czechoslovakia after both countries achieved independence. Many dozens of brewpubs have opened in cities the length of the country, typically selling beers sold as "golden" (sometimes "yellow") and "black". Along with new industrial breweries these are replacing an older tradition of 300 or so small brewhouses producing mostly light beers. In the north these still produce what is known collectively as *bia hơi*, a tradition of light beers racked immediately after fermentation and delivered daily to shack-like bars, where they are served uncarbonated directly from metal kegs emptied in a single session.

COI XAY GIO
Hanoi

Brewpub attached to the Windmill restaurant. The best example from the two dozen or so in Hanoi, typically making only two types of beer, – "Yellow" and "Black". The paler, rustic, fruity, herbal **Sèc** ★★☆ has a mineral palate; while darker **Ðen** ★★☆ has rich sugars and a lot of fruit.

GOLDMALT
Hanoi

A small chain of individually designed pub breweries in Hanoi and the north,

using Czech brewing kit to make Bohemian lagers that include the herbal and modestly bitter **Pilsner 12°** ★★☆; the lightly chocolated **Black** ★★, with a hint of smoke; and the stronger,

golden **Special** ★★☆, with a yeasty, herbal, spicy taste and doughy malt.

HOA VIÊN
Ho Chi Minh City

Pub brewery (1995) with offshoots in Hanoi and beach town Mui Ne. Shares space with the Czech embassy and produces two distinctly Bohemian beers, a *pilsner* called **Lager** ★★★, with a big Saaz nose, bready malts and a long, hoppy finish; and a classic Czech *tmavý* dark lager called **Bia Đen** ★★☆, soft, nutty and a little buttery.

LOUISIANE BREWHOUSE
Nha Trang, Binh Thuan

An Australian-run pub brewery that spills out onto the beach at Nha Trang. Its **Witbier** ★★ has balanced fruit and coriander flavours with a light spicy finish; the rich, woody **Pilsener** ★★☆, which is made with New Zealand hops, has enough bitterness to taste; the pale **Crystal Ale** ★★ has light bitterness and a tropical-fruit character on the palate; while the full-bodied **Dark Lager** ★★☆ is rich and chocolaty.

SINGAPORE

Singapore's tiny land mass belies its prodigious thirst for beer, despite its notoriously high duties on alcohol. While the beer scene is still largely dominated by home-grown Asia Pacific Breweries – brewer of Tiger Beer and owner of the country's largest craft brewery – as well as global players Carlsberg and Heineken, the past decade has seen the rise of a number of microbreweries and brewery pubs, as well as a burgeoning import market.

Evidence of this increasing maturity is the annual Beerfest Asia, first introduced in 2009, which now sees over 30,000 visitors sample some 350 local and international beers over four days. It was joined in 2012 by Singapore Craft Beer Week, a rarity in Asia, which seeks to inculcate the virtues of craft beer to both bar owners and the general populace.

ARCHIPELAGO BREWERY (ASIA PACIFIC BREWERIES)
Singapore

The craft beer division of Singapore's largest brewer, producing a selection of easy-drinking, approachable beers. Its multiple award-winning **Belgian Wit** ★★ is light and citrusy; its **Summer Ale** ★★ features American and New Zealand hops for light bitterness; Kiwi hops add a fruity twist to the otherwise Czech-style **Bohemian Lager** ★★; while toasty toffee, chocolate and caramel notes infuse a highly quaffable **Irish Ale** ★★.

SQUE Rotisserie & Alehouse (6 Eu Tong Sen Street, #01–70 The Central) is Singapore's leader in beer variety, with 10 taps and in excess of 200 bottles in stock, while new ownership spells promise for **Bottles & Taps** (1G Yio Chu Kang Road). **The Good Beer Company** (Blk 335 Smith Street, #02–58 Chinatown Complex) is a bar of a different sort, operated out of a "hawker stand" in Chinatown, allowing patrons to mix craft beer with traditional foods served from the surrounding stands.

BREWERKZ
Singapore

Pioneering brewpub dating from 1997, now bottling and kegging for distribution as far as Bangkok. Signature beers include a lightly bitter **Golden Ale ★★**; Germanic and bone-dry **Pilsner ★★☆**; and balanced, fruity and citrus-hoppy **India Pale Ale ★★☆**. Seasonal **Steam Beer ★★☆** follows canned-peach fruitiness with not insignificant bitterness and a dry, lightly woody finish.

JUNGLE BEER
Sembawang

New brewery still experimenting in a range of styles. The malty, full-bodied **Kiasu Stout ★★☆** exudes rich coffee and chocolate characters; a similarly malt-forward **English Pale Ale ★★☆** combines complexity and quaffability; and a variety of **Tropical Wheat ★★** fruit-infused beers such as Mango & Orange, Mango & Rose and Guava & Soursop pander to local preferences for lighter, sweeter brews.

RED DOT BREWHOUSE
Singapore

Home-grown brewpub with two outlets in the country. Infusion of spirulina adds colour and supposed health benefits to the low-hopped lager **Green Monster ★★**; the crisp **Czech Pilsner ★★** features minimal bitterness and a dry finish; and an estery **Lime Wheat ★★** is refreshingly citrus if somewhat understated.

REST OF SOUTHEAST ASIA

For years now, backpackers have been returning from northern Thailand with Chang Beer T-shirts in tow, leading much of the western public to believe that Thai beer – indeed, Southeast Asian beer in general – begins and ends with that largely unexceptional lager. But there is more to Thailand than Chang, and potentially more to Cambodia and Laos, as well. We're not saying that a craft beer paradise is likely to arise in any of these nations in the near future, but with a handful of breweries and beers now established, and sporadic brewpub sightings becoming of late slightly less so, better beer times do seem to be on the horizon.

BEERLAO (CARLSBERG)
Vientiane, Laos

Co-owned by the Laotian government and Carlsberg, a chain of smallish breweries running the length of Laos producing blond **Beerlao Lager Beer** ★★☆ that in large bottles in its home country holds its delicate, slightly citrus flavour to the last gulp, while elsewhere or in other formats it does not. **Dark** ★★, though short on caramel, makes a change from everything else that is around.

BOON RAWD BREWERY
Bangkok, Thailand

Long-standing regional brewer with solid export sales in its flagship brew, the roundly malty, faintly peppery **Singha** ★★. Seldom-brewed **Singha 70** ★★, created for the brewery's 70th anniversary, mixes florals with rich caramel; while perfumey **Kloster** ★★☆ is slightly easier to find and worth seeking out.

CAMBODIA BREWERY (HEINEKEN)
Phnom Penh, Cambodia

Although Cambodia has its first craft brewery, Kingdom Breweries of Phnom Penh, its products are so far too timid to be included here. However, the country enjoys a legacy from the 19th-century trade in strong porters and stouts, of which the remorseless best is Cambodia Brewery's **ABC Stout** ★★★, which is thick, black, sweet and burnt with a dollop of liquorice, brewed to a stronger recipe than the Singapore original.

STORM BALI
Denpasar, Indonesia

A rare example of a small Southeast Asian brewery of reasonable quality, on Bali. The **Pale Ale** ★★☆ is easy-drinking, vaguely American in style with a light yeastiness; **Red Dawn Bronze Ale** ★★ is light and fruity with good balance; **Black Moon Iron Stout** ★★☆ has a chocolate-fudge palate; and **Sand Storm Golden Ale** ★★ has orange and tropical-fruit notes undermined by a yeasty finish.

TAWANDANG MICROBREWERY
Bangkok, Thailand

Massive brewpub and concert hall with two Bangkok locations and now also open in Singapore, producing acceptable versions of Bavarian standards. **Weisse** ★☆ is bubblegummy, but with a bit of sourness; while the **Lager** ★★ is sweetish and floral. Best is the chocolaty, off-dry **Dunkel** ★★☆.

INDIA

India is not a beer-drinking country. Although growing marginally year-to-year, the country's average annual consumption remains less than 2 litres (3½ pints) per capita, just a tiny fraction of that of every other significant beer-producing nation in the world. (And India's volume production is significant, totalling 18.5m hectolitres of beer in 2011, more than that of Belgium or the Czech Republic.)

Where alcohol is consumed in Indian society, mostly among the middle and upper classes, the drink of choice tends to be spirits, a fact that has contributed to India's United Spirits becoming one of the largest distillers on the planet. United Breweries, part of UB Holdings, is responsible for over half of all the beer consumed in India.

Still, there are signs that this situation is changing, with the rising popularity of imported beers in urban areas and the tentative emergence of a fledgling craft beer sector. A Brewers Association of India has even been formed in the burgeoning beer hub of Bangalore, home to several present and future brewpubs, part of the mandate of which will be to lobby the government to modernize the currently restrictive laws governing brewing.

In 2014, Mumbai finally applauded the long-delayed opening of what is thought to be India's first production craft brewery, Gateway Brewing, which pleased thirsty palates with kegs of a *hefeweizen* called White Zen, the US-styled IPA, and a pale ale named for a common Indian phrase, Like That Only. It followed the opening in 2013 of Mumbai's first brewpub, Barking Deer.

Still in the planning stages are Independence Brewing and EffinGutBeer, both of which will join the pioneering Doolally brewpub in Pune, established when two Indian management school graduates met a German brewer in Singapore. Delhi is also poised to join the craft beer community with the opening of White Rhino, expected sometime in 2014.

THE MIDDLE EAST

Beer brewing likely originated in the Fertile Crescent at the eastern end of the Mediterranean known as the Middle East. There is a tradition going back millennia that craft brewers as far apart as Belgium, the USA and Japan have attempted to recreate in the form of lightly spiced, low-alcohol wheat beers from apparently authentic ancient recipes.

Modern takes on religion and politics dictate an inhospitable climate where alcohol is concerned, though even some states with strong Islamic traditions will allow a handful of respectable bars and restaurants, catering principally to visitors and expats, with reasonable selections of imported beers.

For now, beyond Israel and Turkey, we are only aware of a few small, independent breweries.

TURKEY

Beer is both produced and enjoyed in officially secular Turkey, but that market with a per capita consumption of roughly 12 litres (21 pints) per annum – high for the Middle East, but very low relative to the rest of the world – is dominated utterly by Efes, partly owned by SABMiller, and the Turkish division of Tuborg, part of the Carlsberg Group.

Recent Istanbul brewpub arrival, Bosphorus Brewing Company, British-inspired and with five house taps, was greeted with much enthusiasm, particularly by the expat community, while the five-year-old, five-outlet chain of Taps Restaurants in Istanbul, Ankara and Bursa feeds four core and three seasonal brews to its establishments from a central brewery. Germanic Khoffner Brewery sates thirsts in Antalya, as does the similarly Teutonically inspired Red Tower Brewery in Alanya.

ISRAEL

While the Fertile Crescent may have been the cradle of modern brewing 3000 years ago, it is 21st-century US craft brewers who are credited with kick-starting a trend that thus far has seen around 30 smaller breweries set up in Israel since 2005.

ALEXANDER BREWERY
Emek Hefer, Central District

A small brewery that nevertheless has big aspirations, already seeing its beer served to first-class passengers on El Al flights. The drinkable but dull **Blonde** ★☆ and **Ambrée** ★★ each have Franco-Belgian leanings; the mild, clean and pleasant **Green** ★★☆ is an IPA; and its decent strongish porter, simply called **Black** ★★ is currently a winter brew.

DANCING CAMEL
Tel Aviv

The first and best-known Israeli craft brewer, established in 2005 and run by a US expat, with its own pubs in Tel Aviv. Year-round beers include US pale ale **Patriot** ★★☆ with a citrus Cascade character; refreshing, spicy, Belgian-style white **Hefe-Wit** ★★; sweet and slightly bitter **Midnight Stout** ★★☆ with quite a lot of chocolate; and ever-changing **Golem** ★★→★★★ in various strengths.

HADUBIM
Even Yehuda, Central District

A beer commissioner that is ordering up some of the most interesting, hop-forward beers currently available in the country, brewed at Mivshelet Ha'Am, north of Tel Aviv. Its flagship **Indira IPA** ★★☆ is usually well balanced but can err toward heavy-malty at times; the light and quaffable pale ale **HaDoctor** ★★★ has a lovely Amarillo nose; and the **HaMaka HaRishona** ★★ is a moderately smoked malty red ale.

MALKA
Kibbutz Yehiam, Northern District

This is one of the few local breweries that is known to the Israeli public, based on a kibbutz located northeast of Haifa. Beers include the English-leaning **Admonit Pale Ale** ★★, which has a biscuity nose and some bitterness in the finish; the roasty and coffee'd **Keha Stout** ★★☆; and the stronger, Belgian-leaning **Behira Blond** ★★, which is sweetish, yeasty and citrusy, with added coriander.

NEGEV
Kiryat Gat, Southern District

Small brewery southwest of Jerusalem, making four regular beers that include a sweet and soft, fruity **Amber Ale** ★★; refreshing passion-fruit-infused light amber **Passiflora** ★★; and lighter-bodied but full-flavoured black, oaky **Porter Alon** ★★★.

SHAPIRO
Beit Shemesh, Jerusalem District

The Jerusalemite Beer brewery is located 30km (19 miles) west of its city. Year-round beers include decent, clean, American-influenced **Pale Ale ★★**; the easy-drinking sweetish **Oatmeal Stout ★★☆**; and fruity **Wheat Beer ★★**, one of the better local attempts at a *hefeweizen*. Dark, sweet, heavy and alcoholic **Jack's Winter Ale ★★** is made with oak chips steeped in a well-known bourbon.

SRIGIM BREWERY
Srigim-Li On, Jerusalem District

Founded by two home-brewers who have commercialized the two different line-ups they used to make at home. **Emek Ha'Ela Blond Ale ★★** is an easy-going, English-style pale ale with a dab of spice; **Ronen HaKeha HaMerusha'at ★★☆** is a roasty, hoppy dark ale based on a Californian original; and **Ronen HaHodit HaMekhoeret ★★★** is one of the country's better IPAs, with a high dose of bitterness on a malty backbone.

REST OF THE MIDDLE EAST

With the Arab world still pretty much a no-go area for authentic beer, the small changes in perceptions and values that are brewing's contribution to its modernization are thus far confined to a few small businesses in those states where the next steps to democracy are tentatively established.

961 BEER (GRAVITY BREWING)
Mazraat Yachoua, Lebanon

Craft brewery started as a home-brewing set-up during the 2006 Lebanon war. Basic **Lager ★☆** is dryish and faintly bitter; while the mocha-ish **Porter ★★** is light of body and seems styled to be more refreshing than satisfying. Brewmaster's Select **Lebanese Pale Ale ★★☆** is hop-shy but flavoured with six locally sourced herbs that come through in both aroma and flavour, particularly the thyme and sage.

TAYBEH BREWING
West Bank

Brewery operating for almost two decades in Palestine, which alone makes it worthy of consideration. Beers to choose from include **Golden ★☆**, a lagered ale that tastes like a light pilsner; the roasty **Dark ★★**, a *dunkel bock* that can go fruity and tart; and the new **White ★★**, which has distinct *witbier* spicing. Some beers, particularly the Golden, have been brewed under licence internationally.

AUSTRALASIA

AUSTRALIA

By the 1980s few Australians could give a XXXX about beer, the land of opportunity having succumbed to standardization of the beer industry on a massive scale. Only Coopers Brewery of Adelaide offered a range of beers that fell outside a narrow spectrum of thin, ice-cold, light, pale lagers that were involved in testosterone-fuelled brand battles.

In contrast, the last 15 years has seen the emergence of a nascent Australian craft brewing scene that now boasts well north of a hundred breweries, some attracting investment from the country's successful wineries, making beers in styles from all over the world, with twists that it can increasingly call its own.

In a nation of straight-talkers, most beers are named for the company and beer style, though the description "American" often encompasses both beers made with citrusy, aromatic US hops and those that lead with fruity, tropical antipodean varieties.

2 BROTHERS
Moorabbin, Victoria

Small US-influenced pub brewery at Moorabbin, south of Melbourne. Regulars include **Taxi ★★**, a crisp, hot-weather pilsner; and **Growler ★★**, a medium-bodied American brown ale with satisfying malt depth. Occasionals feature **James Brown ★★★**, a complex Belgian-leaning strong brown ale; and **Guvnor ★★★☆**, a huge barley wine suited to quiet contemplation.

4 PINES BREWING
Sydney, New South Wales

A pub brewery located in the city of Sydney that has recently expanded into a 50-hectolitre facility, which is large even by Australian standards. Its **Kolsch ★★** is an affable, if unchallenging starter beer; the US-style **Pale Ale ★★** is gently bitter; while its dry **Irish Stout ★★★** gained additional publicity when it was researched for its suitability in space travel.

BOOTLEG BREWERY
Wilyabrup, Western Australia

A well-established small brewery located at Wilyabrup in the Margaret River region, standing out among the wineries. Its **Sou West Wheat ★★**, a refreshing, slightly fruity, US-influenced wheat beer is less interesting than its **Raging Bull ★★☆**, which is a robust, intensely malty, not-quite roasty porter.

BREWCULT
Derrimut, Victoria

Using an interesting model of buying tanks to install in differently owned brewery, BrewCult in Victoria is an adventurous but sound stylist. **Hop Zone ★★★** is a surprisingly balanced and sessional IPA with powerful tropical-fruit salad aromas; while the experimental **Acid Freaks ★★** saw the brewer blend a porter with his vinegar-maker brother's balsamic, creating a curious, oily-cocoa-ish body finishing with a pleasing acidic tang and a poke at the sour beer trend.

BRIDGE ROAD BREWERS
Beechworth, Victoria

Small brewery at Beechworth, scene of outlaw Ned Kelly's adventures. Its original **Australian Ale ★★** is a light-bodied pale ale with an aroma of apricots; **Chestnut Pilsener ★★** is a characterful interpretation involving chestnuts and locally grown Galaxy hops; **Bling IPA ★★☆** screams hops as the malt tries to keep up; while the upmarket Chevalier range is led by a brave, authentically tart and phenolic **Saison ★★★**.

BROOKES BEER
Bendigo, Victoria

Regional Victoria is throwing up some reasons to travel beyond Melbourne, not least of which is this brewery. Its **American Pale Ale ★★** uses Mosaic hops over a bold malt body; while the bottle-conditioned **Brown Ale ★★** makes malt the star, oozing with rich chocolate saved from being cloying by the dryly bitter finish.

BURLEIGH BREWING
West Burleigh, Queensland

Larger format craft brewer located on Queensland's Gold Coast, south of Brisbane, making classic styles consistently well. German-style *hefeweizen*, **HEF ★★★**, is the best of its regulars, gaining international recognition; whereas US-style **28 Pale Ale ★★** is biscuity and balanced. More variable annual releases include the unusual but reliably excellent coffee-infused *schwarzbier*, **Black Giraffe ★★★**.

DESTINATION
BRISBANE

Brisbane has undergone a renaissance of late, shaking its "hicksville" image. Its burgeoning craft beer scene is a major part of that change, featuring places like **The Scratch** (8/1 Park Road), an eclectic dive bar with genuine charm, and **Statler & Waldorf** (25 Caxton Street), a new, unpretentious gastropub with a solid selection of local craft beers. Trendy Newstead has two new brewpubs, **Green Beacon** (26 Helen Street) and **Newstead Brewing** (85 Doggett Street), both worthy of a couple of relaxed hours.

CAVALIER BREWING
Derrimut, Victoria

This brewery is one of the new breed to watch, making extremely solid interpretations of classic styles. Its **Pale Ale** ★★☆ is US-inspired and packs a generous hoppy punch; while the **Brown** ★★★ is rich malt with chocolate and a toasty finish. **Courage** ★★☆, a delightfully quaffable golden ale brewed to raise funds for motor neurone disease research, was brewed as a one-off but has become semi-regular due to its success.

COOPERS BREWERY
Regency Park, South Australia

This 1862 family-owned brewery located near Adelaide inspired a generation. Traditional brews include red-labelled **Sparkling Ale** ★★★, arguably Australia's first gift to world brewing styles; though green-labelled **Pale Ale** ★★ is the bigger seller. **Best Extra Stout** ★★☆ is a rich export stout; and the annual red-brown, old English-style **Vintage Ale**, a bit clunky when fresh, ages superbly ★★→★★★.

DESTINATION
ADELAIDE

If Australians did shabby chic **The Wheatsheaf Hotel** (39 George Street) in Thebarton would be it. Not slick or fancy, and aspiring only to be a relaxed place to drink an ever-changing line-up of Australia's best beers. Live music is a bonus too.

FERAL BREWING
Baskerville, Western Australia

One of Australia's best craft breweries, in the Swan Valley near Perth. Its first beer, **Feral White** ★★☆, remains one of Australia's best interpretations of *witbier*; American IPA **Hop Hog** ★★★☆ is consistently a critical and

popular favourite; with **The Runt** ★★★ playing the smaller version. Playing with sour and barrel-aged beers helped create a plausible *Berliner weisse*, **Watermelon Warhead** ★★☆, with help from said fruit.

FORTITUDE BREWING
Mount Tamborine, Queensland

Home-brewing cardiologist teamed up with experienced young brewer for an exciting start-up. Brewing under two labels: Fortitude, for day-to-day session-style beers, and Noisy Minor for its more adventurous brews, such as **Patersbier** ★★☆, a delicate and gently fruity Belgian-inspired blond; and **ANZUS IPA** ★★, a boldly bitter and resinous tropical American-style IPA showcasing hops from Australia, the US and New Zealand.

GRAND RIDGE BREWERY
Mirboo North, Victoria

Early craft pioneer at Mirboo North, some way southeast of Melbourne. **Gippsland Gold** ★★ is a UK-style pale ale finished with Australian and NZ Hops; **Hatlifter Stout** ★★☆ is rich and full despite lowish strength; while **Moonshine** ★★★ is a strong Scotch ale smelling vaguely of Vegemite and tasting of dark fruit and brown sugar. All are best locally.

HARGREAVES HILL
Steels Creek, Victoria

Now back at Steels Creek after being destroyed in the 2009 bushfires, northeast of Melbourne. Its idiosyncratic beers include a New World take on English **ESB** ★★☆; a Bavarian-style

Hefeweizen ★★ with big banana aroma; a light-bodied but flavoursome **Stout** ★★; and annually brewed, bold **Imperial Stout** ★★★ filled with roast malt, with coffee overtones.

HOLGATE BREWHOUSE
Woodend, Victoria

Small brewery at Woodend. Its staple, **Mt Macedon Ale** ★★★, is a beautiful hybrid pale ale, with a citrus aroma despite German hopping, and an unusual malt character; **ESB** ★★☆ is a fine English ale made with East Kent Goldings; **Temptress** porter ★★★ is infused with chocolate and vanilla; and much sought-after annual blockbuster **Beelzebub's Jewels** ★★★ is a Belgian-angled barley wine.

KOOINDA BOUTIQUE BREWERY
Heidelberg West, Victoria

Started as a backyard brewery by two home-brewers, at Rosanna, and come good. Its **American Pale Ale** ★★☆ is a ballsy beer with great malt character; the **Belgian Witbier** ★★ is milky smooth, with coriander and dried, sweet orange peel; while black IPA **Full Nelson** ★★★ is a powerful, resinous, hop-driven beer that balances well.

LITTLE BREWING CO, THE
Port Macquarie, New South Wales

Scrappy little brewery on the northern New South Wales coast, making solid beers that deserve to be better known. The Wicked Elf range includes a citrus, piney US-style **Pale Ale** ★★; a nicely to-style **Pilsner** ★★ with floral but firm bitterness; and a good Belgian interpretation of **Witbier ★★**. The same can be said of its Mad Abbot brand's high-quality interpretations of **Dubbel ★★★**; and excellent, fruity **Tripel ★★★☆**, which manages the Belgian trick of carrying its alcohol well.

LITTLE CREATURES BREWING (KIRIN)
Freemantle, Western Australia

Sizeable operation holding a similar place in the Australian brewing scene to that occupied by SIERRA NEVADA BREWING in the US, its 1999 launch beer, **Little Creatures Pale Ale ★★★**, being a tropically toned homage to its Californian predecessor. Golden-coloured **Bright Ale ★☆** on the other hand is muted; the **Pilsner ★★** is a well-measured light lager; but light, amber-coloured **Rogers' Beer ★★☆** packs satisfying flavour without high strength. Let us hope its new owners do not cut corners.

LORD NELSON BREWERY
Sydney, New South Wales

One of the first Australian pub breweries, based at a beautiful old hotel in Sydney. **Quayle Ale ★★** is an easy-drinking summer ale with restrained bitterness; **Three Sheets ★★** is an Australian pale ale delivering gentle citrus fruits on its nose; and **Nelson's Blood ★★☆** is a creamy smooth, roasty porter.

MALT SHOVEL BREWERY (KIRIN)
Camperdown, New South Wales

The James Squire range is named after but unrelated to Australia's first brewer, and includes: a light and under-hopped **Chancer Golden Ale ★☆**; malty **Nine**

Tales Amber Ale **★★**; more interesting, solid Czech-style pilsner, **Four Wives ★★★**; and inky porter, **Jack of Spades ★★☆**. Also shares production of likely Australia's best lager, **Knappstein Reserve Lager ★★★☆**, blond, Bavarian-styled and complex with wonderfully expressed Nelson Sauvin hopping.

MCLAREN VALE BEER
McLaren Vale, South Australia

Beer commissioner recently turned brewer launched its Vale range with an easy-going Australian pale called simply **Ale ★★**; hit its stride with an **IPA ★★★** that bordered on US-style but showcased hops with summer fruit aromas; then added **DRK ★★☆**, a surprisingly rich *dunkel* for its strength.

MOO BREW
Berriedale, Tasmania

Tasmania's largest craft brewery, well resourced with winery connections but still small. Its **Hefeweizen ★★** is a true-to-style Bavarian wheat beer; **Pilsner ★★** is well rounded, floral and moderately bitter; **Dark Ale ★★☆** is a satisfying American brown ale with rich malt character; while heavy **Stout ★★☆** reaches higher when barrel-aged and released in numbered bottles as annual, limited edition **Imperial Stout ★★★**.

MOON DOG BREWING
Melbourne, Victoria

Arguably the most avant-garde of Australia's new wave, producing beers that can genuinely surprise. Core brand **Love Tap ★★**, a "double lager" – think punchy pine IPA but made with lager yeast – is conventional compared to the once-a-year **Perverse Sexual Amalgam** ★★☆, a barrel-aged wild ale with a sour cherry cough syrup vibe, and the semi-regular **Henry Ford's Girthsome Fjord** ★★, a yeast-driven Belgian-ish strong ale with demerara sugar and stewed fruit body under a contrasting citrus hop nose.

DESTINATION
MELBOURNE

Australia's culture capital is arguably also at the forefront of the nation's beer culture. Despite its name, **The Local Taphouse** (184 Carlisle Street), has had a national influence on beer culture, while the **Great Northern Hotel** (644 Rathdowne Street) is an old-school Melbourne pub with a lovely beer garden stocked with crafty locals. The Brunswick East neighbourhood has developing craft beer cred with **Temple Brewing** (122 Weston Street) and its brewery tap, and **The Alehouse Project** (98 Lygon Street), offering one of the best selections of taps in the city.

MORNINGTON PENINSULA BREWERY
Mornington, Victoria

New small brewery of potential, near Red Hill. Its US-style **IPA** ★★☆ sees Citra, Amarillo and Centennial hops adding stonefruit character; while the **Pale Ale** ★★ is toned down enough to make a session beer; **Witbier** ★★ is big on citrus and spice; and the beautiful English-style **Brown Ale** ★★★, full of toffee and raisins, may appear on hand-pull in specialist beer pubs.

MOUNTAIN GOAT BEER
Melbourne, Victoria

Pioneering 1997 Melbourne craft brewery, with enough success to cause capacity issues. Its fruity, crisp **Steam Ale** ★★ is brewed off-site for now; old-fashioned, grassy, malty English pale, **Hightail Ale** ★★☆, has gone national; and the up-hopped, previously occasional **IPA** ★★☆ has gone full-time. Its seasonal beers are labelled Rare Breed and include strong golden, yeast-spiced **Rapunzel** ★★★, a *tripel* in all but name.

MURRAY'S CRAFT BREWING
Port Stephens, New South Wales

Innovative craft brewery on the New South Wales coast, north of Newcastle, creating numerous beers in hybrid styles. Highlights include golden Anglo-American pale ale **Angry Man** ★★☆; the similarly mid-Atlantic **Icon 2 IPA** ★★★, a boldly hopped double IPA; a Belgian *tripel*, **Grand Cru** ★★★, sent whizzy with lashings of New Zealand hops; and **Heart of Darkness** ★★★, an Australian take on how a Belgian might ape Imperial stout. Put your name down early for a bottle of its ever-changing, annual, limited edition **Anniversary Ale** ★★★, always an intriguing, heavyweight, oak-aged barley wine.

NAIL BREWING
Perth, Western Australia

Founded in 2000 at Perth. One of the first exponents of a distinctively Australian type of pale ale, its starter brew **Nail Ale** ★★ being easy-drinking, with malt and fruit esters; multiple prize-winning, mid-strength oatmeal **Stout** ★★★ has satisfying complexity; while annual, limited edition, Imperial-strength **Clout Stout** ★★★☆ is an evolving classic.

RED HILL BREWERY
Red Hill South, Victoria

Obscure local planning laws mean that this small brewery on the Mornington Peninsula south of Melbourne sits in its own hop garden. A strong range includes light-bodied bestseller **Golden Ale** ★★; a six-week-lagered, clear but unfiltered **Bohemian Pilsner** ★★ with real hop bite and nice malt body; **Scotch Ale** ★★☆ with a complex mix of caramel and dried fruit; and prize-winning seasonal **Christmas Ale** ★★★, brewed like a strong Belgian *dubbel*.

SEVEN SHEDS
Railton, Tasmania

Hidden in tiny Railton, near the north Tasmanian coast, Seven Sheds is run by the elder statesman of Australian beer writing, Willie Simpson. **Kentish Ale** ★★☆ is a rewarding traditional English-style pale ale; **Elephant's Trunk** ★★☆ is a middle-strength, rich and long-finishing, full-flavoured blond that would pass as Belgian; and **Willie Warmer** ★★★ is a medium-strength dark ale spiced with cassia bark and star anise.

STONE & WOOD
Byron Bay, New South Wales

Successful brewery at Byron Bay, a few miles south of Burleigh. Making a name for engaging beers like cloudy Australian pale **Pacific Ale** ★★★☆, which generously expresses Australian Galaxy hop aroma; **Jasper Ale** ★★☆, an English brown

ale with spicy German hop character; and classic *helles*, **Pale Lager** ★★. Impressive flair is added annually with the volcanic-rock-seared, caramelized, faintly burnt, Austrian-style **Stone Beer** ★★★.

TEMPLE BREWING
Melbourne, Victoria

Pub brewery in north Melbourne, recently opened by a former gypsy brewer. Bold but balanced US-style **Pale Ale** ★★ features Amarillo and Cascade; **ESB** ★★☆ is earthy with a dry bitterness; **ESaison** ★★☆ is spiked with Brazilian pepper; while *weizenbock* **Unifikator** ★★★, originally from a collaboration with Bavarian WEIHENSTEPHAN, is now an in-house regular.

YOUNG HENRYS
Sydney, New South Wales

Free-spirited and musically influenced brewery bar with a solid core range and regular seasonals, often made in collaboration with the brewers' favourite bands. Regulars include **Real Ale** ★★☆, an English bitter with biscuity toffee overlaid by citrus nose; and seasonal **Brew Am I** ★★, a zesty fruit-driven American-style pale ale brewed in collaboration with Oz band, You Am I.

DESTINATION
SYDNEY

The Australian Hotel (100 Cumberland Street) is a century-old, colonial-style beer hotel in The Rocks district, gradually building an interest in craftier, broader-based, reliable Australian craft beers.

NEW ZEALAND

Craft brewing in New Zealand since the 1990s has been a series of ups and downs. By the end of the millennium there were some 60 or more breweries in the country, of which about half had closed a mere decade later. Fortunately, waiting in the wings were sufficient young, creative and enthusiastic brewers that by the time the second decade of the 21st century was well underway, Kiwi craft brewing was once again looking forward with hope and promise.

The key to the present and most probably the future of New Zealand craft beer may be found in two elements: contract brewing and native hops. The former, sometimes still derided by certain craft beer aficionados, is practically a New Zealand necessity, considering the variety of costs associated with serving a nation of 4.3m people living on two islands that stretch about 2000km (1240 miles) north to south. The contract arrangement, of which there are many in New Zealand, thus works to the benefit both the contracting brewery – in additional revenue – and the commissioning brewer – in terms of lower costs.

New Zealand's hop industry, on the other hand, has thrived precisely because of the country's isolation, with island-specific varieties such as Nelson Sauvin and Riwaka boasting distinctive tropical-fruit characteristics all their own. Local brewers, skilled as they are in coaxing flavours out of their native hops, have turned these traits into uniquely Kiwi styles, beginning with the perfumey New Zealand pilsner and tropical-fruity New Zealand pale ale, and finishing only at the limit of Kiwi brewers' imaginations.

8 WIRED BREWING
Blenheim, Marlborough

South Island beer commissioners with a deserved reputation for quality and innovation, illustrated by their **Hopwired IPA ★★★☆**, a restrained fruit bowl of a beer credited as the first IPA brewed from all-Kiwi ingredients. Others include **Rewired Brown Ale ★★☆**, a keen balance of nutty malt and fruity-floral hop; **Super Conductor Double IPA ★★★**, an amped-up mingling of US and NZ hoppiness; and **The Big Smoke ★★☆**, an unambiguous smoked porter.

BREW MOON BREWERY
Amberley, Canterbury

Tucked in behind a nondescript café, Brew Moon has been producing English-inspired beers for over a decade. The smooth caramel flavours of **Broomfield Brown Ale ★★☆** are popular with locals; but most accolades are reserved for the orange-marmalade notes of **Hophead IPA ★★★**; and the silky, milk-chocolate decadence of **Dark Side Stout ★★★**.

CROUCHER BREWING
Rotorua, Bay of Plenty

Paul Croucher was a university lecturer who eschewed academia to pursue his love of beer. Signature brands are the juicy, citrusy **Pale Ale ★★★**; classically dry and herbal **Pilsner ★★★**; and bold but balanced **Patriot Black IPA ★★☆**, with coffee notes and a bitter hop kick.

EMERSON'S BREWING (KIRIN)
Dunedin, Otago

Richard Emerson was the originator of the New Zealand pilsner style, hopping his **Pilsner ★★★★** with Nelson-grown Riwaka hops for a flowery and passion-fruity character. Almost as influential is his **Bookbinder ★★★**, a session-strength ale with firm maltiness and a dry finish; while the roasty, faintly briny **London Porter ★★** tends toward the thinner edge of the style. The brewery was sold in late 2012.

EPIC BREWING
Otahuhu, Auckland

Beer commissioner led by Kiwi beer stalwart Luke Nicholas. Best known for big beers like **Hop Zombie ★★☆**, piney, lemony and pearish; **Larger ★★**, a strong pilsner that begins almost honeyed, but finishes with a serious

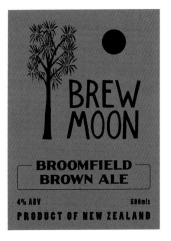

bitterness; the massively citrus, all-US-hopped **Armageddon IPA ★★☆**; and the relatively nuanced **Coffee & Fig Imperial Oatmeal Stout ★★★**, part of the well-named Epicurean series.

FORK & BREWER
Wellington

While the Fork & Brewer range is still developing, perennial favourites at this city centre brewpub in Wellington include the dry grassiness and balance of the **Bohemian Hipster Pilsner ★★★**; and the grapefruit punchiness of **Base Jumper APA ★★★**. Seasonal, speciality and collaboration brews are common with a limited number of kegs supplied to other craft beer venues.

DESTINATION
AUCKLAND

Brew on Quay (102 Quay Street) is a wood-panelled oasis of beer in the heart of the city, with nine draught taps supplementing an extensive selection of bottled beers and a select "Cellar List".

GALBRAITH'S BREWING
Auckland

New Zealand's first modern brewpub, housed in an Auckland building that was once a public library, is renowned for its traditional ales, including the nutty **Bob Hudson's Bitter ★★☆**; the bittersweet yet earthy **Bitter and Twisted ESB ★★☆**; and the spicy, yeasty Belgian monster **Resurrection Tripel ★★★**. Kegs are distributed, as are bottled lagers such as **Galbraith's**

Munich Lager ★★, with a herbaceous nose, lemony and floral hoppiness and a gentle bitterness.

GARAGE PROJECT
Wellington

Self-styled "ongoing project" brewing a seemingly endless variety of ales. No telling what might stick long term, but impressive appearances have been made by honey-ish, perfumey and almost buckwheat-like **Double Summer Ale ★★☆**; boozy toffee **Rum & Raisin ★★★**, aged on rum-soaked raisins; and hop-soaked **Pernicious Weed ★★**, a brew strictly for hop fanatics.

DESTINATION
WELLINGTON

The self-professed Craft Beer Capital of New Zealand has a compact nature, making it easy to walk between a range of high-quality bars. The biggest range of beers in the country is at **Malthouse** (48 Courtenay Place), while the Japanese-themed **Hashigo Zake** (25 Taranaki Street) boasts an almost as impressive number of often obscure ales and lagers. **Rogue & Vagabond** (18 Garrett Street) is quirky and delightful, and **The Hop Garden** (13 Pirie Street) complements fine cuisine with a handful of mostly Kiwi taps.

GOOD GEORGE BREWING
Hamilton, Waikato

Located in a former church, the best offerings from this burgeoning

Hamilton-based brewery include the spicy, navel orange-flavoured **New Zealand White Ale ★★**; the citrus zest and biscuity-flavoured **Sparkling Ale ★★★**; and the punchy **Good George IPA ★★★**, which is bursting with lemony German hops. Good George Brewing is also the official brewer for the Green Dragon pub in the nearby Hobbiton attraction.

HARRINGTON'S BREWERY
Christchurch, Canterbury

Crowned the New Zealand Champion Brewery of 2012, this sizeable operation, based in Christchurch, consistently produces the largest range of beers in the country (with 25+ offerings). The best of those include the bourbon-infused Scotch ale called **Big John Special Reserve ★★★**; the multi-award-winning dark ale **Pig and Whistle ★★☆**; and the zesty orange hop bomb known as **Hop Tremor IPA ★★★**.

INVERCARGILL BREWERY
Invercargill, Southland

This, the southernmost brewery in New Zealand, was founded in 1999. Head brewer Steve Nally produces a tasty English-style pale ale with hints of fruitcake called **Stanley Green ★★☆**; but is better known for his darker brews, including the chocolate/ caramel kiss of **Pitch Black Stout ★★★**; and **Smokin' Bishop ★★★**, which is a seasonal *rauchbier* that is made using malt house-smoked over native Manuka branches. Invercargill is also a major contract brewer, producing beers for the YEASTIE BOYS and MUSSEL INN, among others.

KERERŪ BREWING
Upper Hutt, Wellington

Named after a plump native bird also known as the New Zealand pigeon, this young brewing operation has already expanded once into larger industrial premises. Its balanced, European-inspired brews include a silky, coffee/ chocolate **Moonless Stout ★★★**; the sweet and spicy **Kumara Brown Ale ★★☆**; and the sharp, yeasty Belgian-style strong ale **Velvet Boot ★★☆**.

LIBERTY BREWING/HALLERTAU
Riverhead, Auckland

Two of the country's most acclaimed young brewers have joined forces in Riverhead, north of Auckland city. The combined operations produce a wide variety of beers from the rosters of both companies, including Hallertau's **Luxe Kolsch ★★☆**; and **Statesman ★★★**; and Liberty Brewing's signature **C!tra Imperial IPA ★★★☆**; and **Yakima Monster ★★★**.

MIKE'S ORGANIC BREWERY
Urenui, Taranaki

Nestled in farmland on the North Island of New Zealand, the over-two-decades-old mike's Organic Brewery was only the second fully accredited organic brewery in the country. Its core range includes a quenching, grassy **Pilsner ★★☆**; the famous **Organic Ale ★★☆**, with caramel notes and faultless balance; and the robust raisin and toffee flavours of the whisky-barrel-aged **Whisky Porter ★★★**. mike's also produces a rotating range of excellent non-organic pale ales.

MOA BREWING
Blenheim, Marlborough

A high-profile and sometime controversial brewery located in Marlborough wine country. Its all-Kiwi-hopped **5 Hop** ★★★ combines tropical fruitiness with biscuity malt; two rather than five NZ hops give the **Pale Ale** ★★☆ a citrus, gooseberry-ish character; the vaguely *saison*-esque **Méthode** ★★☆ is bottle-fermented to a spicy crispness; while the darkly fruity, coffee-ish **Imperial Stout** ★★☆ brings strength to the finish.

MUSSEL INN
Onekaka, Tasman

Located on the edge of two national parks on the South Island's Golden Bay, the Mussel Inn operates a brewery that is rightly revered for a single beer, although others are also brewed there. Its amber-hued **Captain Cooker Manuka Beer** ★★★☆ is flavoured to great complexity with tips from the native manuka tree, giving it cinnamon-ish-aroma notes and a leafy-herbal-spicy flavour built on a backdrop of caramel apple malt.

PANHEAD CUSTOM ALES
Upper Hutt, Wellington

While most breweries start small and grow gradually, Mike Neilson, formerly of TUATARA BREWING, sold his family home and poured $750,000 into a new brewery with an ambitious aim of making a million litres of beer within five years. Key automotive themed offerings include a zesty, fruity **Supercharger APA** ★★★; and the balanced, grassy **Quickchange XPA** ★★☆.

PARROTDOG BREWERY
Te Aro, Wellington

The founders of Parrotdog – three twentysomething guys, all named Matt – moved from being homebrewers to Wellington brewery owners in less than four years. Their first beer, **BitterBitch IPA** ★★★☆, rightly remains the flagship product with punchy grapefruit notes and dry, cleansing bitterness. It has been joined by **Bloodhound** ★★, a soft caramel red ale; and the outrageously named **DeadCanary** ★★☆, a contemporary New Zealand pale ale with plenty of tropical fruit and caramel.

RENAISSANCE BREWING
Blenheim, Marlborough

Wine country operation producing elegant, sophisticated beers. Multi-award-winner **Elemental Porter** ★★★ is plummy and mocha-ish; hugely aromatic **Craftsman Chocolate Oatmeal Stout** ★★ remains sessionable despite its big chocolate character; **Tribute Barley Wine** ★★★ offers a mix of whisky-washed orange and maple notes with a warming finish; and **Stonecutter Scotch Ale ★★★☆** offers soothing layers of caramelly, lightly roasty and date- and raisin-accented maltiness, with a drying finish.

THREE BOYS BREWERY
Christchurch, Canterbury

Christchurch operation named for the founder and his two sons, rather than three partners. **Oyster Stout ★★★** is a rich, figgy, lightly smoky ale brewed only when local Southland Bluff oysters are in season; light **Wheat ★★** is a thinnish Belgian-style wheat beer with strong, spicy lemon notes; and the fresh and floral **Pils ★★☆** proves that Kiwi hops aren't only about tropical fruit.

DESTINATION
CHRISTCHURCH

Pomeroy's Old Brewery Inn (292 Kilmore Street), located in a heritage building that formerly housed the original Harrington's Brewery, is a popular destination boasting over 20 craft taps, including its own Four Avenues brands, outstanding food and boutique accommodation next door.

TUATARA BREWING
Paraparaumu, Wellington

Wellington-area brewery recently relocated from the brewer's backyard to somewhat more sophisticated

surroundings. A shortage of American hops led to the fortuitous creation of **Aotearoa Pale Ale ★★★**, bold and fruity with local hops; also Kiwi-hopped, **Bohemian Pilsner ★★☆** is a fine, tropical-fruity example of an emerging NZ style; soft bitterness but high quaffability define the **Munich Helles ★★**; and perhaps overly gentle **Bavarian Hefe ★★** nonetheless offers authentically spicy-banana flavours.

TWISTED HOP, THE
Wigram, Canterbury

This Christchurch brewery was destroyed by the 2011 earthquake, which left the owners loaning other breweries for production while rebuilding their own, newly operational at the time of writing. Beers like the quaffable, tropical fruit **Hopback IPA ★★★**; and toffee-ish dark ale **Twisted Ankle ★★☆** will no doubt benefit further from the stability a permanent home provides.

YEASTIE BOYS
Wellington

Audacious beer commissioners showing a deft hand with utterly unconventional brews like **Rex Attitude ★★**, an intensely phenolic ale made entirely from peated malt; which becomes oddly more balanced and predictably whisky-ish in its stronger guise as **Rex ★★☆**. Flagship is the hoppy porter **Pot Kettle Black ★★★**, evocative of baker's chocolate; while **Hud-a-wa' Strong ★★☆** mixes tropical-fruit notes with toffee and honey-ish malt.

THE WESTERN PACIFIC

The part of the western Pacific styled locally as Oceania is supplied mainly with industrial lagers from locally based breweries that are part of global groups. However, even here a few entrepreneurial smaller breweries are cropping up.

For brewing in real isolation it was hard to beat Stone Money Brewing Company, on the Micronesian island of Yap since 1999, making Manta Gold and Hammerhead Amber, until newly independent Palau, the largest island in the group, gained the Palau Brewing Company and its Red Rooster range of Anglo-American ales.

Port Vila, capital of Vanuatu, the former New Hebrides, has at least one and possibly two brewpubs that sell beers elsewhere, US-leaning Seven Seas joining more UK-bent Nambawan Brewing, both including a porter in their range.

Fiji is now down to just one smaller brewery, a boutique lager maker called Island Brewing, which makes a tasty, crisp Vonu Lager and up-strength but unsubtle Eight.

The Cook Islands are now down to a single small producer, the Matutu Brewing Company at Tikioki on Rarotonga, which makes UK-style Kiva Pale Ale, a German-hopped Mai Lager and draught Matutu, all best sampled locally and fresh.

Unfortunately, at the time of writing, the Norfolk Island Brewery Company is no longer operational.

Finally, further north, on the US dependency of Guam, Great Deep Brewing regularly rings the changes through 16 draught beers, at the Mermaid Tavern in Hagåtña, that would pass muster in any North American brewpub. It has recently been joined on the island by Ishii Brewing Company at Tamuning, which supplies Minagof Pale Ale and IPA to a dozen local bars.

AFRICA

SOUTH AFRICA

The rainbow nation had more than its fair share of obstacles to building a modern beer culture, not least the extraordinary power over all aspects of the beer trade, from ingredients to point of sale, invested until recently in a single producer.

All that is changing, with the emergence of 40 or so new breweries opening across the country since 2011. Lagers are still a staple of breweries old and new, large or small, but drinkers are becoming more adventurous and brewers are responding with hop-forward IPAs, rich stouts and light ales featuring traditional South African herbs and spices.

ANVIL ALE
Dullstroom, Mpumalanga

Tiny pub brewery breaking traditions at Dullstroom, east of Pretoria. **White Anvil ★★★** is made with local *naartje* tangerine, peeled and dried here, then added with ginger and coriander to this fresh, spicy, refreshing and absurdly multi-layered *witbier*; while the regular **Blond Ale ★★☆** is clean and sweet, with a healthy dose of spicy hop.

BOSTON BREWERIES SA
Cape Town, Western Cape

Smart modern brewery making its own beers since 2000 and now contract brewing for numerous aspiring craft brewers. Clean but tasty **Boston Premium Lager ★★** is the backbone; soft, balanced **Johnny Gold Weiss ★★** is tied together by a little acidity in its finish; **Van Hunk's Pumpkin Ale ★★☆** is a sweet and spicy pumpkin pie beer; and dark ruby barley wine, **Loaded Cannon Ale ★★**, offers crème brûlée notes that balance its bold alcohol content.

CAPE BREWING
Paarl, Western Cape

One of the country's largest and most impressive new craft breweries, situated on a popular wine farm. The German-style **Pilsner ★★☆** is crisp, with noble hop character backed by generous malt; while banana dominates in the award-winning **Amber Weiss ★★★**, a slightly sweeter take on a classic *hefeweizen*.

DARLING BREW
Darling, Western Cape

Beer commissioner and wannabe brewer located north of Cape Town, selling beers made by **BOSTON**. These include the orange-tinged *witbier* **Bone Crusher** ★★☆ with nice spiciness and a light body; while the *dunkelweisse* **Silver Back** ★★ has a subtle fruitiness and a character somewhere between coriander and liquorice.

DEVIL'S PEAK
Cape Town, Western Cape

An innovative inner-city brewery that has an über-slick taproom. Its **King's Blockhouse IPA** ★★★☆ is South Africa's hoppiest and currently most impressive beer, American in style with abundant C-hops; the **Woodhead Amber** ★★★ is fresh, with chewy crystal malt and some leafy hop character; and the **First Light Golden** ★★ has light floral hop and slightly doughy pale malts.

DRAYMAN'S
Pretoria, Gauteng

Pioneering 1997 brewery making mostly session beers in both German and British styles. Commonest is so-so light blond **Berghof** ★☆; the most accomplished is an authentic *hefeweizen* called **Altstadt Weissbier** ★★☆, with gentle clove and banana lacing a fresh character; with darker than average, English-style **Goblin's Bitter** ★★☆ not far behind; and pretty passable **Düssel Altbier** ★★ found only on draught.

GILROY
Muldersdrift, Gauteng

Pioneering pub brewery northwest of Johannesburg. The light, low carbonation **Lager** ★☆ is malt-accented; **Favourite Pale Ale** ★★ is malty with a touch of diacetyl; **Traditional Ruby Ale** ★★ has a lot of malt on the nose, with a soft, juicy palate; and unplaceable but mostly English **Serious Dark Ale** ★★ has an appetizing dark-sugar character with light fruitiness.

JACK BLACK'S
Cape Town, Western Cape

Beer commissioner contracting CAPE BREWING to make all-malt **Brewers Lager** ★★☆ with a bready, somewhat sweet aroma that belies its crisp bitterness; **Butcher Block Pale Ale** ★★, an approachable ale with subtle hop character and mild caramel on the nose and palate; and entry level **Skeleton Coast IPA** ★★ with spice on the nose and more malt than hops on the palate, despite a pleasant, lingering bitterness.

MITCHELL'S BREWERY
Knysna, Western Cape

Brewing on the southern Cape coast since 1983 and showcased at its pub on Cape Town's V&A Waterfront. **Bosun's Bitter** ★★ is a soft, subtle, balanced UK bitter with gentle spiciness; **Raven Stout** ★★★ has a chocolaty, fruity nose and sweet chocolate on the palate; and strong, festive Scotch ale **90/-** ★★★☆ has cinammon, caramel and a little smoke, with a touch of dryness in the finish.

PORCUPINE QUILL BREWING
Botha's Hill, KwaZulu-Natal

Small brewery in northwest of Durban brewing lighter Quills, mid-strength African Moon and heavier Dam Wolf brands, represented by sweet, caramel and toasty **Karoo Red** ★★; sweet toffee, slightly nutty African Moon **Amber Ale** ★; and strong, sweet and fruity old ale **Black**

Buck Bitter ★★; and **Wolf in Sheep's Clothing** ★★☆, a strong ale with a leafy hop and subtle apple and plum fruitiness.

SHONGWENI
Hillcrest, KwaZulu-Natal

Small brewery northwest of Durban that is making Robson's beers. **East Coast Ale** ★★ is a slightly fruity pale ale, hopped lightly with Brewers Gold and Challenger; **West Coast Ale** ★★ is slightly stronger and intended to be American but leans more toward malt, with only light bitterness; while the boldest is **Durban Pale Ale** ★★, dry, with a bright hop character and a fair bit of complexity.

STANDEAVEN
Alverstone, KwaZulu-Natal

Brewery near Durban with a range that includes yeasty, lightly hoppy **No 3 Bohemian Pilsner** ★★; **No 5 Press Club Stout** ★★☆ with a hearty body and fudge character; and **No 7 African Pale Ale** ★★ with modest bitterness.

TRIGGERFISH
Somerset West, Western Cape

Family-run brewery with a popular taproom. Produces a wide range, some in bottle. **Hammerhead IPA** ★★ is malt-accented; **Titan Imperial IPA** ★★☆ is big and chewy with no shortage of crystal malt; **Empowered Stout** ★★☆ is buttery and slightly nutty. Starting to play with a range of extreme and experimental brews.

NAMIBIA

Before the era of craft beer, lagers from Windhoek in Namibia were regarded by South Africa as having an edge over its own. Whether Namibian beers continue to impress depends thus far on one entrepreneurial small brewer.

CAMELTHORN BREWING
Windhoek, Khomas

Namibia's only small brewery, in the capital, impacting in South Africa too. Four regular beers include a yeasty **Weizen** ★★ with just a hint of banana; and American amber ale **Red** ★★ with hops imported from Oregon. Seasonal **Summer Ale** ★★☆ has a fruity, juicy, refreshing character; and a tougher dark **Bok** ★★ appears in the winter months.

REST OF AFRICA

While it would be a mistake to say that, outside of South Africa and Namibia, the African continent is a desert for characterful beer, it would not be too much of one. We know of brewpubs scattered here and there – in Kenya and Ethiopia, for instance – but nothing that appears particularly attention-worthy. And while some craft beer aficionados remain enamoured with the legend of Nigerian-brewed Guinness, our limited encounters with the beer have left us less than impressed.

That said, after completing this edition, one of us was off to research the Flying Dodo Brewing Co of Port Louis, on the Indian Ocean island of Mauritius, of which much more next year.

INDEX OF BEERS

1 Enbär *Sigtuna/St. Eriks* 145
Cilindri *Forte, Del* 163
-Dubbel *Pirlot* 34
Monts *St. Sylvestre* 174
Elf Winter Warmer Ale *Dark Horse Brewing* 212
7% *Nokian* 147
am Saint *BrewDog* 108
Barrel Ale *Odell Brewing* 216
-Day IPA *O'Fallon Brewery* 217
Hop *Moa Brewing* 296
Lizard Latin-Style Witbier *5 Rabbit Brewing* 209
Blond *Achel* 29
Vulture Oaxacan-Style Dark Ale *5 Rabbit Brewing* 209
Malheur 34, *North Taiwan* 277, *Rochefort* 41
° *Loterbol* 33
Juli Ale *Frederiksodde Haandbryggerlaug* 136
Rochefort 41
Bruin *Duvel Moortgat* 32
% Sahti *Finlandia Sahti* 146
Street Ale *Four Peaks Brewing* 213
) *Malheur* 34, *Rochefort* 41
) Bitter Years *Black Oak Brewing* 240
) e Lode *Opperbacco* 167
)% Strong Sahti *Finlandia Sahti* 146
3° *Sessler* 183
4° *Sessler* 183
° La Verguenza *Menaresta* 166
3rd Anniversary Old Ale *Karl Strauss Brewing* 198
4 Carat Gold *Liverpool Organic Brewery* 99
)K Golden Ale *Brewfist* 161
3 Pale IPA *Burleigh Brewing* 286
)/- Belhaven Brewery *(Greene King)* 108
3 IPA *Lovibonds Brewery* 95
)/- Belhaven Brewery *(Greene King)* 108, *Caledonian Brewing (Heineken)* 109, *Stewart Brewing* 109
)-Acre Hoppy Wheat Beer *Boulevard Brewing* 211
)/- *Mitchell's Brewery* 301
) Minute IPA *Dogfish Head Brewing* 223
) Shilling *Odell Brewing* 216
100 Nøgne Ø142
)9 *Loire* 121
)0s Old Ale *Chiltern Brewery* 93
!9 *Squatters Pubs & Beers* 219
#5 State Stout *EPIC Brewing* 212
)00 EBC *Stronzo Brewing* 139
)75 *Windsor & Eton Brewery* 106
581 *Herbsthäuser* 71
#72 India Pale Ale *PEI Brewing/ The Gahan House* 244
311 Pre-Prohibition Lager *Fort George Brewery* 205
)42 Hammer Brand *Barghoeve* 127
)45 *Fuller's* 94

1851 Bik & Arnold Dubbel *Muifelbrouwerij* 131
1863 *Hydes Brewery* 97
1872 Porter *Elland Brewery* 93
1882 Gueuze *Girardin* 44
1882 Kriek *Girardin* 44
1892 *Robinsons* 102
1913 Cornish Stout *St Austell Brewery* 103
1919 Choc Beer *Krebs Brewing* 231
Ðen *Coi Xay Gio* 277

A

Abbaye de St Bon-Chien *BFM* 171
Abbey *New Belgium Brewing* 216
Abbey Ale *Břevnovský* 175, *Ommegang (Duvel Moortgat)* 225
ABC Stout *Cambodia Brewery (Heineken)* 280
Abner Double IPA *Hill Farmstead Brewery* 224
Abominable Winter Ale *Hopworks Urban Brewery* 205
Abraxas *Perennial Artisan Ales* 217
Absolvinator *Meinel-Bräu* 58
Abstrakt *BrewDog* 108
Abt 12 *St Bernardus* 35
Abt 12° *Westvleteren* 37
Ace of Spades Imperial IPA *Hopworks Urban Brewery* 205
Acid Freaks *BrewCult* 286
Adam *Hair of the Dog Brewing* 205
Admonit Pale Ale *Malka* 283
Aecht Schlenkerla Rauchbier Urbock *Schlenkerla (Heller)* 60
Affumicator *Gänstaller-Bräu* 55
African Pale Ale *Shiga Kogen Beer* 269
Ageless *RedWillow Brewery* 102
Aiblinger Schwarzbier *Maxlrain, Schlossbrauerei* 52
Aile *Okell's* 101
Akane Red Ale *Zakkoku Kobo* 270
À la Belge Saison *À la Fût* 239
Alba Weizen *Coruja* 253
Aldona Udriene *Jovaru Alus* 157
Ale *Black Sheep Brewery* 91, *McLaren Vale Beer* 289
Alebrije *Jack* 249
Alfa Brown Ale *Soma* 260
Alica *Civale* 162
Alienor Blanche *Aliénor* 117
All Blacks *Crooked Moon* 135
Aloysius *Kuchlbauer* 66
Alpaïde *Nieuwhuys* 34
Alpha King *Three Floyds Brewing* 220
Alt *Bamberg Bier* 252, *Füchschen* 74, *Schmitz Mönk* 77, *Uerige* 75, *Tazawako* 270, *U Bulovky* 181, *Uerige* 77
Alt-Amberger Doppelbock *Winkler* 69
Altbairisch Dunkel *Ayinger* 49
Altbayrisch Dunkel *Schönram, Private Landbrauerei* 52
Altbier *Kürzer* 75, *Southampton Publick House* 226
Alternator *Metalman Brewing* 116
Alt-Fränkisch *Herbsthäuser* 71
Alt Fränkisches Lagerbier *Adler Bräu* 62
Altfränkisch Klosterbier *Weissenohe, Klosterbrauerei* 62
Altitude 6 *Abbaye des Rocs* 38
Alt Nicht Filtiert *Uerige* 77
Altpieschener Spezial *Watzke* 82
Altstadthof Maibock *Altstadthof* 62
Altstadthof Schwarzbier *Altstadthof* 62
Altstadt Weissbier *Drayman's* 300
Alt-Sumbarcher Dunkel *Gessner* 79

Alvinne Extra Restyled *Alvinne* 29
Amalgamator IPA *Beachwood BBQ & Brewing* 195
Amargator IPA *Chingonería, La* 249
Amarillo *Crouch Vale Brewery* 93, *Molen, de* 131, *Oppigårds* 145
Amber *Abita Brewing* 228, *Alaskan Brewing* 202, *Oakshire Brewing* 207
Amber Ale *Bell's Brewery* 210, *Joli Rouge* 121, *Negev* 283, *Oh! La! Ho Beer* 268, *Porcupine Quill Brewing* 301, *Swan Lake Beer* 270, *Szot* 260
Amber Boy *AleBrowar* 183
Ambergeddon *Ale Asylum* 209
Amberger Pils *Winkler* 69
Amber Lady *Dama Bier* 253
Amber Lager *Patagonia (AB InBev)* 258, *Strahov, Klášterní pivovar* 180
Amber Road *Baxter Brewing* 222
Amber Spezial *Binkert Brauhaus* 54
Amber Weiss *Cape Brewing* 299
Ambrata *Maltus Faber* 166
Ambrée *Alexander Brewery* 283, *Ancelle* 118, *Caussenarde* 118, *Dubuisson* 39, *Gaillon* 120, *Garland* 120, *St Alphonse* 124, *St Germain* 124, *St Rieul* 124, *Theillier* 124, *Vallée de Chevreuse* 125
Ambrée au Cassis *Trois Fontaines* 125
Ambrosia *Half Acre Beer* 214
Amburana Lager *Way Beer* 255
American Brown Ale *Outland* 122
American Dark Ale *Stadin* 148
American Darling Good Time Lager *Pretty Things Beer & Ale Project* 215
American India Pale Ale *Júpiter* 254
American IPA *Kuhnhenn Brewing* 215
American Pale Ale *Brookes Beer* 286, *Dark Star Brewing* 93, *Gourmet Calavera* 249, *Júpiter* 254, *Klein Duimpje* 130, *Kooinda Boutique Brewery* 288, *Mestiza Cerveza Gourmet* 259, *Stadin* 148, *Way Beer* 255, *White Gypsy Brewing* 116
American Strong Ale *508 GastroBrewery* 221
Amiral Benson *Mont Salève* 122
Ammestout *Beer Here* 135
Amnesiac Double IPA *Phillips Brewing* 237
Ancient Nipponia *Kiuchi* 267
Andreasbräu Pils *Andreasbräu* 70
Angel's Share *Lost Abbey/Port Brewing* 198
Angerwirts Weizen *Pyraser* 67
Angry Angel *Big Boss Brewing* 228
Angry Boast *Hopfanatic* 188
Angry Boy Brown Ale *Baird Brewing* 265
Angry Goat *Rahr & Son Brewing* 232
Angry Man *Murray's Craft Brewing* 290
Animator *Paulaner (Heineken)* 52
Ankerla Dunkel *Ankerbräu* 78
Anker Pils *Ankerbräu* 78
Anna Hill Farmstead Brewery 224
Anniversary Ale *Murray's Craft Brewing* 290
Anniversary Barley Wine *Uinta Brewing* 220
Anniversary Series *Firestone Walker Brewing* 197
Anno 1050 *Weltenburger* 69
Antenne Tripel *Ramses Bier* 132
Antidepressant *Strahov, Klášterní pivovar* 180
Anti-Hero IPA *Revolution Brewing* 217
Antius *Guineu* 151
Antošův Ležák *Antoš* 175
ANZUS IPA *Fortitude Brewing* 288
Aooni *Yo-Ho Brewing* 270
Aotearoa Pale Ale *Tuatara Brewing* 297
Aphrodisiaque *Dieu du Ciel!* 240

Apocalypse IPA *10 Barrel Brewing* 201
Appia *Colorado* 252
Apricot *Cascade Brewing Barrel House* 203
Apricot Au Poivre Saison *Nebraska Brewing* 216
Archa *Kaltenecker* 182
Arcolator *Graf Arco* 65
Arctic Circle Ale *Malmgårdin* 147
Arctic Devil Barley Wine *Midnight Sun Brewing* 206
Året Runt 4.5% *Nokian* 147
Arkell Best Bitter *Wellington County Brewery* 245
Armageddon IPA *Epic Brewing* 294
Armored Fist Imperial CDA *Boneyard Beer* 202
Arrogant Bastard *Stone Brewing* 201
ArtigianAle *Bi-Du* 160
Asam-Bock *Weltenburger* 69
asty Lady *Eem, De* 128
Atak Chmielu *Pinta* 185
Atlantik-Ale *Störtebeker Braumanufaktur* 82
Atlantis IPA *Kaltenecker* 182
Aubeloun *Pleine Lune* 123
Audace *32 Via dei Birrai* 159
Audit Ale *Westerham Brewery* 106
Aufwind *Bosch* 73
Augsburger Herren Pils *Riegele* 67
Augustijn Blond *Van Steenberge* 36
Augustinian *Growler Brewery, Nethergate* 95
Augustinus *Huber, Familienbrauerei* 85
Aura *Lariano* 165
Aurea *Domus* 151
Au Sapin *Dauphiné* 119
Australian Ale *Bridge Road Brewers* 286
Austrian Amber Lager *Loncium, Privatbrauerei* 86
Auswandererbier 1849 *Faust* 64
Autumnal Fire *Capital Brewery* 211
Autumnal Mole Stout *Ska Brewing* 218
Autumn Maple *Bruery, The* 196
Aux Noix *Dauphiné* 119, *Lutine, La* 121
Avalanche *Fyne Ales* 109
Avatar Jasmine IPA *Elysian Brewing* 205
Aventinus Weizen-Eisbock *Schneider* 68
Avenyn Ale *Dugges* 143
Axe Edge *Buxton Brewery* 92
Aztec Ale *Breakside Brewing* 203

B

B27 *Kaltenecker* 182
Baaad Boy Black Wheat Ale *3 Sheeps Brewing* 209
Babêl *Foglie d'Erba* 163
Back Door Bitter *Orso Verde, L'* 167
Back Hand of God Stout *Crannóg Ales* 235
Back in Black *21st Amendment Brewery* 194
Bad Karma *Croocked Moon* 135
Bad Penny *Big Boss Brewing* 228
Bagheera *Bier Haus* 192
Ballistic IPA *Ale Asylum* 210
Balthazar *Alvinne* 29
Baltic Porter *Stallhagen* 148, *Wensky Beer* 255
Baltic Trader *Green Jack Brewing* 95
Bambergator *Fässla* 54
Bamberger Landrauchbier *Meusel-Bräu* 58
Bam Bière *Jolly Pumpkin Artisan Ales* 215
Banks Amber Ale *Banks* 246
Banks Caribbean Lager *Banks* 246
Barabba *Geco* 164
Barbe Bleue *Mélusine* 122
Barcagi Dupla Bak *Fóti* 188

Barkhatnoe *Tomskoe* 192
Barley Wine *Antares* 256, *Daisen G Beer* 266, *Det Lille Bryggeri* 135, *Harvestmoon* 266, *Moku Moku* 268, *Nils Oscar* 144, *Szot* 260, *Yo-Ho Brewing* 270
Barney Flats Oatmeal Stout *Anderson Valley Brewing* 195
Bärni *Felsenau* 171
Barnsley Bitter *Acorn Brewery* 90
Bärnsten *Jämtlands* 143
Barock-Dunkel *Weltenburger* 69
Barrel Aged Shipwreck Porter *Arcadia Brewing* 210
Barrel Full of Monkeys Imperial Stout *Paddock Wood* 237
Barricata 050 *Opperbacco* 167
Bartmann's Kölsch *Hüchelner Urstoff* 75
Base Jumper A *Fork & Brewer* 294
Bastogne Pale Ale *Bastogne* 38
Battle Axe Baltic Porter *Fat Head's Brewery* 212
Baumburger Dunkle Weiße *Baumburg, Klosterbrauerei* 50
Baumé Half Acre Beer 214
Baunti 1609 *Baumgartner* 84
Bavarian Hefe *Tuatara Brewing* 297
Bayer Thrinheim Ungespundetes Landbier *Bayer* 63
BB *Donnington Brewery* 93
BB10 *Barley* 160
Beach Chair Lager *PEI Brewing/The Gahan House* 244
Béal Bàn *Chorca Dhuibhne (West Kerry Brewery)* 114
Bearded Lady *Magic Rock Brewing* 99
Beard of Zeus Barley Wine *Great Lakes Brewing* 242
Beast Double IPA *Storm & Anchor* 172
Bedarö Bitter *Nynäshamns Ångbryggeri* 144
Bede's Chalice *Durham Brewery, The* 93
Bedlam! *Ale Asylum* 210
Beelzebub's Jewels *Holgate Brewhouse* 288
BeerBera *LoverBeer* 165
BeerBrugna *LoverBeer* 165
Beer Geek Breakfast *Mikkeller* 138
Beer Geek Brunch Weasel *Mikkeller* 138
Beerlao Lager Beer *Beerlao (Carlsberg)* 280
Behira Blond *Malka* 283
Belfast Ale *Whitewater Brewing* 113
Belfast Lager *Whitewater Brewing* 113
Belg *Lwówek Śląski* 185
Belge de Saison *Glutenberg (Brasseurs Sans Gluten)* 241
Belgian Ale *Viven* 37
Belgian IPA *Pfriem* 207
Belgian Stout *Shonan* 270, *Van den Bossche* 36
Belgian Strong Dark Ale *Pfriem* 207
Belgian-Style Golden Strong Ale *508 GastroBrewery* 221
Belgian Style Pale Ale *White Birch Brewing* 227
Belgian Style Quad *Alley Kat Brewing* 235
Belgian White *Outsider Brewing* 269
Belgian Wit *Archipelago Brewery (Asia Pacific Breweries)* 278
Belgian Witbier *Kooinda Boutique Brewery* 288
Belle *Devil's Canyon Brewing* 196
Belle d'Été *Bastogne* 38
Bellevue Pils *Brewbaker* 78
Bel Pils *Duvel Moortgat* 32
Bender *Surly Brewing* 219
Benedict Světlý Ležák *Břevnovský* 175

Benedictus *Durham Brewery, The* 93
Benedikt Dunkel *Vasold & Schmitt* 61
Benno *Engelszell, Trappistenbier-Brauerei* 84
Berghof *Drayman's* 300
Berliner Weiss *White Birch Brewing* 227
Berlin IPA *Brewbaker* 78
Bérotte *Vállée du Giffre* 125
Berried Alive *Longwood Brewery* 236
Best Bitter *Bathams* 91, *Black Sheep Brewery* 91, *Granite Brewery* 241, *Picaroons Brewing* 244
Best Bitter Special *Granite Brewery* 241
Bestefar *Haandbryggeriet* 142
Best Extra Stout *Coopers Brewery* 287
Beta Sweet Stout *Soma* 260
Bête Blanche *Elysian Brewing* 205
Bête Noire *Kelham Island Brewery* 98
Bevara *Menaresta* 166
Beyond the Pale *Elland Brewery* 94
Bia Đen *Hoa Viên* 278
Bianca *Brüton* 162, *Maltus Faber* 166
Biancaneive *CitaBiunda* 162
Bianca Piperita *Opperbacco* 167
Bibock *Italiano* 165
Bieken *Boelens* 30
Bière Brut Reserve *Malheur* 34
Bière de Beloeil *Dupont* 40
Big Bad Baptist Imperial Stout *EPIC Brewing* 212
Big Bark *Live Oak Brewing* 231
Big Ben *Thwaites* 105
Big Daddy *Speakeasy Ales & Lagers* 200
Bigfoot *Sierra Nevada Brewing* 200
Bigfoot Russian Imperial Stout *Seasons* 255
Big Job *St Austell Brewery* 103
Big John Special Reserve *Harrington's Brewery* 295
Big Sky IPA *Big Sky Brewing* 211
Big Sound Scotch Ale *Cigar City Brewing* 22
Big Swell IPA *Maui Brewing* 206
Bikini Beer *Evil Twin Brewing* 136
Bilyi Lev *Lvivske (Carlsberg)* 189
Bink Blond *Kerkom* 33
Bio Blanche *Brunehaut* 39
BioColonia *Sünner* 77
Bio-Dinkel Weisse *Unertl, Weissbräu* 53
Biolégère *Dupont* 40
Bio-Weisse *Trunk* 61
B-IPA *Swan Lake Beer* 270
Birra *Prairie Artisan Ales* 232
Birra Madre *Menaresta* 166
Bishop's Farewell *Oakham Ales* 101
Bispens Trippel *Søgaards* 139
Bitch Creek ESB *Grand Teton Brewing* 214
Bittor *Broumov* 175, *Butcombe Brewery* 92, *Buxton Brewery* 92, *Hawkshead Brewery* 96, *Jennings Brewery (Marston's)* 98, *Joli Rouge* 121
Bitter Ale *Strong Ale Works* 274
Bitter American *21st Amendment Brewery* 19
Bitter and Twisted ESB *Galbraith's Brewing* 29
BitterBitch IPA *ParrotDog Brewery* 296
Bitterfly *Hopfanatic* 188
Bitterland *Doppio Malto Brewing* 163
Bitter & Twisted *Harviestoun Brewery* 119
BI-Weizen *Italiano* 164
Bizon Bier *Cnudde* 30
BK *Olmaia, L'* 167
Blåbærstout *Austmann* 141
Black *Alvernæ Brewery* 283, *Belhaven Brewery (Greene King)* 108, *GoldMalt* 277, *Ilkley Brewery* 98, *Lucky Bastard* 178
Black Albert *Struise Brouwers* 36
Blackball Belgian IPA *Karl Strauss Brewing* 19

Black Bavarian *Sprecher Brewing* 218
Blackberry Festive Ale *Townsite Brewing* 238
Black Betty *Beavertown Brewery* 91
Black Bier *Bier Factory* 171
Blackbird Schwarz *Klein Duimpje* 130
Black & Blue Dogfish *Head Brewing* 223
Black Boss Porter *Witnica* 186
Blackbox *Praght* 132
Black Buck Bitter *Porcupine Quill Brewing* 301
Black Butte *Deschutes Brewing* 204
Black Butte Porter *Deschutes Brewing* 204
Black Cauldron Imperial Stout *Grand Teton Brewing* 214
Black Chocolate Stout *Brooklyn Brewery* 222
Black Feet *Milana* 151
Black Giraffe *Burleigh Brewing* 286
Black Golding Starkporter *Närke Kulturbryggeri* 144
Black Hawk *Nomád* 178
Black Hope *AleBrowar* 184
Black Ice *Titanic Brewery* 105
Black Imperial IPA *Dunham (Brasserie Dunham)* 241
Black IPA *Nbeer Pub* 273
Black Jack *Del Ducato* 163
Black Jack Porter *Left Hand Brewing* 215
Black Lager *Linden Street Brewery* 198
Black Lightning *Hambleton Ales* 96
Black Lizard *Maltovivo* 166
Black Moon Iron Stout *Storm Bali* 280
Blackout *Rurale* 168
Black Rebel *CitaBiunda* 162
Black Rock *Dungarvan Brewing* 115
Black Rose *Békésszentandrási* 187
Black Star Double Hopped Lager *Great Northern Brewing* 214
Black Top *New Glarus Brewing* 216
Black Tulip Tripel *New Holland Brewing* 216
Black Walnut Dunkel *Perennial Artisan Ales* 217
Blanche *Caussenarde* 118, *Dauphiné* 119, *Gaillon* 120, *Mont Salève* 122, *Orgemont* 122, *St Rieul* 124, *Tri Martolod* 125
Blanche au Pain d'Épices *Trois Fontaines* 125
Blanche au Caisses (Cinq Cents) *Chimay* 39
Blanche de Chambly *Unibroue (Sapporo)* 245
Blanche de Saisis *Ellezelloise (Légendes)* 40
Blanche des Honnelles *Abbaye des Rocs* 38
Blanchette de Lorraine *Millevertus* 40
Blâthan *Tryst Brewery* 110
Blauwe Bijl *Leckere, de* 130
Bleue (Grande Réserve) *Chimay* 39
Blind Spot *High Water Brewing* 197
Bling IPA *Bridge Road Brewers* 286
Blond Achel* 29, *Cazeau* 39, *De Ryck* 31, *Extraomnes* 163, *Halve Maan, De* 33, *Mommeriete* 131, *Van Eecke* 36, *Viven* 37, *Westvleteren* 37
Blond 8° *Loterbol* 33
Blond Ale *Anvil Ale* 299
Blonde *3 Fourquets, Les* 38, *Alexander Brewery* 281, 283, *Bastogne* 38, *Bzart* 30, *Caussenarde* 118, *Gaillon* 120, *Glutenberg (Brasseurs Sans Gluten)* 241, *Kichesippi Beer* 243, *Lutine, La* 121, *Maltus Faber* 166, *NOLA Brewing (New Orleans Lager & Ale Brewing)* 231, *Rulles* 41, *St Alphonse* 123, *St Feuillien* 42
Blonde Ash *Grain Brewery* 95
Blonde d'Esquelbecq *Thiriez* 124
Blonde du Vexin *Vexin* 125
Blonde Wheat Beer *High Point Brewing (Ramstein Beer)* 224

Bloodhound *ParrotDog Brewery* 296
Bloody Valentine *AleSmith Brewing* 194
Bluebird *Coniston Brewing* 93
Blue Bridge Double Pale Ale *Spinnakers Gastro Brewpub & Guesthouses* 237
Blue Buck *Phillips Brewing* 237
Blue Heron Pale Ale *Bridgeport Brewing (Gambrinus Company)* 203
Bob Hudson's Bitter *Galbraith's Brewing* 294
Bobo's Robust Porter *Big Sky Brewing* 211
Bock *Bamberg Bier* 252, *Bierland* 252, *Blest* 257, *Chuckanut Brewery & Kitchen* 203, *Griess* 55, *Grohe* 79, *Homburger Brauhaus* 80, *Huber, Familienbrauerei* 85, *Kneitinger* 56, *Kraus* 56, *Pfatten* 76, *Plevna* 147, *Schmitz Mönk* 71
Bockbier *Fischer* 64, *Mohrenbrauerei August Huber* 86, *Rothenbach* 59, *Schroll* 60
Bock Bier *Mahr's Bräu* 57, *Texelse Bierbrouwerij* 133
Bock Dunkel *Naabeck, Schloßbrauerei* 66
Bock Hell *Wagner* 61
Bockl Hell *Spalt, Stadtbrauerei* 68
Bock No. 4 *Ebeltoft Gårdbryggeri* 136
Bock Sollator *Meierei* 80
Bodgers Barley Wine *Chiltern Brewery* 92
Bogotá *Bogotá Beer Company* 261
Bohemian Black Lager *Herold* 176
Bohemian Hipster Pilsner *Fork & Brewer* 294
Bohemian Lager *Archipelago Brewery (Asia Pacific Breweries)* 278
Bohemian Pilsner *Red Hill Brewery* 291, *Tuatara Brewing* 297
Bohemian Wheat Lager *Herold* 176
Bok *Aass* 141, *Camelthorn Brewing* 302
Bokbier *Jopen Bier* 129
Bokkige Theodorus *Sallandse Landbier* 133
Bomb! *Prairie Artisan Ales* 232
Bombay by Boat *Moonlight Brewing* 199
Bonator Doppelbock *Weissenohe, Klosterbrauerei* 62
Bone Crusher *Darling Brew* 300
Boneshaker IPA *Amsterdam Brewing* 239
Bones of Oak Stout *Rothhammer* 260
Bonifatius Barrique *Forstner Biere* 84
Bonita *Milana* 151
Bookbinder *Emerson's Brewing (Kirin)* 293
Boris Goudenov *Corrézienne* 119
Born & Raised IPA *No-Li Brewhouse* 207
Boson de Higgs *Hopfenstark* 242
Bossa Nova *Oh! La! Ho Beer* 268
Boston Lager *Samuel Adams (Boston Beer Company)* 225
Boston Premium Lager *Boston Breweries SA* 299
Bosun's Bitter *Mitchell's Brewery* 301
Bourbon County Stout *Goose Island Beer (Anheuser-Busch InBev)* 213
Bourgogne des Flandres Bruin *Timmermans* 45
Bøvelen *Kinn* 142
Bøyla Blonde Ale *Ægir* 141
BPA *Ommegang (Duvel Moortgat)* 225
Bracia *Thornbridge Brewery* 104
Brackie *Bracki Browar Zamkowy (Heineken)* 184
Bracki Rauch Bock *Bracki Browar Zamkowy (Heineken)* 184
Brainless on Peaches *EPIC Brewing* 212
Brakspear Bitter *Brakspear Brewing (Marston's)* 92
Brännskär Brown Ale *Nynäshamns Ångbryggeri* 145

Braunbier *Bosch* 73
Bräunlinger Löwenbräu Weisser Leo *Bräunlinger Löwenbräu* 70
Braustelle Helios *Braustelle* 74
Brave New World *Tempest Brewing* 110
Bravo American Imperial Porter *Backer/3 Lobos* 252
Breakfast Stout *Founders Brewing* 213
Bresse *Maison de Brasseur* 121
Brettanomyces Lambicus *Bayerischer Bahnhof* 78
Brettporter *Brokeriet* 143
Brew Am I *Young Henrys* 291
Brewer's Dark *Lees, J W* 99
Brewers Gold *Crouch Vale Brewery* 93
Brewers Lager *Jack Black's* 301
Brewer's Secret Handshake *Baird Brewing* 265
Brew Free! or Die IPA *21st Amendment Brewery* 194
Březňák Světlý Ležák *Březňák (Heineken)* 175
Bridge Burner Special Reserve Ale *Lakefront Brewing* 215
Bright Ale *Little Creatures Brewing (Kirin)* 289
Brigstow *Arbor Ales* 90
Bristol Hefe *Bristol Beer Factory* 92
British Bulldog *Westerham Brewery* 106
Broadside *Adnams* 90
Brockville Dark *Tryst Brewery* 110
Brodie's Prime *Hawkshead Brewery* 96
Broomfield Brown Ale *Brew Moon Brewery* 293
Brother David's Double *Anderson Valley Brewing* 195
Brother Thelonious *North Coast Brewing* 199
Brown Backer/3 Lobos* 252, *Cavalier Brewing* 287, *NOLA Brewing (New Orleans Lager & Ale Brewing)* 231
Brown Ale *Brookes Beer* 286, *Brooklyn Brewery* 222, *Cerveza de Autor* 259, *Chateau Kamil Bay* 266, *Duck-Rabbit Craft Brewery* 230, *Hell Bay Brewing* 242, *Klein Bier* 254, *Mornington Peninsula Brewery* 290, *Nøgne Ø* 142, *Tübinger* 260, *Upslope Brewing* 220
Brown Porter *Cabesas Bier* 261
Brown Shugga *Lagunitas Brewing* 198
Bruch *Zwickel Bruch* 79
Bruckberger Dunkel *Dorn-Bräu* 63
Bruin *512 Brewing* 228, *Achel* 29, *Smisje* 35, *Van den Bossche* 36
Bruin 8° *Loterbol* 33
Bruisend en Blond *Oersoep Brouwerij* 131
Brune *3 Fourquets, Les* 38, *Abbaye des Rocs* 38, *Bastogne* 38, *Brunehaut* 39, *Rulles* 41, *St Alphonse* 124, *St Germain* 124, *Trois Fontaines* 125, *Val-Dieu* 42
Bruno *Ales Agullons* 150
Brusca *BirrOne* 161
Brut *Charlevoix* 240, *Wäls* 255
Brutal Hops *Rothhammer* 260
Brut Noir *Malheur* 34
Brutus *Maximus* 131
Bucefalo *Maiella* 165
Bucéfalo *Rámuri* 250
Buddy Marvellous *Bryncelyn Brewery* 111
Budějovický Světlý Ležák *Budweiser Budvar* 176
Budvar *Budweiser Budvar* 176
Budvar Dark *Budweiser Budvar* 176
Bufadora *Tijuana Beer* 250
Buffalo 1907 *Van den Bossche* 36
Buffalo Sweat *Tallgrass Brewing* 220
Bundgarn *Skagen* 139
Buorren Bier *Friese Bierbrouwerij* 128
Buried at Sea *Galway Bay Brewery* 115

Burly Wine *Half Pints Brewing* 236
Burning River Pale Ale *Great Lakes Brewing* 214
Burocracy India Pale Ale *Brewfist* 161
Bush de Nuits *Dubuisson* 39
Butcher Block Pale Ale *Jack Black's* 301
Butterfly *Olmo* 167
Butty Bach *Wye Valley Brewery* 107
Búza *Rizmajer* 188

C

Cacao-Porter Criollo *Malmö Brygghus* 143
California *Matuška* 178
California Sunshine IPA *Devil's Canyon Brewing* 196
Canaster Winterscotch *Glazen Toren* 32
Cane and Ebel *Two Brothers Brewing* 220
Canned Wheat *Malmö Brygghus* 143
Cannonball IPA *Magic Rock Brewing* 99
Cantillon Gueuze 100% Lambic *Cantillon* 44
Captain Cooker Manuka Beer *Mussel Inn* 296
Captain's Reserve Imperial IPA *Captain Lawrence Brewing* 223
Capucijn *Budels* 127
Caracole *Caracole* 39
Carib *Carib* 246
Caribbean Rumstout *Hornbeer* 137
Carminia *Karma* 165
Carraig Dubh *Chorca Dhuibhne (West Kerry Brewery)* 114
Carron Oatmalt Stout *Tryst Brewery* 110
Cascade Pale Ale *Saltaire Brewery* 103
Cascadian Dark Ale *Pfriem* 207
Cassis *Brekeriet* 143
Cast Iron Oatmeal Brown *4 Hands Brewing* 209
Caught in a Rip *Rip Current Brewing* 199
Cavatica Imperial Stout *Fort George Brewery* 205
CBS *Founders Brewing* 213
Ceci n'est pas une Belge *Malmgården* 147
Celebration *Sierra Nevada Brewing* 200
Celebrator *Ayinger* 49
Celis White *Van Steenberge* 36
Celtic Stout *Gambrinus* 257
Centennial IPA *Founders Brewing* 213
Centesimale *Karma* 165
Cerevinum *Gusswerk, Brauhaus* 85
Cerise Cassée *Cambridge Brewing* 223
Černý Ležák *Bernard* 175
Cerveja do Amor *Bodebrown* 252
Cerveza de Menta *Cebi-Chela* 262
Cervoise Lancelot *Lancelot* 121
Český Dřhánek *Tomskoe* 192
Chalky's Bite *Sharp's Brewery (Molson Coors)* 103
Chancer Golden Ale *Malt Shovel Brewery (Kirin)* 289
Chapeau Cuvée Oude Gueuze *De Troch* 44
Chapinero Porter *Bogotá Beer Company* 261
Charles River Porter *Cambridge Brewing* 223
Charleston *Townsite Brewing* 238
Château Neubourg *Gulpener* 128
Chekate Esta *Chingonería, La* 249
Cherubijn *Fontein, De* 128
Chestnut Pilsener *Bridge Road Brewers* 286
Chica Americana IPA *Rooie Dop* 133
Chicca *Pausa Cafè* 168
Chicken Killer Barley Wine *Santa Fe Brewing* 218
Chili Tripel *Midtfyns* 138
Chimera *Del Ducato* 163
Ching Ching Berliner Weiss *Bend Brewing* 202

Chiswick Bitter *Fuller's* 94
Chocolate Marble *Marble Beers* 99
Chocolate Stout *Pen-lon Cottage Brewery* 112
Chocolate Vanilla Imperial Stout *Harbour Brewing* 96
Chocolat No 7 *Shimane* 269
Chopin Tripel *Wensky Beer* 255
Choulette Ambrée *Choulette, La* 119
Christmas Ale *Anchor Brewing* 195, *Harveys* 96, *Red Hill Brewery* 291, *Saint Louis Brewery* 217, *St Bernardus* 35
Christmas Bock *Chateau Kamiya* 266
Christmas Leroy *Leroy* 33
Chupacabras *Cucapá* 249
Cingulus Fekete Sör *Rizmajer* 188
Cirilo Coffee Stout *Seasons* 255
Citra *Oakham Ales* 101
Citra Ale *Häffner Bräu* 71
Citra Strong Ale *Häffner Bräu* 71
Citra Weisse *Aqula* 265
Classic *Anker, het* 30, *Baeren* 265, *Schloss Eggenberg* 87
Classic 2.9 *Waldhaus* 73
Classic Old Ale *Hepworth & Co Brewers* 97
Classic Pils *Meinel-Bräu* 58
Classic Wheat Beer *High Point Brewing (Ramstein Beer)* 224
Clelia *Maneba* 166
Cleric's Cure *Three Tuns Brewery* 105
Cloak of St Martin *Brunehaut* 39
Cloister *Durham Brewery, The* 93
Clotworthy Dobbin *Whitewater Brewing* 113
Clout Stout *Nail Brewing* 291
Cluviae *Maiella* 165
Cnudde Bruin *Cnudde* 30
Cobblestone Stout *Mill Street Brewing* 243
Cochonne *Vapeur, à* 42
Coclé *Istmo* 262
CoCoNut PorTer *Maui Brewing* 206
Coconut Pumpkin Sweet Stout *Breakside Brewing* 203
Coffee & Fig Imperial Oatmeal Stout *Epic Brewing* 294
Coffee Rye Stout *Nbeer Pub* 273
Co-Hop V *À la Fût* 239
Cohort Summer Wine Brewery* 104
Columbus *IJ, 't* 129
Columbus Ale *Det Lille Bryggeri* 135
Combined Harvest *Batemans* 91
Comenius Special 14 *Uherský Brod (Lobkowicz)* 181
Commercial Suicide *Jester King* 230
Conductor's Craft Ale *Junction Craft Brewing* 242
Confine *Bi-Du* 160
Conqueror *Windsor & Eton Brewery* 106
Contemplation *Brewery Vivant* 211
Contessa *Amiata* 160
Continuum *Hardknott* 96
Coolship Cerise *Allagash Brewing* 222
Coolship Red *Allagash Brewing* 222
Copper Coast *Dungarvan Brewing* 115
Coriander Black *North Island Brewing* 268
Corinne-Louise *Paradis, Le* 127
Cornish Coaster *Sharp's Brewery (Molson Coors)* 103
Coronator Dunkel *Tettnanger (Krone)* 72
Cosmos *Rothhammer* 260
Courage *Cavalier Brewing* 287

Courage Imperial Russian Stout *Wells & Young's* 106
Coure *Art Cervesers* 151
Cowboy Coffee Porter *Big Sky Brewing* 211
Coyet Ale *Suomenlinnan* 148
Craft Lager *Upslope Brewing* 220
Craftsman Chocolate Oatmeal Stout *Renaissance Brewing* 296
Crazy Canuck Pale Ale *Great Lakes Brewing* 241
Crazy Donkey *Santorini Brewing Company* 189
Cream Ale *Narragansett Brewing* 225
Cream Stout *Antares* 256, *St Peter's Brewery* 103
Crème Brûlée Imperial Milk Stout *Southern Tier Brewing* 226
CREW IPA *CREW AleWerkstatt* 50
CREW Pale Ale *CREW AleWerkstatt* 50
Crocus *Amiata* 160
Crom Hout *Leckere, de* 130
Crooked Tree IPA *Dark Horse Brewing* 212
Cross of Gold *Revolution Brewing* 217
Crystal Ale *Louisiane Brewhouse* 278
Crystal Bitter Ale *No-Li Brewhouse* 207
C!tra Imperial IPA *Liberty Brewing/Hallertau* 295
Cubulteria *Karma* 165
Cucapá Clásica *Cucapá* 249
Cúl Dorcha *Chorca Dhuibhne (West Kerry Brewery)* 114
Cumbrian Five Hop *Hawkshead Brewery* 96
Curator *Ettal, Klosterbrauerei* 50
Curieux *Allagash Brewing* 222
Curmi *32 Via dei Birrai* 159
Curmudgeon Old Ale *Founders Brewing* 213
Cutthroat Pale Ale *Uinta Brewing* 220
Cutthroat Porter *Odell Brewing* 216
Cuvée Alex le Rouge *BFM* 171
Cuvee Ange *4 Hands Brewing* 209
Cuvée-Brut *Duvel Moortgat* 32
Cuvee de Castleton *Captain Lawrence Brewing* 223
Cuvée de Noël *St Feuillien* 42
Cuvée de Ranke *Ranke, de* 41
Cuvée des Fleurs *Southampton Publick House* 226
Cuvée des Jacobins Rouge *Vander Ghinste, Omer* 36
Cuvée des Jonquilles *Baron, Au* 118
Cuvée des Trolls *Dubuisson* 39
Cuvée de Tomme *Lost Abbey/Port Brewing* 199
Cuvée Houblonnée IPA *À la Fût* 239
Cuvée René Grand Cru Oude Gueuze *Lindemans* 44
Cuvée van de Keizer Blauw *Anker, het* 30
Cwrw Madog (Madog's Ale) *Mŵs Piws (Purple Moose Brewery)* 112
Cwtch *Tiny Rebel* 112
Czarny Dąb *Konstancin* 185
Czarny Kur *Widawa* 185
Czech Pilsner *Red Dot Brewhouse* 279
Czech Premium Lager *Herold* 176
Czech Stout *Primátor* 179
Czech Style Pilsner *Berkshire Brewing* 222
Czechvar *Budweiser Budvar* 176

D

Daisy Cutter *Half Acre Beer* 214
Dalešická 11° *Dalešice* 176
Dalešické Májové 13° *Dalešice* 176
Dale's Pale Ale *Oskar Blues Brewery* 217
Dalva *Thiriez* 125
Dama Brun-a *LoverBeer* 165
Danzig *Devils Backbone Brewing* 229

Darach Mòr Stillman's, The 172
Darbyste Blaugies 38
Dark Beerlao (Carlsberg) 280, Brains 111,
    Capital Brewery 211, Taybeh Brewing 284
Dark Abby Devils Backbone Brewing 229
Dark Age Celt Experience, The 112
Dark Ale Hida Takayama Beer 266,
    Moo Brew 289, Muskoka Brewery 244
Dark Arts Porter Trouble Brewing 116
Dark Beast Djævlebryg 135
Dark Energy Hardknott 96
Dark Force Haandbryggeriet 142
Dark Island Orkney Brewery 109
Dark Island Reserve Orkney Brewery 109
Dark Lady Dama Dier 253
Dark Lager King Brewery 243, Louisiane
    Brewhouse 278, Oku Noto Beer 268,
    Strahov, Klášterní pivovar 180,
    Tazawako 270
Dark Mild Taylor, Timothy 105
Darkness Surly Brewing 219
Dark Ruby Hughes, Sarah 103
Dark Side Stout Brew Moon Brewing 293
Das Pils Watzke 82
Dau' Troll 169
Daughter of Autumn Retorto (Birra Piacenza
    di Ceresa Marcello) 168
Daujotų Davra 157
DBA Firestone Walker Brewing 197
DeadCanary ParrotDog Brewery 296
Dead Cat Beer Here 135
Deadicated Amber Devil's Canyon
    Brewing 196
Dean's Beans Coffeehouse Porter Berkshire
    Brewing 222
Death of a Contract Brewer Black IPA
    He'brew (Shmaltz Brewing) 224
Death & Taxes Moonlight Brewing 199
Decadence Marble Beers 100
De Cam Oude Geuze Cam, de 43
Deceit Funkwerks 213
Deep Roots Red Lager Linden Street
    Brewery 198
De Koninck De Koninck (Duvel Moortgat) 31
Delikat Dark Lager Stallhagen 148
Demoiselle Colorado 253
Den Dorstige Tijger Ramses Bier 132
Den Uddøelige Hest Svaneke 140
Denver Pale Ale Great Divide Brewing 214
Dépuceleuse Avery Brewing 210
Der Dunkle Reh Mout Reh 59
Dernière Volonté Dieu du Ciel! 240
Der Weisse Bock Mahr's Bräu 57,
    Schwanenbräu Burgebrach 60
Destilo Emelisse 128
Deuchars IPA Caledonian Brewing
    (Heineken) 109
DeuS Bosteels 30
Deutsches Altbier Mestiza Cerveza
    Gourmet 259
Devil's Ale SanTan Brewing 218
Devil's Kriek Double Mountain Brewery 204
Diable au Corps Brasseurs du Temps, Les 240
Diablo Jerome 258, Summer Wine
    Brewery 104
Diablo Rojo Boneyard Beer 203
Diabolik Fontaines 120
Diabolus Durham Brewery, The 93
Dies Irae Gusswerk, Brauhaus 85
Dinkel Simon 170
DIPA Emelisse 128
Diplom Pils Waldhaus 73
Dirty Stop Out Tiny Rebel 112
Divers Contreras 31

Divina Panil (Birrificio Torrechiara) 167
DM Batemans 91
D'n Osse Bock Muifelbrouwerij 131
Doctor Okell's IPA Okell's 107
Doesjel 3 Fonteinen 43
Doggie Claws Hair of the Dog Brewing 205
Domaine DuPage Two Brothers Brewing 220
Dom's Alt Im Dom 75
Donker Contreras 31, Extraomnes 163
Donkerbruin Vermoeden Berghoeve 126
Donkere Henricus Sallandse Landbier 133
Donker en Diep Oersoep Brouwerij 131
Donner Party Porter FiftyFifty Brewing 197
Doom Bar Sharp's Brewery (Molson
    Coors) 103
Doppelbock Viking Ölgerd 149
Doppel Bock Krenkerup 138, Sprecher
    Brewing 218
Doppelbock Dunkel Andechs,
    Klosterbrauerei 49, Faust 64, St Georgen
    Bräu 51
Dordogne Valley Corrézienne 119
Dorina Troll 169
Dortmunder Snake River Brewing 218
Dortmunder Gold Lager Great Lakes
    Brewing 214
Double Chocolate Stout Wells & Young's 106
Double Cresta Tempest Brewing 110
Double Daddy Speakeasy Ales & Lagers 200
Double Dog Abita Brewing 228
Double Donn Donnington Brewing 93
Double Hop WinterCoat 140
Double IPA Propeller Brewing 244,
    Stieglbrauerei zu Salzburg 87,
    Vakka-Suomen 150
Double Jack Firestone Walker Brewing 197
Double Oatmeal Stout Rooie Dop 130
Double Rocket Mohawk 144
Double Stout Hook Norton Brewery 97
Double Summer Ale Garage Project 294
Double Tempest Amsterdam Brewing 239
Double White Ale Southampton Publick
    House 226
Dounkelis Širvėnos Bravoras 158
Dragon's Milk Ale New Holland Brewing 216
Dragon Stout Desnoes & Geddes 246
Dreadnaugh Three Floyds Brewing 220
Drenkeling Pampus 132
Dreu'na Piva Old Ale Wensky Beer 255
DRK McLaren Vale Beer 289
Drovers 80/- Tryst Brewery 110
Dryhop Hornbeer 137
Dry Stout Breakside Brewing 203
Dubbel Artezan 184, De Ryck 31, Goeye
    Goet, 't 128, Gourmet Calavera 249,
    Halve Maan, De 33, Little Brewing Co,
    The 289, Triest 36, Wäls 255
Dubbelbock Brand (Heineken) 127
Dubbel+Dik 7 Deugden, De 126
Dubbel Klok Boelens 30
Dubbel Tarwe Friese Bierbrouwerij 128
Dubults Širvėnos Bravoras 158
Duchessa Borgo, Birra del 161
Duchesse de Bourgogne Verhaeghe 37
Dudes Barley Wine Toccalmatto 169
Due Bamberg Bier 252
Duet Alpine Beer 195
Duivels Bier Boon 43
Dulcis Succubus Trou du Diable 245
Dunkel Augustiner-Bräu 49,
    Bergschlößchen 78, Blé d'Or, Le 276,
    Eisenbahn (Kirin Brazil) 254, Joker Bar 192,
    Kloster Machern 80, Kneitinger 66,
    Maisel 57, Märkl 66,

Otaru Brewing 268, Reberg 274,
    Reindler 67, Roppelt 67, Rothenbach 59,
    Tawandang Microbrewery 280, Weisse,
    Die 88, West Brewery 111
Dunkel Bock Otaru Brewing 268
Dunkle Gose Goslar, Brauhaus 79
Dunkler Bock Gessner 79
Dunkles Hops & Barley 80
Dunkles Exportbier Mülhaupt 71
Dunkles Hefe-Weißbier Karg 51
Dunkles Hefeweizen Gutmann 51
Dunkles Lagerbier Mühlonbräu 58
Dunkles Nektar Abadessa 251
Dunkles Weissbier Jacob 66
Dupla Köleses Bandusz 187
Durban Pale Ale Shongweni 301
Düssel Altbier Drayman's 300
D'uuvaBeer LoverBeer 165
Duvel Duvel Moortgat 32

E

e Croucher Brewing 293
Earl Grey IPA Marble Beers 100
East Coast Ale Shongweni 301
Eastern Lightning Typhoon Brewery 274
East India Pale Ale Brooklyn Brewery 222
Eau de Pierre 2 Mondes 120
Ebel's Weiss Two Brothers Brewing 220
Ebenezer Ale Bridgeport Brewing
    (Gambrinus Company) 203
Echt Kriekenbier Verhaeghe 37
Edel-Export Hell Spalt, Stadtbrauerei 71
Edelguss Gusswerk, Brauhaus 85
Edel-Märzen Naabeck, Schloßbrauerei 66
Edel Pils Egg 84, Hebendanz 55, Jacob 66
Edel-Pils Herbsthäuser 71,
    Kneitinger 66, Metzler 80, Reckendorf,
    Schlossbrauerei 59
Edelstoff Augustiner-Bräu 49
Edelweiss Hofbräu Zipfer (Heineken) 88
Edinburgh No 3 Scotch Ale Stewart
    Brewing 110
Edmund Fitzgerald Porter Great Lakes
    Brewing 214
Edward Hill Farmstead Brewery 224
Eejit's Oatmeal Stout 1516 Brewing 83
Eem Bitter Eem, De 128
Eem Kerst Eem, De 128
Eesti Rukki Eil Õllenaut 153
Eichator Doppelbock Eichhofen,
    Schlossbrauerei 63
Eiche Schlenkerla (Heller) 60
Eichhofener Spezial Dunkel Eichhofen,
    Schlossbrauerei 63
Eifeler-Böckchen Gemünder 74
Eifeler-Landbier Gemünder 74
Eight Point IPA Devils Backbone Brewing 229
Eisbock Otaru Brewing 269
Elderflower Blonde Saltaire Brewery 103
Elemental Porter Renaissance Brewing 296
Elephant's Trunk Seven Sheds 291
Elevated IPA La Cumbre Brewing 215
Elfstedenbier Friese Bierbrouwerij 128
Elijah Craig FiftyFifty Brewing 197
Eliščino Královské Kaštanomedový Speciál
    13° Rambousek 179
Elissa IPA Saint Arnold Brewing 233
Elizabethan Ale Harveys 96
Elk Lake IPA Bend Brewing 202
Elliot Ness Amber Lager Great Lakes
    Brewing 214
EloWehnä Nokian 147
Embra Stewart Brewing 109
Embrasse Dochter van de Korenaar, De 32

Emek Ha'Ela Blond Ale *Srigim Brewery* 284
Empowered Stout *Triggerfish* 301
Enebær Stout *Grauballe* 136
En Folie *Vapeur, à* 42
English Ale *Hell Bay Brewing* 242
English IPA *Brimmer* 265
English Pale Ale *Jungle Beer* 279
English Session Brown *Breakside Brewing* 203
Entire Stout *Hop Back Brewery* 97
Epic Saison *Wild Beer* 106
Eric's IPA *Camba Bavaria* 50
Eric's Porter *Camba Bavaria* 50
ER India Pale Ale *Falke Bier* 254
Erstes Forchheimer Export-Hefe-Weissbier *Hebendanz* 55
ESB *Boundary Bay Brewery & Bistro* 203, *Fuller's* 94, *Green Man Brewing* 230, *Hargreaves Hill* 288, *Holgate Brewhouse* 288, *Malmgårdin* 147, *Propeller Brewing* 244, *Temple Brewing* 291, 302
Especial Mars *Contreras* 31
Espresso *Dark Star Brewing* 93
Espresso Coffee Stout *Kiuchi* 267
Espresso Stout *Emelisse* 128
Essex Boys Bitter *Crouch Vale Brewery* 93
Estaminet *Palm* 34
Estivale *Rulles* 41
Etlars IPA *Frederiksodde Haandbryggerlaug* 136
Etoile du Nord *Thiriez* 124
Eucharius Märzen *Weissenohe, Klosterbrauerei* 62
Eugene *Revolution Brewing* 217
Euleteul Zomer *Fontein, De* 128
Euphoria Pale Ale *Ska Brewing* 218
Europa *Domus* 151
Everett Porter *Hill Farmstead Brewery* 224
Everyman's IPA *Societe Brewing* 200
Evil Cousin *Heretic Brewing* 197
Evil Twin Red Ale *Heretic Brewing* 197
Exkluziv 16° *Primátor* 179
Exodus Porter *Sweetwater Brewing* 233
Expedition Stout *Bell's Brewery* 211
Explorer *Adnams* 90
Exponential Hoppiness *Alpine Beer* 195
Export *Abadessa* 251, *Eichhorn* 54, *Fuchsbeck* 64, *Hirsch* 65, *Hirschen-Bräu* 71
Export Dunkel *Andechs, Klosterbrauerei* 49, *Reutberg, Klosterbrauerei* 52
Export Hell *Hebendanz* 55, *Reutberg, Klosterbrauerei* 52
Export Stout London 1890 *Kernel, The* 98
Exterminador *Backer/3 Lobos* 252
Extra *Contreras* 31, *Smisje* 35, *Westmalle* 37
Extra 8° *Westvleteren* 37
Extra Ale *Longwood Brewery* 236
Extra Bruin *Achel* 29
Extra Brune *Maltus Faber* 166
Extra Hop *Italiano* 164
Extra IPA *Mohawk* 144
Extra Pale Ale *Junction Craft Brewing* 242, *Summit Brewing* 219
Extra Special Bitter *Hopshackle Brewery* 97
Extra Stout *Pike Brewing* 207, *Praght* 132
Extra Vecchio *Opperbacco* 167
Ex Voto *Butcher's Tears* 127

F

Faithless *RedWillow Brewery* 102
Fa La La La La *Double Mountain Brewery* 204
Fallersleber Schlossbräu *Fallersleben, Altes Brauhaus zu* 79

Fallersleber Weizen *Fallersleben, Altes Brauhaus zu* 79
Falstaff *Vitzthum, Privatbrauerei* 87
Fancy Lawnmower Ale *Saint Arnold Brewing* 211
Fantastic Voyage *Perennial Artisan Ales* 217
Farfars Favorit *Søkildegaard* 139
Farm Hand *Brewery Vivant* 211
Farmhand Ale *Driftwood Brewing* 235
Faro *Tilquin* 45
Faro Lambic *Lindemans* 45
Farro *Petrognola, la* 168
Farrotta *Almond '22 Beer* 160
Fastenbier *Schlenkerla (Heller)* 60
Fat Scotch Ale *Silver City Brewing* 208
Fat Tire *New Belgium Brewing* 216
Fat Tug IPA *Driftwood Brewing* 236
Favourite Pale Ale *Gilroy* 300
Fear Milk Chocolate Stout *Brewfist* 161
Febbre Alta *Troll* 169
Fellowship Porter *Redemption Brewing* 102
Feral White *Feral Brewing* 287
FES Stout *Partizan Brewing* 101
Festbier *Hirsch* 65, *Lindenbräu* 57, 61, *Meister* 58, *Scheubel* 59, *Seßlach, Kommunbrauhaus* 60, *Wagner* 61
Festive Ale *Sweetwater Brewing* 233
FestiveAle *Beau's All Natural Brewing* 239
Fest Lager *Narragansett Brewing* 225
Festtags Weisse *Mahr's Bräu* 57
Fievre d'Abricot *La Cumbre Brewing* 215
Fievre de Cacao *Thiriez* 125
Figgy Pudding *Block 15 Brewery & Restaurant* 202
Filo d'Arianna *Pasturana* 168
Filo di Fumo *Pasturana* 168
Filo Forte *Pasturana* 168
Fil Rouge *Pasturana* 168
Fimbulvinter *Närke Kulturbryggeri* 144
Finchcocks Original *Westerham Brewery* 106
Fin du Monde *Unibroue (Sapporo)* 245
Finesse *Dochter van de Korenaar, De* 32
Fireman's #4 *Real Ale Brewing* 232
First Angel *Eutropius* 32
First Light Golden *Devil's Peak* 300
Fish Eye IPA *Ballast Point Brewing* 195
Five *Upright Brewing* 208
Five Bridges *Mordue Brewery* 101
Fizzy Yellow Beer *Green Flash Brewing* 197
Flagship *Hook Norton Brewery* 97
Flagship Brüton *Brüton* 161
Flama *Art Cervesers* 151
Fledermaus 13° *Dalešice* 176
Flekovský Tmavý Ležák *U Fleků* 181
Flemish Kiss *Commons Brewery* 204
Flora Sambuco *Menaresta* 166
Floridian Hefeweizen *Funky Buddha Brewery* 230
Fluffy White Rabbits Triple *Pretty Things Beer & Ale Project* 225
Forår *Fanø* 136
Foreign Style Stout *Upslope Brewing* 220
Forest Bacuri *Amazon Beer* 251
Fort Dansborg IPA *Søgaards* 139
Fortuna Czarne *Fortuna* 185
Fortune Cookie Tripel *Bellwoods Brewery* 239
Fortyniner *Ringwood Brewery Marston's* 102
Four *Upright Brewing* 208
Four Grain Stout *Herslev* 137
Fourth Dementia Olde Ale *Kuhnhenn Brewing* 215
Four Wives *Malt Shovel Brewery (Kirin)* 289
Fracture Double IPA *Amsterdam Brewing* 239
Fraîcheur du Soir *Trois Dames* 173

Fraké *San Paolo* 169
Frambuesa *Blest* 257
Fraoch Heather Ale *Williams Bros. Brewing* 111
Frappadingue *Garrigues* 120
Freaky *Alvinne* 29
Freaky Wheaty Grabanc *Armando Otchoa* 187
Fred *Hair of the Dog Brewing* 205
Freestyle Fridays *Arbor Ales* 90
Freigeist AbraxXxas *Braustelle* 74
Fresh *Wild Beer* 106
Fresh Chios Beer *Chios Micro* 190
Friar Weisse *Franciscan Well (Molson Coors)* 115
Friday's Pale Ale *Septem* 190
Friska *Barley* 160
Fritzale India Pale Ale *Braustelle* 74
Früh Kölsch *Früh* 74
Full Boar Scotch Ale *Devil's Canyon Brewing* 196
Full Circle *New Holland Brewing* 216
Full Moon Pale Ale *Alley Kat Brewing* 235
Full Moon Pale Rye Ale *Real Ale Brewing* 232
Full Nelson *Kooinda Boutique Brewery* 288, *Tiny Rebel* 112
Full Suspension Pale Ale *Squatters Pubs & Beers* 219
Fumée *Tri Martolod* 125
Fünf vor 12 *Forstner Biere* 84
Furious *Surly Brewing* 219
FXA *Gänstaller-Bräu* 55

G

Gaelic Ale *Highland Brewing* 230
Gaelic Pale Ale *Gambrinus* 258
Gael's Blood Potato Ale *Crannóg Ales* 235
Gaffel Kölsch *Gaffel* 74
Gaišais *Abula* 154, *Užavas Alus* 155, *Valmiermuiža* 155
Galbraith's Munich Lager *Galbraith's Brewing* 294
Gale's Prize Old Ale *Fuller's* 94
Gallus 612 Old-Style Ale *Schützengarten* 172
Galway Bay Ale *Galway Bay Brewery* 115
Gama Pale Al *Soma* 260
Gambrinus Weisse *Dom-Bräu* 63
Gamma Ray *Beavertown Brewery* 91
Gårdbryg *Ebeltoft Gårdbryggeri* 135
Gaspar *Alvinne* 29
Gassa d'Amante *Forte, Del* 163
Gathering Storm *Leeds Brewery* 99
Gato Malo *Tamarindo Brewing Company* 263
Gattomao *Dada* 163
Gauder-Bock *Zillertal Bier* 88
Generaal *Dilewyns* 32
Generál *Vyškov* 181
Generation Ale *Shepherd Neame* 104
Genesis Dry Hopped Session Ale *He'brew (Shmaltz Brewing)* 224
Geordie Pride *Mordue Brewery* 101
Georgia Brown *Sweetwater Brewing* 233
Gerica *BirrOne* 161
German Doppelbock *White Gypsy Brewery* 116
German Pils *Invicta* 254
Ginger Beer *Phillips Brewing* 237
Gippsland Gold *Grand Ridge Brewing* 288
Gleipner *Midtfyns* 138
Gluttony *Amager* 134
Goblin's Bitter *Drayman's* 300
God is Goed *Oersoep Brouwerij* 131
God Lager *Nils Oscar* 144
Gold *Hembacher* 65, *Prairie Artisan Ales* 232
Golden *Taybeh Brewing* 284, *Yria* 152

Golden Ale Brewerkz 279, Eisenbahn (Kirin Brazil) 253, Guayacan 259, Oppigårds 145, Otro Mundo 258, Red Hill Brewery 291, Zip's Brewhouse 188
Golden Best Taylor, Timothy 105
Goldenen Adler Ungespundetes Lager Goldeneh Adler 55
Golden Harvest Commons Brewery 204
Golden Monkey Victory Brewing 227
Golden Pilsner Moku Moku 268
Goldfassl Spezial Ottakringer 86
Gold Lager Stoudt's Brewing 226
Gold Leaf Lager Devils Backbone Brewing 229
Gold Miner Sudwerk 172
Gold Pilo Fäcela 54
Golem Dancing Camel 283
Göller Rauchbier Göller 64
Good George IPA Good George Brewing 295
Görchla Höhn 55
Gorlovka Acorn Brewery 90
Gose Krebs Brewing 231
Gossamer Half Acre Beer 214
Göteborgs Porter Oceanbryggeriet 145
Goudblond Budels 127
Gouyasse Triple Géants (Légendes) 40
Graaf Dicbier Muifelbrouwerij 131
Grabanc IPA Armando Otchoa 187
Grafentrunk Festbier Graf Arco 65
Gramarye Heretic Brewing 197
Grand Amber Browar 184
Grand Baltic Porter Garrison Brewing 204
Grand Crew Malmö Brygghus 143
Grand Cru AleSmith Brewing 194, BFM 171, Hemel 129, Kerkom 33, Murray's Craft Brewing 290, Proef 34, Rodenbach (Palm) 35, Sainte Colombe 123, Southampton Publick House 226, St Feuillien 32, St Rieul 124, Val-Dieu 42
Grand Cru (6.5%) Strubbe 35
Grande Dame Oud Bruin Trois Dames 173
Grand Q 1516 Brewing 83
Granitbock Hofstetten 85
Granite Hardknott 96
Grapefruit St Peter's Brewery 103
Grapefruit IPA North Island Beer 268
Grätzer Krebs Brewing 231
Great Northern Porter Summit Brewing 219
Greco Domus 151
Green Alexander Brewery 283
Green Cap Butcher's Tears 127
Green Cow IPA Seasons 255
Green Devil IPA Oakham Ales 101
Green King IPA Greene King 95
Green Elephant IPA Laurelwood Public House & Brewery 206
Green Monster Red Dot Brewhouse 279
Greenwich Gueuze 508 GastroBrewers 221
Greg Hair of the Dog Brewing 205
Greg American Foreign Stout Hopfenstark 242
Gregorius Engelszell, Trappistenbier-Brauerei 84
Greifensteinquell Landbier Specht 81
Griottines Rouget de Lisle, La 123
Grosa Jerome 258
Growler 2 Brothers 285
Grozet Williams Bros. Brewing 111
Grüner Pils Schönram, Private Landbrauerei 52
Gubna Imperial IPA Oskar Blues Brewery 217
Gudeløs Djævlebryg 135
Güdenhoppy Pils Fat Head's Brewery 212
Güera Tijuana Beer 250
Guerrilla IPA Olmo 167
Gueuze Tilquin 45

Guldenberg Ranke, de 41
Gulden Draak Van Steenberge 36
Gumbalhead Three Floyds Brewing 220
Gutstoutas Širvėnos Bravoras 158
Guvnor 2 Brothers 285
Gypsy Porter Kocour 177
Gypsy Tears Ruby Ale Parallel 49 Brewing 237

H

H10op5 Bi-Du 160
Hadmar Bierwerkstatt Weitra 84
HaDoctor HaDubim 283
Haferbier Adlerbräu 70
Hairy Eyeball Lagunitas Brewing 198
Halcyon Wheat Tallgrass Brewing 220
Hallertauer Hopfen-Cuvée Herrngiersdorf, Schlossbrauerei 51
Hama-Cisco Thrash Zone Labo 270
Hamaguri Stout Outsider Brewing 269
HaMaka HaRishona HaDubim 283
Hammerhead IPA Triggerfish 301
Hammurapi +21 Fóti 188
Hampshire Ale Geary Brewing (DL Geary Brewing) 223
Hangover Santa Armando Otchoa 187
Hans Bier Haus 192
Hans Pils Real Ale Brewing 232
Hanssens Artisanaal Oude Gueuze Hanssens 44
Hardcore IPA BrewDog 108
Harlot Societe Brewing 200
Haru Urara Moku Moku 268
Harvest Ale Lees, J W 99, Muskoka Brewery 244
Harvest Dance Wheat Wine Boulevard Brewing 211
Hatlifter Stout Grand Ridge Brewery 288
Hausbräu Seßlach, Kommunbrauhaus 60
Hausbrauerbier Rittmayer 59
Haver Bier Commons Brewery 204
Haverstock Pirlot 34
Havgus Fanø 136
Hawaii 90 Wee Heavy Maui Brewing 206
Hayride Autumn Ale Blue River Brewing 222
Hazed & Infused Boulder Beer 211
Hazelnoot Porter Klein Duimpje 130
Hazelnut Coffee Porter Saltaire Brewery 103
Házmela Rusa Chingonería, La 249
Headcracker Woodforde's Norfolk Ales 107
Head Hunter India Pale Ale Fat Head's Brewery 212
Heady Topper Alchemist, The 221
Hoart of Darkness Murray's Craft Brewing 290
Heavy Water Beavertown Brewery 91
Hecht Alt Neustädter Hausbrauerei 81
Heer Mommeriete 131
HEF Burleigh Brewing 286
Hefe-Pils Winkler Bräu 69
Hefe Weiss Sprecher Brewing 218
Hefeweissbier Weihenstephan 53
Hefeweissbier Dunkel Weihenstephan 53
Hefe-Weißbier Naturtrüb Paulaner (Heineken) 52
Hefeweizen Dry Dock Brewing 212, Grasser 55, Gutmann 51, Hargreaves Hill 288, Moo Brew 289, Reberg 274, Tree Brewing 238, Zehendner 62
Hefe Weizen Reindler 67
Hefe-Weizen Freilassing, Weißbräu 51, Hirschen-Bräu 71, Pflugbrauerei 72
HefeWeizen Live Oak Brewing 231, SanTan Brewing 218

Hefeweizen Dunkel Bauhöfer 70
Hefe-Weizen Dunkel Freilassing, Weißbräu 51
Hefe-Weizen Hell Herbsthäuser 71
Hefe-Wit Dancing Camel 283
Heizer Schwarzbier Bayerischer Bahnhof 78
Hele Sillimäe Ölletehas 154
Hell Blé d'Or, Le 276, Fuchsbeck 64, Homburger Brauhaus 80, Hütten 65, Kloster Machern 80, Schloss Eggenberg 87, Surly Brewing 219, Weisse, Die 88
Helle Fränkische Hefe Weisse Hütten 65
Helle Gose Goslar, Brauhaus 79
Heller High Water Kichesippi Beer 243
Heller Katherein-Bock Grasser 55
Helles 1516 Drewing 83, Abadocca 251, Chateau Kamina 266, Joker Bar 192
Helles Hefe-Weißbier Karg 51
Helles Lagerbier Mülhaupt 71
Hells Camden Town Brewery 92
Hell's Belle Big Boss Brewing 228
Hellwoods Bellwoods Brewery 239
Helse Engel Hemel 129
Helsinki Porttteri Suomenlinnan 148
Hel & Verdoemenis Molen, de 131
Helvick Gold Dungarvan Brewing 115
Hemp Hop Rye O'Fallon Brewery 217
Henley Dark Lovibonds Brewery 99
Hennepin Ommegang (Duvel Moortgat) 225
Henry Ford's Girthsome Fjord Moon Dog Brewing 290
Hercule Stout Ellezelloise (Légendes) 40
Herfstbock Goeye Goet, 't 128
Herrgårdsporter Skebo Bruksbryggeri 146
Hibernatus 3 Fourquets, Les 38
Highhops Maximus 131
Highlander Fyne Ales 109
Hightail Ale Mountain Goat Beer 290
High Watermelon 21st Amendment Brewery 194
Higsons Best Bitter Liverpool Organic Brewery 99
Hini Du An Alarc'h 118
Hippaheikki TESB Teerenpeli 148
Hirschen-Trunk Kraus 56
Historic Porter Hopshackle Brewery 97
Hivernale Franche, La 120
HivernAle Montseny 152
HMS Victory Amber Dry Dock Brewing 212
Hobgoblin Wychwood Brewery (Marston's) 107
Hofblues Hofbrouwerije, 't 33
Hofnar Hofbrouwerije, 't 33
Hofstettner Kübelbier Hofstetten 85
Hoftrol Hofbrouwerije, 't 33
Hog Heaven Avery Brewing 210
Holly Hop Bryncelyn Brewery 111
Holy Cow Dugges 143
Holzfass Schloss Eggenberg 87
Holzfassbier Locher 172
Hommel Bier Perennial Artisan Ales 217
Honey Badger Stronzo Brewing 139
Honey Beer Blé d'Or, Le 276
Honey Ma Gold Great Leap Brewing 273
Honey Spice Tripel Sharp's Brewery (Molson Coors) 104
Honey Weizen Bock Shimane 269
Honkers Goose Island Beer (Anheuser-Busch InBev) 213
Hooksett Ale White Birch Brewing 227
Hooky Mild Hook Norton Brewery 97
Hooligan Brown Ale Laurelwood Public House & Brewery 206
Hooligan Stout Old Schoolhouse Brewery 207

Hopadillo IPA *Karbach Brewing* 231
Hopalicious *Ale Asylum* 210
Hoparazzi *Parallel 49 Brewing* 237
Hopback IPA *Twisted Hop, The* 297
Hop Circle IPA *Phillips Brewing* 237
Hop Cretin IPA *Tofino Brewing* 237
Hop Devil *1516 Brewing* 83
HopDevil *Victory Brewing* 227
Hopfelia *Foglie d'Erba* 163
Hopfen *Urban Chestnut Brewing* 220
Hopfen IPA *Trout Brewing* 220
Hopfen-Gold Pils *Staffelberg-Bräu* 61
Hopfenmalz *August Schell Brewing* 210
Hopfenpflücker *Pyraser* 67
Hopfenweisse *Trois Mousquetaires, Les* 244
Hopfest *Ugly Duck Brewing* 140
Hopfix *Beer Here* 135
Hop God *Nebraska Brewing* 216
Hophead *Dark Star Brewing* 93
Hop Head *Porterhouse Brewing* 118
Hop Head Black IPA *Tree Brewing* 238
Hop Head Double IPA *Tree Brewing* 238
Hop Head Imperial IPA *Tree Brewing* 238
Hophead IPA *Brew Moon Brewery* 293
Hop Head IPA *Tree Brewing* 238
Hop Hog *Feral Brewing* 287
Hophorn *Hornbeer* 137
Hopitoulas IPA *NOLA Brewing (New Orleans
  Lager & Ale Brewing)* 231
Hop Juju Imperial IPA *Fat Head's Brewery* 212
Hop Karma *Terrapin Beer* 233
Höpken Pils *Suomenlinnan* 148
Hop Knot IPA *Four Peaks Brewing* 213
Hop Lava IPA *Double Mountain Brewery* 204
Hop Lunch *Stronzo Brewing* 139
Hop Manna IPA *He'brew (Shmaltz
  Brewing)* 224
Hop met de Gijt *Natte Gijt, de* 131
Hopmouth Double IPA *Arcadia Brewing* 210
Hop Notch IPA *Uinta Brewing* 220
Hoponius Union *Jack's Abby Brewing* 224
Hop Ottin' IPA *Anderson Valley Brewing* 195
Hoppen *Jopen Bier* 129
Hoppy Face Amber Ale *Zhůřák* 182
Hop Riot IPA *High Water Brewing* 197
Hop Rising *Squatters Pubs & Beers* 219
Hop Rod Rye *Bear Republic Brewing* 196
Hopsecutioner *Terrapin Beer* 233
Hop Session Ale *White Birch Brewing* 227
HopShock IPA *SanTan Brewing* 218
Hopsinjoor *Anker, het* 30
Hopslam *Bell's Brewery* 210
Hopslave *Thrash Zone Labo* 270
Hop's Marie-Magdeleine *Paradis, Le* 123
Hop Sun *Southern Tier Brewing* 226
Hoptimist *Rodenburg* 132
Hop Tremor IPA *Harrington's Brewery* 295
Hopulent IPA *EPIC Brewing* 212
Hop Vader *Beachwood BBQ & Brewing* 196
Hop Venom Double IPA *Boneyard Beer* 202
Hopwired IPA *8 Wired Brewing* 292
Hopworks IPA *Hopworks Urban Brewery* 205
Hop Yard Pale Ale *Garrison Brewing* 241
Hop Zombie *Epic Brewing* 293
Hop Zone *BrewCult* 286
Horn's Bock *3 Horne, De* 126
Horny Devil *AleSmith Brewing* 194
Horny Toad Cerveza *Coop Ale Works* 229
Hösl Whiskey-Weisse *Hösl* 65
House IPA *Shiga Kogen Beer* 269
Howling Gale Ale *Eight Degrees Brewing* 115
HPA *Wye Valley Brewery* 117
Hradební Tmavé Pivo 10° *Poličce, Měšťanský
  pivovar v* 179
Hr. Frederiksen *Amager* 135

Huardis *Nieuwhuys* 34
Hüchelner Urstoff *Hüchelner Urstoff* 75
Hud-a-wa' Strong *Yeastie Boys* 297
Huitzi Midwinter Ale *5 Rabbit Brewing* 209
Huma Lupa Licious IPA *Short's Brewing* 218
Human Cannonball *Magic Rock Brewing* 99
Humleguf *Søkildegaard* 139
Humming Ale *Anchor Brewing* 195
Humulus Ludicrous *Half Pints Brewing* 236
Hvede *Bøgedal* 135

I

IBA *Leckere, de* 130
Iceberg *Titanic Brewery* 105
Ichor *Sly Fox Brewing* 226
Ichtegems Oud Bruin *Strubbe* 35
Icon 2 IPA *Murray's Craft Brewing* 290
Idjit *Dugges* 143
IJndejaars IJ, 't 129
IJwit *IJ, 't* 129
Illusion *Moor Beer* 100
Immort Ale *Dogfish Head Brewing* 223
Immortal IPA *Elysian Brewing* 205
Impasse Saison *Crux* 204
Imperator Baltycki *Pinta* 185
Imperial *Harveys* 96, *Schans, de* 133
Imperial Biscotti Break *Evil Twin Brewing* 136
Imperial Brown Stout *Kernel, The* 98
Imperial Chocolate Stout *Sankt Gallen* 269
Imperial Eclipse Stout *FiftyFifty Brewing* 197
Imperial Hatter *New Holland Brewing* 216
Imperial IPA *Boundary Bay Brewery &
  Bistro* 203, *Garrison Brewing* 241,
  Invicta 254, *Viven* 37
Imperial Java Stout *Santa Fe Brewing* 218
Imperial Milk Stout *Charlevoix* 240
Imperial Oatmeal Stout *Boundary Bay
  Brewery & Bistro* 203
Imperial Pelican Ale *Pelican Pub &
  Brewery* 207
Imperial Pilsner *Břevnovský* 175
Imperial Red Ale *Ise Kadoya* 267
Imperial Russian Stout *Klein Duimpje* 130,
  Liverpool Organic Brewery 99
Imperial Stout *Arcadia Brewing* 210,
  Artezan 184, *Bierland* 252, *Great Leap
  Brewing* 273, *Hargreaves Hill* 288,
  Harvestroom 266, *Lagunitas Brewing* 198,
  Minerva 250, *Minoh Beer* 267, *Moa
  Brewing* 296, *Moo Brew* 289, *Nøgne Ø* 142,
  Shonan 269, *Silver City Brewing* 208,
  Swan Lake Beer 270, *Wellington County
  Brewery* 245
Imperial Tequila Ale *Minerva* 250
Imperial Vanilla Coffee Porter *Ugly Duck
  Brewing* 140
Imperial X-mas Porter *Fanø* 136
Independence *Bristol Beer Factory* 92
India Ale *Nils Oscar* 144
India Black Ale *Invicta* 254
Indian Entre *2 Mondes* 120
Indian Lady IPA *Dama Bier* 253
Indian Tribute *Oppigårds* 145
India Pale Ale *Ægir* 141, *Artezan* 184,
  Avery Brewing 210, *Brewerkz* 279, *Brew,
  The* 273, *Bridgeport Brewing (Gambrinus
  Company)* 203, *Harbour Brewing* 96,
  Joli Rouge 121, *Marble Brewery* 216,
  Meantime Brewing 100, *Nøgne Ø* 142,
  North Island Beer 268, *Ried'86, *Saranac
  Beer (Matt Brewing)* 226, *Schönram,
  Private Landbrauerei* 52, *Shepherd
  Neame* 104, *Strahov, Klášterní pivovar* 180,
  Trois Dames 173

India Pale Ale Citra *Kernel, The* 98
Indica *Colorado* 252
Indira IPA *HaDubim* 283
Infinite Wit *Nebraska Brewing* 216
Iniquity *Southern Tier Brewing* 226
Ink *Camden Town Brewery* 92
Innkeeper Bitter Lager *Outsider Brewing* 269
Innovation *Adnams* 90
In the Curl IIPA *Rip Current Brewing* 199
In Your Pale Face IPA *Svaneke* 140
I O Boiko *Kurkliy Bravoras* 157
Ionian Epos *Corfu Beer* 189
IPA *512 Brewing* 228, *Buller* 257, *Butcombe
  Brewery* 92, *Geary Brewing (DL Geary
  Brewing)* 223, *Granite Brewery* 241,
  Green Man Brewing 230, *IJ, 't* 129, *Iwate
  Kura* 267, *Lagunitas Brewing* 198, *Leckere,
  de* 130, *McLaren Vale Beer* 289, *Mornington
  Peninsula Brewery* 290, *Mountain Goat
  Beer* 290, *Odell Brewing* 216, *Oku Noto
  Beer* 268, *Propeller Brewing* 244, *Stone
  Brewing* 201, *Swan Lake Beer* 270,
  Sweetwater Brewing 233, *Triest* 36
IPA2 *Sprecher Brewing* 218
IPA Belge *Dunham (Brasserie Dunham)* 241
IPA Hobo *Ticino Brewing* 173
Ipane Brune *Franche, La* 120
IPAs *Acorn Brewery* 90
IPA Saison *Valášek* 181
Ipè *San Paolo* 169
Iris *Cantillon* 44
Irish Ale *Archipelago Brewery (Asia Pacific
  Breweries)* 278
Irish Dry Stout *Mestiza Cerveza Gourmet* 259
Irish Pale Ale *Galway Hooker* 115
Irish Red Ale *Way Beer* 253
Irish Stout *4 Pines Brewing* 285, *Carlow
  Brewing* 114, *Galway Hooker* 116
Iron Buddha Blonde *Great Leap Brewing* 273
Iron Thistle *Rahr & Son Brewing* 232
Isaac *Baladin, Le* 160
Isid'or *La Trappe* 130
Island Bere *Valhalla Brewery* 110
Island Hoppin' IPA *St John Brewers* 247
Island Red *PEI Brewing/The Gahan House* 244
Íslenskur Úrvals Stout *Viking Ölgerd* 149
Isseki Nicho *Shiga Kogen Beer* 269
Ivan the Terrible Imperial Stout *Big Sky
  Brewing* 211
IV Saison *Jandrain-Jandrenouille* 40

J

Jabby Brau Session Lager *Jack's Abby
  Brewing* 224
Jack Chocolate Sweet Stout *Jack* 250
Jack Clown Smile *Jack* 250
Jack D'Or *Pretty Things Beer & Ale
  Project* 225
Jackie Brown *Mikkeller* 138
Jack of Spades *Malt Shovel Brewery
  (Kirin)* 289
Jack Stout *Jack* 250
Jack's Winter Ale *Shapiro* 284
Jacobite Ale *Traquair House Brewery* 110
Jacobus RPA *Jopen Bier* 129
Jai Alai IPA *Cigar City Brewing* 229
Jaipur IPA *Thornbridge Brewery* 104
Jamaica Red *Mad River Brewing* 198
Jambe-de-Bois *Senne* 42
James Brown *2 Brothers* 285
Jan De Lichte *Glazen Toren* 32
Janis Porter *Naparbier* 152
Jan Kubis *DUM Cervejaria* 253
Japanese Classic Ale *Kiuchi* 267

Jarl *Fyne Ales* 109
Jasper Ale *Stone & Wood* 291
Jenlain Ambrée *Duyck* 119
Jet Star Imperial IPA *No-Li Brewhouse* 207
JHB *Oakham Ales* 101
Jihoměšťan *Jihoměšťský* 176
JJJ IPA *Moor Beer* 100
Jockomo IPA *Abita Brewing* 228
John Barleycorn *Mad River Brewing* 198
Johnny Prael, de 132
Johnny Gold Weiss *Boston Breweries SA* 299
Jonge *Girardin* 44
Jorvik *Rudgate Brewery* 102
Josefi-Bock *Reutberg, Klosterbrauerei* 52
Jubilator Maxlrain *Schlossbrauerei* 52
Jubiläums Festbier *Hebendanz* 55
Jubiler 16,80 *Vyškov* 181
Juhlaolut *Lammin Sahti* 147
Juleøl 4.5 *Aass* 141
Juleøl 6.5 *Aass* 141
Jules Avec *Berentsens* 142
Julöl *Jämtlands* 143, *Oceanbryggeriet* 145
Juniper Pale Ale *Rogue Ales* 208
Junkerbier *Felsenau* 171

K

Kaigan Beer *Akashi* 265
Kalamazoo Stout *Bell's Brewery* 211
Kama Citra *Beer Here* 135
Kanapinis Tamsus *Taruškų Alaus Bravoras* 158
Karbachtoberfest *Karbach Brewing* 231
Karel *Nomád* 178
Karl Straus Amber *Karl Strauss Brewing* 198
Karoo Red *Porcupine Quill Brewing* 301
Karumina *Hida Takayama Beer* 266
Katarinas Mild *Kragelund* 137
Katarinas Stout *Kragelund* 137
Kawka *Widawa* 186
Kazbek *Jihlavský Radniční* 176
KBS *Founders Brewing* 213
Keefe's Irish Stout *Granite Brewery* 241
Keesmann Bamberger Herren Pils *Keesmann* 56
Keha Stout *Malka* 283
Kellerbier *Baeren* 265, *Binkert Brauhaus* 54, *Bruckmüller* 63, *Eichhorn* 54, *Gänstaller-Bräu* 55, *Greess* 55, *Hummel-Bräu* 56, *Kaltenhausen, Hofbräu (Heineken)* 85, *Reichenbrand* 81, *Roppelt* 59, *Schmitz Mönk* 71, *Schwanenbräu Burgebrach* 60
Keller Bier *St Georgen Bräu* 61, *Wiesen, Bürgerliches Brauhaus* 69
Kellerbier Ungespundet *Mahr's Bräu* 57
Keller No. 5 *Buchhöfer* 70
Kellerpils *Drei Kronen (Memmelsdorf)* 54
Keller-Pils *Adlerbräu* 70
Keller-Pils *Bräunlinger Löwenbräu* 70, *Tettnanger (Krone)* 72
Keller-Teufel *Baisinger BierManufaktur* 70
Kellertrunk *Meusel-Bräu* 58
Kemurihige Stout *Hideji Beer* 267
Kentish Ale *Seven Sheds* 291
Keptinis *Čižo Alus* 157, *Kupiškio Alus* 157
Kerckomse Tripel *Kerkom* 33
Kerstbier *Slaghmuylder* 35
Kerstbombenbier *Leidsch Bier* 130
Kerst Pater Special Christmas *Van den Bossche* 36
Kerstvuur *Pirlot* 34
Kerzu *An Alarc'h* 118
Keserü Méz *Fóti* 188
KeTo RePorter *Borgo, Birra del* 161
Key Lime Pie *Short's Brewing* 218

Khoppig *Berghoeve* 127
Kiasu Stout *Jungle Beer* 279
Kili Wit *Logsdon Farmhouse Ales* 206
Killani Russian Imperial Stout *Brew, The* 273
Killarney *Bayern Brewing* 210
Kill Your Darlings *Thornbridge Brewery* 104
Kilt Lifter Scottish-Style Ale *Four Peaks Brewing* 213
King Heffy Imperial Hefeweizen *Howe Sound Brewing* 236
King's Blockhouse IPA *Devil's Peak* 300
King Titus *Maine Beer* 225
Kiwanda Cream Ale *Pelican Pub & Brewery* 207
Kiwi IPA *Aquila* 265
Kloster *Boon Rawd Brewery* 280
Klosterbräu *Schützengarten* 172
Kloster Dunkel *Ettal, Klosterbrauerei* 50
Kloster-Urdunkel *Irseer Klosterbräu* 65
Kloster-Urtrunk *Irseer Klosterbräu* 65
Knappstein Reserve Lager *Malt Shovel Brewery (Kirin)* 289
Knoblach Weißbier *Knoblach* 56
Knockmealdown Porter *Eight Degrees Brewing* 115
Kodiak Imperial Stout *Storm & Anchor* 172
Koeke Blond *Struise Brouwers* 36
Kokutou Sweet Stout *Sankt Gallen* 269
Köleses *Bandusz* 187
Kolsch *4 Pines Brewing* 288
Kölsch Antares 256, *Chuckanut Brewery & Kitchen* 203, *Double Mountain Brewery* 204, *Junction Craft Brewing* 242, *Saint Louis Brewery* 217, *Sünner* 77
Komes Porter *Fortuna* 185
Koniec Świata *Pinta* 185
Konrad's Stout *Lervig* 142
Korbinian *Weihenstephan* 53
Korenwolf *Gulpener* 128
Koruna Česka *Mikulinetsky* 189
Kout 10° *Kout na Šumavě* 177
Kout 14° *Kout na Šumavě* 177
Kout 18° *Kout na Šumavě* 177
Kozlak *Amber Browar* 184
Krakatoa *Retorto (Birra Piacenza di Ceresa Marcello)* 168
Kräusen *Faust* 64
Kreuzberger Klosterbier Dunkel *Kreuzberg, Klosterbrauerei* 66
Kriek *Cantillon* 44, *Cascade Brewing Barrel House* 203
Kriek Cuvée René *Lindemans* 44
Kriekenlambiek *Bzart* 30
Kronabier *Drei Kronen (Scheßlitz)* 54
Kronen-Bier *Tettnanger (Krone)* 72
Kronen Bier Keller Pils *Russ, Kronenbrauerei* 72
Kronen Bier Naturels-Bock Hell *Russ, Kronenbrauerei* 72
Kronen Bier Spezial Hell *Russ, Kronenbrauerei* 72
Kronen-Pils *Laupheim, Kronenbrauerei* 71
Kronen-Spezial *Laupheim, Kronenbrauerei* 71
Kross 5 *Ross Cerveza Independiente* 259
Krüger *Tomskoe* 192
Krug Lagerbier *Krug* 56
Kruk *Widawa* 186
Krušovice Černé *Krušovice (Heineken)* 177
Kuldne Eil *Õllenaut* 153
Kumara Brown Ale *Kererü Brewing* 295
Kupfer Spezial *Winkler Bräu* 69
Kurstadt Weizen *Häffner Bräu* 71

Kurt *Ticino Brewing* 173
Kvasničák *Svijany* 180
Kvasnicový Ležák Světlý *Valášek* 181

L

La 5 *Olmaia, L'* 167
La 9 *Olmaia, L'* 167
Labareda *Coruja* 253
La Bavaisienne Blonde *Theillier* 124
La Bella Mère *Millevertus* 40
La Bionda *Manerba Brewery* 166
La British *À la Fût* 239
La Buteuse *Trou du Diable* 245
La Douce Vertus *Millevertus* 40
La Folie *New Belgium Brewing* 216
La Fosse Blonde *Fontaines* 120
La Gavroche *St Sylvestre* 124
Lager *961 Beer (Gravity Brewing)* 284, *1516 Brewing* 83, *Brooklyn Brewery* 222, *Gilroy* 300, *Gleumes* 75, *Hoa Viên* 278, *Hopworks Urban Brewery* 205, *Kundmüller* 57, *Tawandang Microbrewery* 280
Lager Ahumada *Gülmen* 258
Lagerbier *Fässla* 54, *Fischer* 64, *Friedel* 64, *Penning-Zeissler* 59, *Roppelt* 67, *Schwanenbräu Burgebrach* 60, *Zehendner* 62
Lagerbier Hell *Augustiner-Bräu* 49
Lagerbier Ungespundet *Hönig* 55
Lager Hell *Kraus* 56
La Granja Stout *Nørrebro* 138
Lágrimas Negras *Rámuri* 250
La Gruette *Loire* 121
La Gueule Noire *Loire* 121
Lake Effect IPA *Great Lakes Brewing* 241
Lakeland Gold *Hawkshead Brewery* 96
Lakrids Porter *Det Lille Bryggeri* 135
La Mancina *Forte, Del* 163
La Mancina XL *Forte, Del* 163
Lambic Experimental *Hanssens* 44
Lambicus Blanche *Timmermans* 45
Lambiek *Bzart* 30
La Messe de Minuit *Brasseurs du Temps, Les* 240
La Meule *BFM* 171
La Moneuse *Blaugies* 38
La Montagnarde *Abbaye des Rocs* 38
La Mummia *Montegioco* 167
Landbier *Scholl* 60
Landbier Dunkel *St Georgen Bräu* 61
Landlord *Taylor, Timothy* 105
Landsort Lager *Nynäshamns Ångbryggeri* 145
L'Angelus Blonde *Lepers* 121
La Petrognola *Petrognola, la* 168
La Pétroleuse *Brewer's Art, The* 222
Larger *Epic Brewing* 293
La Roja *Jolly Pumpkin Artisan Ales* 215
La Saison Haute *Brasseurs du Temps, Les* 240
La Schwortz *Matten* 122
La Sylvie'cious *Paradis, Le* 122
La Tchanquée Brune *Entre Deux Bières* 120
Late Red *Shepherd Neame* 104
Latitude *Orkney Brewery* 95
Latzenbier *Schumacher* 77
Laukinių Aviečių *Piniavos Alutis* 158
Lauvas Pacietíba *Malduguns* 155
Lava *Melzer* 80, *Ölvisholt Brugghús* 149
La Ventre Jaune *Rouget de Lisle, La* 123
La Verguenza Summer IPA *Menaresta* 166
L'Brett d'Or *Crooked Stave Brewing* 212
Lead Dog Ale *Yukon Brewing* 238
Leann Folláin *Carlow Brewing* 114

Lebanese Pale Ale *961 Beer (Gravity Brewing)* 284
Lectio Divina *St Somewhere Brewing* 233
Le Freak *Green Flash Brewing* 197
Légère *Vapeur, à* 42
Leidsch Aaipiejee *Leidsch Bier* 130
Lemon Ale *Karma* 165
Lenins Hanf *Neustädter Hausbrauerei* 81
L'Ensemble *Dochter van de Korenaar, De* 32
L'Entre 2 *Entre Deux Bières* 120
Leodis *Leeds Brewery* 99
Leonhardi Bock *Autenried, Schlossbrauerei* 63
Leo's Early Breakfast IPA *Dunham (Brasserie Dunham)* 241
Le Perouse White *Maui Brewing* 206
Lepers 6 *Lepers* 121
Lepers 8 *Lepers* 121
Le Petit Prince *Jester King* 230, 232
Leroy Stout *Leroy* 33
Le Serpent Cerise *Snake River Brewing* 218
Levitation Ale *Stone Brewing* 201
Ležák *U Bulovky* 181
Ležiak Svetlý 12° *Urpiner* 183
Ležiak Výčapný Tmavý 11° *Urpiner* 183
Libertas *CRCB* 262
Liberty Ale *Anchor Brewing* 195
Liborator Stout *Sudwerk* 173
Life *33 Acres Brewing* 235
Light Ale *Harbour Brewing* 96
Lilith *Brüton* 162
Lilly Bock *Rhanerbräu* 67
Limburgs Tripel *Fontein, De* 128
Lime Wheat *Red Dot Brewhouse* 279
Linksmieji Vyrukai *Davra* 157
Liquid Gold *Captain Lawrence Brewing* 223
Liquorice Stout *Svaneke* 140
Lisbeth *Officina della Birra* 172
Little Creatures Pale Ale *Little Creatures Brewing (Kirin)* 289
Little General IPA *Great Leap Brewing* 273
Little Korkny Ale *Nørrebro* 138
Little Scrapper IPA *Half Pints Brewing* 236
Loaded Cannon Ale *Boston Breweries SA* 299
Local 1 *Brooklyn Brewery* 222
Local's Light Beer *Short's Brewing* 218
Loch Down Scotch Ale *Arcadia Brewing* 210
Loffelder Dunkel *Staffelberg-Bräu* 61
Loki IPA *Paddock Wood* 237
Lolland og Falster Guld *Krenkerup* 137
London Pale Ale *Meantime Brewing* 100
London Porter *Emerson's Brewing (Kirin)* 293, *Meantime Brewing* 100
London-Style Porter *Propeller Brewing* 244
Long White Cloud *Tempest Brewing* 110
Loose Cannon IPA *Heavy Seas Beer* 224
Lop Lop *Dada* 163
L'Oro Di Napoli *Maneba* 166
Lost River Baltic Porter *Bellwoods Brewery* 239
Lotus IPA *Ilkley Brewery* 98
Lou Pepe *Cantillon* 44
Lovecraft Beer *Gourmet Calavera* 249
Love & Flowers *Mélusine* 122
Love Tap *Moon Dog Brewing* 289
Lowrider Ale *Cucapá* 249
LowRYEeder IPA *Sweetwater Brewing* 233
Lucky Jack *Lervig* 142
Lug-Tread Lagered Ale *Beau's All Natural Brewing* 239
Lümina *Civale* 162
Lunch *Maine Beer* 225
Lundings Porter *Frederiksodde Haandbryggerlaug* 136
Lunik *Pleine Lune* 123
Lupulus *Charlevoix* 240, *Montseny* 151

Lurcher Stout *Green Jack Brewing* 95
Lust *Eisenbahn (Kirin Brazil)* 254
Luxe Kolsch *Liberty Brewing/Hallertau* 295
Lwówek Książęce *Lwówek Śląski* 185
Lychee Beer *North Taiwan* 277
Lynchburg Natt *Ægir* 141
Lys #1 *Bøgedal* 135

M

Maclir *Okell's* 101
Mad Elf *Tröegs Brewing* 227
Mademoiselle Aramis IPA *Mont Salève* 122
Mad Goose *Purity Brewing* 102
Mad Hatter IPA *New Holland Brewing* 216
Mad Meg *Jester King* 230
Madonas Bodnieku Gaišais *Madonas Alus* 155
Mad Tom IPA *Muskoka Brewery* 243
Maduro Brown Ale *Cigar City Brewing* 229
Magaryčių Alus *Kupiškio Alus* 157
Magnus *Croce di Malto* 162
Mahogany Ipa *Doppio Malto Brewing* 163
Maibock *Bauhöfer* 70, *Rizmajer* 188, *Summit Brewing* 219
Mai Bock *High Point Brewing (Ramstein Beer)* 224
Maiden Fields *Sante Adairius Rustic Ales* 200
Maiden the Shade IPA *Ninkasi Brewing* 206
Malacrianza *CRCB* 263
Malagrika *B94* 160
Maldita Vida *Treintaycinco* 263
Maldon Gold *Mighty Oak Brewing* 100
Malpais Stout *La Cumbre Brewing* 215
Malportada *Treintaycinco* 263
Malta *Montseny* 151
Malta Cuveé *Montseny* 151
Mama's Little Yella Pils *Oskar Blues Brewery* 217
Mamba Porter *Ramses Bier* 132
Manchester Bitter *Marble Beers* 99
Mango & Ginger *Garrison Brewing* 241
Manns Brown *Marston's* 100
Maple Bacon Coffee Porter *Funky Buddha Brewery* 230
Ma Première Blonde Pilsner *À la Fût* 239
Maracaibo Especial *Jolly Pumpkin Artisan Ales* 215
Marcowe *Ciechan* 185
Mareridt *Djævlebryg* 135
Marian Maid *Bors* 187
Märkator *Märkl* 66
Marlin Porter *Ballast Point Brewing* 195
Marshal Zhukov's Imperial Stout *Cigar City Brewing* 229
Mary *Prael, de* 132
Mary Jane *Ilkley Brewery* 98
Märzen *Augustiner Bräu (Kloster Mülln)* 83, *Göss (Heineken)* 84, *Joker Bar* 192, *Meinel-Bräu* 58, *Wagner* 61
Masaniello *Maneba* 166
Masham Ale *Theakston* 104
Mash Pipe *Bellwoods Brewery* 239
Mass Rising *Jack's Abby Brewing* 225
Matchlock Mild *Rudgate Brewery* 102
Matilda *Goose Island Beer (Anheuser-Busch InBev)* 213
Matthias *Maiella* 165
Maudite *Unibroue (Sapporo)* 245
Maximator *Augustiner-Bräu* 49
Mazel *Na Rychtě* 178
McGrath's Irish Black Stout *Clanconnel Brewing* 113
Meadowlark IPA *Pretty Things Beer & Ale Project* 225

Mean Old Tom *Maine Beer* 225
Meantime *Rothhammer* 260
Medeno *Kratochwill* 186
Medieval *Backer/3 Lobos* 252
Meibock *3 Horne, De* 126, *Mommeriete* 131
Meierei Hell *Meierei* 80
Meisterpils *Huber, Familienbrauerei* 85
Meister Vollbier *Meister* 58
Melange A Trois *Nebraska Brewing* 216
Melchior *Alvinne* 29
Melkmeisje *Pampus* 132
Mellite *Der* 119
Melon Beer *North Taiwan* 277
Mélusine Bio *Mélusine* 122
Memoriae *Maltovivo* 166
Meriken Beer *Akashi* 265
Merman *Caledonian Brewing (Heineken)* 109
Messiah Nut Brown Ale *He'brew (Shmaltz Brewing)* 224
Mestreechs Aajt *Gulpener* 128
Méthode *Moa Brewing* 296
Met Pijp *Prael, de* 132
Mexican Imperial Stout *Gourmet Calavera* 249
Mezza Petrognola *Petrognola, la* 168
Micherla *Müller* 58
Midnight Bell *Leeds Brewery* 98
Midnight Porter *Rodenburg* 132
Midnight Stout *Dancing Camel* 283
Mikulin Svitle *Mikulinetsky* 189
Mild *Harveys* 96, *Hobsons Brewery* 97, *Partizan Brewing* 101, *Surly Brewing* 219, *Titanic Brewery* 105
Mild Ale *Bathams* 91
Mild West *Arbor Ales* 90
Milk Stout *Bristol Beer Factory* 92, *Duck-Rabbit Craft Brewery* 230, *Falkon* 176, *Left Hand Brewing* 215
Mill Lane Mild *Hogsleys Brewery* 97
Miloud *Lariano* 165
Miodowe *Ciechan* 185
Mirror Pond Pale Ale *Deschutes Brewing* 204
Mischief *Bruery, The* 196
Mitchell's Extra Special Bitter *Spinnakers Gastro Brewpub & Guesthouses* 237
Mjølner *Herslev* 137
Mochaccino Messiah *To Øl* 140
Mocha Porter *Rogue Brewing* 208
Modus Hoperandi IPA *Ska Brewing* 218
Modus Operandi *Wild Beer* 106
Moenen *Hemel* 129
Moinette Blonde *Dupont* 40
Mojo IPA *Boulder Beer* 211
Mojo Risin' *Boulder Beer* 211
Molly's Chocolate Stout *Hilden Brewing* 113
Monasterium *Falke Bier* 254
Monkey's Mango First IPA *Slow Boat Brewery* 274
Montezuma Imperial Stout *508 GastroBrewery* 221
Montserrat *Guineu* 151
Moonless Stout *Kereru Brewing* 295
Moonraker *Lees, J W* 99
Moonshine *Grand Ridge Brewery* 288
Moose Drool Brown Ale *Big Sky Brewing* 211
Móri *Ölvisholt Brugghús* 149
Morimoto Soba Ale *Rogue Ales* 208
Mork *#8 Bøgedal* 135
Mørk Mosebryg *Grauballe* 136
Morküno *Morküno Alus* 158
Morning Glory *Retorto (Birra Piacenza di Ceresa Marcello)* 168
Morsporter *Leidsch Bier* 130
Mosaic IPA *Community Beer* 229
Mosaic Pale Ale *Pfriem* 207

Mother of All Storms *Pelican Pub & Brewery* 207
mOtley Brew *Otley Brewing* 112
Mr. Pineapple *SanTan Brewing* 218
Mt Macedon Ale *Holgate Brewhouse* 288
Mühlen Kölsch *Malzmühle* 75
Müller's Lagerbier *Pinkus Müller* 76
München *Augsburger Bier* 252
Mundaka *Olmo* 167
Munich Dunkel *Wensky Beer* 255
Munich Helles *Tuatara Brewing* 297
Munich Red *West Brewery* 111
My Antonia *Boira, Birra del* 161
My Bitter Wife IPA *Great Lakes Brewing* 241
Mysingen Midvinterbrygd *Nynäshamns Ångbryggeri* 145

N

Nachtflug *Bosch* 73
Nail Ale *Nail Brewing* 290
Namahage *Aqula* 263, 265
Närke Slättöl *Närke Kulturbryggeri* 144
Native Amber *Coop Ale Works* 229
Natsumikan Lager *Hideji Beer* 267
Natt Porter *Ægir* 141
Naturperle *Locher* 171
Naughty Nellie *Pike Brewing* 208
Nectar *32 Via dei Birrai* 159
Nefiltrētais *Tērvete, Agrofirma* 155
Negra *Jerome* 258
Negra Stout *Beagle* 257
Nelson *Alpine Beer* 195
Nelson Sauvignon *Mikkeller* 138
Nelson's Blood *Lord Nelson Brewery* 289
Nelson's Revenge *Woodforde's Norfolk Ales* 107
Neustadt Hell *Neustädter Hausbrauerei* 81
Neuzig *7 Deugden, De* 126
New World *Samuel Adams (Boston Beer Company)* 225
New Zealand White Ale *Good George Brewing* 295
Nicobar IPA *Gusswerk, Brauhaus* 85
Nieuw Ligt *Hemel* 129
Nightmare *Hambleton Ales* 96
Night Märzen *Beau's All Natural Brewing* 239
Night Porter *Rodenburg* 132
Nine Tales Amber Ale *Malt Shovel Brewery (Kirin)* 289
Ninkasi *Wild Beer* 106
No 1 Blanche *Simon* 170
No 3 Bohemian Pilsner *Standeaven* 301
No 5 Press Club Stout *Standeaven* 301
No 6 Porter *Baltika (Carlsberg)* 191
No 7 African Pale Ale *Standeaven* 301
No 8 Pschenichnoye *Baltika (Carlsberg)* 191
No 9 Barley Wine *Coniston Brewing* 93
Noble King *Jester King* 233
Noble Pils *Samuel Adams (Boston Beer Company)* 225
Noblesse *Dochter van de Korenaar, De* 32
No Boundary IPA *High Water Brewing* 197
No Crusts *Funky Buddha Brewing* 230
Nocturna *Kamun* 165
Noël *Cazeau* 39, *Simon* 170
Noël Christmas Weihnach *Verhaeghe* 37
NoHopLimit *Hopfanatic* 188
Noir de Dottignies *Ranke, de* 41
Noire *Cazeau* 39
Nora *Baladin, Le* 160
Nor' Easter: Winter Warmer *Captain Lawrence Brewing* 223
Norfolk Nip *Woodforde's Norfolk Ales* 107

Northamptonshire Bitter *Hoggleys Brewery* 97
Northumberland *Austmann* 141
Norwegian Wood *Haandbryggeriet* 142
Noscia *Maltovivo* 166
Nostradamus *Caracole* 39
Novello *Sallandse Landbier* 133
Noviluna *Maiella* 165
Nubia *Orso Verde, L'* 167
Nugget Nectar *Tröegs Brewing* 227
Nuisement *Der* 119
Nuit de Goguette *Garrigues* 120
Nut Brown Ale *Black Oak Brewing* 240, *Smith, Samuel* 103, *Spinnakers Gastro Brewpub & Guesthouses* 237
Nutcracker *Black Oak Brewing* 240
Nytårsøl *Søkildegaard* 139

O

O1 *Otley Brewing* 112
O3 BOss *Otley Brewing* 112
Oak Aged *La Trappe* 130
Oak Aged Yeti *Great Divide Brewing* 214
Oaked Arrogant Bastard *Stone Brewing* 201
Oaktoberfest *Black Oak Brewing* 240
Oaky Loki *Paddock Wood* 237
Oasis *Tallgrass Brewing* 220
Oatmeal Porter *Highland Brewing* 230
Oatmeal Stout *Boundary Bay Brewery & Bistro* 203, *Four Peaks Brewing* 213, *Hell Bay Brewing* 242, *Saint Louis Brewery* 217, *Shapiro* 284, *Smith, Samuel* 103, *Summit Brewing* 219, *WinterCoat* 140
Oberland Export Weissbier *Unertl, Weissbräu* 53
Obscura *Yria* 150
Obscur Désir *Brasseurs du Temps, Les* 240
Occasum *Kamun* 165
Ocean *33 Acres Brewing* 235
Ocean India Pale Ale *Oceanbryggeriet* 145
Ochr Tywyll y Mŵs (Dark Side of the Moose) *Mŵs Piws (Purple Moose Brewery)* 112
O'Dark:30 *Oakshire Brewing* 207
Off Leash *Crux* 204
O.G. 1043 *Carrobiolo, Birra del Convento* 162
O.G. 1045 *Carrobiolo, Birra del Convento* 162
O.G. 1056 *Carrobiolo, Birra del Convento* 162
O.G. 1111 *Carrobiolo, Birra del Convento* 162
O-Garden *Otley Brewing* 112
Ogham Oak *Celt Experience, The* 112
Ogre Sörr *Rékésszentandrási* 187
Oh Boy *Bryncelyn Brewery* 111
Ohne Filter Extra Herb *Waldhaus* 73
Okell's Bitter *Okell's* 101
Økologisk India Dark Ale *Herslev* 137
Oktoberfest *Buller* 257, *High Point Brewing (Ramstein Beer)* 224, *Lakefront Brewing* 215, *Saint Arnold Brewing* 233
Oktoberfest Märzen *Paulaner (Heineken)* 52
Ola Dubh *Harviestoun Brewery* 109
Olavur *Okkara* 138
Ol'Cattywhompus *White Birch Brewing* 227
Old 5X *Greene King* 95
Old Bawdy Barley Wine *Pike Brewing* 207
Old Boy *Parallel 49 Brewing* 237
Old Brewery Bitter *Smith, Samuel* 103
Old Brown Dog *Smuttynose Brewing* 226
Old Cellar Dweller *Driftwood Brewing* 236
Old Chub Scotch Ale *Oskar Blues Brewery* 217
Old Deuteronomy Barley Wine *Alley Kat Brewing* 235
Old Empire *Marston's* 100
Old Engine Oil *Harviestoun Brewery* 109
Old Foghorn Barley Wine *Anchor Brewing* 195

Old Freddy Walker *Moor Beer* 100
Old Growler *Growler Brewery, Nethergate* 95
Old Hooky *Hook Norton Brewery* 97
Old Jack *Doppio Malto Brewing* 163
Old Knucklehead *Bridgeport Brewing (Gambrinus Company)* 203
Old Man *Coniston Brewing* 93
Old Moor Porter *Acorn Brewery* 90
Old Peculier *Theakston* 104
Old Rasputin Russian Imperial Stout *North Coast Brewing* 199
Old Scrooge *Three Tuns Brewery* 105
Old Thumper *Ringwood Brewery (Marston's)* 102
Old Thunderpussy *Magnolia Gastropub & Brewery* 199
Old Tom *Robinsons* 102
Old Viscosity *Lost Abbey/Port Brewing* 198
Ol' Fog Burner Barley Wine *Garrison Brewing* 241
Omer *Vander Ghinste, Omer* 36
Ond *Bevog* 84
Ondineke Oilsjtersen Tripel *Glazen Toren* 32
Ootje *Volendam* 133
Oppale *32 Via dei Birrai* 159
Op & Top Molen, de 131
Ör *Trouble Brewing* 116
Orange Grove Ale *Craftsman Brewing* 196
Örebro Bitter *Närke Kulturbryggeri* 144
Oregon Brown Ale *10 Barrel Brewing* 201
Organic Ale *mike's Organic Brewery* 295
Organic Baba Black Lager *Uinta Brewing* 220
Organic Dark Lager *Freedom Brewery* 94
Organic Deranger Imperial Red *Laurelwood Public House & Brewery* 206
Organic English Lager *Freedom Brewery* 94
Organic Lager *Mill Street Brewing* 243
Origin *He'brew (Shmaltz Brewing)* 224
Original *Dark Star Brewing* 93, *Everards* 94, *Hydes Brewery* 97, *Maisel* 57, *Pfaffen* 76
Originális *Tērvete, Agrofirma* 155
Original Lammin Sahti *Lammin Sahti* 147
Original Leipziger Gose *Bayerischer Bahnhof* 78
Original Pinkus Obergärig *Pinkus Müller* 76
Original Premium Pils *Drei Kronen (Scheßlitz)* 54
Original Ritterguts Gose *Hartmannsdorfer Brauhaus* 79
Orkiszowe z Czosnkiem *Kormoran* 185
Orkiszowe z Miodem *Kormoran* 185
Orkney Blast *Highland Brewing* 109
Orkney IPA *Highland Brewing* 109
Oro de Calabaza *Jolly Pumpkin Artisan Ales* 215
Oroincenso *Officina della Birra* 172
Orus *Art Cervesers* 151
Orval *Orval* 40
Oscar Wilde *Mighty Oak Brewing* 100
Osiris Pale Ale *Sun King Brewing* 219
Øster *Volendam* 133
Ott Edel-Pils *Ott* 58
Ottmar Weisse *Meusel-Bräu* 58
Ott Obaladara *Ott* 58
Oudbeitje *Hanssens* 44
Oude Faro *Cam, de* 43
Oude Geuze *Boon* 43, *Bzart* 30, *Oud Beersel* 45
Oude Gueuze Mariage Parfait *Boon* 43
Oude Gueuze *3 Fonteinen* 43, *Mort Subite (Heineken)* 45, *Timmermans* 45
Oude Gueuze Tilquin à l'Ancienne *Tilquin* 45

Oude Kriek *3 Fonteinen* 43, *Boon* 43, *Cam, de* 43, *De Troch* 44, *Hanssens* 44, *Mort Subite (Heineken)* 45, *Oud Beersel* 45, *Timmermans* 45
Oude Lambic *Girardin* 44
Oude Lambiek *Cam, de* 43, *Oud Beersel* 45
Oude Quetsche *Tilquin* 45
Ouro Preto *Falke Bier* 254
Outback Old Ale *Bend Brewing* 202
Outback X Old Ale *Bend Brewing* 202
Outcast IPA *Crux* 204
Outer Darkness *Squatters Pubs & Beers* 219
Over Ale *Half Acre Beer* 214
Ov-ral Wild Yeast IIPA *To Øl* 140
Oyster Stout *Arbor Ales* 90, *Iwate Kura* 267, *Marston's* 100, *Porterhouse Brewing* 116, *Three Boys Brewery* 297
Ozzy *Brewer's Art, The* 222

P

P2 *Worthington's (Molson Coors)* 107
PA *Fork & Brewer* 294
Paas- *Slaghmuylder* 35
Pacific Ale *Stone & Wood* 291
Pacific Pioneer Porter *Sudwerk* 173
Päffgen Kölsch *Päffgen* 76
Paint It Black *Flying Couch* 136
Pakkaspaavo *Teerenpeli* 148
Pako's Eye P-A *Snake River Brewing* 218
Palate Wrecker *Green Flash Brewing* 197
Pale *Camden Town Brewery* 92, *Leeds Brewery* 98, *Pike Brewing* 207
Pale 31 *Firestone Walker Brewing* 197
Pale Al *Croucher Brewing* 293
Pale Ale *4 Pines Brewing* 285, *Alaskan Brewing* 202, *Ballast Point Brewing* 195, *Bierland* 252, *Black Oak Brewing* 240, *Brimmer* 265, *Camba Bavaria* 50, *Cavalier Brewing* 287, *Coopers Brewery* 287, *Dr. Beer* 273, *Eisenbahn (Kirin Brazil)* 253, *Gæðingur Öl* 149, *Geary Brewing (DL Geary Brewing)* 223, *Green Man Brewing* 230, *Guayacan* 259, *Heidenpeters* 80, *Humanfish Brewery* 186, *Ise Kadoya* 267, *Jolly* 276, *Little Brewing Co, The* 288, *Metalman Brewing* 116, *Minerva* 250, *Moa Brewing* 296, *Mornington Peninsula Brewery* 290, *Outsider Brewing* 269, *Rana Dorada* 262, *Rapa Nui* 260, *Ratsherm* 81, *Saranac Beer (Matt Brewing)* 226, *Shapiro* 284, *Sierra Nevada Brewing* 200, *Sigtuna/St. Eriks* 145, *Storm Bali* 280, *Temple Brewing* 291, *Tübinger* 260, *Upslope Brewing* 220
Pale Ale Américaine *Glutenberg (Brasseurs Sans Gluten)* 241
Pale Ale Centennial *Kernel, The* 98
pale ales *Partizan Brewing* 101
Pale Lager *Stone & Wood* 291
Pale Rider *Kelham Island Brewery* 98
Paliūniškis Medutis *Su Puta* 158
Pallet Jack IPA *Barley Brown's Brewpub* 202
Palm Speciale *Palm* 34
Palo Santo Maron *Dogfish Head Brewing* 223
Pamola Xtra Pale Ale *Baxter Brewing* 222
Pandora *Maximus* 131
Panduren Weisse *Rhanerbräu* 67
Panil Ambrè *Panil (Birrificio Torrechiara)* 167
Panil Barriquée *Panil (Birrificio Torrechiara)* 167
Panil Barriquée Sour *Panil (Birrificio Torrechiara)* 167
Pannepot *Struise Brouwers* 36
Pappy's Dark *Block 15 Brewery & Restaurant* 202

Pappy Van Winkle *FiftyFifty Brewing* 197
Paracelsus *Stieglbrauerei zu Salzburg* 87
Paradox *BrewDog* 108
Paragon Apricot Blonde *Dry Dock Brewing* 212
Pardubický Porter *Pernštejn* 178
Påsköl *Stallhagen* 148
Passiflora *Negev* 283
Passionfruit Berliner Weisse *Funky Buddha Brewery* 230
Patagonia Foreign Stout *Berlina* 257
Patagonia Golden Ale *Berlina* 257
Patagonia's Bohemian Pilsner *Patagonia (AB InBev)* 258
Patersbier *Fortitude Brewing* 288
Patriot *Dancing Camel* 283
Patriot Black IPA *Croucher Brewing* 293
Patulo Alus *Kupiškio Alus* 157
Pauwel Kwak *Bosteels* 30
Payback Porter *Speakeasy Ales & Lagers* 200
Peach Berliner Weisse *Perennial Artisan Ales* 217
Peaches & Crème *Short's Brewing* 218
Peat Porter *Moor Beer* 100
Pecan *San Paolo* 169
Pecan Porter *512 Brewing* 228
Péché Mortel *Dieu du Ciel!* 240
Peche 'n' Brett *Logsdon Farmhouse Ales* 206
Pecora Nera *Geco* 164
Pedigree *Marston's* 100
Peeper *Maine Beer* 225
Pelikán *Nomád* 178
Perigosa *Bodebrown* 252
Perle dans les Vignes *Artzner* 118
Perle des Îles *Artzner* 118
Perles Noires *Rouget de Lisle, La* 123
Pernicious Weed *Garage Project* 294
Perverse Sexual Amalgam *Moon Dog Brewing* 290
Peters Jul *Grauballe* 137
Petrognola Nera *Petrognola, la* 168
Petroleum *DUM Cervejaria* 253
Petrus Aged Pale *De Brabandere* 31
Petrus Dubbel Bruin *De Brabandere* 31
Phister de Noël *Flying Couch* 136
Phoenix Pale Ale *Sly Fox Brewing* 226
Pie Noire *Sainte Colombe* 123
Pig and Whistle *Harrington's Brewery* 295
Pihtla Õlu *Taako* 154
Pikantus *Erdinger Weißbräu* 50
Pikeland Pils *Sly Fox Brewing* 226
Pilegrim *Kinn* 142
Pilgertrunk *Kreuzberg, Brauhaus am* 56
Pilota Nakts *Malduguns* 155
Pils *Augustiner-Bräu* 49, *August Schell Brewing* 210, *Baumgartner* 84, *Eichhorn* 54, *Freedom Brewery* 94, *Gleumes* 75, *Grohe* 79, *Joli Rouge* 121, *Lagunitas Brewing* 198, *Manerba Brewery* 166, *Märkl* 66, *Mühlenbräu* 58, *Pflugbrauerei* 72, *Pyraser* 67, *Rana Dorada* 262, *Reh* 59, *Rhanerbräu* 67, *Rothenbach* 59, *St Michaelis (Brauhaus Eutin)* 82, *Stoudt's Brewing* 226, *Three Boys Brewery* 297, *Vakka-Suomen* 149, *Wagner Bräu* 61, *Wiesen, Bürgerliches Brauhaus* 69
PILS *Pausa Cafè* 168
Pilsen *Blest* 257
Pilsener *Bayern Brewing* 210, *Goeye Goet, 't* 128, *Louisiana Brewhouse* 278, *Ratsherm* 81, *St Georgen Bräu* 61, *Wippra* 82
Pilsener Premium *Fuchsberg, Schlossbrauerei* 64

Pilssimus *Forschungsbrauerei* 50
Pilsner *Brewerkz* 279, *Cape Brewing* 299, *Capital Brewery* 211, *Chuckanut Brewery & Kitchen* 203, *Croucher Brewing* 293, *Dr. Beer* 273, *Emerson's Brewing (Kirin)* 293, *Griess* 55, *Hops & Barley* 80, *Jolly* 276, *King Brewery* 243, *Kross Cerveza Independiente* 259, *Little Creatures Brewing Co, The* 288, *Little Creatures Brewing (Kirin)* 289, *Löwenbräu Buttenheim* 57, *mike's Organic Brewery* 295, *Mojiko Retro Beer* 268, *Moo Brew* 289, *Müller* 58, *Oku Noto Beer* 268, *OPA Bier (Joinville)* 255, *Penning-Zeissler* 59, *Reberg* 274, *Shimane* 269, *Steam Whistle Brewing* 244, *Yokohama* 270, *Zip's Brewhouse* 198
Pilsner 12° *GoldMalt* 277
Pilsner Urquell *Pilsner Urquell (SABMiller)* 179
Pilz *Live Oak Brewing* 231
Pink IPA *Almond '22 Beer* 160
Pinkus Jubilate *Pinkus Müller* 76
Pisař Pšeničné Pivo *Purkmistr* 179
Pitch Black Stout *Invercargill Brewery* 295
Plain Porter *Porterhouse Brewing* 116
Pliny the Elder *Russian River Brewing* 199
Pliny the Younger *Russian River Brewing* 200
Plum Ale *Outsider Brewing* 269
Podwójny *Fortuna* 185
Poe Brown Ale *Pública Condesa* 250
Poleeko Gold Pale Ale *Anderson Valley Brewing* 195
Polotmavý Ležák 11° *Bernard* 175
Poperings Hommelbier *Van Eecke* 36
Pöröly *Békésszentandrási* 187
Portari *Okkara* 139
Porter *961 Beer (Gravity Brewing)* 284, *Afanasius* 191, *Antares* 256, *Bell's Brewery* 211, *Brimmer* 265, *Duck-Rabbit Craft Brewery* 230, *Grain Brewery* 95, *Haandbryggeriet* 142, *Highland Brewing* 109, *Lvivske (Carlsberg)* 189, *Narragansett Brewing* 225, *Nøgne Ø* 142, *Oh! La! Ho Beer* 268, *OPA Bier (Joinville)* 255, *Sigtuna/St. Eriks* 145, *Slow Boat Brewery* 274, *Swan Lake Beer* 270, *Viven* 37
Porter 22 *Ciechan* 185
Porter Alon *Negev* 283
Porter Baltique *Trois Mousquetaires, Les* 244
Porteresa *B94* 160
Porteris *Aldaris (Carlsberg)* 154
Porter Special *Fheltoft Gårdbryggeri* 135
Portteri *Laitilan* 146
Post-Colonial IPA *Hopfenstark* 242
Posthörnla *Hönig* 55
Postiljon *Jämtlands* 143
Postman's Knock *Hobsons Brewery* 97
Pothole Filler Imperial Stout *Howe Sound Brewing* 236
Pothole Porter *Half Pints Brewing* 236
Pot Kettle Black *Yeastie Boys* 297
Potrójny *Fortuna* 185
Pow Town Porter *Townsite Brewing* 248
Prairie Ale *Prairie Artisan Ales* 232
Pramdrager Porter *Kragelund* 137
PranQster *North Coast Brewing* 199
Pravda Bohemian Pils *Ninkasi Brewing* 206
Pray For Snow *10 Barrel Brewing* 201
Premium *Lobkowicz* 177, *Primátor* 179
Premium Pils *Reichenbrand* 81
Premium Pils No.1 *Spalt, Stadtbrauerei* 68
Prestige *Dubuisson* 39
Prima Lux *Kamun* 165

Prima Pils *Victory Brewing* 227
Primus *Fuchsbeck* 64, *Live Oak Brewing* 231
Prince of Darkness Black IPA *Sigtuna/ St. Eriks* 145
Prior *Van Eecke* 36
Prior 8 *St Bernardus* 35
Profanity Stout *Williams Bros. Brewing* 111
Profonde Blonde *Franche, La* 120
Proper Job *St Austell Brewery* 103
Proud Stronzo *Stronzo Brewing* 139
Proving Ground IPA *Magnolia Gastropub & Brewery* 199
Provo Girl Pilsner *Squatters Pubs & Beers* 219
Pruccia *Birliner Weiss 4 Hands Brewing* 209
Pšeničné Pivo *Pivovarský Dům* 179
Pšeničné Pivo 13° *Matuška* 178
Pszeniczne *Ciechan* 185
Pszeniczniak *Amber Browar* 184
Public Ale *Community Beer* 229
Publican Porter *Short's Brewing* 218
Pullman *Hepworth & Co Brewers* 96
Pumking *Southern Tier Brewing* 226
Pumpkin Ale *Jihlavský Radniční* 176, *Saint Louis Brewery* 217
Pumpkin Beer *O'Fallon Brewery* 217
Pumpkineater *Howe Sound Brewing* 236
Pumpkin Lager *Lakefront Brewing* 215
Punchy Kout 10° *Kout na Šumavě* 177
Punk IPA *BrewDog* 108
Punto G *BirrOne* 161
Pupil IPA *Societe Brewing* 200
Pura Ale *Ales Agullons* 150
Pure Hoppiness *Alpine Beer* 194
Pure Ubu *Purity Brewing* 102
Purkmistr Světlý Ležák *Purkmistr* 179
Pursuit of Hoppiness *Grand Teton Brewing* 214
PVK *Olmaia, L'* 167

Q

Quadrupel *Halve Maan, De* 33
Quadruppel *Wäls* 255
Quaffit Stout *Simon* 170
Quayle Ale *Lord Nelson Brewery* 289
Quickchange XPA *Panhead Custom Ales* 296
Quilmes Cristal *Patagonia (AB InBev)* 258
Quintine Blonde *Ellezelloise (Légendes)* 40

R

Raban *Häffner Bräu* 71
Racer 5 IPA *Bear Republic Brewing* 196
Racer X *Bear Republic Brewing* 196
Raggle Taggle *Butcher's Tears* 127
Raging Bull *Bootleg Brewery* 286
Raid Beer *To Øl* 140
Raison d'Etre *Dogfish Head Brewing* 223
Ramnesia *Pen-lon Cottage Brewery* 112
Ram Tam *Taylor, Timothy* 105
Ranger IPA *New Belgium Brewing* 216
Raptor *Matuška* 178
Rapture *Magic Rock Brewing* 99
Rapunzel *Mountain Goat Beer* 290
Rare Vos *Ommegang (Duvel Moortgat)* 225
Raspberry Eisbock *Kuhnhenn Brewing* 215
Ratinger Alt *Ratinger Brauhaus* 76
Ratz Ambrée *Ratz* 123
Räuber Weisse Dunkel *Wiesen, Bürgerliches Brauhaus* 69
Rauch *Fujizakura Heights Beer* 266, *Krenkerup* 138, *Kundmüller* 57, *Mojiko Retro Beer* 268, *Tazawako* 270
Rauchbier *Bamberg Bier* 252, *Emelisse* 128, *Fischer* 64, *Trois Mousquetaires, Les* 244
Rauchbier Bock *Spezial* 60

Rauchbier Lager *Spezial* 60
Rauchbier Märzen *Schlenkerla (Heller)* 60, *Spezial* 60
Rauchbock *Fujizakura Heights Beer* 266
Räucherator Doppelbock *Hummel-Bräu* 56
Räucherla *Hummel-Bräu* 56
Rauchweizen *Schlenkerla (Heller)* 60
Raudonyyų Dobilų *Piniavos Alutis* 158
Räuschla *Knoblach* 56
RAV Amber Ale *Berentsens* 142
Raven Stout *Mitchell's Brewery* 301
Ravnsborg Rød *Nørrebro* 138
Real Ale *Young Henrys* 291
Real Ale Bitter *Corfu Beer* 189
Re Ale *Borgu, Birra del* 161
Reality Czeck *Moonlight Brewing* 199
Really Cool Waterslides IPA *3 Sheeps Brewing* 209
Rebelde *Orso Verde, L'* 167
Rebel IPA *Samuel Adams (Boston Beer Company)* 225
Rebel Kent the First Amber Ale *3 Sheeps Brewing* 209
Rebel Red *Franciscan Well (Molson Coors)* 115
Rebuffone *Manerba Brewery* 166
Red *Camelthorn Brewing* 302
Red Ale *Camarada* 249, *Glutenberg (Brasseurs Sans Gluten)* 241, *Kraken* 258, *Marble Brewery* 216, *Sigtuna/ St. Eriks* 145, *Tübinger* 260
Red Barn Ale *Lost Abbey/Port Brewing* 198
Red Chair NWPA *Deschutes Brewing* 204
Red Dawn Bronze Ale *Storm Bali* 280
Red Donkey *Santorini Brewing Company* 189
Redemption *Russian River Brewing* 200
Red Eye Flight *Tempest Brewing* 110
Red Fox IPA *Matten* 122
Red Hammer *Paddock Wood* 237
Rédor Pils *Dupont* 40
Red Racer ESB *Central City Brewing* 235
Red Racer IPA *Central City Brewing* 235
Red Racer Pale Ale *Central City Brewing* 235
Red Seal Ale *North Coast Brewing* 199
Red Shield *Worthington's (Molson Coors)* 107
Red's Rye PA *Founders Brewing* 213
Red Stripe *Desnoes & Geddes* 246
Redwood *Grain Brewery* 95
Regenator *Falter* 64
Re Hop *Toccalmatto* 169
Reininghaus Jahrgangs Pils *Göss (Heineken)* 84
Remembrance Beer '14-'18 *Eutropius* 32
Rendezvous Porter *Old Schoolhouse Brewery* 207
Reprieve Schwarzbier Lager *Two Brothers Brewing* 220
Reprise Centennial Red Ale *4 Hands Brewing* 209
Republika *Windsor & Eton Brewery* 106
Reserve Special Black Ale *Dark Horse Brewing* 212
Resination *Hopshackle Brewery* 97
Restoration *Hopshackle Brewery* 97
Restoration Pale Ale *Abita Brewing* 228
Resurrection *Brewer's Art, The* 222
Resurrection Tripel *Galbraith's Brewing* 294
Retribution *High Water Brewing* 197
Rewired Brown Ale *8 Wired Brewing* 292
Rex *Yeastie Boys* 297
Rex Attitude *Yeastie Boys* 297
Rhub'IPA *St Germain* 124
Rieder XXX Weisse *Ried* 86
Riegele Speziator *Riegele* 67

Riesling Style *Kaltenhausen, Hofbräu (Heineken)* 86
Riggwelter *Black Sheep Brewery* 91
Rila *Minerva* 250
Riner *Guineu* 151
Rinkusteinur *Okkara* 139
Ripper *Green Jack Brewing* 95
Ritter 1645 Ur-Märzen *Ritter St Georgen* 67
Rivale *Trois Dames* 173
Riverwest Stein Beer *Lakefront Brewing* 215
Rivière d'Ain *Maison de Brasseur* 121
Robert the Bruce *Three Floyds Brewing* 220
Robinia *San Paolo* 169
Robust Porter *Smuttynose Brewing* 226, *Vallée du Giffre* 125
Rodenbach *Rodenbach (Palm)* 35
Rodeo Clown Double IPA *Karbach Brewing* 231
Rodersch *Bi-Du* 160
Röðull India Pale Ale *Ölvisholt Brugghús* 149
Rogers' Beer *Little Creatures Brewing (Kirin)* 289
Roggen-Weizen *Störtebeker Braumanufaktur* 82
Rogue Farms Dirtoir Black Lager *Rogue Ales* 208
Rogue Farms OREgasmic Ale *Rogue Ales* 208
Roja *Cadejo* 263
Roja India Pale Ale *Beagle* 257
Rökporter *Nils Oscar* 144
Ronen HaHodit HaMekhoeret *Srigim Brewery* 284
Ronen HaKeha HaMerusha'at *Srigim Brewery* 284
Rookbock *Mommeriete* 131
Rosarito Beach *Tijuana Beer* 250
Rosdel *Nieuwhuys* 34
Rosé de Gambrinus *Cantillon* 44
Rosée d'Hibiscus *Dieu du Ciel!* 240
Rosenburg Pils *Sperber Bräu* 69
Rotbier *Ratsherrn* 81
Rotes Zwickl *Ottakringer* 86
Rothaus Hefeweizen *Rothaus* 72
Rothaus Märzen Export *Rothaus* 72
Rothaus Pils *Rothaus* 72
Rouge Hop *Summer Wine Brewery* 104
Rouge (Première) *Chimay* 39
Rough Snuff *Midtfyns* 138
Route 66 *Manerba Brewery* 166
Rowing Jack *AleBrowar* 183
Royale *Palm* 34
Royal Extra Stout *Carib* 246
Royal Ionian Pilsner *Corfu Beer* 189
Røyk Uten Ild *Haandbryggeriet* 142
RPM IPA *Boneyard Beer* 202
Rrose Sélavy *Dada* 163
Rubia Ale *Beagle* 257
Rubia al Vapor *Szot* 260
Ruby Irish Red Ale *White Gypsy Brewery* 116
Ruby Mild *Rudgate Brewery* 102
Ruby Red Ale *St Peter's Brewery* 103
Rudais Rudens *Maldugus* 155
Rugporter *Amager* 134
Ruination IPA *Stone Brewing* 201
Rum & Raisin *Garage Project* 294
Runa *Montegioco* 167
Russian Imperial Stout *White Gypsy Brewery* 116
Ruud Awakening IPA *Old Schoolhouse Brewery* 207
Rychtář Natur *Rychtář (Lobkowicz)* 180
Rye IPA *Lervig* 142
RyePA *FiftyFifty Brewing* 197
Rye Pale Ale *Terrapin Beer* 233

S

SA *Brains* 111
Saaz of Anarchy *Bi-Du* 160
Safe Harbour Christmas Ale *Slow Boat Brewery* 274
SA Gold *Brains* 111
Saint Botolph's Town *Pretty Things Beer & Ale Project* 225
Saint Léon Blonde *Saint Léon* 123
Saison *Bridge Road Brewers* 286, *Charlevoix* 240, *Funkwerks* 213, *Schans*, de 133, *St Feuillien* 42
, *Zip's Brewhouse* 188
Saison Athene *St Somewhere Brewing* 233
Saison À Trois *Invicta* 254
Saison Bernice *Sante Adairius Rustic Ales* 200
Saison Brett *Boulevard Brewing* 211
Saison Cazeau *Cazeau* 39
Saison de Dottignies Ranke, de 41
Saison de l'Epeautre *Blaugies* 38
Saison de Pipaix *Vapeur*, à 42
Saison d'Erpe Mere *Glazen Toren* 32
Saison Dupont *Dupont* 40
Saison du Tracteur *Trou du Diable* 245
Saison Framboise Zinfandel *Dunham (Brasserie Dunham)* 241
Saison One *Shiga Kogen Beer* 269
Saison Rue *Bruery, The* 196
Saisons *Partizan Brewing* 101
Saison Station 55 *Hopfenstark* 242
Saison St Médard *Baron, Au* 118
Saison Vielle Artisanal *Crooked Stave Brewing* 212
Saison Voisin *Géants (Légendes)* 40
Saison Vos *Sly Fox Brewing* 226
Sakura Kobo *Aqula* 265, *Chateau Kamiya* 266
Salada *Lariano* 165
Salaus Alus *Kupiškio Alus* 157
Salinae *Mister Drink* 166
Salty Dog *Toccalmatto* 169
Salvator *Paulaner (Heineken)* 52
Samurai *Great Divide Brewing* 214
Samuraj *Kocour* 177
Sand Storm Golden Ale *Storm Bali* 280
Sandy *Petrognola, la* 168
Sans Culottes *Choulette, La* 119
Sansho Porter *Zakkoku Kobo* 270
Santería *Camarada* 249
Saphir Bock *Schönram, Private Landbrauerei* 52
Sara's Ruby Mild *Magnolia Gastropub & Brewery* 199
Sarcophagus *Fontaines* 120
Šariš Tmavé 11° *Šariš (SABMiller)* 183
Sas Pils *Leroy* 33
Savu Kataja *Vakka-Suomen* 149
Sawtooth Ale *Left Hand Brewing* 215
Saxo *Caracole* 39
SBA *Donnington Brewery* 93
Scarfiun *Geco* 164
Scarlet Lady Ale *Stoudt's Brewing* 226
Schaarbeekse *3 Fonteinen* 43
Schiehallion *Harviestoun Brewery* 109
Schlossbräu Trausnitz Pils *Herrngiersdorf, Schlossbrauerei* 51
Schloss Trunk *Maxlrain, Schlossbrauerei* 52
Schlotfegerla *Kreuzberg, Brauhaus am* 56
Schlüssel Alt *Schlüssel* 76
Schlüssel Stike *Schlüssel* 76
Schmaltz's Alt *August Schell Brewing* 201
Schnickelfritz *Urban Chestnut Brewing* 220
Schörebräu Hell *Schöre* 72

Schörepils *Schöre* 72
Schöre Weisse *Schöre* 72
Schremser Roggen *Trojan* 87
Schumacher Alt *Schumacher* 77
Schwarz *Baeren* 265, *Harvestmoon* 266
Schwarzbier *Bayern Brewing* 210, *Wippra* 82
Schwarze Gams *Loncium, Privatbrauerei* 86
Schwarze Kuni *Simon* 68
Schwarzer Kristall *Locher* 172
Schwarzer Specht *Specht* 81
Schwarzwald Weisse *Waldhaus* 73
Scotch Ale *Blest* 257, *Jolly* 276, *Red Hill Brewery* 291
Screamin' Beaver Oak Aged Double IPA *Beau's All Natural Brewing* 239
Scrimshaw Pilsner *North Coast Brewing* 199
Scullion's Irish Ale *Hilden Brewing* 113
Sculpin IPA *Ballast Point Brewing* 195
Seasonal Hell *21st Amendment Brewery* 194
Seasonal Winter's Day Porter *Septem* 190
Sèc *Coi Xay Gio* 277
Secession Cascadian Dark Ale *Hopworks Urban Brewery* 205
Seckenator *Reindler* 67
Sedgley Surprise *Hughes, Sarah* 103
Seeheld *Pampus* 132
Seiglée *Caussenarde* 118
Seinsheimer Kellerbier *Seinsheimer Kellerbräu* 68
Seizoen *Logsdon Farmhouse Ales* 206
Seizoen Bretta *Logsdon Farmhouse Ales* 206
Seklyčios *Piniavos Alutis* 158
Sella del Diavolo *Barley* 160
Senovinis-Senoliy *Su Puta* 158
Serafijn *Hemel* 129
Serious Dark Ale *Gilroy* 300
Serious Madness *Mad River Brewing* 198
Serpica *CitaBiunda* 162
Serpicata *CitaBiunda* 162
Session Ale (ISA) *10 Barrel Brewing* 201
Session Pilsner *Svaneke* 140
Seta *Rurale* 168
Setembre Ales *Agullons* 150
Seven *Upright Brewing* 208
Seven Giraffes *Williams Bros. Brewing* 111
Severin Extra IPA *Plevna* 147
Shabadoo Black & Tan Ale *Berkshire Brewing* 222
Shallow Grave *Heretic Brewing* 197
Shandon Stout *Franciscan Well (Molson Coors)* 115
Shangrila *Troll* 169
Shapeshifter Series *Cœlt Exporicnce, The* 112
Shark *Widawa* 186
Shark Attack *Lost Abbey/Port Brewing* 198
Shawinigan Handshake *Trou du Diable* 245
Sherwood *Bors* 187
Shipwreck IPA *Liverpool Organic Brewery* 99
Shire Stout *Ramses Bier* 132
Shonan's Chocolate Porter *Shonan* 270
Shredder's Wheat *Barley Brown's Brewpub* 202
Siberia *Ilkley Brewery* 98
Sidabrinė Puta *Šviesus Su Puta* 158
Silber Füchschen *Füchschen* 74
Silent Treatment Pale Ale *No-Li Brewhouse* 207
Silures *Celt Experience, The* 112
Silver Back *Darling Brew* 300
Sinebrychoff & Brooklyn Two Tree Porter *Sinebrychoff (Carlsberg)* 148
Sinebrychoff Koff Porter *Sinebrychoff (Carlsberg)* 148

Singer Bier *Schmitt* 81
Singha *Boon Rawd Brewery* 280
Singha 70 *Boon Rawd Brewery* 280
Single Hop IPAs *Storm & Anchor* 177
Single-Wide IPA *Boulevard Brewing* 211
SIPA *Humanfish Brewery* 186
Siperia Imperial Stout *Plevna* 147
Siren Noire Imperial Stout *Heavy Seas Beer* 224
Sisyphus *Real Ale Brewing* 232
Six *Upright Brewing* 208
Sjolmet Stout *Valhalla Brewery* 110
Skalák Světlý Ležák 12° *Rohozec* 180
Skalák Tmavý 13° *Rohozec* 180
Skawskum *Skagen* 139
Skeleton Coast IPA *Jack Black's* 301
Skinny Green Lager *Brew, The* 273
Skizoid *Toccalmatto* 169
Skjálfti *Ölvisholt Brugghús* 149
Skull Splitter *Orkney Brewery* 109
Skuumkoppe *Texelse Bierbrouwerij* 133
Sky High Rye *Arcadia Brewing* 210
Slánská Pšenka *Antoš* 175
Slava Pilsen *Abadessa* 251
Sleigh'r *Ninkasi Brewing* 206
Sloth *Amager* 134
Smiske Nature-Ale *Smisje* 35
Smoke Ale *Moku Moku* 268
Smoke & Dagger *Jack's Abby Brewing* 225
Smoked Pigasus *4 Hands Brewing* 209
Smoked Porter *Alaskan Brewing* 202, *Captain Lawrence Brewing* 223, *Ise Kadoya* 267, *O'Fallon Brewery* 217
Smoked Rye Beer *Hell Bay Brewing* 242
Smoked Rye IPA *508 GastroBrewery* 221
SmokeJumper Left Hand Brewing 215
Smokeless *RedWillow Brewery* 102
Smokin' Bishop *Invercargill Brewing* 295
Smoky Dark Beer *Strong Ale Works* 274
Sneck Lifter *Jennings Brewery (Marston's)* 98
Snow Ghost Winter Lager *Great Northern Brewing* 214
Sockeye Red IPA *Midnight Sun Brewing* 206
Soft Dookie *Evil Twin Brewing* 136
Solstice Stout *Hoggleys Brewery* 97
Song from the Wood *Foglie d'Erba* 163
Sonne Keller-Pils *Sonne* 72
Sonne Spezial *Sonne* 72
Sonne Weizen *Sonne* 72
Sophie *Goose Island Beer (Anheuser-Busch InBev)* 213
Sorachi Ace Bitter *Mont Salève* 122
Sorte Får Stout *Berentsens* 142
Sort Hveda *Indslev* 137
Sort Mælk *Tø Øl* 140
Sour 050 *Opperbacco* 167
Sour Grapes *Lovibonds Brewery* 99
Southpaw Winter Warme *Boxing Cat Brewery* 272
South Peak Pilsner *La Cumbre Brewing* 215
Southville Hop IPA *Bristol Beer Factory* 90
Southwold Bitter *Adnams* 90
Sou West Wheat *Bootleg Brewery* 286
Spaceman India Pale Ale *Brewfist* 161
Sparkling Ale *Coopers Brewery* 287, *Good George Brewing* 295
Specht Pilsener *Specht* 81
Special *GoldMalt* 278, *Slaghmuylder* 35
Special De Ryck *De Ryck* 31
Spelt Bock *Indslev* 137
Sperber Bräu Zoiglbier *Sperber Bräu* 69
Spezial *Göss (Heineken)* 84, *Mohrenbrauerei August Huber* 86

Spielbacher Spezial Hell *Goldochsenbrauerei* 71
Spitfire *Shepherd Neame* 104
Spithead Bitter *Suomenlinnan* 148
Spotted Cow *New Glarus Brewing* 216
Spring Oddity *Muskoka Brewery* 244
Spring+Tijm *7 Deugden, De* 126
Stalker IPA *Falkon* 176
St Ambroise Imperial Stout *McAuslan Brewing (Brasserie McAuslan)* 243
St Ambroise Oatmeal Stout *McAuslan Brewing (Brasserie McAuslan)* 243
St Ambroise Pale Ale *McAuslan Brewing (Brasserie McAuslan)* 243
St Ambroise Vintage Ale *McAuslan Brewing (Brasserie McAuslan)* 243
Standing 8 Pilsner *Boxing Cat Brewery* 272
St Andrews Ale *Belhaven Brewery (Greene King)* 108
Stanley Green *Invercargill Brewery* 295
Star Island Single *Smuttynose Brewing* 226
Stark-Bier *Störtebeker Braumanufaktur* 82
Starker Ritter *Ritter St Georgen* 67
State Pen Porter *Santa Fe Brewing* 218
Statesman *Liberty Brewing/Hallertau* 295
Stationmaster Stout *Junction Craft Brewing* 242
St Bretta *Crooked Stave Brewing* 212
Steam Ale *Mountain Goat Beer* 290
Steam Beer *Anchor Brewing* 195, *Brewerkz* 279, *Kragelund* 137
SteamPunk Dunkel *Longwood Brewery* 236
Steelhead Extra Stout *Mad River Brewing* 198
Steel Rail Extra Pale Ale *Berkshire Brewing* 222
Steel Toe Stout *Ska Brewing* 218
Steenbrugge Dubbel Bruin *Palm* 34
Steer Weißbierbock *Unertl, Weissbräu* 53
Steer Weiße *Unertl, Weissbräu* 53
Štěpán Světlý Ležák *Pivovarský Dům* 179
Štěpán Tmavý Ležák *Pivovarský Dům* 179
Sternla Lager *Keesmann* 56
St Erwann *Bretagne* 118
Stettfelder Heller Bock *Adler Bräu* 62
Stettfelder Pils *Adler Bräu* 62
St Florian IPA *Silver City Brewing* 208
St Giles *Stewart Brewing* 110
Sticke *Uerige* 77
Stiegl Goldbräu *Stieglbrauerei zu Salzburg* 87
Stiegl Weisse Naturtrüb *Stieglbrauerei zu Salzburg* 87
Stierberg Eispils Monte Torro *Stierberg* 52
Stierberg Hochzeitsbier *Stierberg* 52
Stimulo *Slaghmuylder* 35
Stiprus Tamsus *Su Puta* 158
St Jakobus Blonder Bock *Forschungsbrauerei* 51
St Lamvinus *Cantillon* 44
STLIPA *Urban Chestnut Brewing* 220
St Mungo *West Brewery* 110
Stöffla *Drei Kronen (Memmelsdorf)* 54, *Hembacher* 65
Stone Beer *Stone & Wood* 291
Stonecutter Scotch Ale *Renaissance Brewing* 297
Stoner Brüton 161
Stonewall *Crooked Moon* 135
Stöpfidler Classic *Adler Bräu* 62
StormBock *Texelse Bierbrouwerij* 133
Storm King *Victory Brewing* 227
Stormy Port *Galway Bay Brewery* 115

Stout *Alaskan Brewing* 202, *Cerveza de Autor* 259, *Gæðingur Öl* 149, *Guayacan* 259, *Hargreaves Hill* 288, *Hida Takayama Beer* 266, *Humanfish Brewery* 186, *Iwate Kura* 267, *Klein Bier* 254, *Kraken* 258, *Kross Cerveza Independiente* 259, *Moo Brew* 289, *Nail Brewing* 290, *North Island Beer* 268, *Rapa Nui* 260, *Schans, de* 133, *Sierra Nevada Brewing* 200, *Titanic Brewery* 105, *Zip's Brewhouse* 188
Stout 8 *Maximus* 131
Stouterik *Senne* 41
Stout+Moedig *7 Deugden, De* 126
Stout Noire *Søgaards* 139
St Petersburg *Thornbridge Brewery* 101
Strada S. Felice *Grado Plato* 164
Strawberry *Cascade Brewing Barrel House* 203
Strix Extra *Coruja* 253
Strong Ale *Szot* 260
Strong Pale Ale *Brimmer* 265
Strong Red Ale *Otro Mundo* 258
Strong Suffolk Ale *Greene King* 95
Strubbe Pils *Strubbe* 35
St Terese's Pale Ale *Highland Brewing* 230
Stud *Hambleton Ales* 96
St Victorious Doppelbock *Victory Brewing* 227
St. Wilbur Weizen *Bayern Brewing* 210
Styrian Ale *Forstner Biere* 84
Suitsu Porter *Õllenaut* 153
Su Kanapemis *Taruškų Alaus Bravoras* 158
Sumeček *Kocour* 177
Su Medumi *Jovaru Alus* 157
Summa *Domus* 151
Summer Ale *Archipelago Brewery (Asia Pacific Breweries)* 278, *Camelthorn Brewing* 302, *Narragansett Brewing* 225
Summer Lady *Dama Bier* 253
Summer Lightning *Hop Back Brewery* 97
Summer Saison *Green Flash Brewing* 197
Summer Swelter *Baxter Brewing* 222
Sunburnt Irish Red *Eight Degrees Brewing* 115
Sunday's Honey Golden Ale *Septem* 190
Sunlight Cream Ale *Sun King Brewing* 219
Sunrise Oatmeal Pale Ale *Fort George Brewery* 205
Sunspot Gold *SanTan Brewing* 218
Super *Baladin, Le* 160
Superator *Bruckmuller* 63
Supercharger APA *Panhead Custom Ales* 296
Super Conductor Double IPA *8 Wired Brewing* 292
Super Nebula Imperial Stout *Block 15 Brewery & Restaurant* 202
Supplication *Russian River Brewing* 199
Surette *Crooked Stave Brewing* 212
Suruga Bay Imperial IPA *Baird Brewing* 265
Susan IPA *Hill Farmstead Brewery* 224
Sussex Best Bitter *Harveys* 96
Svart Hav *Kinn* 142
Svátecní Ležák *Bernard* 175
Svátecní Speciál 17° *Broumov* 175
Světlé Výčepní *Zemský* 182
Svetlo *Kratochwill* 186
Světlý Ležák *Štramberk* 180, *Zemský* 182
Světlý Ležák 12° *Krakonoš* 177
Svetlý Ležák 11.5° *Sessler* 183
Sveva *Grado Plato* 164
Šviesus *Butautų Dvaro Bravoras* 156, *Taruškų Alaus Bravoras* 158
Svijanský Rytíř *Svijany* 180
Sweet Cow *AleBrowar* 184

Sweet Vanilla Stout *Sankt Gallen* 269
Sympathy for the Lager *Karbach Brewing* 231
Szilvás *Békésszentandrási* 187

T

T *Eem, De* 128
T8 English Bitter *Typhoon Brewery* 274
Table Beer *Kernel, The* 98
Taddy Porter *Smith, Samuel* 103
Tafelbier *St Michaelis (Brauhaus Eutin)* 82
Taiyo no Lager *Hideji Beer* 266
Tak *Bevog* 84
Tall Tale Pale Ale *Cambridge Brewing* 223
Tally-Ho *Adnams* 90
Talvi *Nnkian* 147
Tamsus *Butautų Dvaro Bravoras* 156
Tandem Double Ale *Pike Brewing* 208
Tank 7 Farmhouse Ale *Boulevard Brewing* 211
Tankhouse Ale *Mill Street Brewing* 243
Tap 4 Mein Grünes *Schneider* 68
Tap 5 Meine Hopfenweisse *Schneider* 68
Tap 6 Unser Aventinus *Schneider* 67
Tap 7 Unser Original *Schneider* 67
Taras Boulba *Senne* 41
Tari Frumi *Rocca dei Conti* 168
Tari Qirat *Rocca dei Conti* 168
Tari Wit *Rocca dei Conti* 168
Tasmanian India Pale Ale *Saint Louis Brewery* 217
Taxi *2 Brothers* 285
Tchec *Klein Bier* 255
Telenn Du *Lancelot* 121
Teleporter *Summer Wine Brewery* 104
Temno *Kratochwill* 186
Temnoe *Afanasius* 191
Tempest Imperial Stout *Amsterdam Brewing* 239
Temporis *Croce di Malto* 162
Temptation *Durham Brewery, The* 93, *Russian River Brewing* 200
Temptress *Holgate Brewhouse* 288
Tempus Doble Malta *Primus* 250
Tempus Dorada *Primus* 250
Ten Fidy *Oskar Blues Brewery* 217
Tentatripel *Montegioco* 167
Terra Incognita *Rodenburg* 132
Terrarossa *B94* 160
Terrible *Unibroue (Sapporo)* 245
Terzo Miglio *Rurale* 168
Teton Ale *Grand Teton Brewing* 214
Teufels Weisse Helles Hefe *Baisinger BierManufaktur* 70
The Big One IPA *Longwood Brewery* 236
The Big Smoke *8 Wired Brewing* 292
The Czar *Avery Brewing* 210
The Dissident *Deschutes Brewing* 204
The Fundamental Blackhorn *Hornbeer* 137
The Reverend *Avery Brewing* 210
The Runt *Feral Brewing* 288
The Vaporizor Pale Ale *Double Mountain Brewery* 204
The Vine *Cascade Brewing Barrel House* 203
Thirsty Lady *Heidenpeters* 80
Thor's Hammer Barley Wine *Central City Brewing* 235
Three Sheets *Lord Nelson Brewery* 289
Tibir *Montegioco* 167
Tiger *Everards* 94
Tipopils *Italiano* 164
Tipsy Tup *Pen-lon Cottage Brewery* 112
Titan Imperial IPA *Triggerfish* 301
Titan IPA *Great Divide Brewing* 214
TKO India Pale Ale *Boxing Cat Brewery* 272
Tlustý Netopýr Rye IPA *Antoš* 175

Tmavý Džbán *Vyškov* 181
Tmavý Ležák *Budweiser Budvar* 176,
  Purkmistr 179, *Štramberk* 180
Tmavý Ležák 11.5° *Sessler* 183
Tmavý Speciál *Jihoměstský* 177
Tmavý Speciál *Sessler* 183
Toasted Porter *Viking Ølgerd* 149
Toccadibò *Barley* 160
Tokyo* *BrewDog* 108
Tokyo Black *Yo-Ho Brewing* 270
Tonneke *Contreras* 31
Topvar 11° Tmavý Výčapný Ležiak *Šariš*
  (SABMiller) 183
Topvar Marina *Šariš (SABMiller)* 183
Torbata *Almond '22 Beer* 160
Torpedo *Sierra Nevada Brewing* 200
Tors Hammer *Ægir* 141
Torwen *Pen-lon Cottage Brewery* 112
Tosta *Pausa Café* 168
Tostada *Milana* 151
Total Domination IPA *Ninkasi Brewing* 206
Total Eclipse Black Ale *Zhůrák* 182
Totality Imperial Stout *FiftyFifty Brewing* 197
Tough Love Imperial Stout *Crux* 204
Tourbée *Mont Salève* 122
Tovarish *Beachwood BBQ & Brewing* 195
Town Crier *Hobsons Brewery* 97
Traditional Ruby Ale *Gilroy* 300
Traquair House Ale *Traquair House*
  Brewery 110
Trawlerboys *Green Jack Brewing* 95
Tribute *St Austell Brewery* 103
Tribute Barley Wine *Renaissance*
  Brewing 296
Tricerahops *Ninkasi Brewing* 206
Trigo *Cabesas Bier* 261, *Gülmen* 258,
  Milana 151
Trigo con Cas *CRCB* 263
Trinitas Tripel *Jopen Bier* 129
Trinity *Redemption Brewing* 102
Trinity IPA *Trinity Brewhouse* 227
Trinity Tripel *Community Beer* 229
Triomphe *Brewery Vivant* 211
Tripè *Lariano* 165
Tripel *Allagash Brewing* 222, *Anker, het* 30,
  Brunehaut 39, *De Ryck* 31, *Dilewyns* 31,
  Extraomnes 163, *Gourmet Calavera* 249,
  Halve Maan, De 33, *La Trappe* 130,
  Little Brewing Co, The 289, *Pirlot* 34,
  Praght 132, *Proef* 34, *Slaghmuylder* 35,
  St Bernardus 35, *Texelse*
  Bierbrouwerij 133, *Westmalle* 37
Tripel-Gueuze 7% *Dilewyns* 32
Tripel Karmeliet *Bosteels* 30
Tripel Klok *Boelens* 30
Triple *Brakspear Brewing (Marston's)* 92,
  Charlevoix 240, *Maltus Faber* 166,
  Orgemont 122, *Rulles* 41, *Stoudt's*
  Brewing 226, *Val-Dieu* 42
Triple 4 Céréales *Caussenarde* 118
Triple Bock *De Brabandere* 31
Triple Chocoholic *Saltaire Brewing* 103
Triple d'Anvers *De Koninck (Duvel*
  Moortgat) 31
Triple Gold Bitter *Skebo Bruksbryggeri* 146
Triple Hop *Duvel Moortgat* 32
Triple White Sage *Craftsman Brewing* 196
Triplexxx *Croce di Malto* 162
Trippel *New Belgium Brewing* 216, *Wäls* 255
Trippelaer *3 Horne, De* 126
Troegenator Double Bock *Tröegs Brewing* 227
Trois Pistoles *Unibroue (Sapporo)* 245
Trooper *Robinsons* 102
Tropical Wheat *Jungle Beer* 279

Tropic King *Funkwerks* 213
Troublette *Caracole* 39
Troyan *Mikulinetsky* 189
Trucht'l'inger Wilderer Weisse *Camba*
  Bavaria 50
Trumer Pils *Trumer Brauerei (Gambrinus*
  Company) 201, *Trumer Privatbrauerei*
  Josef Sigl 87
Trunk *Trunk* 61
Tsar *Buxton Brewery* 92
Tsarina Esra *Molen, de* 131
Tschöl *Maltovino* 166
Tsingtao Lager *Qingdao (Tsingtao)* 273
Tsjeeses *Struise Brouwers* 36
Tsunami Stout *Pelican Pub & Brewery* 207
Tübinater *Tübinger* 260
Tuck Barát *Bors* 188
Tuff Session Ale *Tofino Brewing* 237
Tume *Sillimäe Õlletehas* 154
Tumi Humali IPA *Gæðingur Öl* 149
Tumma *Plevna* 147
Tumšais *Abula* 154, *Užavas Alus* 155,
  Valmiermuiža 155
Turbodog *Abita Brewing* 228
Turmoil Black IPA *Barley Brown's*
  Brewpub 202
Turmweisse *Kuchlbauer* 66
Tuverbol *Loterbol* 33
Twice as Mad Tom *Muskoka*
  Brewery 244
Twisted Ankle *Twisted Hop, The* 297
Twisted Hop *Hilden Brewing* 113
Two Penny *Ticino Brewing* 173
Two Tortugas *Karl Strauss Brewing* 198
Tzara *Dada* 163

U

Uerige DoppelSticke *Uerige* 77
Ugly Pug *Rahr & Son Brewing* 232
Ukrainske Dark *Mikulinetsky* 189
Ultimator *Stadin* 148
Ultra *Pyraser* 67
Ulula *Civale* 162
Ulysses *Foglie d'Erba* 163
Umbel Ale *Growler Brewery, Nethergate* 95
Umbel Magna *Growler Brewery,*
  Nethergate 95
Uncle Mark's Hopfen Weisse *Kichesippi*
  Beer 243
UnEarthly IPA *Southern Tier Brewing* 226
Ünětice 10° *Ünětice* 181
Ünětice 12° *Ünětice* 181
Unfiltered Lager *Mohawk* 144
Ungespundet *Spezial* 60
Ungespundetes Lagerbier *Wagner* 61,
  Wagner Bräu 61
Ungspund's Lagerbier *Knoblach* 56
Union *Meantime Brewing* 96
Union Jack IPA *Firestone Walker*
  Brewing 197
Uno *Guayacan* 259
UP Brand *(Heineken)* 127
Up In Smoke Smoked Porter *Fat Head's*
  Brewery 212
Urban Dusk *Redemption Brewing* 102
Urban Farmhouse Ale *Commons*
  Brewery 204
Urban IPA *Tiny Rebel* 112
Urban People's Common Lager *Linden*
  Street Brewing 198
Urbock 23 *Schloss Eggenberg* 86
Urchon *Géants (Légendes)* 40
Urhell *Fuchsberg, Schlossbrauerei* 64
Urstöffla *Kundmüller* 57

Ursud *Unertl Weissbier* 53
Urtyp Hell *Autenried, Schlossbrauerei* 63
Urweisse *Erdinger Weißbräu* 50
Ur-Weisse *Ayinger* 50
US Red Ale *Stallhagen* 148
Utah Sage Saison *EPIC Brewing* 212
Utopias *Samuel Adams (Boston Beer*
  Company) 225
Uttendorfer Pils *Vitzthum, Privatbrauerei* 87

V

Vaeltepeter *Skagen* 139
Vagebond Vienna *Maallust* 130
VanderGhinste Oud Bruin *Vander Ghinste,*
  Omer 36
Van Hunk's Pumpkin Ale *Boston Breweries*
  SA 299
Vanilla Porter *Dry Dock Brewing* 212
Vánoční Speciál 13° *Ünětice* 181
Van Vollenhoven's Extra *Schans, de* 133
Varniuku *Davra* 157
Vaskne *Sillimäe Õlletehas* 154
Vasold Lager Hell *Vasold & Schmitt* 61
Vauhtiveikko *Teerenpeli* 148
V Cense *Jandrain-Jandrenouille* 40
Vecchia Bastarda *Amiata* 160
Vehnänen *Laitilan* 146
Vehnäolut *Plevna* 147
Veliocasse Ambrée *Vexin* 125
Velvet Boot *Kererü Brewing* 295
Veraguas *Istmo* 262
Verdi Imperial Stout *Del Ducato* 163
Vestkyst *Fanø* 136, *Kinn* 142
Vesuvia *Maneba* 166
Vete-öl *Malmö Brygghus* 143
VIÆMILIA *Del Ducato* 163
Vicar's Vice Olde Ale *Amsterdam*
  Brewing 239
Vichtenaar *Verhaeghe* 37
Victory Ale *Batemans* 91
Vide y Muerte *5 Rabbit Brewing* 209
Vieille Saison *Brekeriet* 143
Viena *Minerva* 252
Vienna Bierland *252, Chuckanut Brewery*
  & Kitchen 203
Vienna Lager *Community Beer* 229, *Devils*
  Backbone Brewing 229, *King Brewery* 243,
  Snake River Brewing 218, *Wensky*
  Beer 255
Vin de Céréale *Rodenbach (Palm)* 35
Vinkenier *Eutropius* 32
Vintage *3 Fonteinen* 43, *Bristol Beer*
  Factory 92, *Rodenbach (Palm)* 35
Vintage Ale *Coopers Brewery* 287,
  Fuller's 94
Vinter *7 Fjell Bryggeri* 141
Vitesse Noir *Hardknott* 96
Vitus *Weihenstephan* 53
Viva la Wita *Pinta* 185
Vivre Pour Vivre *Falke Bier* 254
VI Wheat *Jandrain-Jandrenouille* 40
Vixnu *Colorado* 253
Vlaskop *Strubbe* 35
Vogelbräu Pils *Vogelbräu* 73
Vojtěch *Na Rychtě* 178
Vølenbock *Volendam* 133
Vollbier *Friedel* 64, *Grasser* 55,
  Lindenbräu 57, *Scheubel* 59
Vollbier Hell *Hirsch* 65
Vortex IPA *Fort George Brewery* 205
Vrouwe *Mommeriete* 131
Vüdü *Italiano* 165
Vuurdoop *Berghoeve* 127
Vuur & Vlam *Molen, de* 131

W

Waase Wolf *Boelens* 30
Wabi *Orso Verde, L'* 167
Wälder Senn *Egg* 84
Wallace Amber *Seasons* 255
Wapa *Cadejo* 263
Warmiński *Kormoran* 185
Watermelon Warhead *Feral Brewing* 288
Watershed IPA *Oakshire Brewing* 207
Watou's Witbier *Van Eecke* 36
Wayan *Baladin, Le* 160
Weedwacker *Saint Arnold Brewing* 233
Wee Heavy *Antares* 256, *Bodebrown* 252
Wee Mac Scottish-Style Ale *Sun King Brewing* 219
Weesensteiner Schlossbräu Original *Weesenstein, Schlossbrauerei* 82
Wehnäbock *Vakka-Suomen* 149
Weiherer Keller-Pils *Kundmüller* 57
Weihnachtsbier *Füchschen* 74
Weihnachts-Bock *Zehendner* 62
Weiss *Blé d'Or, Le* 276
Weissbier *Camarada* 249, *Jacob* 66, *Jihoměstský* 177, *Reckendorf, Schlossbrauerei* 59, *Unertl Weissbier* 53
Weißbier *Erdinger Weißbräu* 50, *Simon* 68, *Spalt, Stadtbrauerei* 68
Weissbier Bock *Baumburg, Klosterbrauerei* 50, *Unertl Weissbier* 53
Weißbier Bock *Zillertal Bier* 88
Weissbier Dunkel *Andechs, Klosterbrauerei* 49
Weissbier Hell *Andechs, Klosterbrauerei* 49
Weissbier Premium Gold *Falter* 64
Weisse *Laupheim, Kronenbrauerei* 71, *Otaru Brewing* 268, *Patagonia (AB InBev)* 258, *Tawandang Microbrewery* 280
Weizen *Andorfer, Weißbräu* 63, *Autenried, Schlossbrauerei* 63, *Baeren* 265, *Bierland* 252, *Binkert Brauhaus* 54, *Bruch* 79, *Camelthorn Brewing* 302, *Daisen G Beer* 266, *Fujizakura Heights Beer* 266, *Gleumes* 75, *Grohe* 79, *Hida Takayama Beer* 266, *Hops & Barley* 80, *Kaltenecker* 182, *Kloster Machern* 80, *Lindenbräu* 57, *Mojiko Retro Beer* 268, *North Taiwan* 277, *OPA Bier (Joinville)* 255, *Stadin* 148
Weizenbier *Primátor* 179, *Roppelt* 59
Weizenbock *Fujizakura Heights Beer* 266, *Göller* 65, *Gutmann* 51, *Matuška* 178, *Reckendorf, Schlossbrauerei* 59, *Rittmayer* 59, *U Bulovky* 181
Weizen-Bock *Andorfer, Weißbräu* 63, *Autenried, Schlossbrauerei* 63, *Ayinger* 50, *Hummel-Bräu* 56, *Jacob* 66, *Karg* 51
Weizen Falk Dunkles Falk *Bruckmüller* 63
Weizen Strong *Mojiko Retro Beer* 268
Weizentea *Grado Plato* 164
Weldoener Blond *Maallust* 130
West Ashley *Sante Adairius Rustic Ales* 200
West Coast Ale *Shongweni* 301
West Coast IPA *Green Flash Brewing* 197, *Outland* 123
Westmalle Dubbel *Westmalle* 37
Wheach *O'Fallon Brewery* 217
Wheat *Dr. Beer* 273, *Three Boys Brewery* 297
Wheat Beer *Shapiro* 294
Wheat Wine *Daisen G Beer* 266
Wherry *Woodforde's Norfolk Ales* 107
Whisky Porter *mike's Organic Brewery* 295

White *Allagash Brewing* 222, *Taybeh Brewing* 284
White Ale *Kiuchi* 267, *Oh! La! Ho Beer* 268, *Viking Ölgerd* 149
White Ant *Brew, The* 273
White Anvil *Anvil Ale* 299
White Bark Wit *Driftwood Brewing* 236
White IPA *Saranac Beer (Matt Brewing)* 226
White Joker *Yokohama* 270
White Label *Emelisse* 128
White Rabbit *Olmo* 167
White Shield *Worthington's (Molson Coors)* 107
White Weizen *Hideji Beer* 267
White Wife *Valhalla Brewery* 110
Wholesome Stout *Wye Valley Brewery* 107
Whoop Pass DIPA *Silver City Brewing* 208
Wijs *7 Deugden, De* 126
Wild Boar *Buxton Brewery* 102
Wildebeest *Wild Beer* 106
Wild Mule *Rooster's Brewing* 102
Wild Swan *Thornbridge Brewery* 104
Willie Warmer *Seven Sheds* 291
Willy *Prael, de* 132
Windjammer *Metalman Brewing* 116
Windsor Knot *Windsor & Eton Brewery* 106
Winged Nut *Urban Chestnut Brewing* 220
Winter De Koninck *(Duvel Moortgat)* 31, *Smisje* 35
Winter Ale *St Peter's Brewery* 103
Winterkoninckse *Kerkom* 33
Winterlude *Del Ducato* 163
Winternacht *Fóti* 188
Winter Storm *Heavy Seas Beer* 224
Winter-Traum *Weltenburger* 69
Winter Warmer *New Glarus Brewing* 216, *Rahr & Son Brewing* 232, *Wells & Young's* 106
Winter Wheat *High Point Brewing (Ramstein Beer)* 224
W-IPA *Minoh Beer* 267
Wisconsin Belgian Red *New Glarus Brewing* 216
Wit *512 Brewing* 228, *Artezan* 184, *Harvestmoon* 266, *St Bernardus* 35
Witbier *Jolly* 276, *Little Brewing Co, The* 289, *Louisiane Brewhouse* 278, *Mornington Peninsula Brewery* 290
Witbier Taperebá *Amazon Beer* 251
Witch's Rock Pale Ale *Tamarindo Brewing Company* 263
Wittekerke *De Brabandere* 31
Wolf in Sheep's Clothing *Porcupine Quill Brewing* 301
Wolf Pils *Wolf* 69
Wolf Urtyp Dunkel *Wolf* 69
Woodhead Amber *Devil's Peak* 300
Woolly Bugger Barley Wine *Howe Sound Brewing* 236
Workhorse IPA *Laurelwood Public House & Brewery* 206
Workie Ticket *Mordue Brewery* 101
Working For Tips *Moonlight Brewing* 199
Workingman Mild *Revolution Brewing* 217
Worthington's E *Worthington's (Molson Coors)* 107
Wrassler's XXXX *Porterhouse Brewing* 116
Wreckless IPA *RedWillow Brewery* 102

X

X *AleSmith Brewing* 194
XB *Batemans* 91, *Theakston* 104
X-mas *Triest* 36

X-Porter *Malmgårdin* 147
XX *Greene King* 95
XXA India Pale Ale *Bier Factory* 171
XX Bitter *Ranke, de* 41
XXX *Three Tuns Brewery* 105
XXXX Hydes Brewery* 97
XXXX Porter *Ringwood Brewery (Marston's)* 102
Xyauyù *Baladin, Le* 160

Y

Yago *Daisen G Beer* 266
Yakima Monster *Liberty Brewing/Hallertau* 295
Yamamomo Ale *Zakkoku Kobo* 270
Yankee *Rooster's Brewing* 102
Yellow Donkey *Santorini Brewing Company* 189
Yeti Imperial Stout *Great Divide Brewing* 214
Yippee IPA *Picaroons Brewing* 244
Yokohama Lager *Yokohama* 270
Yona Yona Ale *Yo-Ho Brewing* 270
Yorkshire Stingo *Smith, Samuel* 103
Young's Bitter *Wells & Young's* 105
YPA *Rooster's Brewing* 102
Yperman *Leroy* 33
Yuan Jiang *Qingdao (Tsingtao)* 273
Yukon Gold *Yukon Brewing* 238
Yukon Red *Yukon Brewing* 238
Yukyu no Toki *Akashi* 265
Yule Ale *WinterCoat* 140
Yunnan Amber Ale *Boxing Cat Brewery* 272
Yuzu Garden Temple Ale *Baird Brewing* 265
Yuzu White *Minoh Beer* 267

Z

Zagara *Barley* 160
Zaison *Brewery Vivant* 211
Zakkoku Weizen *Zakkoku Kobo* 270
Žatecký Gus Černý *Baltika (Carlsberg)* 192
Záviš 12° Poličce, Měšťanský pivovar v* 179
Zeos Pilsner *Chios Micro* 190
Zest Extraomnes* 163
Zhigulyovskoe *Tomskoe* 192
Ziggy Zoggy Summer Lager *Silver City Brewing* 208
Zinnebir *Senne* 41
Zipfer Pils *Zipfer (Heineken)* 88
Zipfer Urtyp *Zipfer (Heineken)* 88
Zoe Maine Beer* 225
Zoigl *Gänstaller-Bräu* 55
Zona Cesarini *Toccalmatto* 169
Zonker Stout *Snake River Brewing* 218
Zümi *Bandusz* 187
Zundert *Kievit, Trappistenbrouwerij de* 129
Zunga *Townsite Brewing* 238
Zuster Agatha *Muifelbrouwerij* 131
Zware Dobbel *Budels* 127
Zware Jongen Tripel *Maallust* 130
Zwergla *Fässla* 54
Zwet.be *3 Fonteinen* 43
Zwickel Bergschlößchen* 78, *Hembacher* 65, *Urban Chestnut Brewing* 220
Zwickelbier Kreuzberg, Brauhaus am* 56, *Meister* 58
Zwickelpils *Gänstaller-Bräu* 55
Zwick'l *Reh* 59
Żytnie *Konstancin* 185
Żywe *Amber Browar* 184
Żywiec Porter *Bracki Browar Zamkowy (Heineken)* 184
ZZ+ *Naparbier* 152

ACKNOWLEDGEMENTS

We have each been fortunate over the years to have met and got to know many of the world's best beer writers and consumer champions, though neither of us understood how grateful we would one day become for their knowledge, wisdom and insights until the time came to compile this book.

We wish to thank the following for their invaluable help in compiling our regional and national information:

Germany: Steve Thomas (*www.german-breweries.com*)

Austria: Conrad Seidl (*www.bierpapst.com*)

UK & Northern Ireland: Des de Moor (*www.desdemoor.co.uk*)

France: Elisabeth Pierre (*www.lafilledelorge.com*)

Netherlands: Tim Skelton (*www.facebook.com/tim.skelton.399*)

Denmark: Henrik Papsø (*www.facebook.com/henrik.papso*)

Sweden: Per Forsgren & Andreas Fält (*twitter.com/BAambassador*)

Finland: Patrik Willfor & Heikki Kähkönen

Spain & Argentina: Max Bahnson (*www.pivni-filosof.com*)

Lithuania: Martin Thibault (*www.lescoureursdesboires.blogspot.co.uk*)

Italy: Lorenzo Dabove (*www.kuaska.it*)

Switzerland: Laurent Mousson (*libieration.blogspot.co.uk*)

Czech Republic: Evan Rail (*www.evanrail.com*)

Poland: Tomasz Kopyra & Jan Lichota (*www.bractwopiwne.pl*)

Hungary & Eastern Europe: Péter Takács

USA: Stan Hieronymus (*www.appellationbeer. com*), Lisa Morrison (*www. beergoddess.com*), John Holl (*www.johnholl.com*) & Jay Brooks (*www.brookstonbeerbulletin.com*)

Brazil: Kathia Zanatta (*www.institutodacerveja.com.br*)

Chile: Felipe Pizarro (*www.sommelierdechile.cl*)

Latin America: Joe Stange (*www.thirstypilgrim.com*)

Japan: Mark Meli & Tim Eustace

China & Taiwan: Michelle Wang (*www.hopsmagazine.com*) & Elaine Hseih (*www.facebook.com/elainecraftbeer*)

Singapore: Daniel Goh (*www.facebook.com/goodbeersg*)

Israel: Barak Meiri

Australia: Matt Kirkegaard (*www.brewsnews.com.au*)

New Zealand: Neil Miller (*www.beerandbrewer.com*)

South Africa: Lucy Corne (*www.lucycorne.com*)

Far-flung outposts: Josh Oakes (Editor-in-chief, *www.ratebeer.com*)

We also wish to thank Jan Bolvig, Erik Dahl, Joris Pattyn, David Cryer, Doug Donelan, Junghoon Yoon, Chul Park, Bill Miller, Troy Zitzelsberger, Ankur Jain, Navin Mittal, Benjamin Johnson, Manuele Colonna, Luca & Ivan at Domus Birrae in Rome, Luis Garcés and the Fairmont Mayakoba Resort.

PICTURE CREDITS

Octopus Publishing Group would like to acknowledge and thank all those breweries and their agents, credited on the page, who kindly supplied labels for use in this book.

Additional picture credits
Alamy/Jim Holden 18; Corbis/REUTERS/Luke MacGregor 11; Getty Images/Flash Parker 8, Gary Moss Photography 14.